# JFD LANIER
## AMERICA'S FORGOTTEN
## PATRIOT AND FINANCIER

BILL BRUGGEN
R. DAVID CART

LANIER MANSION
Foundation

# About the Authors

Bill Bruggen is a thirty-three year employee of the Indiana Department of Natural Resources, the last twenty of which have been as an Assistant Director of the Division of Museums and Historic Sites. This is his third book.

David Cart is the former Curator of the Lanier Mansion State Historic Site in Madison, Indiana. He was awarded the "Nancy Hanks Award of Excellence" by the American Association of Museums in 1998. Also that year he left state employment to pursue other interests. He now operates a successful restoration business in Deputy, Indiana.

Library of Congress Cataloging in Publication Data:

Bruggen, Bill., 1939-
JFD Lanier: America's Forgotten Patriot and Financier

Cover Design: Gary Schmitt
Published by: Lanier Mansion Foundation

Library of Congress Catalog Card Number:
ISBN: 1-884125-80-8

Printed in the United States of America and published with Cooper Publishing Group, LLC, P.O. Box 562, Carmel, IN 46032.

10 9 8 7 6 5 4 3 2 1

# CONTENTS

Acknowledgments                                                          v

A Prologue ". . . to respect scrupulously the rights of
others, but always to be firm in the assertion of my
own."                                                                    ix

1. "Lost forever around the first bend in the road. . ."    1

2. "A monument to his memory, more lasting than a
   granite or marble shaft."                                            8

3. "I suffered incurable hurts"                                        14

4. "An irreparable loss . . ."                                         23

5. "To the State Bank of Indiana- more corruption
   than money"                                                          35

6. ". . . to relieve me of a pecuniary difficulty . . ."              53

7. ". . . implicated in 'deeds of darkness"                            64

8. "Wealth, talent and reputation . . ."                               77

9. "We are doing a fine business already . . ."                        87

10. "A melancholy accident. . ."                                      101

11. "Our pecuniary prospects look gloomy"                             112

12. "I must get out of this scrape the
    best way I can"                                                    125

13. "I suffered not a little anxiety . . ."                           136

14. "I would make any sacrifice before I would
    do an unjust act"                                                  147

15. "We are as completely cornered as ever a set
    of men were . . ."                                                 160

16. ". . . the credit of the State is gone forever . . ."            178

17. "It is rumored that Lanier is opposed to specie payment . . ."   186

18. ". . . his improper connections with brokers, shavers and swindlers . . ."   193

19. "A robbery of a most daring and successful character . . ."   208

20. "Mr. Sering is too sick to travel to the trial . . ."   220

21. ". . . sweating and snakeroot were recommended . . ."   226

22. ". . . no longer be worthy of their respect and confidence."   240

23. "Hurrah for the railroad."   254

24. "This is annihilating time and space."   263

25. "We not unfrequently negotiated a million of bonds daily."   276

26. "A period of great general depression and discouragement . . ."   286

27. "The white trash of the South spawned on Illinois"   299

28. "The events of last night in Washington will strike with profound horror the whole American people."   315

29. ". . . a gentleman of your distinguished and well-merited reputation . . ."   330

Notes   348

Bibliography   384

Sketch of the Life of J.F.D. Lanier   387

Family Tree   444

# Acknowledgments

Contrary to the popular conception, authors do not hide in a garret and emerge six months later with a book. It takes the help of many individuals to produce a book. At the risk of leaving out some important contributors, we list those who we feel helped make this book possible.

Without the Lanier Mansion Foundation agreeing to finance the publication of the book it would be just a reference text at the Lanier Mansion.

David Mc Daniel and Wayne Machan were great proof-readers and acted as sounding boards for many ideas of presenting the work. They never gave bad advice.

Diana Lanier Smith deserves special mention. She is a great, great granddaughter of JFD Lanier, and agreed to edit the book. Her long experience in the literary field polished the work of two inexperienced authors.

Alan January and Steve Towne, and other librarians of the Indiana State Archives and spent valuable time finding old records. Mr. Towne was especially helpful in explaining the "Stover Fraud." Librarians at the Indiana State Library were equally helpful in retrieving the many references used in this book.

Many members of the Indiana Department of Natural Resources, Division of Museums and Historic Sites, shared their expertise to fill in gaps in the story. Most notable of these were Richard Gantz, Executive Director, Orbin Ash, Historic Sites Construction Manager, and Kevin Hereford, Historic Consultant.

The Lanier Mansion Foundation, in addition to funding most of the outstanding restoration of the Lanier Mansion, funded a research trip to New York City, and provided constant encouragement. Gil Daniels, trustee of the foundation, and Scott Davis constantly supported the effort.

The entire staff at the Lanier Mansion State Historic Site gave enthusiastic reviews of the work in progress and urged us on when the task looked impossible.

# Author's Notes

The decision to reprint Mr. Lanier's biography as an appendix to this book has allowed us to expand the scope of the book and include not only some of the background surrounding Mr. Lanier's success, but some information on what was going on in Indiana and the country. The book is not a classic biography, and may offend purists. Mr. Lanier's autobiography was a true "sketch" of his life and dealt with only the high points of a very active life. Since he intended the book "for the use of his children only," he detailed only the results of what papa did when he went off to work. He did not delve into details or his behind-the-scenes maneuvering. We have attempted to highlight these aspects of his life. They reinforce his understanding of human nature and spotlight his strong moral character.

His autobiography also did not include any of his private life. There was no need, his family knew all about his private life. We have attempted to weave in as much of the family's daily life as we could. The births and deaths were easy. Because Mr. Lanier was such a private person, other details were very hard to find. We admit that we have extrapolated some events, and have made "educated guesses" about how he would have reacted to other events. Our hope is that we made a great man human. Only our readers can judge our success.

# A Prologue
## "... to respect scrupulously the rights of others, but always to be firm in the assertion of my own."
— JFD Lanier

*Character is the engine of action; it transcends life. James Franklin Doughty Lanier's character was taking shape over 200 years before he was born. Its influence continues over 200 years after his death. His legacy is more than a mansion on the Indiana shore of the Ohio River. It is a large family that has spread his ethics and moral fiber across the country.*

The Laniers were a noble family in France dating from at least the thirteenth century. Nicholas Lanier I was born in Rouen, France ca 1535, or at least prior to 1540. He was a Huguenot, and court muscian to King Henri II of France in 1559-1560. Nicholas emigrated to England in 1561. It is not known why Nicolas left France and emigrated to England, but perhaps he was a casualty of the early disagreements between Protestants and the Catholic monarchy that would lead to civil war twenty years later. The Huguenots were a politically powerful religious group that preached independence, freedom and personal rights. They were leaders in the rebellion.

Nicholas' musical ability came to the attention of the English king, and three generations of Laniers were court muscians. Laniers intermarried with Italian court muscians during those years. John Lanier,* a decendant of Nicholas, emigrated to America about 1656.

He apparently settled in Charles City County (later Prince George County, Virginia.) In 1683 a land warrant was given to John Lanier and Peter Wycke for 482 acres of land on the south side of the James River. All Laniers in America can trace their ancestry back to John Lanier, his four sons and fifteen grandchildren.

One of John's grandsons, Sampson, married Elisabeth Washington, George Washington's aunt.[1] Sampson moved to North Carolina; where his youngest son, James, became a successful planter. When revolution broke out, James acted on his family convictions. During the Revolutionary War, he served as a Ensign in Col. William Augustine Washington's light cavalry. William Washington was George's oldest nephew. James and William fought in the battles of Cowpens, Eutaw Springs, Gilford Court House, and Kings Mountain.[2]

James returned to the coastal plantation he loved. He and his wife, Sarah Chalmers Lanier settled in to raise a family.[3] James found to his dismay, that the revolution had not secured the rights of all men. Despite the lofty words of the Constitution, not all men were equal. Slavery thrived in North Carolina. While state law provided that any slave-holder could free his slaves at any time, in practice the law never worked. Those who freed their slaves faced unfair competition and economic disaster. Without universal abolition, the North Carolina law was an empty promise.

James Lanier opposed slavery from the depths of his heart. When the efforts of Quakers, and others failed to reform the social order of North Carolina, and as of tobacco farming exhausted the land, he and his brothers, Isham and Henry, decided to leave for the West to claim their share of lands set aside as payment to Revolutionary War soldiers. James left behind his oldest son, Alexander.

---

*Later genealogical investigation has shown that, in his autobiography, J.F.D mis-identified this ancestor as Thomas Lanier.

The Lanier brothers settled near Nashville, Tennessee. In June 1789 the brothers moved again, this time to Bourbon County, Kentucky. James became Prothonotary, or County Clerk of Bourbon County. Not content, James moved a final time to Falmouth, in Pendleton County, Kentucky, and we shall see how fraudulent land speculation and imperfect titles beset the Laniers and many others in Kentucky. [4]

Americans paid for their precious rights on the installment plan. James' generation made two payments. In 1794 he joined Mad Anthony Wayne's campaign against the Indians, and then returned to Pendleton County to live out his life.[5]

The Lanier brothers represented a new concern that fretted the minds of the Federalists. Western expansion was eroding their base of power. By 1790 the trickle of people that continually leaked through the Allegheny Mountains had increased to a steady flow. These pioneers were independent. They rallied to Jefferson's Democrat-Republican Party, finding a voice in Andrew Jackson.

# 1.
## "Lost forever around the first bend in the road . . ."

*Alex Lanier did not stay long in North Carolina. Soon after his son was born he took his family on the dangerous journey to join his father and uncles in Kentucky. It was the first of several journeys Alex made to calm his restive soul.*

On November 22, 1800, in the town of Washington, Beaufort County, North Carolina, Drusilla Doughty Lanier struggled through the delivery of her first child. Birthing was dangerous to both mother and child at the opening of the nineteenth century. No record of Drusilla's trial remains, but the fact that she had no more children indicates a problem birth with lasting consequences.

Both mother and child did survive, however, and Drusilla presented Alex with a son, that looked and sounded healthy. They named the boy James Franklin Doughty Lanier to honor not only his paternal grandfather, but also his maternal ancestry.[1]

Drusilla did not recover quickly from the ordeal. In her weakened condition, Drusilla and Alex would have to be constantly vigilant to protect against any of a score of diseases that could prove fatal. Cholera, typhoid, smallpox, diphtheria, undulent fever, pneumonia, scarlet fever, tuberculosis, and influenza were certainly prominent among the destructive diseases. Measles, mumps, and whooping cough, while not lethal normally, could prove deadly to someone in a weakened condition. Even the Auge, a malarial fever, so common that many did not consider it an illness, could be dangerous to Drusilla.

Alex planned to follow his father James west after the child was born. Stories of the promised land beyond the mountains beckoned. Tales of the earth's bounty — rich black soil, untapped deposits of lead and iron, mountains of precious salt — became the gospel of the disenchanted. Miners and millers; coopers and cabinetmakers; farriers and farmers could all gain a fortune. The West knew no social class. Perspiration could make any man a prince.

Still, the decision to cross the mountains was not an easy one. Not all of Alex's neighbors thought leaving was wise. For every story of prime land and riches beyond the mountains, there were two about the dangers. The land itself was an enemy. The great forests shut out sunlight and dampened sound. Sloughs and sinkholes sheltered vermin and disease. The vast green void swallowed up any traveler that ventured from the trail. The fear, the quiet, and the loneliness drove some over the edge of sanity. If you survived the forest, savages lurked behind every tree brutally murdering all that trespassed on their sacred ground. Only the most desperate or daring would take the risk.

Christmas came and went and still Drusilla was weak. As spring approached, she slowly regained her strength and took on her full share of the family burden. The trials of the winter faded and the hope of a new start in Kentucky buoyed their spirits. Drusilla even let thoughts of more children brighten her hours of sewing and mending before the evening fire. Butchering, smoking, and salting a supply of meat took on added urgency for Alex as he anticipated the move westward.

Alex set the date for leaving, and the rituals of departure began. They visited friends for the last time. There was no deception about the finality of the good-byes. People seldom returned from beyond the mountains.

Decisions on what to take and what to leave must have been painful. The first items packed were necessities of survival. Food to last until the next harvest, and a supply of fresh seed

2

were critical. A good ax, a brace and bit, a froe, bullet molds, and the spinning wheel, were high priority items. A keg of nails and another of gun powder would be priceless in the West. They left behind many prized possessions. The beautiful table and chairs, as well as the heirloom grandfather clock went to a friend or relative. They were too heavy for the overburdened wagon. Bolts of cotton cloth or serviceable linsey-woolsey were more important than a fancy party dress. Drusilla did not complain about giving up the trappings of a southern lady. She retained her most important possession — her character.

As excited as Alex and Drusilla were, it was a sad time when they finally released the wagon brake and clucked up the horses. All their worldly possessions that could not fit in a narrow, short wagon, remained at the home place, lost forever around the first bend in the road.

Talk of a major passage into the wilderness had been rampant for years. The flood of pioneers breaking through the mountains begged for it, and military necessity demanded it. As early as 1784, George Washington felt a water link between the Potomac and Ohio Rivers vital to consolidate the new nation. Washington, the general, spoke of the military necessity of protecting the pioneers and the country's remote borders. Washington the nation builder, argued that a connection was necessary to bind East and West with the strong sinew of commerce.*

Washington suggested his plan to both Governor Benjamin Harrison of Virginia and his friend Thomas Jefferson. He begged Jefferson to set aside his states' rights views and allow the federal treasury to construct the passageway. Jefferson agreed that a water link was desirable, but could not agree that the federal government should fund it.[2]

There was general agreement to the need for transportation ties to the western lands. The arguments centered on the mode of transportation, and who would pay the cost. Some championed canals while another faction favored toll roads. Many believed that clearing the rivers as general channels of commerce would suffice. Some argued the federal government should pay,

---

* It is of interest to note that another General elected president, Dwight Eisenhower used the same military and commerce arguments in proposing the Interstate Highway System 170 years later.

while others thought transportation improvements were the state's responsibility.

The debate raged without a solution for years, so that when Alexander Lanier left North Carolina, in 1801, he made his way over an unimproved track that taxed the fortitude of both horse and human. Roads were almost non existent. Narrow trails led from the settled, civilized margin of the ocean into the Blue Ridge Mountain wilderness. Deep holes threatened wheel rims. High stumps reached for wagon beds. Most river fords were unmarked, making each crossing an adventure.

On a good day the Laniers, like all travelers, covered ten to twelve miles. Many travelers used old campsites hacked out of the tangled brush along the track. Too often, however, a crude grave marker along the trail testified to a broken heart and a dead dream.

Westward pioneers encountered a few returning wagons. The occupants would pass stone faced, reliving some horror. Few words would pass between the travelers. Those facing the morning sun prayed for the widening of the track that signaled civilization. They hoped the wilderness would close behind them and shut out forever the memories of fear and failure. Those going west prayed that they would not encounter, or could overcome, the tragedy that deeply etched the ghost faces that passed.

Alex's arrival in Falmouth, Kentucky, set off a celebration capped with a heartfelt prayer of thanksgiving. They had passed the first test and were among the strong survivors. Children were especially prized on the frontier, so young James was the center of attention.

Alex had the intelligence needed. He turned his efforts to land speculation. The prospects were good. People flooding through the gaps in the mountains needed land. The soil along the forks of the Licking River was deep and rich. Once cleared, the land made good farmland. Someone who knew the value of land, and was fair and honest, could double his money in a month. Alexander met those qualifications.

The future looked bright as the new century celebrated its second birthday and the new country its Twenty-sixth. Thomas Jefferson, the "people's president," was in firm command of the country after a quarter century of Federalist rule. It looked like a new beginning for the country as well as for Alexander Lanier.

When Jefferson assumed the presidency he inherited a debt of eighty-three million dollars from the Federalist Administrations. The primary goal of the new administration was to control the fiscal situation and pay off the mammoth national debt. The major sources of revenue for the new nation were customs tariffs and sporadically collected excise taxes. An increase in customs revenue made it possible to repeal all of the excise taxes except the one on salt.[3] Jefferson felt that the country had to expand westward to survive. The only extravagance he would permit himself was the purchase of Louisiana from France, and the cost for Lewis and Clark to explore the purchase.

He was correct. Americans were moving West, and land speculation boomed. Land speculation required cash for land purchases. The national bank was the best source of currency. The U.S. Bank issued its own credit paper or "Promissory Notes" of varying denominations. Any U.S. Bank branch, and all public land offices accepted these notes at face value.

There were few U.S. Bank branch offices in the West, however, and U.S. Bank notes were not always available. This lack of bank notes was a major problem. Specie — gold and silver coin — was the most universally accepted currency. U.S. coins seldom appeared west of the mountains. The few coins found on the frontier were Spanish, French or English. This foreign specie was also in very short supply, and could not support even the day-to-day transactions on the frontier.

Private commercial banks, many chartered by the states, sprang up to fill the currency void. In theory, state charters provided some control over bank operations. In practice, the control was ineffective. The U.S. Bank offered the best control of state banks. It heavily discounted the notes of poor banks, while accepting the notes of sound banks at face value. As a land speculator, Alexander needed the banks. It was risky business. If the bank notes he accepted were not honored, he had traded his land for a handful of worthless paper.

Most people had little education, and could not understand banking. The majority of day-to-day transactions involved barter. Even land sales sometimes involved bartering. Alex would accept quantities of grain, ore, and even livestock, if no currency was available. At some point Alexander reluctantly accepted two black slaves as payment for a debt. Alex had inherited the Lanier abhorrence of slavery and would not trade human beings like chattel. He treated these men as hired hands, and dreamed of one day setting them free.[4]

Another problem plagued land speculators in Kentucky. The Land Ordinance passed Congress in 1785, and prescribed precise measurements for land surveying. Kentucky, however, stuck to the old system of "metes and bounds" surveying. Deeds used geological features to describe boundaries. A typical deed description might read:

> Beginning at the old oak tree measuring 32 inches in diameter; and running in an easterly direction 500 paces to the rock pile, then north west 716 paces crossing John's creek between the two blazed cottonwood trees to a point on the old salt lick trail, then following the trail until it turns due north then southwesterly 156 paces to a thicket of hickory trees. Follow the blazed line to where it comes out on the prairie then south over Indian camp hill to the old oak tree.

Descriptions using this system were extremely difficult to determine on the ground. Even after finding the "old oak tree," the directions were imprecise. Without compass degrees, what was "an easterly direction"? How did "north" differ from "due north"? How long was a pace? A short legged man took a much shorter pace than a long- legged man.

If this piece of land was difficult to find on the ground, it was impossible to lay out on a plat map. It was not uncommon for two or more people to claim the same piece of land. The first one that could provide the County Recorder of Deeds with a description was the legal owner. Sometimes two or three different buyers purchased the same piece of land. Often these sales were honest mistakes. Some were intentional frauds. This deception devastated Alex. JFD, in his autobiography, states that his father lost much land in Kentucky due to imperfect titles.[5]

Margaret, affectionately called Peggy, was James and Sarah Lanier's youngest child. She was born in 1784 just before James moved west. Reacquainted in Kentucky, Alexander and Peggy became close friends. Peggy must have been difficult to control. It appears she had a stubbornness that was much like her father. James was probably too close to see it or appreciate it.

Peggy became pregnant. It was a family scandal. Despite intercession by Sarah, James Lanier remained belligerent. He became livid at the mention of Peggy's name, and dangerous at any reference to James Street, the father of her child. The Laniers

6

defamed Street, and many in Falmouth shunned him. Peggy truly loved James Street and defended him before her father's wrath. Banned from the Lanier house, and forced to choose between father and lover, Peggy married Street days after their daughter, Sarah Hubbard Street, was born. The couple moved to Eaton, Ohio, to start a new life. Alexander rode along side the departing wagon for several miles, promising to keep in touch.

The feud with his daughter affected James Lanier more than he would admit. His health entered a long decline. Alex's admonitions and Sarah's loving care could not spark a fight in the old man. He died in 1806. This was the first death young James experienced close at hand.

Jeffersonian economics were healing the U.S. Treasury. The pinch purse policies of Jefferson's administration cut the federal debt almost in half. Congress repealed the salt tax in 1807. [6] The country's finances may have been improving, but the fortunes of Alexander Lanier were at a low point. His confidence bludgeoned by financial losses; his spirit battered by the death of his father; Alex sought a change.

Letters from Peggy described prime land protected by the provisions of the Land Ordinance. By 1807 Alexander decided he had to leave Kentucky to survive. He loaded his wife, son, and mother, along with what few possessions could fit into the small wagon, and headed north. James alternately rode in the wagon or trudged behind it with his father and the two slaves.

7

# 2.
## "A monument to his memory, more lasting than a granite or marble shaft."
— The History of Preble County 1881

*Alexander moved his small family north to Eaton, Ohio, where James and Peggy Street had made a home. In Ohio, James would grow and learn. Alexander would find success and recognition.*

Eaton was a small settlement on the edge of the frontier, 44 miles as the crow flies north of the Ohio River and the metropolis of Cincinnati. It was at least double that distance on the tortuous trails that were either axle deep in mud, or so dry that hoof and wheel raised a smother of dust. The area was growing rapidly, and prospects appeared good.

Once north of the Ohio River, Alex immediately freed the two slaves he had acquired but not wanted. Kentucky outlawed the freeing of slaves, so Alexander and the two bonded men waited until they had safely crossed the river. Freeing his two slaves rather than selling them before reaching Ohio represented a considerable loss of income. Years later, JFD would recall with pride his father's adherence to principle over profit.[1]

Hamilton County, Ohio was huge and unmanageable. It in-

8

cluded both Cincinnati and Eaton. Soon after the Alexander Lanier family arrived, voters approved splitting Hamilton County. The new county became Preble County, and the City of Eaton officially recognized as the county seat.[2]

Undaunted by his disastrous land speculation efforts in Kentucky, Alex began purchasing land in Ohio. Ohio and most other western states used the new surveying method prescribed in the Land Ordinance of 1785. This ordinance required that a grid system be superimposed over the land features and be based on exact compass readings and precise linear measurements. It allowed for unequivocal deed descriptions and land registration.[3] By 1805 the U.S. government had surveyed the area encompassing Ohio and Indiana using the new system. In 1811, Isham Lanier, Alex's uncle, succumbed to his nephew's descriptions of deep black soil in Ohio. He purchased a prime piece of farmland from Alexander.[4]

Meanwhile, Jefferson led the fight against the national bank established during the administration of Washington. His Democrat-Republicans carried on the battle. Believing a national bank gave the federal government too much power, they favored private local banks. As the bank charter was due to expire in 1811, Jefferson's successor, Madison, led the fight to suspend the charter.

Being a westerner, Alex favored many Democrat-Republican policies, but disagreed with the party's stand on the national bank. A stable banking system was of prime importance to Alexander's land speculation. He had personal experience with unstable private banks, and strongly favored the national bank. James listened as his father and mother discussed the banking issue. It was his introduction to finance.

The discussion in the Lanier household was one-sided, but debate on the issue in Congress was fierce. Albert Gallatin, Secretary of the Treasury under Presidents Jefferson and Madison, realized the value of a national bank and spoke for it in the face of party disapproval. The vote in the House of Representatives was sixty-four to sixty-three in favor of indefinite suspension of the bank's charter. The Senate split evenly on the question. Madison's vice president, George Clinton, cast the deciding vote against the bank. The Democrat-Republicans had finally won their twenty year struggle against the national bank. With it went the hope of a national paper currency.

Alex's fears were realized. Without the policing function of the U.S. Bank, problems with the private banking system developed almost immediately. Anyone with a printing press, and a political ally could set up a bank. Regulations were minimal and haphazardly enforced. There were few rules governing the amount of specie a bank needed to maintain as a reserve against its loans. Many private banks dangerously over extended their notes.[5] Most people avoided the banks as if they were pest houses. Many people called bankers "rag merchants" because the paper currency they tried to peddle was less valuable than the rags used to make the currency.

The exchange of notes for gold and silver specie took place only at the bank counter. To remain solvent, bankers circulated their notes far from the bank. Poor roads and arduous travel conditions were allies of the bankers. The idea was to distribute notes so far from home that a wildcat could not find its way to the bank counter. Such disreputable practices earned the name "wildcat banking."

Since there was no national bank, income from federal land sales went into private banks. These deposits paid U.S. government expenses, or were forwarded to the federal treasury on demand. Often the private banks loaned out these federal funds and could not meet treasury demands. Private banks paid the federal obligations in their own bank notes. Since the value of private bank notes depended upon the reputation of the issuing bank, many merchants would not accept them. Heavy discounts ensued. The federal government lost millions of dollars to unscrupulous bankers and through the need to discount local currency.

Alex prospered despite the problems. The local bank was sound, and its notes accepted with little discount. He purchased many parcels of land in and around Eaton between 1810 and 1817. Most of these parcels he sold for a profit of between 300 and 500 percent, only three or four years after purchase. The family did not sell the last parcel in Eaton until years later after Alexander's death.[6]

Alex also made a name for himself in local politics. The citizens of Preble County elected him Clerk to the original Board of County Commissioners and he served as Clerk of the County Court for most of the years he lived in Preble County.[7] The land records of Preble County between 1810 and 1817 are replete

10

with instances where Alexander served as a witness to deeds. This not only testifies to his popularity and credibility among the people, but to the fact that he took his offices seriously. Keeping close to the volatile land prices also helped him become a very successful land speculator. The *History of Preble County*, published in 1881, has high praise for Alexander Lanier:

> Major Lanier, in addition to his fine social qualities was a superior scholar and a remarkably energetic man. He contributed largely to the organization of the county; and being the first clerk of the board of commissioners, he drew up all their forms, and so admirably arranged all the details of business in that department of county affairs, that the same is substantially followed to the present day. He did the same thing in the office of the clerk of courts, originating his own forms from the nature of the business in hand, and the old records yet attest his admirable executive ability. In this respect he was the master pioneer of the county . . . The name of this worthy man and prominent pioneer stands perpetuated in the county, in the name of "Lanier" township . . . It is a standing monument to his memory, more lasting than a granite or marble shaft.

Alexander had several business interests. He went into the sawmill business with Dennis Pottenger in 1810. He also went into the mercantile business about this time with a Mr. Begaau. Although he enjoyed the mercantile business, the store was not as successful as his other ventures, and he soon sold his interest.[8]

Alex and Drusilla knew education was critical to success, and were determined that James obtain the best education possible. He enrolled in the local school as soon as the schoolmaster would take him. School gave exercise to his blooming mind, but did not relieve him of family responsibilities. As an only child, James had more responsibilities than boys who came from larger families. It was at this time that JFD began to develop his ability to organize his time and handle many tasks at once. The school disappointed mother and pupil, however. In JFD's own words:

> **"While at Eaton I attended the village school for about eighteen months. It was kept by a Mr. Stevens, who taught only the rudiments of an English education."**[9]

Although JFD's formal schooling was suspect, about this time his parents probably began teaching him the rudiments of gentlemanly behavior. Learning to sit at the table quietly for 30 minutes is difficult for a seven year old. Chances are, most of

11

the time he used his knife and fork properly, and obeyed the Cardinal Rule of chewing quietly with his mouth closed. Like most boys, he, no doubt, enjoyed watching his father carve the meat and looked forward to the day carving lessons would start. It would have been like Drusilla to make a game of teaching him to escort her to the table.

Alex and Drusilla were not "Sunday Christians." They practiced Christian virtues every day. The Laniers attended the Presbyterian church when available. If there was no Presbyterian church close, a Methodist meeting house would suffice. The Golden Rule was the family guide. Alex and Drusilla had strong morals and ethics. They believed the Laniers were well born and therefore had high responsibilities and obligations. They preached this virtue of "Noblesse Oblige" to their son.

On March 4, 1812, the County Commissioners voted to subdivide the county into more manageable units, splitting the two townships into smaller units. Lanier Township became the largest of these new units. Alexander's sense of humor, so vital on the frontier, stands out in a story about the formation of another township that same day.

> An Early Quaker settlement was made at a point now called West Elkton; and these Friends became desirous to have a new township established, and to this end they petitioned the Commissioners, wherein they claimed that Lanier township as it then stood, was too large for the convenience of the settlers to attend the polls and transact their township business. . . . but as the settlers were then few in number, the petition was overruled. Mr. (Samuel) Stubbs was made the spokesman in the second effort. He appeared before the Commissioners and after reviewing his former argument for a new township, he concluded by saying: "now friends, we think we are right in making this request, and we also believe that we ought to have a township gratis. This latter remark so pleased Alexander C. Lanier, then clerk of the Board, that he remarked to the Commissioners "Let him have it and call it Gratis." The commissioners at once assented to the suggestion; and this incident is the origin of the name the township now bears.[10]

The townships of Lanier and Gratis as well as a community named Gratis survive to this day in Preble County.

The sawmill, his land speculation, and his pay as clerk of court and clerk of the county commissioners, allowed the family to live well. Alexander built the first frame house in Eaton. Frame construction looked suspicious to many people. They felt it was not as sturdy as solid log construction. Alexander took people on tours of the house and pointed out its advantages. Converts were good customers for the sawmill. Later, he built the second brick house in Eaton, one block west of the center of town on Main Street between Barren and Beech Streets.[11]

Life was good for the Laniers. Alex was well established and highly respected. The family was living comfortably. The future held promise. As is often the case, however, the future does not always conform to one man's plan.

# 3.
# "I suffered incurable hurts"
—Alexander Lanier 1814

*Alexander was successful, and Drusilla was happy in Eaton. At 10, James was still a care free boy. He worked hard, but would go off and fish, or play with other boys whenever he could sneak away. Thousands of miles from Eaton, belligerent governments and piracy on the high seas would change the Laniers' lives forever.*

By 1812, the after-shocks of the war on the coast reverberated on the western frontier. England allied herself with the Indians who carried the fight to the settlers. William Henry Harrison led the fight in the West. Alexander Lanier felt a strong obligation to defend the country that had allowed him to prosper; the land that had sheltered his family. It was his turn to take up the sword. Drusilla did not object, we surmise she understood the responsibility; she shared the obligation.

James listened to their conversations and absorbed the lesson. He wanted to go to war along with his father. Alex smiled inwardly, but patiently explained that James was more valuable at home. He had to become the man of the house and help his mother in his father's absence. Drusilla argued that she could not survive without James' help.

His father needed two horses, so James happily gave up his horse for the cause. Walking everywhere would be inconvenient, but James did not miss the hours of care the horse required. As an adult, a stable boy would be one of his first luxuries.

At the age of eleven, JFD left whatever childhood he had enjoyed and became an adult. It was at this time that the sobriety of life began to shape his character. That JFD Lanier was a serious man, seldom displaying a ready humor, can be traced to this beginning.

Alex received a commission of major in the Ohio Militia.[1] Of average height, he had a full head of dark hair that ran out from under his hat down the back of his neck. Although the normal tasks of living contributed to muscle and stamina, Alex's profession did not require strenuous exercise. His stomach slumped slightly. At the head of the column of troops, however, he stood tall. The new uniform added to his military bearing. Drusilla stitched each seam double strong with a full measure of love to protect him from harm. Drusilla's heart fluttered anew as her handsome major marched off to war. James was very proud of his father, running alongside his horse until ordered back to his mother's side. They both watched until the column was out of sight and the last curls of dust settled back on the road.

Drusilla continued James' home schooling after Alex left. After the evening meal was the best time for mother and son to talk. She could converse while knitting or mending. James could clean candlesticks or fix a broken implement while talking with his mother. Like most boys, James brought home the slang of the streets. Drusilla quickly reproved vulgar words and phrases. They would debate the common questions of the time. She forced James to defend his position and to consider alternates. Most importantly, Drusilla taught him the art of listening attentively. In the early 1800's there was nothing that marked a gentleman more than his ability to remain silent and listen closely.

James, no doubt, began to notice girls about this time. With his father gone, Drusilla answered his ill disguised questions on the subject. Deciding he needed to learn to dance Drusilla taught him reels and waltzes. With no other means to provide the music she would hum the tunes as they danced. JFD enjoyed the lessons and was a good pupil. They constantly missed their husband and father, however, and never neglected him in evening prayers.

Placed under the command of Major General John L. Gano, Alex commanded a unit charged with supplying the string of defenses from Lake Erie westward to Fort Wayne, an outpost at the confluence of the Maumee and St. Joseph Rivers. Alexander also commanded Fort St. Clair, just outside Eaton. He put his organizational skills to good use in supplying the troops with the necessities of war.[2]

An army can only march if it has supplies; only fight if it has powder. Major Lanier supplied the necessities of success to General William Henry Harrison. A friendship forged amid whistling shot and among exploding shells developed between the two men. Pay voucher records show that Alex served from September 1, 1812, to October 20, 1812. His pay was $82.25 for the period, plus $16.45 for forage for two horses, and $32.40 for his own subsistence.[3]

At home things were not going well. Margaret Street became ill in the spring of 1813. Drusilla cared for her sister-in-law and her three children who were eleven, eight, and three years old. The youngest was James Lanier Street, named for his grandfather in a desperate attempt at heavenly reconciliation. On April 13, Margaret died. It was a hard blow for Alex and Drusilla. For James it was the second close relative to die. He was learning to cope with death at an early age.[4]

The War of 1812 wrecked the careful spending policy nurtured by the Democrat-Republicans. The monetary system, with state banks as the keystone, was not up to the task of financing the war. Inflation spiraled upward, and banks quit paying out specie. Unredeemable bank notes were worthless. The unstable banks paid tremendous discounts to survive. In 1814, currency discounts from some southern banks reached 23% at Baltimore.[5]

Writing a review of the history of the U.S. Bank in 1829, Albert Gallatin stated that the federal government issued $80,000,000 in bonds to realize $34,000,000 in cash to finance the war. [6] Gallatin stated unequivocally that, had the national bank been in operation, the suspension of specie payments would have been avoided. Gallatin insisted that the outlay of cash needed for the war would have been little more than the $34,000,000 actually spent.[7] Wars make strange allies. One of the major purchasers of U.S. bonds to finance the War of 1812 was the American representative of the British banking house of Baring Brothers.[8]

The cost of the war ballooned the National Debt to $127,335,000. This amounted to a staggering $15 for every man, woman, and child in the country. Annual government expenditures of about 11 million dollars more than tripled to 35 million dollars after the war. The war forced Congress to enact new taxes on land, dwellings and slaves in 1813. Still, spending outstripped revenue. In 1814, the tariff rates increased and the taxes imposed just the year before were doubled. The number of items subject to tax also increased.[9]

The war also caused chaos in the Lanier family. In addition to the increased workload, less money was available. James felt the need to supply the family with monetary support while his father was away. At age 13, he went to work for Cornelius Van Ausdall, who owned the largest store in Eaton.[10]

James was beginning to fill out. He had well-defined muscles thanks to the need to chop and carry the family wood supply as well as garden plowing and numerous other chores. Later paintings suggest young James was of average height and well proportioned. It appears he resembled his mother's side of the family more than the Lanier line. His light hair curled naturally framing a high forehead. He carried his head high, creating a prominent chin. He had his father's intense eyes. James never developed a wit to match his father, and his smile, while genuine, seldom reached his eyes.

Working at Van Ausdall's store had a profound effect on JFD:

> . . . I served as clerk in the store of a Mr. Cornelius Van Ausdall, an immigrant of Dutch descent from Hagerstown, Maryland, and a very worthy man. I believe he is still living (1867 — He was, Van Ausdall died in 1870). I have always looked upon my service with him as one of the most valuable periods of my early life. It taught me to be industrious, active, methodical and the value, if I may use the word, of small things. I was brought into contact with all varieties of people, had to turn my hand to every kind of work, and learned how to be respectful and obliging to all . . . [11]

This was James' initiation to the world of commerce. The business of the store reflected the problems of the "hard money" policy practiced by the Democrat-Republicans:

. . . The stock in the store consisted chiefly of light cotton goods, twists (of thread), buttons, and the smaller articles of hard and tinware, and other articles suited to the primitive condition of the people with whom we dealt. The greater part of the trade consisted of barter. The most valuable articles received in exchange for goods were peltries of one kind or another. . . The only money then in circulation was silver-Spanish coins chiefly, received by way of New Orleans . . . [12]

He goes on to support General Washington's assessment of almost thirty years earlier; explaining that travel between the Ohio frontier and the Eastern seaboard was so arduous that farmers shipped surplus crops to New Orleans:

. . . The route to the eastern markets was up the Ohio River to Pittsburgh and Wheeling, in keel-boats; thence by wagons to Philadelphia or Baltimore. There was in those days, neither roads nor steam boats in the West. The cost was too great to allow the transportation of the produce of the Western country to market, except a small amount of flour, corn and provisions sent down the river in arks or flatboats to New Orleans. Nearly everything produced in the family was consumed in it . . . (Spanish coin) was packed on horses when the merchant went east to make his purchases, and the lighter kinds of goods were brought back in the same manner. The trip to and from the Eastern states was then an affair of greater magnitude and peril, and required a greater length of time than that at present (1871) between New York and San Francisco; or between New York and Europe. The country was wholly without good roads, and almost the only mode of travel, as of transporting merchandise was on the backs of horses and mules . . . [13]

The tie between the western states and New Orleans would grow in the next 50 years and have a profound influence on public attitudes at the outbreak of the Civil War.

With his father gone, James had to be the host of the house. Drusilla undoubtedly taught him to serve soup and fish, and to carve various cuts of meat. Using everyday glasses and water, James and Drusilla could have practiced serving and drinking wine at the table. This training would serve him well in later years, when serving wine in the opulence of his beautiful mansion on the river.

Alexander served in the army again from August 21, 1813, to Feb. 20, 1814. He commanded Lanier's Independent Battalion of the Ohio militia.[14] During December of 1813, Alex commanded Fort St. Mary on the St. Mary's River, about 70 miles north and east of Eaton. On December 8, he ordered a sunken ferry boat

18

raised and put back in service. The partially raised boat began to fall back into the water. Alexander jumped into the water to add his strength to keep the craft afloat. As the heavy boat heeled over, Alex strained to keep the gunwale above the surface. Pain ripped through his arms, back, and thighs. Major Lanier suffered what he described as "incurable hurts," sustaining a serious hernia.[15]

He continued on duty despite intense pain. Not knowing he was injured; General Gano ordered Alex to attend a Courts Marshal in January of 1814.[16] The court was at Fort Meigs near Chicago. Not wanting to shirk his duty, Alex attended the court proceedings, and continued to endure the hardships of winter in the field until discharged in February of 1814. The injury would plague him the rest of his life. He earned a disability pension, which paid him $12.50 per month from March 5, 1814, until his death on March 25, 1820.[17]

Drusilla and James barely recognized Alex when he arrived home. His eyes were lifeless and his hair was turning prematurely white. He slumped in the saddle in obvious pain. The condition of her husband appalled Drusilla. She immediately marched him to bed; then set about nursing her husband back to health as he had tended to her 14 years earlier.

Alex continued James' education when he returned. He taught his son that personal appearance was an advertisement of character. Clothes did not need to be new, but they should always be clean and well fitting. Black coats were proper. At that time, black was a very expensive color to produce. Less expensive black garments would fade to a rusty brown, but still marked a man as respectable even if he was poor. Bright coats and brocaded vests were for bar room drummers and others of dubious character. Jewelry was the advertisement of sin. No matter what the temperature, a fully buttoned vest and dress coat were proper attire. Perspiration was a small price to pay for propriety.

William Henry Harrison earned the task of negotiating a peace treaty with the Indians. He visited Eaton with the intention of having his friend share the triumph. Seeing Alex's condition, he invited James to represent the family. Alex felt honored; James excited, and Drusilla privately dubious. According to his biography, James acted as a special aide to General Harrison, sharing the general's tent at Greenville, Ohio.[18] He observed the

19

great Indian chiefs at the treaty grounds outside Greenville, and shared the common distrust of the race.

The war and the fiscal situation spotlighted the deficiencies of a "hard money" economy. James listened as his mother and father complained about local banks and yearned for the return of the U.S. Bank. He overheard Van Ausdall, his employer, bemoan the lack of currency, and the dismal roads. He listened with reverence to his father's stories about General Harrison. A Federalist mentality was beginning to develop.

The need for a national bank became apparent to many, and Secretary of the Treasury Dallas recommended it in 1814. His concept passed the House of Representatives without difficulty by a vote of 66 to 40. Compromises weakened the concepts during writing of the actual bill, however. On December 5, 1815, President Madison vetoed the bill as unworkable, but conceded the constitutional authority to establish a bank. This was the first break in the opposition of the bank by the Democrat-Republicans.[19]

Immediately after the veto on January 8, 1816, John C. Calhoun introduced a new bill. His bill was very close to what Secretary Dallas had proposed in 1814. Henry Clay, who in 1811, had voted against the first bank, supported Calhoun's bill. Daniel Webster opposed the bill. This issue would springboard those three Congressmen into a prominence they would maintain until the eve of the Civil War. The bill passed on March 14, 1816, and chartered the Second National Bank. Its charter was to run until 1836.[20]

At home, Alex struggled to regain his health and reestablish himself in the community. James accompanied his father whenever he could. Starting in 1814, JFD's name shows up as witness to some of his father's purchases. James was an attentive pupil; Alex a lucid teacher. He explained how to evaluate land; how to sell the virtues of the tract. James learned the proper form for a deed and the legal shortcuts in filing the papers.

Alex passed along several moral and ethical rules that were inviolate. He was always fair and honest. He never allowed a man's politics or religion to influence a business deal. Alex never spoke ill of a man in public. Government service was an inviolate public trust. These were lessons that James learned well, and practiced all of his life.

If James recognized any weaknesses, it was that his father

was too trusting; too forgiving. Alex seldom insisted on his own rights. These were the same shortcomings that had led to disaster in Kentucky. When James protested, Alex would explain that the culprit would have to answer to his own conscience, a much sterner judge than any court of law.

Once the war ended, consumers purchased the goods scarce during the war. Cotton and other commodity prices soared. Farmers needed more land to meet the pent-up demand. They looked to the fertile land in the West. More and more settlers were venturing across the Mississippi River. There was no prime land for sale near Eaton, so the great westward migration bypassed the community. Alex became restive.

Despite his infirmities, Alexander continued with his civic duties. He was clerk of the county commissioners when the commissioners approved the second courthouse. The building would cost $532.95, and under the watchful eye of Alexander Lanier funds began to be raised in 1816. The grand structure opened in 1820, but only after the Lanier family moved west.[21]

With his father home, James was able to resume his schooling. He boarded at an academy at Newport, Kentucky. In his autobiography, James praises the teachers, Morse and Jones, commenting that he derived much from their instruction.[22] His father's decision to move once again interrupted James' schooling.

Alexander, well respected in Eaton, could have lived out his life in comfort among numerous friends. He was not one, however, to settle for predictability and comfort. He was adventurous and ambitious, traits he passed on to his son. Alex was aware of the flow of wagons heading west, and friends in Cincinnati spoke often of the many boats headed down the Ohio River. The treaty of Greenville made the land west of Ohio safe for settlement. Now was the time. If he acted quickly, he could amass a fortune.

Indiana had recently gained statehood with all the legal protection that status offered. On the long rides, and around the campfires of war, General Harrison boosted the Indiana Territory. He dreamed of being the first governor of the new state with large plantation-like farms populated with settlers from the South. Harrison lost the election to Jonathan Jennings, and the Quaker-small farmer coalition, but that did not diminish his love of this land. He maintained a mansion in Vincennes, and his op-

21

timism about Indiana sparked Alex's imagination.

Drusilla felt encouraged by her husband's renewed interest. As he planned the move, his strength grew and he scanned the *Niles Weekly Register* for news from the land offices in Indiana. His eyes regained their shine as he talked of Indiana. The truss, so tightly wrapped each morning seemed to keep the pain at a tolerable level. The move would be a hardship on her and James, but it was a tonic for Alex, so they would gladly strike out again.

Madison, a town on the edge of civilization with access to the Ohio River, the greatest commercial artery in the West, was an obvious choice for a home. It was ready to boom, and Alex wanted to be part of the expansion. The town included families that had called Virginia, Kentucky, South Carolina, and other southern locales home. Alexander and Drusilla would be comfortable with other expatriates from the South.

The Laniers were not alone as they headed west. Some historians dubbed the period 1814-1819 as the "Great Migration." Indiana grew by more than 100,000 souls in the ten year span 1810 to 1820; more than seventy-five per cent of that increase coming in the last half of the decade.

*Niles Weekly Register*, a well-respected Baltimore paper that specialized in migration stories and western news, reported in February 1815:

> Our monthly returns from the several land offices in Ohio and Indiana Territory, exhibit an unparalleled sale of public lands, since the pacification of the Indian tribes in that quarter . . . The main road through the state I am told, has been almost literally covered with waggons (sic) moving out families.[23]

# 4.
# "An irreparable loss. . ."

—Madison Courier 1820

*Alexander and his family arrived in Madison in the fall of 1817 full of life and hope. Within three years he would lose both. James did not like the town, but would survive sorrow and find love in his new home.*

Madison perched precariously on the slippery bank of the Ohio River. Its two main streets reached up the hillside like two strong arms grasping to keep the town from slipping back into the fast moving current. Madison disappointed JFD. He observed that Indians roamed freely as close as twenty miles north of town. He estimated the population of the town to be

> ". . . about 150 people. It had been so recently settled that it was still a forest - the trees that were not standing almost covered the ground where they fell. It was wholly without streets or any improvements fitted to make it an attractive or agreeable place."[1]

Others were not so harsh in their appraisals, closely matching Alex's assessment:

Madison . . . (has) many local advantages. Being at the extreme northern line of the great bend of the Ohio River, is nearer to the rich and fertile districts of the central part of the state than any other important town on the river.[2]

One of the attractions for Alex was the Farmers and Mechanics Bank. It was one of the two major banks in the state. It was a well run, honest bank. The board of directors and officers were all prominent citizens whose goal, in addition to making money, was to help the town prosper. The bank enjoyed a better reputation than did the other major bank in the state, the First State Bank of Indiana, which was headquartered in Vincennes.[3]

The first Lanier house in Madison was smaller than the one they left in Eaton, but the prospects were bright. Alex was a hard worker and James and Drusilla would do more than their share.

Alexander opened a dry goods store at the corner of Second and Main streets. Supplying the burgeoning population seemed the fastest way to riches. Storekeeping is not an ideal occupation for a man with a festering hernia, but Alex was not one to dwell on the negative. Perhaps, with his experience of supplying the army during the war, Alex thought shopkeeping would suit him. Perhaps Mr. Van Ausdall's success and James' training inspired him.

Alexander immediately made friends in Madison. A. A. Meek, a general under Harrison, had settled in Madison. He was a lawyer and dabbled in land speculation. Milton Stapp was another soldier that had returned to Madison after the war. The group readily accepted James because he had accompanied General Harrison at the treaty grounds. He enjoyed listening to the soldiers talk about the war and, with prompting, told about the treaty negotiations.

Soon after moving to Madison, James continued his education at a private school taught by **"a very superior person from the Eastern States."**[4] When James was not in school, he was a big help to his father at the store. Alexander and Drusilla continued to impress upon James that he had an elevated station in life, and needed to know the social graces. They reinforced the necessity of listening. It was never necessary to laud yourself. "Praise your friends and let your friends praise you" was an adage that both parents preached and practiced.

But Alexander picked a poor time to start a new business.

The *Indiana Republican* and the *Madison Courier* carried this advertisement in November 1817.

## NEW STORE

The subscriber offers for sale in the house formerly occupied by R.S. Mixtor in Madison, a general assortment of MERCHANDIZE consisting of

Fine and course Cloths
Cassimeres
Pellisse Cloths
Imperial Cords
Vesting
Velvets
Domestic Cottons
Irish Linens
Imperial Shiftings
Dimites
Calicoes
Chintz
Cambrics
Joconet
Leno
Mulmul Muslins
Book &
 India
Bed Ticking
 Bombazetts
Suspenders
Checks
Ginghams
Jeans
Silks
Silk Shawls
Silk Handkerchiefs
Cotton Shawls
Mourning Shawls
Bandana
Madrass
Pulicat                Handkerchiefs
Naval and
Fancy Ribbons
Morocco and full-trimmed Shoes
Groceries
Hardware
Cutlery
Queensware
Tinware
Hats&c
Jamaica Spirits
Wines
Candles &c

ALL of which will be sold at a moderate advance on the Philadelphia prices for Cash or such Country Produce as I may find beneficial. Peddlers may find it to their interest to give him a call.

ALEXANDER C. LANIER
Madison, Nov. 1                47-tf

By 1817 overproduction of commodities was outstripping the demand, and the first signs of economic weakness were evident to those who looked closely.

Europe was purchasing less from the United States. In 1816 customs receipts of the federal government were $36 million dollars. They dropped steadily until 1823 when they reached $13 million. The U.S. Treasury suffered an additional loss from land sales. Receipts for public land sales hit $3,274,000 in 1819, but by 1820 receipts dropped a staggering 50% to $1,635,000. Americans became more self sufficient and purchased fewer goods from overseas. In 1818, imported goods totaled $121 million. In 1819, imports dropped to $87 million.

As small as Madison was, there were several other stores in town. Advertisements for Alex's competitors, David McClure, J. & A.G. Reed and John Sheets appear often in the Madison papers.

James found himself drawn to the Sheets store. Sheets' sister-in-law, Elisabeth Gardner, clerked during busy times. Elisabeth was visiting from Lexington, but she was in no hurry to return home. It seemed that she was always the one that waited on James. It annoyed Alex that James knew more of what was going on at the Sheets store than his own, until Drusilla told him the reason.

Alex seemed bedeviled with customers that failed to pay their debts. Merchants carried their own accounts and had to make collections. Alex was trusting and forgiving, but many people took advantage of his good nature. His last recourse was the courts. As reluctant as he was to sue customers, Jefferson County records disclose that he took numerous debtors to court.[5] This pained Alex almost as much as his hernia, and Drusilla privately wished they were back in Eaton where debts were important trusts.

During the time that Alexander was struggling to establish his store, Indiana was struggling to establish itself as a state. The capitol was at Corydon, 90 miles down the Ohio River from Madison. Most of the 60,000 inhabitants of the state lived in close proximity to the river. As JFD noted, Indians controlled the majority of the lands in the northern two thirds of the state.

Government was minimal. Governor Jonathan Jennings, Lieutenant Governor Christopher Harrison, and a part-time legislature ruled with relatively few problems. Christopher Harrison was no relation to William Henry; having come from an aristocratic family in Maryland. His first home in Indiana had been just west of Madison, near Hanover. Jennings led the Democrat Republicans, while William Henry Harrison spoke for the Federalist party. Political parties did not have structure. What division there was, centered on the ideas of individuals rather than party platforms. The Laniers could be forever counted in the Harrison column.

Political debate centered on protection from the Indians, education, and the locating of a new state capitol closer to the geographical center of the state. The most divisive political discussions in Indiana dealt with the need for internal improvements. While the debate raged, farmers suffered and the state lay undeveloped.

The Eastern Seaboard hungered for the surplus produce of Indiana, but there was no way to transport the bounty. The Ohio River was the only dependable means of transportation for the state. Shipping upriver was impossible in the days before the steamboat, so Indiana's only outlet was New Orleans. Some grain did find its way from there to the east coast, but it was indeed a long and costly route. Traffic was brisk when the river behaved. The March 8, 1818, edition of the Madison *Indiana Republican* noted that the river was high and the weather was pleasant. Thirty-four boats had passed Madison on March 5 alone.

In the fall and winter the river was often low or frozen. Even if the Ohio River was passable, the vast fertile prairie between the Great Lakes and the river lacked adequate transportation. Roads were impassable much of the year and the rivers were undependable. What good was the golden harvest if it rotted on the wharf waiting for the waters of some river to rise or recede? Who would purchase a hogshead of wheat infested with meal worms or slime rot on the tortuous overland trip from Indiana to Maryland?

Under intense pressure from all sides, the federal government finally agreed to allot five percent of the revenue from land sales to construct roads. The federal government held two percent for national roads, and three percent accrued to the states for their use. The Indiana legislature appointed Christopher Harrison agent of "the Three Per Cent Fund." Politicians planned great projects for this fund. Governor Jennings stated in 1818:

> The internal improvements of the state forms a subject of the most serious importance and deserves the greatest attention. It increases

27

the value of the soil, leads to culture and refinement, induces immigration, broadens the horizons of the people and prevents feuds and political broils. With the three percent fund it is within your power to lay the foundation of a system coextensive with the state.[6]

Jennings was wrong on one point: the internal improvement struggle was going to produce one of the most serious "political broils" in the state's history. The three percent fund was of little value. It was usually overdrawn because of inflated estimates of revenue. Actual collections seldom kept pace with the grand plans.[7]

Shippers needed a canal around the Falls of the Ohio at Louisville to make the Ohio River navigable. The Indiana Legislature chartered a company to build the canal in 1818. The project was one of the few in the U.S. that did not draw the interest of foreign investors.[8]

The backers of the canal then organized a lottery. Lotteries were popular means of raising funds because they appealed to men's gambling instincts. Even if they did not win, the men felt their money was going to a good cause. One of the most famous lotteries raised about $80,000 for Thomas Jefferson who was in danger of losing Monticello.[9] The lottery did not help the canal, however. Despite a mammoth construction effort, the Falls of the Ohio Canal project failed.[10]

Alex built one of the first brick buildings in Madison and moved the store into the first floor. The family lived on the second floor. He reasoned that having his store and living quarters in the same building would save money. In addition, a brick building was a great investment. Drusilla loved the large front living room that had an excellent view.

To enlarge his business, Alex opened an auction service. As early as March of 1818, advertisements in the *Indiana Republican* proclaimed that he held consignment auctions every Wednesday and Saturday.

As in Eaton, Alex gained respect in the community and became secretary of the Royal Arch Masons. Alex allowed the Grand Lodge of Indiana Free and Accepted Masons to use the big room on the second floor for meetings. The Masons were the most powerful fraternal organization in the United States. Both Alexander and JFD were members. The structure, known as the Schofield House is still standing today as a Masonic museum.[11]

As inflation spiraled upward, Alex borrowed more money.

His income never caught up with his debt. More customers defaulted on their bills, and the future looked bleak. It was evident that the country was drowning in a depression. Alex was one of thousands of businessmen caught in the economic whirlpool. The federal government was struggling also. The U. S. Bank, in concert with the secretary of the treasury, moved to improve the government's deteriorating fiscal condition. It declared that beginning July 1, 1818, it would accept only specie as payment for federal drafts. Panic rippled through the West. Banks did not have the specie to pay, and many failed. Discount rates for those that survived reached as high as seventy-five percent.[12]

Until the specie order, the Farmers and Mechanics Bank ranked as one of the safest banks in the Northwest. The U.S. Land Office accepted its notes at par or face value. According to John Sering, the Farmers and Mechanics Bank cashier:

> This bank continued to pay specie until its notes were refused at the Land Office, when its payment became only an accommodation to brokers. Even after that we have continued to furnish our people such paper as is taken at the land office in exchange for our notes.[13]

William Hendricks, a strong Democrat-Republican, represented Indiana in the U.S. Congress. He was a resident of Madison who knew first hand the reputation of the bank. He argued against the order, asking that the Farmers and Mechanics Bank be exempted from the specie order and was "entitled to the fullest confidence" of the government. The secretary of the treasury yielded to the political pressure. When the Vincennes bank failed in 1820, he named the Farmers and Mechanics Bank as the repository for federal funds. The bank served in this capacity from October of 1820 to October of 1821.[14]

Storekeeping was not for James. The instant wealth his father forecast had not developed. The family was worse off than they had been in Eaton. As James matured, it became clear to him that the law was the keystone of success. Honesty, integrity, truth, and faith formed the cornerstones of life, but only the courts protected these virtues. His father was living proof that virtue alone could not guarantee success.

Early in 1819, James began to study law in the offices of A.A. Meek. Since Meek was on the board of directors of the Farmers and Mechanics Bank, James could not help absorbing some banking lessons from Meek. Being a Brigadier General in the 5th

LOST
THE tenth volume of Mavor's Universal History. Any person having it in their possession, will confer a favor on the undersigned by informing him of the same, or leaving it at Gen. Meek's Law office.
*JAMES F.D. LANIER*
*August 18th 1819*

BRIGADE ORDERS.
Major John Sheets, has been appointed Brigade Quartermaster, and is to be obeyed and respected accordingly.
By order of Gen. Meek,
JAS. F. D. LANIER, aid.
January 7th, 1820

BRIGADE ORDERS
Having received official information, that the 6th Regt. in the 5th brigade Indiana militia, contains more than its legal number of companies, the Field officers of said brigade will meet at the court house in Switzerland county, on the 8th day of Oct. Next, for the purpose of dividing said Regiment according to law.
By order of the Gen.
JAS. F. D. LANIER, *Aid.*
Sept. 6th, 1819
The Independent Examiner, and Indiana Oracle, will please give the above a few insertions

**Several notices signed by James Lanier appeared in the Madison papers during the time he studied with General Meek.**

Indiana Militia Regiment, Meek made James a captain in the militia. The only military service he performed was in the Indiana Militia.[15]

John Sheets was surviving the depression, and proving to be an intelligent businessman. In 1819 he built one of the first pork processing plants in Madison. It was the forerunner of a thriving industry for the city.[16] James Lanier watched Sheets' business operation closely, hoping to discover ideas that would help his father. It also gave him an excuse to see Elisabeth on a regular basis.

The summer of 1819 was exceptionally hot and dry. On Sunday, August 22, church services were unbearable. Men sweated freely and women fanned themselves incessantly to keep from fainting. The blistering sun reinforced sermons that threatened the fires of damnation. At 5:00 P.M., the thermometer stood at ninety-eight degrees.[17]

By August and September the Ohio River was so low that river traffic was at a standstill. No goods came in; no produce hauled out.[18] The situation reinforced the need for more dependable means of transportation. The drought effectively embargoed the city until the spring rains once again filled the river.

This local catastrophe deepened the depression for Madison and other river towns. Only the most necessary goods reached the town over the narrow trails. This was the crowning blow to Alex's mercantile efforts. Faced with the drought and the realization that James would not be a storekeeper, he sold the store to William Robinson, newly arrived from Baltimore.

The sale of the store greatly reduced Alexander's debts, but lowered the family's standard of living. The auction business, and Alex's war pension brought in some money, but most of James earnings went to support the family.

Late in 1819, General William Henry Harrison honored James and his family by offering the boy an appointment to West Point. James admits that he wanted to attend the Academy, but turned the offer down at the request of his mother. In his autobiography he states:

> **At this period, General Harrison, afterward President of the United States, and who was a warm and lifelong friend of the family, procured for me a cadetship at West Point. I was very eager to accept the appointment, but relinquished it, seeing that my mother was greatly distressed at the thought of my leaving home, I being her only child.**[19]

His mother's wishes would weigh heavily on the final decision. Drusilla had proven to be a sage advisor. James did not have a rugged constitution. He and Drusilla had only to look at Alex to witness the ravages that military life could inflict. James had chosen a profession and was well into his studies with General Meek. There was one other overwhelming factor. James Lanier was in love.

The fiscal panic, the deterioration of his father's business, even the shabby appearance of Madison could not weigh down James' spirit. The sun shone brighter, the breeze blew sweeter, and the future beckoned without fear. Elisabeth Gardner was two years older than James. She was born in Augusta County Virginia where her family owned large tracts of land. Like the Laniers, the Gardners had moved west in 1802 settling in Lexington, Kentucky. Her father was a leader in that community.

Elisabeth made an immediate impression on Alex and Drusilla. She exhibited the grace and charm of the old south. She was beautiful by any measure, and could have had any man in Madison for her husband. She was a head shorter than James, but her wit and friendliness surpassed his. She was prim and

31

lady-like around Alex and Drusilla, but teasing and playful with James. She forced him to be less serious and to be more sociable. His interest in dancing revived. He suddenly enjoyed picnic lunches in hidden coves along the river.

Drusilla saw in Elisabeth reflections of her youth. Alexander saw the breeding that would maintain the family stature. James saw lifelong happiness with Elisabeth. They married on December 7, 1819.[20] They moved in with Alex and Drusilla.

Drusilla had hoped that without the responsibility of the store; Alex would slow down and take better care of himself. Alexander's health was deteriorating, and although Drusilla and James did not want to admit it, they worried. No matter how tightly he wrapped the truss, pain was a constant companion Alexander would admit to short episodes of pain or discomfort. He would pass them off as being brought on by changes in the weather; by the muddy streets; or by slippery stairs. Everything was to blame, from poorly made wagon springs to ill fitting boots.

Alex would heed no suggestions that he slow down or concede to the pain. He knew that once he gave up he would die. James quit arguing with his father, realizing that the exchanges were more painful to Alex than the hernia. The British, the war, General Gano, William Henry Harrison, and the St. Mary's River where Alex suffered his injury all took their share of Drusilla's silent wrath. She knew better than to accuse them openly, as Alex would brook no condemnation of his comrades in arms or their cause.

Alexander's main occupation, when he could work, was administering sales, and as a consignment auctioneer. Despite his constant pain, he trav-

> Departed this life on the 25th ultimo, near Lancaster Ky. after a long and extremely painful illness, Maj. A.C. Lanier of this place, aged 42 years.
>
> In this solemn and afflicting Providence, his wife and family have sustained an irreparable loss, and society a very valuable member. Maj. Lanier was a worthy patriot and enjoyed whilst living, universal respect. He was a member of the Royal Arch Chapter of Madison and a pious member of the Methodist Episcopal Church. Possessed as he was of many amiable qualities, his memory and worth will live though he is gone. He was interred on the 27th in Lancaster, by the brethren of the Masonic fraternity in due Masonic order.

On April 13, 1820, the Madison Courier printed a long obituary; an honor reserved for the most prominent citizens in that time.

eled a wide circle in this chore, as his honesty and humor were in demand. On March 25,1820, while in Lancaster, Kentucky, administering a sale, Alexander died of complications brought on by his war injury.

Even though he could see his father's death coming, the news hit James hard. Never one to show his emotions publicly, he found a secluded spot on the river bank and let his emotions free in a flood of tears.

Drusilla turned to James as the head of the family. He was responsible for making all of the arrangements to eventually return Alex's body to Madison, and for the local funeral. He visited the Third Street Graveyard and picked a grave site. The cemetery was small, hemmed in by the frequent flooding of Crooked Creek. James decided to purchase several burial plots. Everyone involved was understanding about the payments. They accepted James' word without hesitation. Alex's sterling reputation automatically passed on to James.

Although never admitting it, Alex knew for some time that he was losing his last battle. Well before his death he prepared a detailed Will.:

> being weak in body but of common mind and memory calling to mind that is appointed for all men ever to die, deem it precedent to make some disposition of the small property of which I may die possessing. I give my body to it's parent (sic) earth wishing it to be deposited decently and Masonically.[21] Alex's will declared that his debts be paid. He bequeathed to his "beloved wife Drusilla Lanier her choice of the beds, a silver watch, and her saddle and bridle."[22]

To JFD he left his silver plate and his sword "(hoping he will use it only in the defence of his country)" all his books and maps, and one feather bed. He split up his furniture between Drusilla and JFD, with Drusilla getting first choice. He also commanded that Drusilla live with James and cautioned James:

> And I do hereby declare that no bargain which my son shall make shall ever operate as to deprive my said wife from the use of the house and land on which I now live unless she deprives herself by marrying again. Whenever she is a widow she may enter upon and occupy said house and land indefinitely with my said son.[23]

This was his final loving attempt to take care of Drusilla. It was one final lesson to his son that responsibility extends beyond the grave.

This left young James responsible for his mother and new wife, and with debts from his father's failed businesses. He had only his father's treasured sword for protection. The future looked bleak, but James shouldered the responsibility with determination. In the midst of despair he had learned a great lesson. If he was honest with people, they would be helpful and understanding. His father had been right, kindness, and honesty were powerful allies. A father's reputation was a priceless legacy.

# 5.
## "To the State Bank of Indiana-more corruption than money"
### —Richard Daniel, June 1821

*With new responsibilities, James redoubled his efforts to establish himself. During the next seven years, he would build the foundation of respectability, honesty and integrity that anchored his entire life. JFD would become a respected lawyer; would begin building a political base; and would be introduced to banking and finance.*

James needed additional income. He had learned enough from Meek to start his own practice. Milton Stapp offered him office space. Later that same year Elizabeth presented James with a baby boy. True to family tradition they named the child Alexander Chalmers Lanier.[1] It was bittersweet to James and Drusilla that Major Lanier did not live to see his namesake.

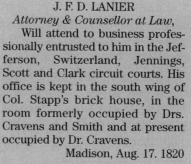

J. F. D. LANIER
*Attorney & Counsellor at Law,*
Will attend to business professionally entrusted to him in the Jefferson, Switzerland, Jennings, Scott and Clark circuit courts. His office is kept in the south wing of Col. Stapp's brick house, in the room formerly occupied by Drs. Cravens and Smith and at present occupied by Dr. Cravens.
Madison, Aug. 17. 1820

**In August this advertisement appeared in the *Indiana Republican***

35

Fiscal problems continued to plague the nation and the state. The First State Bank of Indiana at Vincennes was in the middle of the fiscal maelstrom that was sweeping the country. The decision of the U. S. Bank not to accept state paper currency stripped away the veneer of respectability from the State Bank and exposed the deep layers of corruption.[2]

Directors had made improper loans to themselves. They had poured bank funds into pet projects that were unprofitable even to the novice observer. The bank failed to pay state debts with funds deposited for that purpose. Several investigations of the bank produced unfavorable reports. Legislators who had a stake in the bank blocked these reports. In 1821, Samuel Merrill, a respected member of the legislature from Switzerland County, led one such investigation. The information gathered was incriminating, and although political maneuvering shelved the official report, the results of the investigation became common knowledge.[3]

At a banquet given to honor a visit by William Henry Harrison in 1821, Richard Daniel offered a toast that spoke volumes about the financial situation in Indiana.

"To the State Bank of Indiana - more corruption than money."[4]

State Treasurer Lane finally demanded that the First State Bank turn over all of the state funds on deposit. While the bank stalled, an independent audit showed the deposits illegally loaned, and were not available. The incensed public demanded action. In June of 1822, the Legislature closed the bank, declaring that it was insolvent. Partially because of his efforts to clean up the bank mess, Sam Merrill won the election for state treasurer that same year. He served until 1834.[5]

Lawyers have forever been closely tied to politics, so discussions before and after court sessions often centered on political topics. The corruption outraged James Lanier. He could tolerate neither ignorance nor stupidity. Alex's insistence that public service was an honor and a trust remained deeply ingrained in his son. Reluctant to speak ill of anyone, JFD fumed internally.

JFD would forever distrust those that had perpetrated the bank fraud. His friends urged him to run for office. The legislature needed his moral standards to clean up the corruption in Corydon. James considered the suggestion, but did not want to be beholden to a party or its ideology.

Banking concerns were not the only legislative problems. Hoosiers pressed the legislature to provide a fledgling transportation system. In 1821 it appropriated $10,000 into a road fund. Road designs mandated a width of 100 feet, built to the specifications of the National Road. In actuality there was little construction, and the roads were little more than trails. The roads offered minimum clearance for wagons and promised rough rides and deep ruts.[6]

Most of the money went to farmers who maintained a section of road near their land. The farmers earned $1.50 per day for their efforts. Although it was a very good wage, the farmers gained little benefit as the money returned to the state at tax time.[7]

James worked hard at his law practice. The fiscal situation in the country did not deter him. It was at this time that he developed the philosophy and plan that was to guide him successfully for the rest of his life. He states the philosophy in his autobiography:

> I was diligent, strove to be respected, and made it a point to be punctual in every duty and appointment. It was early my purpose of life to respect scrupulously the rights of others, but always to be firm in the assertion of my own. My diligence and fidelity in every engagement gave me the command of whatever money I wanted, as it was well known that I would never allow my liabilities to exceed my means. While in the practice of law, I made the causes of my clients my own. Success or defeat consequently gave me more pleasure or pain than it did them.[8]

To this strict plan he added an unwavering moral code passed down from his parents. The teachings of the church and the Masons reinforced the code. His parents had also nurtured a strong sense of community within James. From his own experience he realized the importance of education. He knew that Madison needed an educated citizenry to become an important city. The state legislature's continued refusal to fund education disappointed James. When the city decided to establish the Madison Academy in 1821, he became one of the first subscribers.[9]

JFD found that he could work best behind the scenes, **"making the causes of clients (and friends) my own."** He had no visible ego, and readily gave others credit for joint successes. Others might gain the spotlight, but he gained a solid friendship. Those friendships would pay dividends for years to come. Lanier became very influential, and many of the projects that he promoted benefited both his reputation and his bank account.

James' reputation in the community was rising, and his public pronouncements all gained thoughtful consideration. His wife and mother did not fear him, however. Drusilla and Elisabeth were friends and co-conspirators. They often combined efforts to bend James to their will, knowing just how far they could push. He complained bitterly about the two-pronged attack on his home rule, but secretly admired the skillful manipulations of the two women he loved.

JFD never established a close bond with Alexander. From earliest childhood, Alexander was carefree. He never took his father's instructions as seriously as they were given. Perhaps he had the Gardner personality. Increasingly frustrated in his attempts to guide Alexander, and busy with a variety of businesses, James left the raising of Alexander to the women. He knew Elisabeth would provide the love, and Drusilla the direction needed to make Alexander a worthy son.

James immersed himself in the business community of Madison, and Madison was the busiest community in Indiana. An outbreak of cholera was the one event that could stop the transaction of business in the thriving city. In August of 1821, it swept through the Ohio River Valley. Those stricken seemed chosen by some deadly lottery. A person would notice a slight fever at breakfast, suffer vomiting, diarrhea and dehydration after lunch, and be dead before dinner. Fear of cholera was so great that most people avoided all outside contact during an outbreak. Families moved to the country if possible. Businesses closed. Stage coaches from cities experiencing an outbreak were stopped at the city limits of "clean" towns.

Cholera was violently contagious. Infected food and drinking water were the causes, but germs and microbes were unknown so the tainted food and water never became suspects. There was little treatment. Drinking large quantities of water sometimes relieved the dehydration. An infected water source hastened death. If the water happened to be clean, the patient might survive.

Madison became a ghost-town during the epidemic. Shops closed; streets stood deserted; houses shuttered against the invasion of the disease. Mourning wreaths on doors of houses and businesses charted the progress of the disease. James followed all of the precautions, and admitted fearing the disease only to himself. The Lanier family survived, but they knew many families touched by the cold hand of death.

The fiscal strife in the country was doing almost as much damage as cholera. It was a hot political issue, and was hitting close to home. The Farmers and Mechanics Bank was dealt a staggering blow when the U. S. Bank refused its notes. It did not collapse completely, however, as did so many private banks in the West and South. In September of 1821, tired of waiting for the Farmers and Mechanics bank to die from strangulation, treasury secretary Crawford wrote to John Sering the cashier:

> It is presumed from the punctuality with which your bank has always made its transfers that the surplus has already been placed to the credit of the Treasurer of the United States. The Treasurer has accordingly been instructed to draw on you in favor of the Bank of the United States at Louisville for $140,000.00.[10]

This blow did not kill the bank as Crawford had anticipated, but it did put the bank in a coma. The directors closed the doors, but vowed to reopen when the financial situation improved.[11] As a director of the bank, the actions of the secretary of the treasury disturbed General Meek. Meek felt the move politically motivated, and not in the best interest of the United States or Indiana. Perhaps now the Democrat-Republicans would lose the trust of the people of Jefferson County.

General Meek was in poor health, a condition he jokingly blamed on the Democrat-Republicans. He continued to advise James, but could no longer work. Henry P. Thornton was a respected Madison store keeper, attorney and political figure. In August, Lanier and Thornton decided to combine their practices. In November, the House of Representatives elected Mr. Thornton Assistant Clerk.[12]

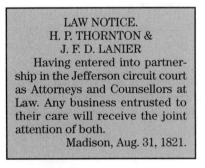

LAW NOTICE.
H. P. THORNTON &
J. F. D. LANIER
  Having entered into partnership in the Jefferson circuit court as Attorneys and Counsellors at Law. Any business entrusted to their care will receive the joint attention of both.
  Madison, Aug. 31, 1821.

**The Madison papers carried this announcement of the Thornton-Lanier partnership.**

Just before James' twenty first birthday, his friend and men-

39

tor, General Meek passed away. With his new partner away in Corydon, and left without his legal guide, James decided he had to attend college and obtain a law degree. The birth of another child, Elizabeth Frances, on February 26, 1822 delayed his plans, but did not cancel them.[13] James struggled with the decision. To his surprise and joy, Elisabeth and Drusilla encouraged James to go. They could manage the house and children. The savings the family had accumulated would suffice.

Still James delayed. Was it fair to make the women suffer for his benefit?

Despite the increasing family responsibilities, James did not shirk from public service. One of his earliest efforts to help the community was to serve as the secretary of the Madison Library Society. With no public school system, libraries were a major opportunity for education in most communities

**His service as Secretary of the Madison Library Society is just one example of James dedication to the community.**

LIBRARY NOTICE.
Pursuant to a resolution of the directors of the Madison Library society, suits will be commenced against all persons who are found in arrears after the 1st day Of March next. This is therefore to notify all delinquents to said institution that they may expect the visit of an officer if their arrears are not paid up before the above date.
By order of the directors,
J. F. D. LANIER.
Secretary
February 4th, 1822
P.S. As the society is at this juncture hard pressed for funds, it is to be hoped that the debtors to said institution will avail themselves of the above notice to make immediate payments

Many of J.F.D's friends and acquaintances were rising in state politics. In addition to Thornton, Milton Stapp represented Jefferson County in the 1822 session of the General Assembly. He, like JFD, was an independent thinking Federalist. Fellow

40

Madison lawyer, William Hendricks became Governor and served from December 1822 until February 1825.

Hendricks was a dedicated Democrat-Republican and JFD was a devout Federalist. Although they ate at different political tables, they shared a common menu. Progress was primary; party was secondary. Lanier and Hendricks became lifelong friends and would build houses across the street from one another in Madison.

Fellow Democrat-Republicans differed in their opinion of Hendricks. Some supported him.[14] Others felt he was an opportunist, that his main goal was to seek higher office. This election would certainly be different than his uncontested election as governor.[15]

The Madison muscle in the legislature pushed through an appropriation of $6,347.00 for a road from Madison, through Vernon and Columbus to Indianapolis.[16] James realized that Madison was fast becoming a center for political power. Lawyers dominated the political ranks and that was another incentive for James to complete his academic requirements for a law degree. Lanier sounded out his friends. The lawyers were unanimous in their recommendation that he attend school. John Sheets offered to contact friends at Transylvania College in his behalf. James applied to Transylvania. If accepted, he would leave after laying of the cornerstone for the new Masonic hall.

The Masons were a strong organization. John Sheets, was Grand Master of the Madison Lodge. Influential people filled the rolls of the lodge. The organization continued to grow. They needed a new meeting hall; a building of their own. James attended the laying of the cornerstone. The Masons placed several coins in the cornerstone. Some minted as early as 1797 and 1802, and others as late as 1821. The final item in the cornerstone was a copper plate stating the following message in both English and Latin.

> This cornerstone of Union Lodge #2 held at Madison was laid by John Sheets most worshipful Grand Master of Grand Lodge of Indiana on 25th day of July 1822 agreeable to ancient form and usage. C.S. Jeferes engraver [17]

Transylvania College in Lexington, Kentucky accepted James into Law School. Shortly after the Masonic Lodge corner-

41

stone dedication, he left for Lexington. Records show that James received his LB Degree in 1823.[18] The choice of schools is not surprising given that Elisabeth's family were influential citizens of the town. In addition, Alexander had maintained business friends in Lexington until his death. Transylvania was a well-respected school, outshining both Hanover College and the recently founded Indiana University. The school attracted a faculty of outstanding scholars. A degree from Transylvania would open many doors for the young lawyer.

James probably stayed with his in-laws, reducing room and board expenses. It is not unlikely that James met Henry Clay, a resident of Lexington, and the Todds, who were another leading family.

Elisabeth and Drusilla remained in Madison with the two children. Times were tough, but so was Drusilla. The sacrifices were of little consequence. She was realizing her life-long goal of seeing her son obtain the most advanced education possible. Elisabeth revealed a stubborn character in the face of poverty, refusing help from the Sheets or her parents. The two women grew as close as mother and daughter while James was in Lexington.

Immediately after graduation, James returned to Madison, and renewed his efforts on the judicial circuit. He remained an avid political spectator, and followed the political battles closely. He was a strong supporter of Henry Clay, the perennial Federalist candidate for president.

Riding the court circuit was physically demanding. It was almost as taxing as the military campaigns Drusilla recommended James avoid. Sanford Cox gives a good description:

> To witness a troop of those early attorneys entering a village as they traveled the circuit, themselves and their horses bespattered with mud and their huge port-manteaus surmounted with overcoat and umbrella, they resembled the forlorn hope of a company of mounted rangers . . . or a caravan emerging from the desert of Sahara blackened with heat and covered with dust. . . .
>
> Their long rides on horseback along blind paths and dimly defined roads, crossing unbridged streams, sleeping in the open air, as they frequently had to do, and leading colts and: driving steers home, taken on fees fully developed their physical and intellectual energies, and gave them a vigor and self reliance possessed by but a few of our more modern students.[19]

There was truth in Cox's words. Many men who rode the

court circuit exhibited great physical and intellectual energies. Hugh McCulloch, a contemporary of Lanier's on the Indiana State Bank Board, and later Comptroller of the Currency and Secretary of the Treasury under President Lincoln, was one example. Abraham Lincoln, himself a circuit rider in Illinois, was another. McCulloch had this to say about riding the circuit:

> In those long journeys through sections but sparsely settled, these circuit riding lawyers were frequently under the necessity of stopping for the night at cabins lighted only by candles or by blazing wood in the ample fireplaces, and to while away the time story telling was resorted to, in which not only memory but imagination was brought into lively exercise. To be a good story teller under such circumstances was a necessary qualification for agreeable companionship. To this practice is the country indebted for many of Mr. Lincoln's apt and original stories.[20]

JFD was not a story teller of note, and while he may have honed his intellectual energies on the court circuit, he did not enjoy it, as he relates:

> **The only mode of traveling in those days was by horseback. On most of the routes traveled we were guided by trails or blazed lines, which were often preferable to what were called roads, which, from the friable nature of the soil, were speedily so cut up as to be almost impassable, particularly in the wet seasons of the year. The rivers were crossed in log canoes, and by swimming our horses, when they could not be forded . . . I found the labor and anxiety of my profession too much for my strength, which led me to give it up as soon as other satisfactory openings presented themselves.[21]**

A temporary opening soon presented itself. Despite the best intentions of the board of directors, the Farmers and Mechanics Bank was never able to reopen as the depression deepened. The directors decided to shut down operations in such a way that all obligations be met; no investors lose money; and all terms of the charter fully discharged.[22] The directors called upon two men with unblemished reputations to accomplish the task. Milton Stapp was familiar with all of the depositors, and brought years of experience to the team. James Lanier, with a new law degree, contributed current legal opinions and innovative ideas. James had little knowledge about bank operations, but following General Meek's advice of several years earlier, asked detailed questions of both Stapp and John Sering, the bank cashier.

43

The plan Lanier and Stapp devised for closing the bank met with the directors' wishes, but involved some risk on their part. The two men purchased the bank's loans at current, or slightly discounted value. This gave the directors the cash needed to pay off all the bank's creditors. Lanier and Stapp probably converted the bank loans to personal loans. This allowed the two men to gain the interest due on the loans as profit. The risk, of course, was that the debtors would not pay off the loans. The depression hightened the risk, but the fact that the debtors were all well known to Stapp and Lanier mitagated the problem. This is JFD's first practical experience in banking.[23]

Young James became better acquainted with both Stapp and John Sering during the closing of the bank. Sering brought all of the bank records to the meetings and had intimate knowledge of the operations. He seemed flattered that Lanier asked his advice and opinion on many issues. The cashier was one of the early settlers of the town whom everyone liked.

When the conversation strayed from banking, John Sering would often steer it to the history of the town and toward politics past and present. It was evident to Lanier that Sering considered himself an excellent Federalist who coveted state-wide office.

The fact that the bank's currency continued to be honored for the commerce of Madison was a testament to the bank directors and their promise to re-open the bank when conditions improved. His successful closing of the bank with no one suffering loss, established James as a well-respected lawyer. Power and money were gravitating to Madison. It was fast becoming a center for butchering, lumbering and iron production. Its location on the Ohio River allowed for the easy shipping of those commodities to the South and West. Madison became Indiana's link to the world, and JFD was in the middle of it.

In 1824, Henry Thornton went from assistant clerk to principal clerk of the Indiana House of Representatives. James became his assistant clerk. JFD, who was looking for an alternative to riding the circuit, now contemplated a career in politics.[24]

The Indiana legislature was a part time body sitting two or three months per year. The sessions started in December or January and ran through February. It convened during a slow time for farming and business. The Clerk of the House of Representatives and his assistant kept a journal of the House proceedings,

44

and read the bills. These responsibilities required diligence and great attention to detail. Public office was a duty, not a profession, so members served their terms and retired, giving others a chance at service.

Given the normal election turnover, JFD, who served in the clerk's office for several terms, became a stable influence. Legislators often asked him to help with one problem or another. He unfailingly practiced his creed of scrupulously respecting the rights of others, exercising diligence and fidelity in every engagement, and making the causes of his clients his own. He became well respected as an honest broker.

James gained many friends by his actions. Through his office he befriended powerful businessmen who wanted legislation passed. The circle of powerful individuals in Indiana was rather small at that time, and James made a point to become well acquainted with as many as possible.

Most legislators were older than James and liked young Lanier. He was serious and a quick learner. He seemed genuinely interested in their projects, would keep a confidence, and was not threatening. James was building for the future. He recalls his stint as clerk in his autobiography:

> My good offices were often availed of in the drawing up of motions and bills and in the guiding the conduct of members on the floor . . . It enabled me to form an intimate acquaintance with all the leading men of the state, many of whom, in after life were not slow to reciprocate the good offices I had done them.[25]

As involved as he was in politics Lanier did not forget his other civic duties in Madison. He was still active on the library board, with local schooling efforts and in the church.

He traveled to Louisville, Kentucky, with a group of Masons, to meet the Marquis de Lafayette, who was touring the U. S. The talk that evening revolved around the near disaster the Marquis' party had suffered a few days earlier. During a night passage up the Ohio, the boat began to take on water. Lafayette and his son escaped to the Indiana shore in Perry County without injury.[26]

JFD commented to the Marquis that his ancestors came from France, and that he was a relative of George Washington. Lafayette was gracious and attentive, but must have marveled at the Washington family virility after meeting so many relatives of the great general during his travels. Eighteen twenty-four was a good year for JFD, and was capped off when Elisabeth presented him with his third child, Drusilla Ann, born December 21, 1824.[27]

State government moved from Corydon to Indianapolis in time for the 1825 session. There were two stagecoach "roads" in Indiana at the time. One ran from Madison to Indianapolis, and the other from Indianapolis to Centerville.[28] The quality of the highway or the dependability of the coach service did not impress James. He preferred horseback to the undependable stagecoach, but still the trip was laborious. In his autobiography he states the trip from Madison to Indianapolis took **"three days of exhausting travel on horseback."** By 1870 James noted the trip took 4 hours in the relative comfort of a train coach.[29] Today it takes just under two hours by automobile.

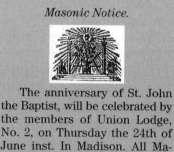

*Masonic Notice.*

The anniversary of St. John the Baptist, will be celebrated by the members of Union Lodge, No. 2, on Thursday the 24th of June inst. In Madison. All Masonic brethren who are in good standing are invited to attend and participate in the festivities of the day.

JAMES F. D. LANIER, Sec'y.
Madison, June 3d, 1824

**James continued his dedication to the Masonic cause.**

Lanier was in a position of power. He would write the bills as requested but, using the skills of persuasion and logic honed in the court room, he could often persuade legislators to include language he favored. He was gaining favor in both parties without being tied to the political dogma or destiny of either.

The talk of opening the rivers in the state to navigation and building canals was the major topic of conversa-

The Legislature of Indiana convened at Indianapolis, on Monday the 10th inst.

In the Senate James Dill was elected secretary, John H. Farnham assistant secretary, Rollin C. Dewer enrolling clerk, & John Medcamp, doorkeeper. In the house of representatives, Steven C. Stevens was elected speaker, Henry F. Thornton, clerk, James F.D. Lanier, assistant clerk & Amariah Porter, doorkeeper.

We are informed that William W, Wick of Indianapolis, presiding judge of the 5th judicial district is elected secretary of state — Goodlet is re-elected presiding judge of the fourth judicial district

Indiana Republican Jan 20, 1825

**The *Indiana Republican* announced J.F.D's election to assistant clerk of the 1825 legislature.**

tion in the crossroads taverns, in town meeting halls and in the legislature. There was an "enormous surplus" of farm products that rotted in the field for lack of transportation. Other states were very successful in constructing internal improvements and were getting rich in the process.*[30] Why not Indiana?

Backers touted the Wabash River as a major artery of commerce. When linked to the Ohio River it would "exhibit one grand theater of splendid and successful exertion" equal not only to the Mississippi, but to the Thames, the Nile and the Danube![31]

The Whitewater River Valley was one of the earliest areas inhabited by settlers from the East. The river drained directly into the Ohio. A strong faction in southeastern Indiana had been demanding a canal along the Whitewater River for years. In talking with the proponents of water transportation, James quoted President Washington's dream of a water link between the Potomac and Ohio Rivers.

Other factions wanted a network of toll roads as the centerpiece of the internal improvements package. They argued that roads were less expensive than either canals or railroads, and could reach large portions of the state, not accessible by river. Many boosters prophesied that their projects would pay back the initial investment almost immediately and would garner so much revenue that taxes would be unnecessary.[32]

Lanier was in a prime position to hear and carefully weigh all of the internal improvement arguments that raged in the legislature. He helped all sides of the issue, writing legislation and legislative "memorials" to the federal government for all of the proposed improvements. He made no enemies, and kept his personal opinions to himself. James had great self confidence. He never contemplated making wrong decisions.

The $3.50 per day the legislature paid him, along with the income from his law practice and investments, gave JFD a good income for that time period. Elisabeth and Drusilla formed a good partnership and were able to obtain their share of the family wealth to run the household. Still there was a surplus which James invested in real estate, following his father's example. Land was again rapidly rising in value.[33]

---

*The individual states borrowed more than $225,000,000 for internal improvements, and only New York paid her debts from proceeds of the improvements.

47

Each legislative session brought new examples of successful projects in other states. The Erie Canal in New York, and the Miami & Erie Canal in Ohio were often used as examples. Railroads in Maryland, and Virginia, and even in England were all wildly successful according to the reports. And of course there was the National Road.[34]

The National Road was an unqualified success. Often called Gallatin's Road, because Secretary of the Treasury Gallatin championed it in the face of strong Democrat-Republican opposition, it was the greatest wagon road in the world. Begun in 1806, it reached Wheeling, Va. by 1818 and began rolling across Ohio, headed for St. Louis. By 1834 it had reached Columbus Ohio.[35]

The design called for an 80 foot wide cleared right-of-way and a crushed stone track 40 feet wide and 10 inches deep. At least a score of freight companies as well as a dozen stage lines operated on the road. Under the best conditions the stage coaches could average 15 miles per hour. Well-respected coach drivers and freight teamsters worked all along the route. Passenger coaches, freighters, and immigrant wagons shared the road.[36]

Droves of hogs, cattle and sheep moved eastward between the tree line and the wagon track, eastward against the flow. The first great American cattle drives were not in the far west, but from the farms of the Midwest to the slaughterhouses along the National Road.[37]

Men that had lost everything but their dreams trudged westward pinched between the grinding wagon wheels and sharp hooves. During the summer and fall, the road was never asleep.

Many enterprises sprung up along the road. Inns were prevalent. Some just tents to shield the travelers from dust and dung. Weary drovers rented pens to corral the herds while they slept. Blacksmiths, wheelwrights, and carpenters did a lively trade. At the foot of every steep hill and beside each bottomless mud hole a brace of teamsters stood ready to help heavy wagons over the obstacle — for a price. No doubt some entrepreneurs even constructed their own hazards so that they could come to the aid of a struggling wagon. The National Road became a prime example of what Indiana needed.

Hoosiers are basically conservative, and there were many naysayers. In 1822 Governor Hendricks cautioned that "the interest in canals has waned, but we should keep them in mind and wait until the resources of the State increase."[38] Hendricks did not believe the state was in a healthy financial condition. In 1825 the state debt stood at $27,000, with the annual income at $40,000.[39] The tax rolls stood at less than 35,000 people. Many argued that the state could not stand the massive expense of internal improvements.

Talk continued but there was little progress. The politicians found that verbal investment required no cash outlay, but paid dividends at the ballot box. Lanier had mixed feelings. He was a fiscal conservative, but could see the advantage of a well-managed investment. The question was, could the state manage the investment?

By 1825, the people tired of talk. They were willing to take the financial risk. Farmers felt particularly disadvantaged. They turned out Hendricks and elected James Ray. Opponents called him haughty and overbearing. He was a strong internal improvements advocate, that bullied the Legislature in that direction. It was exactly what the electorate wanted. Ray was a visionary who dreamed that Indianapolis would be the hub of a great railroad network that stretched to every major city in the state.[40] James Lanier would remember that vision.

Lanier had visions of his own. He wanted to be a powerful force in Madison business and politics. Following his father's example, James was developing varied business ventures. His plan was to use politics to further his business interests. By spreading his interests he was maximizing his opportunity and minimizing his risk. He was always looking for good deals on distressed land, and was discussing business partnerships with a variety of people. JFD was in demand as a business partner. He had boundless energy and political connections as well as legal expertise to contribute to an alliance. He had a reputation for fiscal responsibility.

In June 1825 he paid $1,000 for a prime piece of river front land.[41] He could not afford to buy out the ferry operation that ran from the land, but planned to do that in the future. He moved his growing family to a good sized house on the northeast corner of the property.

The house was a full front Federal design, with an ell extending along one side. It was one of the largest houses in town, and provided the luxury of bedrooms for Drusilla as well as

James and Elisabeth. There was no need for a bed in the parlor. Alex could have a bedroom of his own and the girls could share another. It was definitely a step up in the world. There was an outbuilding that James converted to a carriage house. When finances permitted, JFD purchased a town carriage and hired a coachman. Thus he was able to fulfill one of his earliest dreams; turning the laborious task of caring for his horses over to someone else.

JFD was happy that the 1826 legislature finally approved some modest internal improvements. Several new roads were authorized along with clearing of the Wabash River to improve navigation. The Legislature directed B.I. Blythe, the new commissioner of the three per cent fund, to pay for these improvements from the fund.[42]

The three percent fund was continually overdrawn, but few worried. The potential for profit from the internal improvements seemed unlimited and largely untapped. Taxes from expanded commerce would wipe out any temporary deficit in the fund. Time-and a little faith-were the solutions to the problem.

With the Masonic hall finally completed, plans for its dedication began. A notice in the *Banner* announced the dedication. JFD Lanier signed the notice as Secretary.

The Democrat-Republicans found a way to take some credit for internal improvements without spending any money. A provision of the treaty with the Potowatomie Indians, concluded in 1826, provided for a federal land grant to construct a road from the Ohio River to Lake Michigan. Congress ceded a section of land straddling the route for its full length to the state. The Indiana Legislature promptly authorized construction of the "Michigan Road," stretching from Madison on the Ohio, through Greensburg, Shelbyville, Indianapolis, Logansport, South Bend and finally to Michigan City. The design followed that of the National Road. Sale of the land along the road would pay for the construction. The increase in land values close to the road would more than repay the federal Government for their generosity.[43]

James liked the idea. He saw the potential of making money by purchasing land along the road's proposed route. Land adjacent to the road was highly prized. Settlements would spring up adjacent to the road. Crops grown on land bordering the road would have the best access to the markets. His father's training would give him an advantage in locating prime pieces of land.

He wished the legislature had acted earlier. He needed a dependable link between Indianapolis and Madison now. Elisabeth was expecting their fourth child. Legislative business beckoned to him from Indianapolis, but family needs tugged at him from Madison.

As was the custom before births, Elisabeth set up the bedroom with special bed drapes and other accessories soon after January 1, 1827. Here she would remain until the baby was born. She would run the household, receive guests and take her meals all in relaxed, anticipatory comfort.

On February 25, 1827, James and Elisabeth welcomed their third daughter, Margaret Downing Lanier, to the family.[44] James showed no disappointment at not having a second son. Even though Elisabeth complained often of being weak and of suffering sundry illnesses, Drusilla must have marveled at Elisabeth's stamina and strength to have borne four children.

The Michigan Road was a success along its southern route, living up to expectations. The route followed the old road, so the expense of improvements was reasonable. With Indiana's best port at the southern terminus, the road was an immediate success.

Not so, north of the Capital. Disputes and political arguments over the exact route; outright fraud; and the excessive costs of crossing the swamps of northern Indiana eventually exhausted the construction funds. Finishing the Michigan Road became a liability to the state.[45]

The economy began a downward cycle in 1827. Indiana, Ohio and Illinois were producing great quantities of farm produce. Since there were few good east-west roads, the only outlet for midwestern produce was New Orleans. The only dependable shipping season was the spring. With no storage facilities, and with a crop made perishable by warmer weather, the New Orleans markets overflowed with produce. This oversupply became known as the "Wabash Glut." The prices for farm commodities fell drastically.[46]

Once again the citizens cried for a year-round route to the eastern markets. Many felt that canals were the most sensible form of internal improvements. They argued that money spent for canal construction was primarily for labor and would stay in the state. Canals would last forever with little maintenance. The Wabash and Erie Canal became the priority project.[47]

To bolster their argument, canal advocates pointed out that from one-half to two-thirds of the capital for railroads would be used to purchase rails and engines built out of state. Railroads needed rebuilding every 20 years, they argued.

The Indiana delegation in Congress included ex-governors Jennings in the House of Representatives, and Hendricks in the Senate. Hendricks had overcome his early reluctance and now pushed for a major canal in the state.[48]

# 6.
## "... to relieve me of a pecuniary difficulty ..."
— JFD Lanier April 20, 1829

*Beginning in 1828, James Lanier became very involved in politics. The next few years confirmed his belief that he could be much more effective behind the scenes than if he held public office. He truly wished to promote those projects he felt best served Indiana, and could more easily choose his battles and his comrades in arms if not tied to a political party. The major project involved a transportation system for the state.*

In an effort to swing Indiana into his vote column for the upcoming presidential election, Henry Clay pushed a Federal land grant through Congress encompassing the route of the Wabash & Erie Canal. In January 1828, Indiana accepted the land gift. As with the Michigan Road, proceeds from the sale of land along the canal route were to pay for construction.[1]

The Indiana Legislature appointed a three man Board of Canal Commissioners to oversee the project.[2] The authority of the board was unclear. For a year accomplishment was nil. The Indiana legislature had powerful railroad interests that blocked

53

canal appropriations for an entire session. In addition, it was an election year, and legislators were reluctant to increase taxes to initiate the canal, even though the return was "guaranteed."[3]

The 1828 election was a vicious contest. Political parties were beginning to take shape, but were still closely identified with their heroes. The Democrat-Republicans became "Jackson men." The Federalists evolved into the Whigs or "Adams-Clay men."[4] They felt Jackson was vulnerable and campaigned long and loud against him. Democrat-Republicans were confident and kept up a drum-beat of support for their man. Politics became a neighborhood sport in most towns.

January 1828 was very mild and shipping on the Ohio River continued all month long. On the 14th, General Jackson passed Madison on a river boat.[5] Although he did not stop, loyal Democrats lined the riverbank acknowledging their hero.

A heavy snowstorm and cold snap in late February momentarily slowed river traffic and reminded everyone that winter still had Madison in its grip.[6] Residents dug for additional blankets and coats. Thick hoar-frost coated the insides of windows. Low wood supplies disappeared, and many residents planned to head for the nearby forests on restocking missions when the weather broke.

LAW NOTICE
J. F. D. LANIER & WM. SHEETS,

**A**TTORNIES and Counsellors at law, have entered into partnership, and will practice in conjunction with the county of Jefferson. Any business that may be placed in their hands shall receive their joint attention. Office on Main cross Street opposite Mr. Pugh's Hotel, where one of the firm can always be found.
*Madison, March 22, 1828*

TOWN LOTTS
To Sell On Good Terms.

**T**he undersigned is authorized by power of attorney, to sell several valuable building lots in Madison, on the most liberal terms. One lot, No. 65; in the old town, can be divided to advantage into two parts if it should be wished. The undersigned is also authorized to sell lot No. 107, on which is situate the tavern house now occupied by John Irwin. There is also several other valuable buildings on said lot. Persons wishing to purchase lots in Madison will find it to their advantage in calling on me.
J. F. D. Lanier.
April 17th, 1828

**The newspaper was the only method of mass advertising available in the 1820's**

Although James was enjoying the political game, he still had to earn a living. His family was growing. Law partnerships were fluid. The papers often carried advertisements announcing new alliances and separations. On March 22,1828, the Madison *Courier* carried the announcement shown below. The firm did general legal business, but James was especially proficient in the legal aspects of land sales. Each time he assisted in a successful legal land sale, he knew his father would be proud.

The improved road between Madison and Indianapolis allowed weekly mail and coach service between the two most important towns in the state. The service began in late June 1828. The stages left Madison and Indianapolis at 6:00 A.M. and 7:00 A. M. respectively Thursday mornings. Both arrived at Columbus at noon on Friday. They left Columbus at 1:00 P.M., arriving at their respective destinations at 5:00 P.M. on Saturday. The fare was 6 1/4 ¢ per mile. The cost of a one way trip was about $5.60. James much preferred the coaches to horseback. Horseback travel might be faster, but stages, with their heavy leather springs were certainly more comfortable and less debilitating.[7]

It was well that travel to Madison was improving, because the town was prospering. A traveling reporter wrote back to his newspaper:

> Madison is the most populous town in the state, and from its position must eventually secure to itself the trade of a great portion of the interior of Indiana. It contains from 13 to 1500 inhabitants; is handsomely situated on the high bank of the Ohio river, and is principally built of brick. There is a handsome courthouse, a (sic) Presbyterian and Methodist meeting houses, a Masonic Lodge and a market house, all of brick, and a large frame building for the schools. Two cotton factories, each with 84 spindles, 2 oil mills, 3 tan yards, 15 stores, 3 drug stores, printing office and etc. The business done here is already very considerable, the goods for many counties in the interior here being received (from the boats).[8]

Times were good according to the *Banner*. Flour was selling for $2.00 per hundredweight and was scarce. Wheat brought 50¢ per bushel, corn 25 to 37 1/2 ¢ per bushel and was also in short supply. Sweet potatoes sold for 37 1/2 ¢ and Irish potatoes 25¢ per bushel. Beef and pork brought 2-3¢ per pound. Chickens went for 62 1/2-75¢ per dozen. Butter was 8-12¢ per pound with lard bringing half of that. The *Banner* thought the prices quite good and stated: "surely the farmers can not now complain of 'hard times' or say they can not get anything for their produce."[9]

Lanier had learned from his father that financial diversity equated to fiscal security. He always put surplus money to work immediately. Banks were not safe, and even if they were, they did not pay interest. He invested every extra dollar he could. Depending on the business climate, he either purchased land, or invested in business.

He gladly gave "top billing" to his business partners; "Thornton & Lanier"; "Stapp and Lanier." James kept a tight rein on the operation of the business. He knew good business practices were more important than the sign board.

James was quick to see an opportunity. He discussed opening a Commission House with Milton Stapp. Commission agents were much like modern day distributors. They purchased goods from the East and the South, and resold them in the interior of the state. They also sold state produce in the South or East. James did not want to run a retail store as his father and Van Ausdall had; he preferred a wholesale operation. Madison was a perfect place for such a business.

Milton Stapp decided to run for lieutenant governor as an independent, rather than challenge for the Whig nomination. Lanier supported his friend and pushed the cause of Henry Clay. Not only had Clay shown his support for Indiana's internal improvements, he was a strong backer of the U.S. Bank.

In the state elections, held in early August, Hoosiers readily split their ticket. J. B. Ray, a Democrat, returned to the governor's chair. In a close race not certified until weeks after the election, Milton Stapp gained the second spot.[10] Whigs

The following gentlemen are candidates for the offices which are to be filled by the next legislature.

FOR SECRETARY OF STATE
*HENRY P. THORNTON,*
*WILLIAM W. WICK.*

AUDITOR OF PUBLIC ACCOUNTS
*B. I. BLYTHE,*
*MORRIS MORRIS,*
*HARVEY GREG,*
*BENJAMIN F. WALLACE,*
*JOHN SCOTT.*

PRINCIPAL CLERK
*J. F. D. LANIER*

ASSISTANT CLERK
*WILLIAM H. HURST,*
*WILLIAM SHEETS,*
*AUSTIN W. MORRIS*

**The legislature voted to fill many state offices. The Madison *Banner* carried the slate.**

won most of the other state offices. The voters retained Samuel Merrill as state treasurer.

The legislature appointed H. P. Thornton secretary of state. JFD ran unopposed for principal clerk of the House of Representatives and installed William Sheets as his assistant, thus keeping the clerk's office within the law firm.[11]

In Jefferson County, Gamaliel Taylor, a Democrat, became sheriff, John Sering, a Whig, went to the House of Representatives along with David Hillis. The voters elected Nathan Palmer, a Madison Democrat to the state senate.[12] In the national election, later in the fall, Jackson carried the state.

James was happy. His star appeared to be on the rise. He did not neglect his family, and actively participated, with Elisabeth and Drusilla, in their social education. JFD began to teach Alex the art of carving at the table. At eleven, Alex should learn the skill. Dinners were learning experiences for all of the children as the girls gained the social graces. Alex considered the practices old fashioned, and criticized them once, suffering his father's wrath. Alex found his grandmother more tolerant of his complaints than his father.

Fiscal constraint ruled Indiana. The state balance sheet was in the black. The revenue generated by land taxes and poll taxes was sufficient to finance normal government operations. By 1831 these taxes would generate $37,000 per year. Local issues of transportation, schools, and protection from the Indians still dominated the legislature. Hoosiers were involved and interested in government. Political debate was a common sport and people believed in the political process.

Responsible citizens were organizing committees to oppose social evils the government failed to address. Lanier drank in very controlled moderation. Men of character and social responsibility would drink a glass or so of wine with dinner, and perhaps a brandy after dinner, but no more. Beer was unacceptable at any time. James abhorred the increasing public drunkenness that was a national scandal. Men drank beer and wine at all hours of the day. It was not unusual for men to show up drunk for work, and common for workers to become drunk on the job.

The Temperance Society of Marion County was organized on October 3, 1828. Its goal was "to discontinue the use of ardent spirits, except as medicine, both by precept and example." James M. Ray was Secretary. Many prominent citizens were members including Dr. Isaac Coe and Calvin Fletcher.[13] Lanier and Stapp were active in the Jefferson County temperance organization. In December of 1829 the State Temperance Society was formed. Jeremiah Sullivan was elected president, and JFD Lanier was installed as secretary.[14]

The Indiana Colonization Society began in Indianapolis on November 4, 1829. It was an auxiliary of the American Colonization Society whose purpose was to colonize "the free people of colour of the United States on the coast of Africa." Samuel Merrill, Calvin Fletcher, Dr. Isaac Coe, James Morrison, and James Ray were all founding members.[15] Lanier had a strong family history of hating slavery, and supported the ACS.

JFD continued to be active in the Masonic Lodge. During the winter of 1828-29 he attended a meeting and ran into General John Tipton. Tipton was a strong Democrat. From 1819 to 1822 he served in the Indiana Legislature in Corydon. In 1823, President Monroe appointed him the government agent for the Indians in northern Indiana. Tipton and JFD spent a pleasant evening discussing mutual political friends and enemies.

James found a way to put their rekindled acquaintance to profit. On April 20, 1829, he wrote to Tipton inquiring if a contract to furnish the Indians with supplies was possible. He suggested a figure of $1,000.00 and went on to explained why he suggested that amount of money:

> . . . to relieve me of a pecuniary difficulty which I now labor under. Two men in Ohio have had to pay $500.00 as the security of my father and one of them is poor . . . altho the estate of my father is insolvent, I feel myself under an <u>honorary</u> obligation to pay them . . . Your compliance will confer an obligation to be remembered and repaid . . . I have an aged mother and wife and four children to support. I unburden myself to you confidentially. This letter has been kept a secret . . . [16]

The letter is unusually revealing. Seldom does Lanier "unburden" himself in public. His father stated in his will that he wanted his debts paid. Since debts do not pass from father to son, JFD emphasized the "honorary obligation." The fact that he did not pay the debt for eight years although Lanier admits to having ". . . a good income for the time" is evidence that he must have invested every free dollar and was probably "land poor" most of the time. Perhaps he only used his father's debt as an excuse to obtain the contract.

Former Governor Hendricks wrote to Tipton supporting JFD. Tipton did offer James a contract. In a letter dated October 20, 1829, he stated that a Mr. Marshall and James Lanier will share a $3,000.00 contract. By that time, James has more reason to need the contract. On July 23, 1829, James and Elizabeth's second son, John James Lanier, was born.[17] JFD was always as good as his word. He and Tipton cooperated on several ventures and became close friends. They exchanged political opinions until Tipton died several years later.

At six o'clock in the morning of Wednesday, August 12, 1829, a "very severe hurricane" whistled through Madison, causing considerable damage. According to the *Banner*, fences, trees and roofs all suffered severe damage. The strong winds completely destroyed some buildings. The Presbyterian Church lay in ruin. Thankfully, no lives were lost.[18]

The 'hurricane' was the talk of Madison for the rest of the week. Most families grew tired of chicken and pork dinners, as the dead animals served one final good purpose. Church attendance rose dramatically in the following weeks.

Two weeks later, on August 24, William Henry Harrison, now one of the nation's leading Whig spokesmen, appeared in Madison in connection with a court case. James sat near the general in the courtroom and talked to him at length after the court proceedings. Lanier headed a committee including John Sering, and Milton Stapp, that persuaded Harrison to return to town for a banquet two days later. Over 80 people attended the banquet, and many others watched the proceedings through the open windows of Pugh's Hotel. Judge Eggleston presided, and JFD sat at the head table. After the 13 customary toasts, General Harrison gave a "brief but pertinent and highly impressive speech of some 25-30 minutes that was interrupted several times by hearty and repeated plaudits" according to the *Banner*.[19] Democrats felt the visit by Harrison was a more serious calamity than the recent tornado.

Whiskey continued to be the Devil's draught. Children turned into beggars and wives worse. Preachers traced most of the nation's problems back to the bottle. The temperance movement was as strong politically as it was morally. Candidates that harbored any hope of success came out against demon rum. Saloon campaigning continued late at night and only at the back door. On September 30, 1829, Milton Stapp, President of the

Madison Temperance Union, suggested that a meeting be held in Indianapolis to form a statewide organization.[20]

Drinking was not the only vice rampant in Madison. Crime was on the increase. It appeared that men were losing their moral values. James was vocal on the issue, and his friends persuaded him to run for prosecutor of the Third Indiana District. He could use his law skills and instill values back into the community at the same time.

In September, Milton Stapp, Lanier, and Gamaliel Taylor were appointed as a committee to build a new jail in Madison.[21] James, running for prosecutor, and Gamaliel, the Jefferson County Sheriff, had a vested interest in a new jail. JFD won the election. It was the only political office he ever pursued. He served during 1829 and 1830.

The off-year election did not generate much heat, and winter came early to Indiana. When the cold weather settled in, men followed the example of nature. Squirrels and beavers stored food for the winter. Men stocked the root cellars and laid up a supply of firewood. As animals hibernated, families sealed their shutters and shut off unnecessary rooms. Families grew closer together to share meager heat and conserve wood and coal.

Water froze within ten feet of roaring fireplaces. Mittens were worn indoors, supplemented by heavy gloves if one ventured out. On February 2, 1830, the mercury in the thermometer was barely visible, standing at $-10°$.[22] Iron hinges and implements cracked like egg shells. Men ventured along the Madison wharf for emergencies only. The river sheeted with ice. Children dared younger siblings to touch their tongue to harness rings and laughed when the small fry came away bleeding. It was a lesson never forgotten.

Later that month the legislature introduced a bill that described the State Penitentiary as a "moth at the State treasury." The bill proposed making the prison a paying proposition by establishing a "rolling penitentiary." Several specially constructed wagons would house inmates, guards and cooks. The inmates would work on the roads. While working, the prisoners carried a six foot long chain attached to a "40 weight" bar. The bill stated that John Sering, the current postmaster at Madison, be contracted to supply the wagons.[23]

The administering of smallpox vaccine became a political

issue in Louisville.[24] Madison watched the outcome of the debate closely. Protection against smallpox would be a miracle, but treatment by a "vaccine" was radical. Was it another medical hoax or a heaven sent blessing?

Late in July 1830, Henry Clay made a visit to Cincinnati. The Madison Whigs invited Clay to stop in town on his way down river to Louisville. A committee, composed of JFD, John Sering, Dr. Tilton, John Woodburn, R. Reuben, and C.P.J. Arion, journeyed to Cincinnati to extend the invitation. The verbose invitation praised Clay for his ". . . consistency, firmness, . . . zeal, and unrivaled eloquence in behalf of the 'American System' and of the best interest of our country and of mankind in general . . ." Despite the heaps of praise, Clay was forced to turn down the invitation because of his tight schedule.[25]

In August of 1830, JFD, Milton Stapp and others came out strongly for Henry Clay once again. The Whigs hoped Jackson had lost favor in Indiana because of his obvious hatred of the U.S. Bank, and because he reneged on his pledge to assist Indiana with internal improvements. Stapp announced for governor, running again as an Independent. He was opposed by Noah Noble of Indianapolis who ran on the Whig ticket.

Political battling left the legislature unable to do the state's business. Disgusted Indiana voters threatened changes. Perhaps new blood would solve the problem. Fear of being turned out caused the politicians to act. In 1830 the legislature reorganized the Board of Canal Commissioners and gave them clear powers.

Surveys began, and land sales along the route of the Wabash and Erie Canal commenced. Only 42,000 acres sold. The price per acre averaged a disappointing $1.75. The terms of the sale allowed only twenty-five down with payments over 17 years. The initial land sale garnered less than $75,000, and a mere $20,000 in cash.[26]

The original estimate for construction of the Wabash and Erie Canal was $1,100,000. The task of designing the canal and arranging for construction overwhelmed the Board of Canal Commissioners. The commissioners neglected their fund raising responsibilities. The project inched along.[27]

The legislature stepped in to get the project moving. They appointed three fund commissioners just to manage the canal finances. The fund commissioners mandate was to borrow con-

**JFD continued his private practice while he was prosecutor, and his name appeared often in connection with land sales. At times he resorted to a Sheriff's sale to settle a claim.**

struction funds by issuing bonds. The bonds would pay six per cent interest. Land sales, tolls, and the prestige of the State of Indiana would back the bonds.

The fund commissioners were above reproach. Samuel Hanna, from Fort Wayne, was a successful teacher, businessman, and Judge of the first Circuit Court in Allen County. He served as a state representative from 1826 to 1831, and again in 1840. He represented Allen County in the State Senate between 1832 and 1834, and would serve as state treasurer from 1847 to 1850. He was a friend of JFD Lanier from his days in the legislature. Years later the two would collaborate in financing the railroad that served Fort Wayne.[28]

Nicholas McCarty, originally from Virginia, was a prominent businessman in Indianapolis. He knew many businessmen in the East, and could use his contacts to expedite borrowing. The third member of the fund commissioners was J.F.D's long time friend, court opponent, and future bank messenger, Judge Jeremiah Sullivan. He served on the bench in Jefferson County for many years and served on the Indiana Supreme Court from 1837 until 1846.[29] Lanier was very happy with the fund commissioners. He was optimistic that the long awaited internal improvements would now proceed.

Another important topic in the Indiana Legislature centered around establishing a state bank. When Jackson forced the U.S. Bank to close, there would be a need for fiscal control. A state bank was the best solution. The experience with the First State Bank in Vincennes caused many people to be skeptical.

JFD followed the bank discussion closely. Working with the Farmers and Mechanics Bank had whetted his appetite for banking. His father had convinced him long ago that a bank was necessary to promote commerce. A safe and honorable bank interested Lanier. He took no side in the debate, but listened and learned.

Calvin Fletcher, who represented Indianapolis in the legislature, opposed the 1831 Bank bill as unconstitutional. Fletcher knew his constituents favored the plan. Rather than vote against their wishes or against his conscience, he resigned his seat.[30] The bill failed to win a majority.

# 7.
# "... implicated in deeds of darkness"
—William Hendricks March 5, 1831

*Politics consumed Hoosiers in the 1830's. The destiny of the state seemed to be at stake. Every man had an opinion on Indiana's future and was not afraid to voice it. The politicians tried to keep pace with the electorate. Factions rose into coalitions and splintered into fragments as voters' opinions changed. Statesmen tried to steer a steady course among the debris.*

The state bank was an important topic in the 1830 legislature, and internal improvements always brought loud and opinionated arguments in the chambers. The most vicious battles, however, centered on the election of a U.S. senator. The Democrat-Republicans differed in their opinion of Hendricks. The *Indiana Journal* of 12/1/1830 editorialized "Hendricks was well regarded and almost certain to be reelected." Madison Democratic leaders despised Hendricks, however. Michael Bright, by then editor of the short-lived *Madison Herald*, hated Hendricks. Even after the election the feud continued. N.B. Palmer, a strong Democrat, made it known to Jackson that many Democrats did not want Hendricks to control patronage in Indiana.[1] Hendricks fought back. He wrote to the president stating that Bright and Palmer were implicated in "deeds of darkness, . . . unprincipled and unworthy of your patronage" because they opposed Jackson's appointments the previous summer.[2]

These Democrats tried to persuade General Tipton to run against Hendricks. Although interested, Tipton decided at the last minute not to run if Ratliff Boon entered the race.[3] JFD watched the bitter struggle with more than just a passing interest. Both Hendricks and Tipton were friends.

On Sunday, December 12, 1830, Lanier wrote to Hendricks from Indianapolis. JFD arrived on the 10th after "**. . . a most disagreeable trip, much snow and rain.**" He had planned to come earlier, but was confined to bed for ten days with an "**. . . affliction in the head I never entirely recovered.**" He went on to explain that the legislature was going to vote for senator on the 18th.

> **Dewey, Law, and Blackford are trying to be brought forward in opposition to you. They can not agree among themselves which should move nor can they concentrate anything like a serious opposition to you. It is in the mouth of everyone that you will most certainly be elected and probably on the first ballot. Tipton is not here and is not opposing you.**[4]

As Tipton had surmised, Boon became Hendricks' chief rival. The General Assembly elected Hendricks on the fourth ballot.[5] Hendricks' election caused an uneasy truce in the Democrats' camp. After the election, the *Indiana Democrat* (Indianapolis), which had strongly opposed Hendricks, stated "he is guided in his official acts by principles instead of by blind devotion to parties and to men."[6]

The other Indiana senator, James Noble, died in office in February 1831. General Tipton hoped to fill the unexpired term, but Governor Ray appointed Whig Robert Hannah. This forced Tipton to wait until December 1831 when the Indiana Legislature would vote on the office.

The campaign for governor began in earnest in May 1831. Noah Noble and David Wallace ran on the Whig ticket. James Read and Amos Lane were the choice of the Democrat-Republicans. Milton Stapp ran as an Independent.[7]

When the dust had settled, Noble and Wallace had beaten

Read and Lane. Stapp came in a distant third.[8] James had mixed emotions. He wanted his friend to win, but at least the Democrat-Republicans had lost. Noble would continue Governor Ray's push for internal improvements.

Noble had served in the State Legislature in 1824. As assistant clerk of the House of Representatives, James had helped Noble craft several pieces of legislation. They found several common interests. Both men were Masons and both believed that education was the cornerstone of success. Noble authored a bill providing for free education for all Hoosiers, and Lanier was as disappointed as Noble when the General Assembly defeated the bill.[9]

As involved as he was in politics, Lanier always kept his eyes open for land deals. James owned, and was living on the eastern edge of River Block 9. Two founders of Madison, Jacob Burnet and John Paul, owned two other parcels of the block. After Paul died, JFD approached his heirs about selling the parcel. The heirs agreed, but Lanier made the sale contingent upon Burnet selling his land. Burnet lived in Cincinnati, and James made the trip to talk to him. Burnet, who had sold the first parcel to Lanier, had lost interest in Madison. He readily agreed to James' offer.

In September of 1831 Lanier purchased Burnet's sixty foot wide strip of land, adjacent to his own, that ran from First Street to the Ohio River. He paid Burnet $300 for the parcel. In October he completed the negotiations with the Paul estate. He paid the estate $500 for a parcel that was 148 feet wide running from First Street to the high water mark on the Ohio River. James now owned the entire River Block 9. The land sat on the western edge of town and was a prime industrial site. JFD intended to hold the land as an investment..

Madison continued to prosper. It is difficult to tell which came first, political or commercial power. By the fall of 1831, however, it was evident that Madison was a force in both arenas. The *Madison Republican* was constantly extolling the virtues of the town. As early as 1828, the newspaper saw the bright future of the town.

> There have already been commenced within a few days 12 or 13 three story buildings, all of brick, besides many others of two or one story, which have been commenced or are in a state of great forwardness. From present appearances and calculations now made, it

66

is expected that from forty to fifty buildings will be erected in Madison this season[10]

Political muscle was also evident. The opponents of Jackson combined under the banner of the National Republicans in an effort to break the string of defeats, but kept the same old Henry Clay as their candidate.

Almost every action of government or subject that affected large segments of the population became intense political issues - small pox vaccinations, banking, education, treatment of the Indians, temperance, sale of state bonds, and a host of others. Political debates were hostile. Libel was common; groundless accusations frequent; character assailed with impunity. It was often difficult to tell whether charges were valid or the product of political assassination.

Newspapers were by design partisan. Editors became paid political operatives. There was no attempt at balancing news stories. If a citizen wanted a different viewpoint it was up to him to purchase a different paper.

Although deeply involved in Whig/Republican politics, James Lanier's opinions enjoyed respect in both parties. He stood ready to help his Democrat friends in matters of principle and when there was no chance of a Republican gaining office. He stood for those projects that he felt would benefit the state no matter which party championed them. It is a tribute to his honesty, and integrity that the opposition press never personally attacked him. The Democrat papers in the state violently disagreed with many projects championed by Lanier, and were not above harpooning other participants by name. These attacks never listed JFD.

In late November 1831, James' uncle, Dr. James Walton Lanier arrived in Madison. He had been living in Warren County Ohio. He was two years younger than his brother Alex.[11] JFD's house was big enough for Dr. James to have an office and bedroom on the first floor. Once his uncle took up residence in Madison it became even more important that JFD use his full set of initials. At this point he carefully signed his name "James F.D. Lanier."

Dr. James arrived in Madison just in time for the annual political brawl. The two Democrat factions girded for another of their famous fights. The state senate would vote to fill Noble's unexpired term. They would surely replace Hannah, but with whom? These annual political battles evoked greater anticipation than the Kentucky Fighting Cock Championships. The Hendricks faction and the Tipton faction hurled insults and charges at one another. Politicians made outlandish promises, and unenforceable deals. Disaster loomed if the opponent won.

No matter how desperate their troops became, the commanders did not enter the battle. Hendricks remembered that Tipton stood mute in 1830. In November of 1831 he returned the favor. He wrote a confidential letter to Tipton pledging to not oppose the general's senate bid. Hendricks observed that Tipton was the "Wabash candidate" and had many Adams Clay men under personal obligation. If Tipton could unite the Jacksonians, he could win.[12]

On James' 31st birthday, this ad appeared in the *Madison Banner*.

Uniting the Jacksonians was a near impossibility. The struggle had been so bitter that many Democrats would never vote for Tipton. Hendricks was right; Tipton needed the help of the Adams-Clay men. One of the Adams-Clay men that Tipton had under personal obligation was Lanier. On the first ballot, Tipton received only one vote. As "favorite sons" dropped out Tipton gained strength. The bargaining was intense. Behind the scenes, Lanier used all of his persuasive powers. After seven ballots, Tipton finally won.[13]

With the election out of the way, the legislature got down to business. In January 1832, the legislature authorized the fund commissioners to sell bonds totaling $200,000 for the construction of the Wabash and Erie Canal. It was a disorganized effort, with very little control and few records maintained. The com-

## REPUBLICAN.

### MADISON, APRIL 21, 1831.

#### - COMMERCIAL -

We take pleasure in calling the attention of our vendors, especially those at a distance, to the present situation and future prospects of Madison. We do this not merely because we are citizens of the place, and interested in its prosperity, but because we think that a large portion of the interior of the state will be greatly benefited by its advancement. It is well known that merchants in the interior, as well as many of the farmers, have formerly procured their goods at Cincinnati and Louisville. The reason of this was, that until recently, a general assortment could not be procured at this place. We can assure them, however, that this difficulty is now removed. From information obtained from those whose statements may be relied on, we can assure our friends in the country, that at least THREE TIMES the amount of goods imported in any former year, have been ordered this spring, and that as good an assortment, and on as good terms, may now be procured here as at Cincinnati or Louisville. Indeed there is no good reason why they should not be sold here as low as at either of these places. House rent, and living generally, can be procured at a lower rate, and the cost of transportation of the goods is about the same. Produce for exportation will command as good a price here as at those places, with a saving of time and expense of transportation.

We feel confident that that people of Indiana will prefer dealing with their own citizens, when they can be as well accommodated as they can be in a neighboring state. There is a mutual dependence between the towns on the river and the interior, and both will be greatly benefited by commercial intercourse. Large lots of goods are daily arriving from either New York, Philadelphia, Baltimore or New Orleans. We hope the merchants convenient to this place, will, before they lay in their stock for the season, visit Madison, and ascertain on what terms they can purchase. We are sure that if they do, they will save themselves the trouble and expense of going any further to procure supplies. Our old merchants, generally have increased their stock of goods this spring, and many of them are now prepared to sell largely by wholesale, besides several new stores which will also do business on quite a large scale.

### N. REPUBLICAN MEETING

At a large meeting of the National Republicans at the court house in Madison on the 15th of Oct. inst. James H. Wallace, Esq. was called to the chair, and W. Lyle, appointed Secretary. Whereupon the following resolutions were adopted:

*Resolved*, That this meeting highly approve of the course of their National Republican friends in various parts of the Union, in electing delegates to meet in National Convention at Baltimore on the second Monday in December next, for the purpose of nominating a suitable person, entertaining principles tending to advance the Internal Improvement of our country, and a system of domestic industry, as a candidate for the next presidency.

Resolved, That this meeting also approve of the State Convention to be held by the National Republicans of this State at Indianapolis, on the first Monday in December next, for the purpose of choosing delegates to represent this state in the above named National Convention.

*Resolved*, That this meeting do now proceed to the election of three delegates to represent the National Republicans of this county in the Indianapolis Convention.

*Resolved*, That HENRY CLAY, of Kentucky, from his distinguished talents, tried patriotism, sterling integrity, warm attachment to the cause of Home Industry, (as evidenced by his hearty support of Internal Improvements, & Domestic manufactures,) and his eminent public services generally, is the decided choice of this meeting as a candidate for the next presidency.

*Resolved*, That in case of a resignation, or a refusal to act of any of the delegates now appointed, the other delegates shall have power to fill said vacancy.

And J. F. D. Lanier, Joseph G. Marshall and Joseph H. Cravens Esqrs. were elected delegates, pursuant to the 3d resolution.

*Resolved*, That the proceedings of this meeting be published in the Indiana Republican.

And the meeting was adjourned.

JAS. H. WALLACE, Ch'n.

W. Lyle, *Sec".*

October 12, 1831

These two articles, appearing in the *Madison Republican* in 1831, testify to the commercial and political prominence of Madison missioners left many of the details to Dr. Isaac Coe, an Indianapolis physician who was commission secretary. He set up a sales office in New York City. Two other sales agents were Milton Stapp and Lucius Scott.[14] These men were upstanding and honest. It appeared these moves solved the problems with the internal improvements.. Still Lanier worried about the lack of records and control, and the inclination of the commissioners to loan income rather than pay bills.

February 1832 brought the highest flood waters on record to the Ohio Valley. The Ohio River seemed angry about other methods of transportation being planned to replace it. The towns of Lawrenceburg and New Albany drowned under ten to twenty feet of water. Flood waters covered eighty percent of Cincinnati and large sections of Louisville.

In Madison, the rampage reached a high water mark of 64.2 feet. According to the *Banner*, only about a dozen worthless houses on the "first bottom" suffered flood damage. The important parts of town, constructed on the "second bottom," were well out of reach of the frothing flood. The newspaper went on to brag that this second level protected Madison against the wild river better than any other town.[15]

The appointment of Taylor pleased JFD. He knew that Gamaliel would do a fair and honest job. Lanier was happy to pledge security for Taylor's $2,000 bond. A suit filed against Taylor forced James to pay the judgment, but when a counter suit prevailed, JFD retrieved his money.[16]

During the March term of the Jefferson Circuit Court, the case of Adam Moderwell came before the bar. The charge against Moderwell was allowing ". . . excrement, blood, entrails and filth . . . of slaughtered hogs" to lie around his slaughterhouse and pollute Crooked Creek.[17] Both Lanier and Milton Stapp testified against Moderwell.

Perhaps the testimony at the trial convinced Stapp and Lanier that pork processing was a lucrative venture. Later in the month they purchased a modern slaughterhouse in Madison. It was an efficient plant that posed none of the problems of the Moderwell operation. The plant was within a block of James' waterfront property. The prospects looked good. There was a steady supply of hogs available in the counties north of Madison, and an expanding market for pork among the plantations of the South. Transportation costs were negligable. The plant pur-

In February 1832, Jackson appointed Gamaliel Taylor U.S. Marshal for Indiana. The *Banner* put the best light on the appointment.

chased hogs at the front door of the pork house after having been driven through town by farmers. Steamboats loaded directly out the back door of the plant.

Lanier and Stapp enjoyed a solid partnership and decided to open a store in March 1832. JFD sent Milton and his brother on a purchasing trip to the East. Their first stop was to see Robert Buchanan, an influential Cincinnati businessman. In 1828, Lanier had collected a debt in Madison for Robert Buchanan. A friendship grew between the men when they discovered a mutual interest in horticulture James asked Buchanan to write letters of introduction to merchants in Baltimore and Philadelphia.[18]

It appeared to be a good time to begin a business. Shipping rates on the river were the lowest in history. When Alex had opened his store in 1817, shipping costs from Pittsburgh to Louisville were $1.00 per hundred pounds of goods. Of course shipping up-river was much more expensive. It cost $4.00-$5.00 to ship the same cargo from New Orleans to Louisville. The extra distance and difficulty of moving against the current accounted for the difference in cost. By 1833 it cost only $0.30 per hundred pounds to ship goods from Pittsburgh to Louisville, and $0.62.5 to ship from New Orleans to Louisville.[19] The steamboat had revolutionized shipping.

The low shipping rate gave new urgency to building transportation routes to the Ohio River. The Wabash and Erie Canal would run through the heart of Indiana, from Fort Wayne to the

71

Ohio River at Evansville. It joined a canal across Ohio to Lake Erie. Shippers could send goods east either way on the canal. Digging on the Wabash & Erie Canal began in March of 1832 amidst great optimism. Finally the "wind work" of the politicians ceased, and the real work begun. All opposition to internal improvements washed away with the beginning of the canal. If Ohio could build a canal from Lake Erie to the Ohio River, a distance of 250 miles, surely Indiana could do the same. Advocates pushed for a canal from Leavenworth to Lake Michigan.[20]

The railroad interests also benefited from low shipping rates. The 1832 General Assembly chartered 12 joint stock companies to build railroads throughout the state. If Hoosiers were betting Indiana's future on internal improvements, they wanted to hedge their bets.[21]

Tipton's election in December of 1831 was only to fill the unexpired term of Senator Noble. In 1832 the seat would come open again and the Legislature would vote for someone to serve for an entire term. With barely a year's rest, the political circus would take center stage again. On May 11,1832 Lanier wrote to General Tipton stating that even though they had political differences, he would back Tipton for the Senate. National-Republican votes would again be crucial.[22]

JFD also stated in that letter he was getting some pressure to run for the Indiana House of Representatives. He declined because his business interests would suffer. What he did not say was that he enjoyed manipulating political deals in the shade of the State House. If he held office, his influence with the Democrats would diminish.

The summer of 1832 was a busy one for the nation. Congress passed an early extension of the U.S. Bank Charter. Hendricks and Tipton angered Jacksonian Democrats when they both voted to retain the national bank. Lanier was proud of his friends. President Jackson vetoed the bill, setting up a confrontation between the pro-bank and anti-bank forces in the coming election.

As progressive as the western states were becoming, there was still a threat from Indians in the back country. That threat became real in Illinois. Indians led by Chief Black Hawk went on a rampage, and western states mustered troops to defeat them. Senator Tipton called for Indiana volunteers. Governor Noble called the militia into service and asked Tipton and Hendricks to secure federal pay for the force. The senators informed Noble that Congress had authorized "the raising of 600 mounted rangers for the protection of the northwestern frontier." Two hundred of these men would come from Indiana.[23] The Indians in northern Indiana were barely under control, and "Indian fever" spread through the state. Frightened citizens called for their immediate removal. Under pressure, the Potawatomi sold most of their land to the government. They and the Miami retreated to small reservations in the state.[24]

The sale of bonds for the Wabash and Erie Canal was not progressing. Many states were attempting to sell bonds to finance their own internal improvements. It was a buyer's market. Higher interest rates and extended payment schedules enticed investors. Capital in the United States was evaporating. Even the massive vaults of Europe emptied at an astounding rate in response to the demand.

In an effort to obtain scarce capital, Dr. Coe allowed J.D. Beers & Co. of New York to purchase $100,000 of the canal bonds with a bid that read "one hundredth per cent above any other bid." Having their price based on other bids made the J.D.Beers bid illegal. In addition it was not the low bid. The fund commissioners accepted this questionable bid because they felt it was advantageous to the state. J.D. Beers was a well-known company vouched for by Dr. Coe. J.D. Beers was permitted to make only a small down payment on the bonds.[25]

When they collected cash, the fund commissioners immediately loaned it out to take advantage of the high interest rates. Newspapers praised the loans as examples of wise business practice. Lanier frowned on the scheme. Not only did it violate the law, but the cash was not available to pay construction bills. It appeared to Lanier that the state was allowing its liabilities to exceed its means.

On August 20, 1832, another girl was born to James and Elizabeth Lanier. They named her Mary. Elizabeth did not know whether it was more taxing to have a child in the frigid winter or the roasting summer.[26]

Meanwhile, the directors of the Farmers and Mechanics Bank reached a compromise with the secretary of the treasury which allowed the bank to reopen. They appointed JFD cashier.

James believed that history provided many valuable lessons. Before he became involved in the bank, JFD wanted to know as

The directors of the Farmers and
Mechanics Bank reached a
compromise with the secretary of
the treasury in July. This allowed
the bank to reopen in the latter days
of September. The good news was
reported in the *Banner*

much about the profession as possible. He asked friends to explain the history of banking in the U.S. He read what limited information was available in the Madison Library. JFD reviewed
the early history of the National Bank. The national bank debate
was one of the early battle grounds between the Federalists and
the Democrat-Republicans, the origin of Jackson's loathing of
the bank. The lawyer in Lanier became engrossed in the legal arguments of the banking issue.

He reviewed Hamilton's argument on the side of the strong
central government, and how that became the "implied powers"
or "loose construction" argument for interpreting the Constitution.[27] Thomas Jefferson's argument against the bank impressed
him equally. It became the "strict construction" argument for interpreting the Constitution.[28]

James appreciated George Washington's method of resolv-
ing the issue. Washington approved the bank plan, siding with
Hamilton, the cabinet officer who had the most direct involvement and responsibility. The Bank of England was the model
for the U.S. National Bank. Congress chartered the National
Bank to operate for twenty years. For the most part, the bank
worked well.[29]

JFD enjoyed the political compromise that traded southern

votes for the bank in exchange for moving the national capital to a government district carved from southern states. Congress did not approve of paper currency, but did order the minting of U.S. coins. As a sop for losing the federal Capital, the mint stayed in Philadelphia.[30]

James had learned how banking had fared in Indiana from his friend John Sering when they closed the Farmers and Mechanic's Bank. Lanier talked to Samuel Merrill and obtained the inside details of the failure of the First State Bank. J.F.D's personal experience with Van Ausdall, and his father's failures now came into sharp focus. He now understood the battle that Calvin Fletcher had waged in the legislature over revival of the state

*Administrator's Sale*

By virtue of an order of the Probate Court within & for the county of Jefferson and state of Indiana, at the last term thereof, the undersigned as the administrator of the estate of

**DANL. GREGG**

Late of said county, dec'd on Saturday the 30th day of June next, will proceed to sell (for the purpose of paying the debts of said estate,) all the following parts or parcels of lot numbered sixty-three, (63) as designated on the plat of the original town of Madison, Indiana, bounded as follows, viz.

Beginning at the prime corner of said lot formed by Main and Main-Cross streets, thence northwardly on Main street, fifty-six feet to a four foot alley, thence westwardly, parallel with Main street fifty-six feet, to Main-Cross street, thence eastwardly with Main-Cross street to the beginning corner.

*Also,*

One other parcel of said lot situate on the west of Dr. Howes', twenty-four feet, binding on J. F.

D. Lanier's, lot containing about nineteen by fifteen feet. On the first of the above described premises, there are

*TWO FIRST RATE NEW THREE STORY BRICK TENEMENTS,*

intended to be finished for business houses. Also, one two story brick tenement, row in the occupancy of George W. Bantz as a saddler's shop, the said Bantz having an unexpired lease thereon. One fourth of the purchase money will be required in hand, the balance in installments of one, two and three years, with interest. Bond and good security must be given.

THE ABOVE COMPRISES TWO OF THE *BEST STANDS*

For business in Madison, and is the only property of the kind for sale.— Persons desirous of buying such property, will do well to embrace the present opportunity. I shall sell in parcels to suit purchasers. A plat of the premises can be seen at my office. A clear and indisputable title will be given.

J. F. D. LANIER.

Madison, May 22, 1832.

All through this period, JFD continued his law practice, specializing in land sales.

bank. He agreed with Fletcher; a bank had to be honest and sound. In order to serve the citizens, and operate successfully, a bank's operations had to be above reproach.

The lure of banking excited James. After trying several different business ventures, he found his niche. The more he studied, the more he realized that his natural mentality and lifestyle fit that of a banker. His honesty was the paramount ingredient to good banking. His principle of never letting his liabilities exceed his means was critical. His experience with the law would help him write sound rules and regulations. His powers of persuasion learned in the court room would be invaluable in the bank. The biggest drawback to the practice of law was the tribulations of travel. Surely running a bank would not entail nearly as much.. He realized that a combination of political influence and financial control could make him a very powerful man.

Lanier continued his political involvement. In September 1832, Madison was the site of a massive anti-Jackson rally. The *Banner* reported that it was the largest public meeting ever held in Jefferson County, proving that political hyperbole is as old as campaigns themselves. It is a sure bet that James was near the front rank of the throng.[31]

On his thirty second birthday, James wrote a letter to his friend Buchanan in Cincinnati. In it he acknowledged receiving a petition from Buchanan through John Lodge, co-owner of the *Republican Banner*. The petition favored the closing of the U.S. Bank. Lanier stated that he and Lodge were against the closing. Not wanting to anger his friend, JFD promised to make the petition available to those that wished to sign it, and then forward the document to Washington.[32]

# 8.
# "Wealth, talent and reputation . . ."
## —Madison Republican Banner

*The poor always outnumber the rich, and in the fall of 1832 they again flocked to the ballot boxes electing Andrew Jackson. Indiana was solidly in the column of the winner. JFD had strongly opposed Jackson, and his victory was a bitter pill. Jackson's victory, however, was to set in motion a series of events that would propel James Lanier into prominence on both a state and national level for the remainder of his life.*

Tipton stood for re-election to the U.S. Senate. In the year he had served he had garnered few Democrat friends. Those that opposed Tipton asked Hendricks for help, but he refused. Voting began on December 9,1832. On the first ballot, Tipton received 32 votes and Boon 24. Whispered deals filled the dark corners of the chamber; promises overflowed the cloakroom. Again and again the clerk called the role. Still there was no majority for either candidate. The legislature recessed, but the political fighting and finagling proceeded far into the night. Tipton supporters went to bed thinking they had their man elected.

The first role call on the morning of the 10th showed that the

Tipton coalition had faltered. Groups of two and three men huddled throughout the chamber. Tally men for each faction counted and recounted the votes. More roll calls; more deadlocks. Finally on the nineteenth ballot, Tipton prevailed. The legislators recessed, exhausted. Some left the chamber to celebrate. Some left to brood.[1]

James continued his law practice along with his responsibilities at the Farmers and Mechanics Bank. In 1833, Spier Tipton, John's son, came to Madison to study law with Lanier. JFD took a liking to the boy and sent good reports to his father. At 19, Spier wanted to marry. JFD supported the decision in a letter to Senator Tipton in January 1834. Lanier reported that the girl was a very respectable citizen of Madison, and that Spier felt he would do better in his studies if he married. James recalled that he married at 19 and "have always thought it one of the most fortunate events of my life."[2]

Jackson could not wait for the Charter of the U.S. Bank to expire. He decided to hasten the bank's death. In a letter to his cabinet he stated "The President considers his re-election as a decision of the people against the bank." He instructed his secretary of the treasury to begin withdrawing federal funds from the bank, but not to deposit federal receipts.[3]

The Whig members of Congress were in an uproar. Opposition papers called for Jackson's impeachment. Even some of his own cabinet thought "Old Hickory" had gone too far. William Duane, secretary of the treasury, refused the order and fell victim to Jackson's wrath. . Two other appointees would not carry out the order, and Jackson removed them also. Jackson finally appointed Roger B. Taney — later Chief Justice — to the post. Taney did not actually withdraw funds, but refused to deposit federal revenue in the bank, while requiring the bank to pay government expenses. This action was enough to strangle the bank.[4]

Congress refused to confirm Taney, and the battle continued.[5] It became obvious that Jackson would crush the U.S. Bank any way he could. Indiana politicians began taking sides and making plans for the U.S. Bank's demise.

While Jackson battled in Washington, Lanier was waging a battle of his own in the Jefferson County court room in Madison. The original plat of the town did not include the area between High Street (First Street) and the river. This acreage was subject to flooding, and John Paul wanted to keep it as "common ground" for the town. In actuality, it protected access to the river for those who purchased land close to the river, but above possible flood damage.[6]

The town trustees wanted the conditions voided so that development of the waterfront could proceed. In 1830 they amended the town charter to include this land. Adjacent landowners sued. In the spring of 1833 the case came to court. JFD argued for the trustees, while Jeremiah Sullivan and Joseph Marshall argued for the landowners. The judge continued the case until the fall session, and James took depositions during the summer.[7] Owning a river block himself, JFD had great interest in the outcome.

Although the court records are incomplete, in 1830, Madison built a floating wharf because the town owned no land to anchor the wharf. By 1836, four permanent landings were graded and improved.[8] This leads to the belief that the town won the suit.

General Tipton and James continued their friendship and kept up an active correspondence. Tipton asked James for help protecting former governor Jennings' property. It was common knowledge that Jennings had a great weakness for distilled spirits. Many people abandoned the former governor. James did not agree with Jonathan Jennings' politics, and condemned his weakness of character. General Tipton stood by Jennings. JFD did not want the office of governor tainted, and had great compassion for innocent victims of the bottle. He also respected Tipton's friendship and agreed to help keep Jennings from becoming destitute.

When Jennings died in August of 1834, Tipton asked Lanier to do the legal work to clear the title of the Jennings farm. He suggested the farm be sold to provide Mrs. Jennings with money. In November 1834, James had all the timber cut and gave the proceeds to Mrs. Jennings. He and Tipton then arranged for the sale of the Jennings farm for $2,200.00, assuring Mrs. Jennings' well being.[9]

It was not until 1834 that the Legislature reestablished a state bank. Early in January, the House of Representatives passed the measure 48 to 23 and the Senate approved it 18 to 11. The law was specific and stringent, attempting to correct all of the deficiencies of the earlier state banking effort. It answered most of Calvin Fletcher's concerns.[10]

The law divided the state into ten banking districts of three counties each. A branch bank served each district. The law provided for two more districts if population and commerce necessitated it. The administrative office was in Indianapolis, but there was no parent bank. The branches had equal power, standing, and responsibility.[11]

Two important provisions tried to correct the faults of the First State Bank. No state officers could serve in any capacity for the bank, and the bank could not deal in real estate. No director or stockholder could give collateral for a loan. A branch president or cashier could not endorse a loan for themselves, each other or anyone else.

The law made the Indiana state bank the repository of all state funds. The legislature amended the state constitution to forbid any banks in the state except the state bank. This provision caused the Farmers and Mechanics Bank of Madison to close.[12]

Each branch would issue its own paper promissory notes, but must accept the notes of any other branch. The issuing branch had to redeem the notes from the branch that collected them. The form of the branch promissory notes would be the same as those used by the Bank of the U.S.[13]

The branch notes were fully convertible currency. Each branch had to exchange its notes for gold or silver coin on demand. Failure to do so was cause for the revocation of its charter. Notes of less than five dollars were illegal. The lawmakers felt this provision would keep specie in circulation. The law required that the branch cashier, and the president of the state bank board sign all notes.[14]

To raise capital for the bank, the legislature authorized the sale of 32,000 shares of bank stock worth fifty dollars each. This placed the total capital of the bank at $1,600,000. The state purchased 1/2 the shares, worth $800,000. Individual shareholders purchased the remaining $800,000, but they had to pay only $18.75 per share. The state loaned shareholders the remaining $31.75, taking as security twice the value of the loan. This made the total state investment in the State Bank $1,100,000 or almost 70% of the total. Shareholders had to pay the state six per cent interest on the $31.75 and also paid the educational fund twelve and one half cents per share annually instead of taxes.[15]

To finance the state share of the stock, the state sold state bank bonds that paid five per cent interest. Most of these bonds sold in the East, and were highly valued throughout the life of the bank. The bank stock was in the care of three commissioners of the "sinking fund." The commissioners received the dividends for the state held bank stock, as well as the principal and interest on loans made to purchase bank stock. Interest on the state bank bonds came from the sinking fund. The sinking fund was a reserve fund that would keep the bank solvent during difficult financial periods.[16]

Although the stockholders had to pay the state 6% on their loan, all of the dividends from the state portion of the stock were credited against the principal of the loan. The term of the stock loans was 20 years, but the bank was so successful, that most stockholders paid off their loans early. The individual stockholders received the entire dividend once the loan closed.[17]

Each branch needed $30,000 in specie on deposit before it could open. No branch could have outstanding debts of more than two times its capitalized value, nor could it issue notes totaling more than one and one-quarter times the capital paid into the branch. The rate of discount was six per cent.[18]

Dividends could vary between branches and depended on branch profits. The dividends of each branch accrued only to the stockholders of that branch. Only the board of directors in Indianapolis could set the dividend for each branch. This provision prevented branch stockholders from milking a branch dry. Profits above the declared dividend went into the sinking fund.[19]

The stockholders of each branch were liable for the debts of that branch up to the par value of their shares. Each branch was liable for the debts of the other branches. This put a tight check on the actions of individual branches, and was designed to promote cooperation between them.[20]

The legislature elected the president and four directors. From these four, the legislature appointed three to be Sinking Fund Commissioners. Each branch elected one director. This group made up the state bank board. This bank board controlled the branches and reported directly to the legislature. The state bank board appointed three directors for each branch and the shareholders of the individual branches appointed seven.[21]

The legislature was to vote for the bank president. Most people thought that Sam Merrill was a shoo-in. He wanted the presidency, and had been an outstanding state treasurer. John Sering also wanted to be president. He contended that his experience with the Farmers and Mechanics Bank made him the best candidate. He appealed to JFD for help. JFD's interest was in the Madison branch, so did not want to risk angering Merrill. He finally agreed to help Sering indirectly.

Lanier reasoned if they could field a strong Democrat, it would siphon off the Democrat votes. Merrill's Whig votes would not be enough for a majority, and Sering might be an attractive compromise. What friendly Democrat could they put forward? Gamialiel Taylor seemed a good choice. If, by some chance he did win, he would also be friendly to Lanier.

Gamaliel Taylor was a well-respected citizen of Madison. He was a strong Democrat known to President Jackson. He was a Presbyterian minister, had been county sheriff, county judge and federal marshal of Indiana. Everyone in Madison loved "Uncle Gam" who "dispensed gospel truths with a pure hand on Sunday, while dispensing civil justice with an even hand during the week."[22]

As Lanier developed the plan he became intrigued by the possibilities. He warned Sering that planning for the Madison branch of the bank was going forward, and running for state president, precluded a branch position. Sering was eager to take the all or nothing risk. Sering and Taylor campaigned on their own. Lanier stayed in the background protecting his standing with Merrill. He felt he could not lose no matter who won the election.

Sam Merrill was too strong. On January 29, 1834, the General Assembly elected Merrill president of the state bank board. He received thirty-seven House votes and fifteen in the Senate. John Sering received fifteen and ten votes respectively, and Gamaliel Taylor received seventeen and three. Merrill's understanding of the pitfalls of state banking and his excellent record as state treasurer carried the day.[23]

Calvin Fletcher won the election for one of the state-wide directors, along with Seton Norris also from Marion County. Lucius Scott from Vigo County and Robert Morrison from Wayne County completed the legislative choices for the board. Calvin Fletcher also became one of the commissioners of the sinking fund.[24]

The first bank board meeting convened on February 13 in Indianapolis. This, and subsequent meetings of the bank board took place at the "Governor's Circle."[25] The legislature designated the house in the circle as the governor's residence, but Indiana's first lady refused to live there, complaining the house afforded no privacy. She refused to hang her washing in public view! Thereafter the building became a location for public meetings.

The board vote for chief cashier ended in a tie. Merrill broke the tie by voting for James M. Ray. The cashier served a four year term. The position required a $50,000 bond. The board also appointed him secretary.[26]

The board delineated the ten districts and proposed branch banks in the following cities: 1. Indianapolis 2. Lawrenceburg 3. Richmond 4. Madison 5. New Albany 6. Evansville 7. Vincennes 8. Bedford 9. Terre Haute 10. Lafayette.[27]

The board then appointed commissioners to obtain subscriptions of stock for each branch. The commissioners had to supply a performance bond of $10,000 each. The commissioners for the fourth district were Nelson Lodge, editor of the *Indiana Republican Banner* in Madison, JFD Lanier, and Milton Stapp.[28] Subscriptions to the Madison branch sold in three hours, the sale exceeding the quota by 145 shares.[29] James Lanier purchased a large block of stock and would eventually own more stock than any other shareholder.

Subscriptions sold at an encouraging rate statewide. At the May 1834 meeting, the bank board authorized the striking of plates for the printing of bank notes, not to exceed $13,200,000.00.[30]

On May 5, JFD and Elisabeth attended the wedding of children of two close friends. Wm. Hendricks Jr. married Margaret Stapp. Suddenly the Lanier children seemed older. Elisabeth dreamed about Alex's and Elisabeth's weddings. James refused to discuss it. Both were far too young to even talk about marriage.

On August 4, 1834, Noah Noble began his second term as governor. Wallace continued as his lieutenant governor.[31] They were now "National Republicans." They hoped that the change of party name would change the party's national fortunes. James was not very active in the campaign. He immersed himself in studying banking and economics so that he could make an immediate contribution to the success of the state bank.

By November the commissioners had all of the money from the stock sales. The Madison branch was ready for business. The stockholders elected Lanier president and Milton Stapp cashier. John Sering's unsuccessful run at the bank presidency relegated him to clerk of the branch. At this point, JFD Lanier's career in banking began in earnest. His training and experience up to this point would serve him well.

At the height of his personal success, however, the cruel realities of life jolted JFD. In August 1834, cholera once again swung its deadly scythe along the Ohio River. Dr. Lanier stood stalwart between his patients and the killer. The disease could turn a robust man into a corpse within days. Dr. Lanier hired a driver and lived in his buggy, sleeping as he traveled between patients. Not even a doctor's knowledge and skill could protect him from the disease. He contracted the illness, and within days, on August 10, he died.[32] The loss devastated the town, and a large number of people turned out to honor the doctor.[33] James opened the grave close to his father and buried the brothers side by side. The epidemic also claimed the son of Michael Bright.

JFD left for his first state bank board meeting less than a month after being elected president of the Madison branch and delegate to the state board. The weather was cold and the road rough. He probably had second thoughts about the amount of traveling his association with the bank would require. On Nov. 13, 1834, James presented his credentials to the board representing the fourth district. The board also confirmed him as president of the Madison branch.[34]

Merrill assigned bank board members to committees at each quarterly meeting. Lanier's assignment was the accounts and business committees. The accounts committee acted on all matters of accounts and claims that came before the board. The business committee acted on items not appropriate to any other committee. Several important resolutions passed at that meeting. The board laid the groundwork for a solid bank system.[35]

The board instructed the bank president to make an arrangement with the U.S. Bank to accept all branch notes at par in the U.S. Bank branches in Cincinnati and Louisville. The U.S. bank could redeem all Indiana notes through either the Lawernceburg or New Albany branches. These branches were closest to Cincinnati and Louisville respectively. According to the rules, the other branches were to reimburse the New Albany and Lawrenceburg branches at par for any of their branch notes the U.S. redeemed.[36]

In August and September 1834, the *Indiana Republican* of Madison published the notice on the right. The editorial below followed on November 13, 1834.

**State Bank of Indiana**

The subscribers for Stock in the several branches of the State Bank of Indiana are hereby notified that they are required to pay the first Installment on each share of their Stock; to the respective Commissioners having charge of the Subscription Books in each District in the town where the Branch Bank to which such stock is subscribed is located and at such public place in said town as the said Commissioners shall direct on Monday, the tenth day of November next .- And also, that on the day succeeding, being the eleventh day of November next, at the usual place of holding elections in such town between the hours of ten o'clock in the forenoon and four o'clock in the afternoon, an election will be held by ballot, for eight Directors on the part of the respective stockholders in each such branch; of which election the Commissioners holding the Subscription Books of Stock in such district are appointed Judges.

By order of the Board of Directors of the State Bank of Indiana, on the 22 day of August, A.D. 1834.

JOSEPH M. MOORE
*Cashier pro. tem.*

The publishers of the several newspapers in each town where a branch of the State Bank is located, are requested to insert the above notice as early as possible and continue the same until the tenth day of Nov. next, and forward a copy of the paper containing the same to this office.

J.M. MOORE
August 29,1834

The Commissioners for the branch of the State Bank of Indiana at Madison, hereby give notice that they will attend at the office of the Madison Insurance Company on the tenth day of November next, for the purpose of receiving from Subscribers for the Stock in said Branch the first installment of $18 75 cits. on each Share in pursuance of the above notice.

NELSON LODGE,
JFD LANIER, *Comm' rs*
MILTON STAPP,
Madison, 2 Sept. 1834

## MADISON BRANCH BANK

The cash on the part of Stockholders in Madison was paid in on the 10th instant without any defalcation. On the 11 the following gentlemen were elected directors on the part of the stockholders: viz.—JFDLanier, John King, Robert Craigg, Benj. Hubbs, Lucius Barber, Wm. W. Page, C.P.J. Arion, and Howard Watts. The directors on the part of the state are Wm. Dutton, Robert Branham, and Williamson Dunn. On the evening of the 11th, all the directors held a meeting and elected JFD Lanier, Esq., *president*—Milton Stapp, Esq., *Cashier*, and John Sering, Esq., *Clerk*. JFD Lanier was also chosen a director of the State Bank, on the part of the Madison Branch.

We know not that it becomes us on this occasion to say anything in praise of the selections, and we need not, and would not, were Madison or Jefferson County, alone concerned; but this is not the case. The people of the whole state, and as many out of it as may handle the paper of the Bank, have a right to know if a good selection has been made? As evidence of confidence on the part of the stock-holders we have been told that the choice of directors was nearly unanimous, while the vote for *president* and *cashier* was entirely so—and as far as we have learned, the whole transactions have been generally approved. It is enough for us to say that the gentlemen elected possess *wealth, talents*, and *reputation*, and their skill and fidelity in the management of Madison Branch cannot be doubted.

85

The board wanted the highest quality notes possible, so turned to a New York City printer. The Merchants Bank in New York City kept the plates for the various Indiana bank notes. This plan safeguarded the plates and stifled any local temptation to print extra branch notes.[37]

Lanier established himself as a leader at this first meeting. He made several motions in connection with his committee duties, and argued his opinions strongly. He had taken it upon himself to purchase a bottle of 'Gold and Silver Test' and a set of gold scales for each branch. The Madison Branch received reimbursement of fifty cents each for the test liquid and $15.55 for each scale.[38]

The board set the salary of the president of the Second Indiana State Bank at $1200.00 per year. Each branch would establish the salary of its officers and director. Each director received $3.00 per day for each meeting day, and $3.00 for every 25 miles traveled going to and coming from the meetings.[39]

The governor issued a formal proclamation on November 19, 1834, that the Second Bank of Indiana would commence the business of banking.[40] Politicians and businessmen agreed that Indiana had now moved from an infant pioneer into a full-fledged brotherhood with the eastern states. The *Indiana Republican* reported in the November 27,1834 issue that "the Madison Branch began discounting on Monday last" (Nov. 21).

The bank opened its first office in the Madison Hotel.[41] The location was perfect, and traffic in and out of the hotel brisk. James worked all day, and into the evening on his 34th birthday. He was happy. The Madison branch opened amid great interest and excitement. It had a bright future. James felt the state of Indiana had given him a wonderful birthday present — a new vocation with a great opportunity for service and wealth.

Well connected politically, and well respected in the community, JFD also had a thriving law practice. Up to now he had invested excess funds in land. He saw a bright future for the bank. A future he could control. He began investing not only his time and talent, but his capital. His talents paid dividends to the bank. The bank reciprocated.

# 9.
## "We are doing a fine business already . . ."
JFD Lanier Nov. 23, 1835

*Although the bank board attempted to remain non-partisan, in 1835 the state bank proved to be an important force in Indiana. Lanier immersed himself in the operations of the bank. He liked the business, realizing it put him at the center of both business and politics.*

The quarterly state bank board meetings settled into a routine. They usually lasted three to four days. The first day entailed setting the agenda, and dividing the members into committees. There were several standing committees.

One reported on the condition of the bank, listing the means, liabilities and dividends. Another dealt with the destruction of defaced bank notes. The board burned defaced bills and deducted them from the branch's balance. Special problems required select committees. After determining committees and assigning agenda items to the committees, the board adjourned and the committees went to work.

The committees normally resolved disagreements. After discussing the problems, the committees reported back to the full board. The full board voted on the committee resolutions. The minute books of the bank board normally recorded only the resolutions and the board votes, not the deliberations of the committees. The minutes from the state bank board meetings contain little discussion and few arguments. Merrrill conducted the meetings in the gentlemanly manner common for the times. Voices seldom rose in anger; veracity seldom challenged..

At the March 1835 meeting of the bank board, all present congratulated James on the birth of his seventh child, another girl, Louisa Morris Lanier. James reported that the baby had been born on January 31, and that mother and daughter were doing fine.[1]

The business meeting commenced, and Samuel Merrill reported that the secretary of the treasury agreed to accept the Indiana bank notes at par. The secretary also designated the Indiana state bank a federal repository. In addition he named Merrill, through the Indianapolis branch, as the U.S. pension agent. The agent had the responsibility of dispersing U.S. military pensions to Hoosiers.[2]

James sat on the committee that dealt with the acceptance of deposits and redemption of bank notes from foreign (out of state) banks including the federal government. In a committee meeting, he made a proposal that caused a rare disagreement within the bank board.

JFD proposed that the branch banks at Madison, Lawrenceburg, Indianapolis, Richmond and Lafayette as the only ones that could accept federal notes. This plan gave a distinct advantage to those branches because they could loan out the deposits until redeemed. Although the branches had to pay the federal treasury two per cent interest on the funds, they could charge six percent on the loans.[3]

The proposal raised the hackles of the branches not included. Varner Clark representing the New Albany branch, Gustave Clark from Bedford, Deming from Terre Haute and Snapp from Vincennes strongly opposed this resolution. They tried several times to amend the proposal, but failed. In desperation they tried other parliamentary moves to defeat the issue, including a call for adjournment. In the end, the resolution passed 9-3. Clark read a statement into the minutes condemning the resolution, stating that it was illegal because it violated the bank charter.[4]

JFD also pushed through a resolution granting the Madison

branch "the power and privilege" to borrow up to $25,000 from any other branch that might wish to lend the money. The Madison branch would pay interest on the money. The $25,000 in effect was additional capital in the Madison branch available for distribution as provided for in the Indiana state bank charter. The loan term was not to exceed five years. Lanier argued that it was good for the banking system. Those branches that did not have demand for loans could put their excess capital to work, and the Madison branch could increase its lending power without violating the charter.[5]

Since Madison was a commercial center, the demand for loans was always strong. JFD realized the state economy was beginning to heat up. Demand for money would soon spread across the state. If other bankers did not recognize the opportunity, he was happy to give any short-sighted branch the opportunity to invest with him.

JFD left the meeting, pleased that all the resolutions he had proposed had passed. He had found a simple means of increasing the capital of the Madison branch. More importantly he had beaten back a challenge and began to establish himself as a force on the bank board.

In court, James had tried to anticipate what action his opponent was going to take, and then planned a counter move. He found the same strategy invaluable in banking. One small deviation from a planned course of action led to a maze of hazards and opportunities. James exercised his mind during the long trips between Madison and Indianapolis finding his way through the financial maze and sorting out the opportunities from the hazards. His forecasts of the fiscal future were surprisingly accurate. His fellow bankers thought him capable of prescience; they did not realize the hours of study JFD put in to every major decision.

Finances for the internal improvements were floundering. Lanier and Milton Stapp held long discussions about the problems. James wanted the canal fund money deposited in the state bank, and under the control of the bank directors. He argued that the funds should be immediately available to pay internal improvement bills.

Milton Stapp disagreed. He felt the fund commissioners should control the money directly. If the banks controlled excess funds, the bank would accumulate the interest. If the fund commissioners loaned the excess money, the internal improvements fund would gain the interest. James tried to warn his friend that loans were risky. Loans would not bring automatic income. Stapp felt he knew the banking business and was willing to take the risk.

The two friends did agree that continuing as branch cashier might prove unethical for Stapp. Documents and letters from the Madison branch show that John Sering became cashier of the branch by May of 1835.[6]

The state bank was proving to be a great success. A second land rush was bringing thousands of new settlers into the state and pouring federal land sales revenue into the bank. Construction projects were bringing hundreds of additional workers into Indiana. Private businesses were borrowing heavily to supply all of the needs of the new settlers, from shingles to scythes.

The depression was a shrinking memory. These good times were reassuring to Stapp. He felt that by investing excess internal improvement money he could earn enough to pay the interest on the bonds. The boom was on throughout the country. Everyone had a scheme to get rich and everyone who had extra money was investing it. Stocks offered to finance new ventures sold overnight.

Chevalier, in his book *Society, Manners and Politics in the U.S.*, told fellow Europeans in 1835:

> Everyone is speculating, and everything has become the object of speculation. The most daring enterprises find encouragement; all projects find subscribers. The principal objects of speculation are those subjects which chiefly occupy the calculating minds of the Americans, that is to say, cotton, land, city and town lots, banks, railroads. . . . Speculation in railroads has hardly been less wild than those in land. The American has a perfect passion for railroads.

The Madison branch was by most measures the most successful of the state bank branches. Lanier insisted that the branch build its own structure as soon as practical and that the structure be strong and solid. The banking house itself had to reflect strength and safety.

The bank charter required that the entire branch board of directors be present whenever discussing loans. The board met at least once each week. JFD chaired the meetings and strongly influenced the board. James took advantage of sound opportunities, but his bankers' mentality demanded judicious risk taking.

The social conduct of branch board members was as important as their fiscal conduct. James continually reminded them that their moral and business conduct reflected the strength and character of the bank. He made it clear there must not even be the appearance of impropriety.

Not only did he chair the loan meetings, Lanier took an active role in the day to day operation of the branch. He learned the banking business from the clerk's stool to the president's chair. He was a borrower as well as a lender. His intimate knowledge of the operation allowed him to contribute mightily, not only to the efficient operation of the branch, but also to the sound policies of the state bank board. His diligent study of the history of finance and banking allowed him to avoid many fiscal traps.

"Discounting" was the normal method of granting loans. If a man requested a $1,000 loan for a year, and the rate of interest was six per cent, the bank would take the interest off the top, giving him $940. This method of loaning money was unlike the practice today whereby the borrower receives entire amount of the loan, with interest deducted from each payment. The discount method slightly increases the actual rate of interest.

Letters of transmittal between the Madison and Indianapolis branches of the state bank show large amounts of money being transferred almost daily in answer to the speculator's needs. Messengers carried these funds on horseback or on the stage. The messengers were not always employees of the bank, but often trusted friends who happened to be traveling between the two cities on other business. There was little concern, and no fear connected with carrying large amounts of currency.

Even short notes reflected courtesy and respect not often shown today. The decimal point was still used between hundreds and thousands as well as between dollars and cents. In many instances the dollar sign was to the right of the amount:

To: B.F. Morris Esq.                                    5/15/35
Cashier

By Mr. Lanier I (send) a package of the notes of your Branch which please apply to credit of this Branch.
      Amount 5.320$
                              very respectfully,

                              John Sering

In 1889, Hugh McCulloch, a long time director of the state bank from Fort Wayne, recalled the common method of transferring money between banks:

> There were in the times of this bank (the state bank of Indiana) no express companies in the West. Money was carried from place to place by its owners or private messengers. It was at quarterly meetings (of the bank board of directors) also that the branches usually obtained their circulating notes. Every director, therefore, in going to or returning from these meetings was under the necessity of taking with him considerable amounts of money and although most of the directors traveled on horseback, and were sometimes two and three days on their way, there was no instance of robbery.

> Fort Wayne was three good days ride from Indianapolis north through the woods. For fifteen years I made the journey on horseback and alone, with thousands of dollars in my saddlebags, without the slightest fear of being robbed. I was well known on the road and it was well known that I had money with me and a good deal of it, and yet I rode unarmed through the woods, and stopped for the night at the taverns and cabins on the way in perfect safety. In what part of the United States would a man dare travel in this way now?[7]

JFD had one advantage over McCulloch because there was a stage line between Madison and Indianapolis. Not that stage travel was effortless; it was not unusual for flooded streams or mud slicked hills to stall the stage.

Calvin Fletcher, a farmer as well as a banker observed that the spring of 1835, was unusually wet. Streams escaped their banks; roads became impassable; planting often delayed. Early corn was either under water or ravaged by army worms.[8]

Poor roads caused JFD to be two days late for the May 1835 meeting of the bank board. Before he arrived, a problem arose. The Lafayette branch refused notes from other branches as payment for federal land purchases in violation of the bank charter.[9] The action of the branch threatened the relations every other branch had with the federal land office. The board threatened strong action against the Lafayette branch.

The problem became moot when Merrill produced correspondence from the secretary of the treasury demanding that one person be designated as the pension agent for the state, and one branch be the depository of all federal funds. In the letter, the secretary reaffirmed Merrill as pension agent. The Indianapolis branch was the federal depository. The Lafayette branch need not accept other branch notes for land purchases.

All land transactions must come through the Indianapolis branch.

The bank board resented treasury secretary Woodbury's intrusion into their business. Since it was very inconvenient for pensioners to travel to Indianapolis, the bank board decided that the local branches would continue to pay the pensions and be reimbursed by the Indianapolis branch.[10]

With that problem resolved, the board moved on to other business. Fort Wayne became the eleventh branch of the Indiana State Bank. The board appointed Sam Lewis, Hugh McCulloch and William Roachdale as commissioners to raise the necessary capital.[11]

After he arrived, James introduced his concerns about the health of the canal funds. He argued that the state, through the state bank, had a large stake in the success of the projects. Lanier proposed that the canal commissioners deposit the proceeds from the sale of the canal bonds in the bank, and the bank be responsible for disbursements.[12]

He reminded the bank board that the state bank was the official depository for all state funds. The canal funds should not be an exception. JFD wanted to make sure the bank controlled the canal funds. He worried that poor money management could lead to problems in the future. Few on the board concurred with the argument that the internal improvement funds needed protection; the value of the land bordering the canal would generate more than enough to finish the project. There was no opposition to his proposal, however; they all realized the funds could generate interest for their branches.[13]

A booming economy and full granaries did not keep the shroud of disease away from Madison. In the summer of 1835, cholera made its annual death march along the Ohio River ravaging the town. Most people retreated behind locked doors. Many businesses closed, and social visits ceased. The streets became deserted. The wharf desolate. River steamers refused to stop. People that had a place to run escaped. In his diary, Calvin Fletcher noted that of 20 cases in Madison; there were 16 deaths. He voiced concern that travelers from Madison would carry the disease to Indianapolis. Sheriffs and town marshals between the two cities would not let Madison passengers leave the coaches. Stage travel then ceased. The final toll would reach 34 before the disease ran its course.[14]

On June 15, William Henry Harrison visited Indianapolis to assess his chances in the next presidential campaign. Harrison declined a public banquet, but did have a private dinner with Calvin Fletcher and other influential Whigs.[15] Lanier did not make the trip to Indianapolis because of the cholera scare, but William Henry knew Lanier's loyalty was unimpeachable.

On June 25,1835, JFD wrote to Sam Merrill asking help for a business transaction, and commented on the cholera epidemic.

> The cholera has, I trust, left forever. No new cases for two days. We have consummated the arrangement with the Bedford Branch (in response to the loan resolution of March) for $20.000. Can I get the money Here to counter 1 July- for 5 years. The (U.S.Bk.) branch in Louisville takes all (the paper) of Evansville, N. Albany, Madison and Lawrenceburg on general deposit and wish to take the Indianapolis Branch provided they will agree to redeem through our branch. Will you talk to them and see what they will do? On yesterday we redeemed $21.000 of the bank of Kentucky. It is better to redeem Ky. Bank than ours As it gives paper better credit.[16]

James was expressing an important tenet in banking of the period. It was critical to the health of the bank to keep its paper in circulation. If citizens were willing to accept Indiana bank paper in exchange for Kentucky paper, it would give Indiana paper wider circulation. James could then exchange the Kentucky paper for U.S. Bank notes, or redeem the paper for specie at the Bank of Kentucky.

James was not one to concentrate his efforts. All his life he made an attempt to diversify his interests and his business ventures. He had learned early in life to manage several ventures at once. Although the bank was doing well, he had not completely given up his law practice. In July the Madison paper carried an announcement that JFD Lanier was entering into a law partnership with Hugh B. Eggleston, son of Judge Miles Eggleston.[17]

Lanier did not spend all his time with business dealings. The Presbyterian chuch had been his church of choice for many years, but in the mid 1830's James sought a new direction. When a group of Madison residents talked of organizing an Episcopal congregation, JFD joined the discussions. James knew many bankers and politicians that had embraced the Episcopalian faith. It was fast becoming the church of the powerful.

Differences between the high church and the low church

stalled formal establishment of a congregation for over a year. Finally, in July of 1835, the Christ Episcopal Church of Madison became a reality. James joined Judge Miles Eggleston, Courtland Cushing, Adolpheus Flint and Isaac Lea on the first board of trustees.. Lea, JFD, James Siddall, N.C. Brace, J.G. Marshall, and E.G. Doan became vestrymen. In addition to these duties, Lanier taught Sunday school. He gave financial support to both the Presbyterian and Episcopal churches.[18]

Using the Indianapolis branch as the sole federal depository was proving awkward. Transfers between the federal banks in either Cincinnati or Louisville required long arduous trips. At the August meeting of the bank board, JFD proposed that the Madison branch be the deposit branch for all federal funds. He reiterated the contents of the June 25 letter to Merrill and confirmed that the Madison branch had a strong working relationship with both the Louisville and Cincinnati Branches of the U.S. Bank. In addition, Madison was much closer to either than Indianapolis. The Indiana bank board did not appreciate Secretary of the Treasury Levi Woodbury dictating policy. They must have taken perverse delight in approving James' plan, and in response the Indianapolis branch transferred one third of its federal deposits to the Madison branch.[19]

James expressed concern that the branches were not judiciously accepting out- of-state bank paper. The condition of out-of-state banks was volatile, and the Indiana state bank stood to lose heavily if it continued to accept poor paper. The board instructed branches to reduce their supply of out-of-state notes or suffer the wrath of the board.[20] Many bankers left the meeting feeling Lanier was jousting windmills. The diversity of banks was what made the system strong. It would take a fiscal panic of unbelievable proportions to drive all of the banks in the country into bankruptcy.

In September 1835, James had a chance to dust off his skill as a land speculator. Land sales for the northern segment of the Michigan Road opened in Laporte, Indiana. William Polke was the Michigan Road commissioner responsible for these sales. Polke was a veteran of the Battle of Tippecanoe, a delegate to the 1816 Constitutional Convention, and a judge in Knox County. Many people flocked to purchase land, but in the first six days only 50,000 acres sold, a number disappointing to promoters. Calvin Fletcher and Sam Merrill made the long trip north. Fletcher purchased solely, or in partnership with others, a total of about 860 acres.[21]

While there is no record JFD was actually present, he certainly had his agents in attendance. John and William Walker, Benjamin and Enoch McCarty, John Saylor, Abraham Hall, and James Laughlin established the Porterville Land Company. All lived in Porter County. The only member of the group not living in Porter County was JFD Lanier. Records show he had a one-fifth share in the venture.[22]

The first record of James' direct participation in land sales in the North is a letter to Polke dated October 17, 1835. Evidently JFD purchased the land sight unseen, perhaps on the advice of his friend John Sering, who had friends in the North.

> **I have purchased of Ben (Ach?) Sec. No. 30 in Township 33 lying north of you and east of the Michigan Road. Will you be good enough to see to it a little and prevent Trespassing by cutting timber as far as you can. Write me your opinion of the land and its value. Please pay taxes as you intend by Mr. Sering for himself and me. To what county does the County of Marshall now belong for judicial purposes.[23]**

Secretary Woodbury interrupted James' land negotiations. The secretary did not appreciate the Indiana state bank ignoring his directive. He once again ordered that Indianapolis be the sole federal depository. To make sure there was no mis-communication he also wrote directly to the Madison branch. In a letter to B.F. Morris dated October 23, 1835, John Sering settled the federal account in the Madison branch, and sent the receipts back to Indianapolis:

> The Secretary of the Treasury has communicated to this branch that the department would prefer to keep but one account in the state and that with your branch, and requests the treasury on the books of this branch be transferred over to the credit of the treasury in your branch. I have this day agreeably to his request ballanced (sic) the treasurer's account by extending to the account of your branch the ballance (sic) due Secry eleven thousand 25/100 dollars/ $11.000.25. This amount you will please charge to this bank and credit the Treasurer's account for money received over by this bank. Yours from the 19th inst. With N Mc C— for 5.000 was duly received.[24]

The argument over the federal depository was important to JFD and he hated to give in to Secretary Woodbury. On December 31, 1835, the U.S. bank would cease to exist. The Indiana state bank would become the federal depository as it was the only legal bank in the state. The designated depository would have a considerable amount of federal funds at its disposal.

JFD was aggressive but not foolhardy. He would yield to Woodbury this time. With the federal depository removed from Madison he tried another idea to increase the branch means. The judicious purchasing of bills of exchange provided one such opportunity. Bills of exchange were loans that used produce or store inventory as collateral. When the goods sold, the borrower repaid the loans. Bills of exchange were safe and turned over quickly. Lanier set up a three-way transaction of these bills of exchange between Indiana, New Orleans, and the eastern banks. This 'triangular trading' was very profitable. Lanier explained the practice in his autobiography:

> One of the most important branches of our banking business was the purchase and sale of exchange made by the internal commerce of the country. At that time the only outlets of the interior, as far west as Indiana, were the Ohio and Mississippi Rivers. New Orleans was the sole port of export. We purchased largely bills drawn against shipments of produce to this port. As these bills were about to mature, it was my custom to go to New Orleans to invest their proceeds, and such other means as our bank could spare in the purchase of bills drawn in New Orleans upon shipments of produce from thence to the Eastern States. The proceeds of the latter bills, at their maturity, supplied us amply with exchange for our Western merchants, in payment of their purchases of merchandise. In this way we were able to turn our capital several times each year, and at a good profit, without the loss, I believe, of a single dollar in any transaction.[25]

Purchasing bills of exchange was a stroke of fiscal genius. Since they never exceeded the value of the goods, they were a safe investment. They were short term, payable upon the sale of those goods. They allowed Indiana farmers to ship farm produce to market, and then provided capital for merchants to purchase supplies in the East. While helping Indiana's farmers, the bank turned over its capital several times a year in safe lucrative loans. It was an excellent example of Lanier benefiting by "making the causes of my clients my own."

Bills of exchange provided additional profit for the state

bank. The Madison branch bank purchased New Orleans bills of exchange at a sizable discount. This discount became a profit when JFD, traveled to New Orleans to cash the bills. The same held true for New York bills of exchange purchased in New Orleans and then cashed in New York. Lanier acted as agent for all of the branches and made regular trips to New Orleans to carry on this trade. He also visited New York City, but less frequently.

However, in at least one instance James did not follow his own advice about careful dealings with out-of-state financial institutions.. When he wrote Morris explaining this opportunity he had just turned 35 years old.

**November 23, 1835**

> By Judge Taylor please send us enough to make out $50.000 including what you sent Mr. Sering by mail a few days ago. If you (think proper) you may send me $20.000 on your own account to be deposited in Louisville Savings Inst. I have just received a letter from them a satisfactory arrangement can be made with them. I will trust you to send us such funds as we neglect to I do not . . . think we should want more of the deposits hereafter; therefore make the above as good as you can. You will oblige me by making out the amount of eastern funds to amt. of $15.000. You sent I think $8.000 by mail and we have but little and there is (much demand) for it. If you think proper to send me $20.000 on your own account in Eastern funds I think the savings will allow you 1/2 per cent for it. We are doing a fine business already and our new capital is nearly subscribed and nearly all to the pork merchants and good bills of exchange. Please have the package prepared for Judge Taylor and he will call for it.[26]

When times were good, everyone was buying, and bank paper was in demand. It was the best of times when a bank could keep its notes in circulation and hoard specie in its vaults. Conversely, if customers demanded specie for paper, a bank's reserves dropped with the speed of a diving hawk.

Toward the end of 1835 it was the best of times in Madison. The Madison branch had exhausted its supply of paper notes, and paper notes from eastern banks were very much in demand at the Ohio River banks. When paper at one branch ran low, they would often draw notes from another bank where it was moving as fast. This helped the second bank by keeping its paper in circulation. Sering wrote to Morris in Indianapolis on December 6:

I have drawn a check on you for $6.000 the reason I give the check is that we (have) no Indiana paper on hands. It is to fulfill a contract made by Mr. Treadway for land. Pay him our paper if you have it. If not any paper Indiana will do. We will replace the (check) to you when Mr. Lanier comes out. Lanier goes . . . tonight to Louisville. in great haste yr servt/ John Sering
It will oblige us to comply as above as we have no paper in hand and the— account shall be returned.[27]

Griffin Treadway owned a hotel in Laporte.[28] He appeared to be a good credit risk. Treadway would prove to be a festering sore for JFD, but at this point James did not realize it.

Lanier went to Indianapolis later in the month and made good on the check mentioned above. Christmas was a major religious holiday, but was not the family holiday it is today. It was not unusual for James to spend Christmas in Indianapolis. The legislature opened in December or early January. James could renew political alliances, visit old friends, and do necessary bank business. JFD spent December 24 in meetings with Calvin Fletcher, James Farrington of Terre Haute, and Achilles Williams of Richmond discussing the bank's strategy in the current legislative session.

Lanier and Fletcher worried that the boom had exhausted the available capital in the state. European capital had been flowing west across the ocean like a golden river. Rumors were circulating that the Bank of England was about to raise interest rates to stem the loss of sterling. The country needed new capital to prevent a disastrous depression. The bankers lobbied the legislature to raise the limit on bank stock a branch could issue. They also requested permission to sell branch stock to out-of-state investors. Bank stock was a good value and would always attract investors.

Later that day JFD and Calvin Fletcher attended a party given by Governor Noble. Calvin Fletcher described it: "Governor Noble had a party and employed stages to carry guests to his house. Very little parade about Chr(i)stmass."(sic)[29] James probably attended church at the new Episcopal Cathedral on the circle on Christmas Day

The year ended on a tragic note. On December 30, news reached Indianapolis of a terrible fire in New York City. Estimates of property damage ranged between $30,000 and $60,000. Many people died. Those with friends in New York wrote hur-

99

ried letters to determine their fate. Many people organized collections of clothing and household goods. Requests to appropriate money to relieve the suffering and begin the rebuilding flooded Congress.[30]

# 10.
## "A melancholy accident . . ."
### Madison Republican Banner April 28, 1836

*JFD was very happy as 1836 dawned. He had found a profession that suited his talents and lifestyle well. At 35 years of age he was a success. His reputation was flawless and his bank account flush. His family was growing and healthy. The U.S. Bank officially closed its doors on December 31, 1835; its charter expired. He looked forward to the challenge of operating without the U.S. Bank.*

James was a very private person. Few references survive that list James or Elisabeth as party guests. Those that do, are business oriented: a party given by a governor, a reception for legislators. The mansion he built in 1844 on the north bank of the Ohio River certainly accommodated large gatherings, and there must have been gala parties in the house. JFD used it most often to entertain small groups of influential friends. These were not the type of social affairs that made the local paper. Lanier's circle of friends appreciated the privacy. They rewarded his discretion with information that allowed him to increase his influence and his means.

James realized that closing the National Bank afforded local bankers a great opportunity to make large profits. It also provided an opportunity for spectacular failure. Without a national bank, and a fully convertible national currency, state banks could greatly affect the money supply and the fiscal health of a region. He resolved to be doubly vigilant for both opportunities and disasters.

Lanier knew there were two ways to create money. The government could print currency of course. Banks also create money when they make loans. When a bank makes a loan of $1,000 it creates an account and credits the borrower with $1,000. No currency is printed or changes hands; no dollars flow into the account. A simple entry in a ledger book creates $1,000. This was both an opportunity and a problem.

As close as they were to Ohio and Kentucky, Madison residents could not obtain loans out of state. Indiana state bank branches were even reluctant to make loans to men living outside their banking district. This gave branch banks a captive clientele, and complete fiscal control within their district. The fact that, unlike a national currency, state notes were not fully convertible outside Indiana strengthened this control.

These factors combined to give the banks and bankers remarkable power. The situation was not without pitfalls. JFD recognized that proper banking practices and appropriate caution were critical to success. He worked at refining the banking practices and became the state bank's conscience.

Because of its power, the Second State Bank of Indiana had many critics. Most were men who were jealous of the power. Some opposed the bank on principle. They did not feel the state should charter a monopoly. Newspapers chose sides and kept up a drum roll of praise or condemnation. Although the Democrat papers of Madison regularly castigated the state bank, they never criticized Lanier personally.

Banking allowed Lanier to practice his life creed to ". . . **(make) the causes of my clients my own. Success or defeat consequently gave me more pleasure or pain than it did them . . .**" This was especially true since he held the maximum number of bank shares allowed by law. While minding other people's money, he was also shepherding his own purse.

James personified the public perception of a respectable banker in every specification. He was fiscally conservative, even under intense speculative pressure. Years earlier he had established a reputation for **"never allowing my liabilities to exceed my means."** He maintained and built upon that reputation. He was industrious, spending long hours at the banking house, available to depositors and borrowers alike. He would never betray a confidence or broadcast the sensitive fiscal condition of his clients.

Being president of the Madison branch, and a power on the state banking board fit his personal lifestyle like a handmade boot. He was friendly, but not fawning; tranquil not tempestuous. His manner, language, and bearing bespoke respectability, knowledge and control. While bank policy dictated that the entire branch board of directors be present during loan discussions, JFD led the board. A nod or a frown determined the success or failure of loan applications.

Whether setting policy for the bank board, interpreting laws, or implementing fiscal practices, the record shows James was incorruptible. Honor, Honesty and Integrity were lifelong companions. Since JFD owned more stock in the state bank than any other individual, sound practices filled his pockets. Poor practices drained them. Survival became another active business partner.

The Madison branch purchased bills of exchange for all branches. On January 9, 1836, Sering wrote to Morris:

> We have this day purchased a bill on N.Y. for $10.000. The money is to be paid out in the Wabash (Valley) in purchasing pork. We are out of Indiana money and theirs is the best kind of operation and best for the people to have their own state paper. I have drawn on you for 8.000 supposing you would have considerable on hand received from the several offices and it is much better to put our own state paper in circulation than to circulate paper of other states. We have a large amount of Cincinnati paper on hand and can place that amount with more if you wish in any of the branches in Cincinnati. If you have the notes of this branch pay them, but any state paper will do.[1]

And on January 21:

> Eastern funds very much in demand on the river and we are nearly out. If you could let us have $10.000 or $20.000 we will give you 1/2 per cent in commission prepaid. Will you let me know if we can have the funds.[2]

To emphasize the dearth of paper on hand at Madison, JFD wrote to the Indianapolis branch:

In late January 1836, flooded by petitions from across the
state, and buoyed by the positive economic situation, the legislature passed the Mammoth Internal Improvements Bill. This
bill consolidated all of the piecemeal transportation efforts into
one massive undertaking. The bill outlined eight major projects.

1. The Whitewater Canal along the Whitewater River in
   southeastern Indiana
2. The Central Canal running from the Wabash River between Fort Wayne and Logansport, south through Munci-
   etown to Indianapolis, along the White River to the forks
   and then to Evansville
3. An extension of the Wabash & Erie Canal from Lafayette
   through Terre Haute then south to meet the Central Canal
   at some convenient point
4. A railroad from Madison through Columbus and Indianapolis, to Lafayette
5. A macadamized turnpike from New Albany to Vincennes
   The road was to pass through Greenville, Fredericksburg,
   Paoli, Mt. Pleasant and Washington.
6. Either a road, or a railroad from Jeffersonville through
   New Albany, Salem, Bedford, Bloomington and Greencas-
   tle, terminating in Crawfordsville
7. Clearing the Wabash River of obstructions to navigation
8. A canal or a railroad across the top of the state from Fort
   Wayne to Michigan City, connecting the towns of Goshen,
   South Bend and Laporte with the Great Lakes.[4]

The legislature appropriated $8.7 million for the first seven
projects, anticipating that the sale of bonds and lands would
raise the immediate cash. This was in addition to the cost of the
Wabash and Erie Canal that added another 1.1 million dollars to
the cost of state improvements. Tolls and other payments would

repay the debt. The lawmakers did not plan to build the northern canal until 1846.[5]

Lanier's persuasive efforts focused on the Madison to Indianapolis rail line. In exchange for the railroad votes, he used his influence to obtain other improvements throughout the state. He also promised to help obtain financing for the projects.

Six additional members joined the canal board and this group became the Internal Improvements Board. Each member was to receive $2.00 per day plus expenses. The fact that John Woodburn was appointed to the board was probably another example of Lanier's hidden influence. Woodburn, in addition to being a director of the Madison branch bank, was a local businessman deeply involved in salt mines and shipping. Woodburn salt preserved tons of meat processed at Madison pork plants, and Woodburn ships carried the meat to the plantations in the South.

The state erupted in joy as news of passage of the bill spread. Great fires illuminated town squares, with speeches and parades adding to the celebrations. Respected papers throughout the nation praised the progressive attitude of Hoosiers. The Boston Atlas extolled Indiana and chastised Massachusetts for its foot dragging.[6] Calvin Fletcher wrote:

> This day the great internal improvements bill passed the House of Representatives . . . This grand project will exalt Indiana among the great nations of the earth. I have a strong desire to see the completion of this splendid system.[7]

Samuel Merrill was against the bill. He felt the fiscal arrangements would ruin the state. Merrill also felt the influx of heathen laborers would disrupt the moral tranquillity of Indiana.[8] JFD withheld judgment. He remembered Washington's plea for a water link between the Potomac and the Ohio rivers. He remembered Governor Ray's vision of Indianapolis as a rail hub. Perhaps Indiana did need a diverse transportation system. The Wabash and Erie Canal had proven that wise planning and astute fiscal control were essential. Jesse Williams was a good man, and John Woodburn was certainly honest. Time would tell.

To bring some order and understanding to the wide range of internal improvements, the legislature appointed Jesse Williams chief engineer. He was a highly qualified man who left his mark on major projects throughout Indiana. A corps of twelve resident engineers assisted Williams. There were as many as seventy five surveyors working on the individual projects. Lead men earned $2.00 per day and their assistants 75¢. The annual cost of survey crews alone totaled $54,000.[9]

The legislature was debating some amendments to the bank charter. Lanier, Calvin Fletcher, Achilles Williams and James Farrington lobbied for the changes that the state bank board of directors wanted. They were very successful in their efforts. The men persuaded the legislature to increase the capital of the bank to $2,500,000, and to allow bank stock to be sold outside the state.[10]

It was evident to Lanier that the state was in danger of over extending itself as Merrill had predicted. It was critical to begin construction of the Madison and Indianapolis Railroad before the legislature realized the fiscal problem. He began lobbying his friends in the legislature.

James missed the February 1836 meeting of the bank board, but was paid $95. for his lobbying efforts.[11] Merrill had done a routine audit of the Lafayette branch and found some disturbing problems. The committee deferred action on the problems to allow the officers of the branch to correct them. The committee did:

> beg leave, however to say that they consider it very important that the teller's daily statement should be so kept as to show at all times the exact amount and kinds of cash in Bank.[12]

The report went on to say that the committee regretted that a misunderstanding between the board and the branch existed, and there was no hostility on the part of the board toward the branch. The board was just doing its job in reviewing the branch — just like it reviewed all branches.[13] No doubt the board member representing Lafayette felt relief when the report escaped the hard eye of Lanier.

Demis Deming, from Terre Haute, joined the committee assigned to review all branches. He found all the reports uniform and correct — except the report from the Madison branch. Deming criticized the Madison report as too abbreviated and consolidated. He admitted that a later report cleared up the questions.[14] It appears that Deming could not resist a cheap shot at JFD while he was not present to defend himself.

106

The Wabash and Erie Canal had cash flow problems. Bond revenues were not accumulating as planned. Commissioners were loaning out the revenue instead of paying bills. Construction continued, and unpaid invoices mounted. The state bank was glad to help. It agreed that any branch could loan the canal fund commissioners up to $30,000 in addition to the $470,250 the bank had already advanced for the project.[15] If Lanier had been at the meeting he would have thrown up a caution flag. The poor fiscal practices of the canal operation confirmed his original fears.

In its continued effort to generate capital, the bank board entertained the idea of paying interest on deposits. They decided to study the idea and obtain branch input before making such a drastic move. The directors also wanted branch input on a proposal to equalize federal deposits between all branches, so that everyone could take advantage of the extra federal money.[16]

The board decided that although the new amendments to the charter allowed discounts up to 2 1/3 the amount of capital paid in, this limit was not automatic. They would set the actual limits allowed for each branch. This would be an effective tool in adjusting the money supply and for controlling branch activities. Finally the directors voted to investigate the possibility of obtaining its own building for meetings and other purposes.[17]

Borrowing and spending continued unchecked. On March 3, 1836, Sering wrote again to Morris:

> We still need eastern funds and will take to the amount of $40,000 and will place that amount to your credit in the commercial bank of Cincinnati immediately with the 1/2 per cent premium.[18]

James efforts on behalf of the Madison & Indianapolis railroad were successful. The legislature gave the project a high priority, and survey crews quickly assembled. Mapping began in March, when the weather moderated.

The railroad and bank were not JFD's only interests. He was still looking for prime land near the Michigan Road. In a letter dated March 2, 1836, he asked William Polke, the Michigan Road commissioner, to be on the lookout for good land. His father's teachings on land selection are evident in his instructions:

> **Your two letters are rec'd. I am desirous of getting some land on one of those larger clear water lakes . . . if the soil is good. I can not now say whether I will go beyond the $3,000 if how-**

ever very good investments beyond that can be made I will be willing to go a little beyond.

It is desirable to use great caution in selection of lands as to soil, timber and location. This I of course submit entirely to your sound judgment — It will also be better to make personal examination as far as you can. Your note to Bates is here rec'd. If possible we will discount it.[19]

In the next two weeks, the rapid deterioration of the fiscal situation surprised James. By March 22 he was retreating. In a letter to Polke he advised that he had purchased a 1/4 interest in a Madison law practice and **"must decline any further land contracts in the north altho they are no doubt good."**[20]

JFD gave another indication of increasing troubles in a letter dated April 15. He explained that the Madison branch could not discount Polke's note. He thought a bank in Cincinnati discounted the note and sent it to Indianapolis for payment. James ended the letter by saying **"Let matters stand about our land until you come in (to Indianapolis). Please bring in with you the Land Office certificates."**[21]

As the credit constriction became apparent, the directors of the Franklin branch bank in Cincinnati were demanding payment from the Indianapolis branch for some outstanding bills or warrants. The Franklin branch bank officers were unwilling to accept notes from the Indiana state bank, or even from Cincinnati banks. They demanded specie. JFD was in a contentious mood, and was happy to help another Indiana branch, while putting the screws to a bank he felt was less than scrupulous. This is one of the few times that his surviving correspondence shows any emotion. In a letter to Morris dated April 19, 1836, he stated:

> In regard to the payment to the Franklin Branch you can command our services. We now have several thousand dollars in Franklin Branch paper and can get more & have requested the— & our merchants to save all they can get for us. We shall also collect all the other Cin. paper we can get. They (the notes) must be paid by the bank in Cincinnati. The matter can easily be explained to the banks in the city. Tell them that the F.B. will not accept their paper as a reason why we call in theirs. They are a real set of sharks in that Franklin Bank. I would like to see them gored a little.[22]

In the same letter he goes on to give his opinion of the secretary of the treasury's attempts to change the agreement with the Indiana state bank.

108

The Secretary of the Treasury is attempting to force us into his terms. That is the same contract he has with the deposit banks. We will be forced to accept or give up the depository. My opinion is we can comply with his wishes without much trouble. If our contract was the same as the other banks he may let us rest.[23]

The next day, JFD was in the office at the Madison branch tending to normal bank business when a man burst into the bank, pushing his way directly to JFD's desk. The wild look in the man's eyes stifled Lanier's first rush of annoyance. There was a terrible accident. The river swept away the Lanier family carriage. Alex and Oliver Sheets, a cousin survived, but there was no sign of little John James or Elisha, the dwarf negro carriage driver.[24]

James sat stunned and speechless, his mind churning. He made the messenger slowly repeat his babbling: "Alex and another unidentified person swam to safety, and are at the doctor's house. A black servant boy and little John James are missing."

JFD rushed to the river's edge on the east side of town. Several people milled around on the shore. A group of men, tied together with a rope, was chest deep in the frigid water, vainly sweeping the shallows. They had difficulty avoiding the boiling current. Several men in a boat searched the deeper water, but they concentrated most of their efforts on keeping the boat from being swept away.

James questioned a few bystanders, but they are unable to add to the story. Few saw the accident. Alex's frantic screams had drawn most people to the scene. A devastated JFD drove home to tell Elizabeth the tragic news.

When Alex recovered from the near drowning and shock, he told his father what had happened. His cousin Oliver heard about the beautiful carriage his uncle James had purchased from Ben Hubbs. Everybody knew it was by far the nicest carriage in town.[25] Oliver begged for a ride. Elisha drove the carriage, and decided the horses needed a drink. They were close to the river so they decided to let the horses drink there. The horses lost their footing and the swift current tipped the buggy over without warning. Alex reached for John James, but he missed. The carriage and horses sank immediately. Alex struggled to shore and gave the alarm. Each time he told the story the 16 year old broke down and finished amidst tears and blubbering.

109

Elisabeth was inconsolable. Drusilla and Elizabeth's maid ministered to her as best they could. The girls wailed and screamed until Drusilla calmed them down and put them to bed. They sobbed into their pillows until their red eyes could produce no additional tears. Friends flocked to the house but could do little but stand a hushed vigil. JFD remained stoic, but his mind ached as he tried to make sense of what had happened.

The river does not give up its captives easily. Each day a boat left the Madison landing, the occupants rowing back and forth, peering into the water and probing the depths for any sign of the carriage or the bodies. Each night they returned with a grim shake of the head. On the 22nd, James had to escape the dark confines of the grieving house. He went to his office for a few hours hoping to lose himself in business. He wrote a few letters. He did not mention the tragedy.

Each day that the bodies remained undiscovered raised Elisabeth's hopes that John James had somehow survived. She pleaded to have men sent along the banks on both sides calling the boy's name. She sat for hours at her bedroom window watching the river. Each flash of color, each far off silhouette brought hope, then disappointment. As long as the body was missing there was hope—wasn't there? A sad nod answered her question, but with eyes that said no. Deep in the black recesses of her mind she knew what JFD and everyone knew. The river had swallowed up John James. It was playing a cruel game and would not yield the body until it had exacted a terrible price from the family.

James went to work each morning, but found himself wandering along the riverbank silently damning the river and the circumstances that caused John James' death. Children's deaths were not unusual. Most of the families in Madison had

*Melancholy Accident*—A son of JFD Lanier, Esq. and his servant, a Negro boy, were drowned in the Ohio, at our landing, on Wednesday afternoon last week. The boy had driven Mr. L's horses, attached to his carriage, into the river to let them drink, when going too far in, the current being very swift, they were suddenly swept away by it into twenty or thirty feet water. The horses and carriage immediately disappeared, and have not been seen or heard of since. There were four persons in the carriage at the time; two saved themselves by swimming; but Mr. Lanier's child and the Negro sunk beneath the waters before any assistance could be rendered. Their bodies have not yet been found.

On April 28, the *Republican Banner* printed the sad story.

lost a child to one of the plagues or illnesses that stalked the West. This was different. This was his child.

Friends tried to console JFD. John Sering, Michael Bright, Milton Stapp and many others spoke in hushed tones to the bereaved father. Gamaliel Taylor spoke as a friend and minister. The kind words did little good. It did not have to happen. The death was caused by someone's carelessness; by someone's stupidity. JFD could not tolerate carelessness or stupidity.

Searchers finally recovered the body of John James. Almost with relief, JFD made the funeral arrangements. The funeral was, of course, at home. The coffin rested on a stand in front of the heavy drapes drawn against the bright sunlight. A candle stood at each end of the small coffin.

The service droned on, drawing from the assembled friends and family the last anguish possible. James Lanier sat stiff and silent. Despite his best efforts to hold them back, tears rolled down his cheeks and dropped unto his black trousers.

A helplessness he had never experienced ate at James' heart on the long slow trip up the hill to City Cemetery; at the table with the empty chair; in the long quiet nights as he lay beside Elisabeth, feeling her silent sobs. His infant son now found the peaceful rest of the rewarded, but JFD felt he would never rest peacefully.

The only relief he could find was at the bank. The means and liabilities, the entries and trial balances demanded his complete attention and he readily gave it. The veil of concentration could shut out, for a few hours at least, the dreadful reality.

Meanwhile the Indianapolis branch helped solve the Franklin branch problem. On April 30, 1836, Sering wrote to Morris:

I have yours of the 25th inst. (this month) The payment of $25.000 to the Franklin Bank will be attended to as you request.[26]

Elisabeth would only find solace in another child. Ten months after John James death, she gave birth to another boy, Charles. James and Elisabeth thanked God for this baby boy. After so many girls, Elisabeth was sure that Charles was a sign from God that He was sorry to have taken James from them. Charles was to have a special place in both Elisabeth's and JFD's hearts.

# 11.
## "Our pecuniary prospects look gloomy."
— Calvin Fletcher December 1836

*In the mid-1800's economic depressions followed booms as surely as fall followed summer. Only the inexperienced speculators felt they could avoid the inevitable down-turn. Lanier knew a recession was coming. The trick was to take full advantage of inflation, but be prepared for the slide. Timing meant the difference between wealth and poverty. He had been successful in the past, could he do it again?*

Land sales were booming throughout the U.S. In 1832 federal land sales totaled only $2,623,000. By 1836, fueled by internal improvement speculation throughout the nation, they would reach $24,877,000 and exceeded the funds collected by tariffs.[1] Indiana was no different from its neighbors. The Internal Improvements Law set off an explosion of speculation.. Land values soared along the routes of the projects. Lots sold in the prairie wilderness for $50.00 to $200.00 each, on land purchased from the government for $3.00 per acre.[2]

By 1835, the Jackson administration retired the national debt, and a surplus began to build. With the U. S. Bank shut down; the federal government did not know what to do with the money. Congress passed legislation designating the surplus federal funds as loans to the states. Secretary of the Treasury Woodbury selected the deposit banks.[3] Few felt the federal government would ever call in these loans. In 1836 William Henry Harrison wrote to Governor Noble:

> I have no hesitation in recommending to your legislature to appropriate every Dollar of the surplus revenue which has been assigned to you. . . . Rest assured that it will never be reclaimed by the U. S. under any circumstances. [4]

This was the high point of the American boom. The demand for cash in America was draining the vaults of Europe. British gold reserves had fallen by almost fifty percent in less than five years. Rumors floated across the ocean that Europe would stop loaning money in the U.S. The rumor became fact. The Bank of England raised interest rates dramatically to recapture their reserves. The flow of European gold began to dwindle.[5]

Nationalists who feared foreign investment was "purchasing" America welcomed the move. They felt the U.S. could fund its own construction. "Hard money" advocates crowed that their predictions of the evils of borrowing had proven true. Lanier and the Indiana state bank board had acted none too soon.

As foreign capital dwindled; the financial picture in the U.S. became clouded. Fiscal experts in Washington feared a recession. President Jackson proposed that all federal land purchases be paid for exclusively in specie. The Whigs labeled the move a politically motivated punitive strike at business interests. Congress defeated the proposal by a narrow margin. Jackson was undeterred.[6]

Lanier spent long hours on the stage between Indianapolis and Madison contemplating the volatile fiscal situation. Inflation was devastating, but Jackson's solution would demolish the bank and Indiana's economy. The vote in Congress had given a reprieve, but Jackson felt so omnipotent he might yet break Congress. The state bank must prepare.

Calvin Fletcher worried also. His example of inflationary prices was close to home. On May 14,1836 he wrote in his diary "This day I bot (sic) a breeding sow and shoate of 100 lbs. Gave $12. Two years ago could have bot (sic) for $4.00."[7]

At the spring 1836 meeting of the bank board, on May 18,

Hugh McCulloch took his seat for the first time, representing the Fort Wayne branch. He was to serve the bank in various capacities for over 20 years.[8] James attended, perhaps glad to escape the sad atmosphere in Madison.

JFD immediately took advantage of the new amendments to the state bank charter. He proposed that the Madison Branch be permitted to increase its capital stock by $60,000. The wording of the resolution guaranteed that the new shares and old shares would be of equal value.[9]

Although they all knew of the new laws, other directors had not seen the need for immediate action. After approving the measure, some directors realized that Lanier's resolution gave the Madison branch a formidable advantage. Delegates introduced hasty proposals to allow the branches at New Albany, Lawrenceburg, Lafayette, Richmond, Terre Haute, Vincennes and Indianapolis to sell additional stock in the amount of $30,000 each. The terms would be the same afforded the Madison branch. Merrill assigned the motions to a committee. Another motion rescinded the resolution for the Madison branch, requesting it be studied by the same committee.[10]

Lanier explained in detail why the increase was necessary at Madison; the type of investors he would seek; and the safeguards he planned to put in place. It was obvious that he had given the plan much thought before proposing the increase. No other branch representative had such a plan or could meet the criteria that JFD had set for the sale of stock. The resolution lost; and the increases of Madison branch stock survived.[11]

Later in the meeting, after detailed plans were submitted, and strict criteria agreed upon, the board resolved that the Indianapolis, Lawrenceburg, and New Albany branches could increase their capital by $45,000.00 each. They agreed to meet the same conditions as the Madison branch.

". . . and your committee as to the other resolutions requesting an increase of capital, ask to be discharged from further considerations"[12]

The resolution quickly passed, and the board went immediately into a discussion of correspondence and expenses for the last three months. The bypassed branches could not reopen the discussion. The representatives fumed at the unreasonable control exercised by the board and silently vowed to get even.

The board discussed bills of exchange. This was the idea that Lanier pioneered to turn over branch capital safely and rapidly. At least one branch polluted the idea. There were indications that the branch manufactured bills of exchange for the sole purpose of paying off bills of exchange previously purchased. The board put a stop to the practice.[13]

The board received and approved the report of the branches. The bank appeared to be doing very well. Branches reported an aggregate profit of $95,423.83 for the six month period ending April 30, 1836. The Surplus Fund stood at $81,203.00. The Indianapolis and Madison branches led the way with a profit of over $12,000 each. The Madison branch paid a dividend of five percent. All of the branches paid at least a four percent dividend except the new Fort Wayne branch.[14]

The report provided a false sense of security. It did not reflect the volatile fiscal situation. Lanier's committee on the condition of the bank tried to raise a warning. Land was selling briskly, and all appeared well, but there were problems ahead. Lanier warned that the European vault door was closing. America would have to survive on its own capital. The U.S. Government would not help as the "hard money" advocates gained power.

Lanier reminded the board that during the preceding three months the secretary of the treasury had called in federal funds at an alarming rate. If he continued to make heavy demands on the bank in the next three months, the drain would be "severely felt." The branches had about $360,000 of federal deposits in their vaults as a result of the land sales.[15] Most of this money was in Indiana bank notes. If Jackson had his way, these notes could not pay the federal drafts. It was critical that the Indiana state bank circulate its paper.

To solve the problem, Lanier strongly suggested the branches collect as much eastern paper as possible. They should stand ready to forward it to Washington at a moment's notice. JFD wanted as much of the federal debt paid with paper as possible before Jackson demanded specie.[16] He reasoned that the treasury was more likely to accept eastern bank notes than Indiana bank notes.

Paying specie to Jackson was a last resort. Silver was the only circulating medium, because gold was over valued in relation to silver. The state bank cached any gold collected in the bank reserve fund. If Jackson's plans went into effect before Indiana paid the debt with paper, it would exhaust the reserve fund and seriously damage the bank. At the end of the lengthy report, the board resolved that the branches reduce their loan total to twice their paid in debt, and approve only those loans that were "most proper . . . and of short dates."[17]

Lanier's plan appears to run counter to modern fiscal policy of loosening credit during a depression. However, with no national bank, and no national currency, each state's paper was valued in relation to that of other states. The U.S. currency market in 1838 acted much like the international currency market does today. With minimum loans, and a strong gold reserve, the Indiana state bank position would be stronger than a bank with depleted reserves. Capital would flow to Indiana. State bank notes would retain their value. Concerned that available capital was exhausted in Indiana, the board empowered the branches at New Albany, Vincennes, Madison, Terre Haute, Lafayette, and Bedford to sell their stock outside the state.[18]

In addition to the external problems, there was still a serious threat at home. The board tried to protect the bank from internal bleeding. They specified that the state bank would not loan the Internal Improvements Fund Commissioners additional money unless they placed all internal improvement cash in the bank. In addition, the state bank board mandated that it must approve all internal improvement drafts.[19]

The next topic discussed was Woodbury's proposed agreement between the U.S. Treasury and the Indiana State Bank. Despite JFD's misgivings, the board bowed its neck. It voted to "not, at present, consent to any alteration of the contract." The board directed Merrill to continue his negotiations with Woodbury.[20]

As he rode home, JFD still worried. He anticipated a depression, but was happy that work would soon begin on the Madison incline. It was a major construction effort designed to allow trains to run to the banks of the Ohio River. Although the most expensive and complicated single project on the line, the cut or incline would allow for the efficient transfer of goods from boats to rail cars.

In a letter to Polke dated June 25, 1836, he mentioned his economic concerns and the incline.

**By all means sell our land. Now is the time. Money is still getting more scarce. We shall soon have some men at work on the hill.**[21]

116

Work on the incline progressed slowly. The summer heat warmed the Ohio River valley like a sauna. The strongest stevedores called for the water boy after less than an hour of loading freight. In town, perspiration stained the clothes of even the most genteel women. Hot blasts of air that surely emanated from the devil's own furnace replaced the inviting breezes of spring. Infrequent rains teased gardens, and raised steam from tile roofs and the rock faces that glared down on Madison.

Pedestrians watched their footing to avoid animal dung and trash that littered the streets. They made circuitous detours to avoid packs of dogs that foraged for an existence. Peddlers hawked their goods from pushcarts. Horse drawn drays and heavy wagons pulled by broad shouldered oxen crowded the streets. Dust clouds rose to second story windows and invaded every room.

Roaches, beetles, spiders, and other crawling vermin marched through houses spoiling flour, decimating cloth, and spreading disease. Flies, bred for strength in stable manure piles, invaded the best houses and marked lamps, mirrors and polished tables with their droppings. Clouds of mosquitoes attacked robust men and defenseless infants with equal vigor.

The Fourth of July was the major national holiday. In Madison, throngs took a river steamer to Hanover to attend the annual picnic where religion and patriotism vied for attention. Politicians measured their patriotism by the length of their speeches. Ministers proved their righteousness by the fervor of their sermons. JFD sat his family squarely between the pulpit and the podium.

James reinforced his decision to sell the land and gave Polke detailed instructions on July 7:

> **Contracts are now made to work on the hill. You will please enter in** (the Land office records) **Mr. Sering's or my name a good pc.of Michigan road land as named to you. Sell land enough to pay our debt and hold the residue. I am convinced that now is the time to sell as to price I leave that to you. Advise me occasionally how you get on.**[22]

In July 1836, while Congress was in recess, President Jackson used his whip. He mandated what Congress would not approve, and issued his famous "Specie Circular." It stated that only specie be accepted for federal land purchases. Despite the Specie Circular, Woodbury could not call in funds because of the surplus. The conflicting federal policy caused massive turmoil. Most banks chose to take the easy path, electing to continue business as usual. Some actually increased loans in anticipation of the federal disbursement.[23]

The bank board called a special meeting for July 27 to discuss the Specie Circular and the federal surplus disbursements. JFD was not able to attend. He wrote to B.F. Morris with instructions:

> Finding I can not attend the next State Board I resign my appointment and have you appointed to represent us at the next Board. Our branch is unanimously in favor of retaining the (federal) deposits under the new law. The plan to give the most satisfaction would be for each branch to retain its portion and pay the interest. If all will not agree to this we are willing to receive more than our portion. If it is thought best to make the River Banks the depositories, we are willing to act as one, make all expenses of transfer as a joint concern. There is no doubt but what we can make money by retaining the deposits and paying the interest required. Finally do whatever you think is best in the circumstances and we will be content.[24]

In a separate letter to the board, Lanier reported all $60,000 in new bank stock sold. He expected full payment by October.

The bank board adopted most of the ideas JFD had proposed to Morris. They agreed to accept the surplus distributions under the terms set forth by the secretary of the treasury. The board fought for some concessions from Woodbury. As part of the agreement, they demanded state bank notes of $10.00 and above be accepted as payment for federal debts including land purchases. In addition, they asked the secretary to designate the branches at Madison and Lawrenceburg as the federal direct deposit branches, and to void that designation for other branches.[25]

A final resolution of the bank board allowed the Indianapolis branch to increase its capital by $45,000. The board denied the Lafayette branch the same privilege. There were still questions about the banking practices at Lafayette.[26]

Not all of JFD's deals turned out to be sound. The arrangements with the Bank of Northern Kentucky, begun in November 1835 when the future looked bright, turned sour. On August 20, 1836, Lanier wrote to Morris:

> Mr. Nesbitt (cashier) is positively misunderstanding me and I think willfully. I stated to him distinctly that you could not at present spare him any specie that you had to furnish $91.000 in silver for the Ind. (Canals?) That we could not at this time because a new stock was about to be paid in which would be

118

mostly in paper. I regret that Mr. Nesbitt should have misunderstood me.[27]

Despite the tightening fiscal vise, James rejoiced when actual construction of the Madison and Indianapolis Railroad began on September 16, 1836. The first leg was from the north edge of Madison to Graham, a distance of seventeen miles.[28]

The stretch from the Ohio River to the flats above Madison was one of the most difficult engineering and construction challenges of the entire internal improvements scheme. Two cuts through solid rock, one 100 feet deep and the other 125 feet deep provided access to the river. The cuts would be about 7,000 feet long, and the roadbed laid on a grade of 5.89%, making it the steepest non-cog rail line in the United States. Digging at the cut also began in September but progress was slow.[29]

The Whigs were desperate to win the White House in 1836, and they tried a unique idea. They put forward different candidates in different sections of the country. The Whigs thought that these popular candidates would beat Van Buren in each section. No Whig would win a nationwide majority, but the election would end up in the House of Representatives where the Whigs would unite behind a single choice.

William Henry Harrison was one of the Whig candidates. James worked tirelessly for his old friend. His personal friendship and confidence in William Henry came through as a passionate endorsement. Jackson was gone. Martin Van Buren was an eastern snob, not in tune with the needs in the West. Surely the Whigs could easily defeat him.

Also in September of 1836, the Portersville Land Company plans were coming to fruition. The company offered to donate alternate lots in the townsite of Portersville, plus an additional 40 acres outside the townsite, and some cash, if the County Commissioners would pick Portersville as the County seat.[30]

Lanier wrote to Benjamin McCarty giving his approval to the deal, and giving McCarty Power of Attorney for his share of the land.

**September 21 1837**

Sir, I do hereby approve your doings thus far in laying out and selling lots in the Portersville, Porter County, Indiana, so far as I am concerned, viz one fifth, and do hereby authorize you to go on and make such additional sales in said town as you

119

may proper, at and for such price as you may think most to the advantage of the properties. . . .

It would be best for you to make title to the purchaser on payment of the purchase money. I would in no case make title unless the purchase money is paid or otherwise secured beyond doubt. I wish you would occasionally drop me a line informing me how you are getting along and prospects.

Yours Very respectfully,
JFD Lanier[31]*

There were several other offers made to the Commissioners, but they voted for the Portersville site. The name of the town became Valparaiso at a later date.

Payments to the Northern Bank of Kentucky were coming due and the bank was demanding specie. On October 14, 1836, JFD was beginning to yield to the pressure applied by Mr. Nesbitt. He wrote to Morris:

It will be best to pay the No. Bank of Ky. some specie at payment of the 80.000 25 next month. I shall go to Louisville to night and will tell Mr. Nesbitt that they shall have some specie.[32]

More complications arose. On October 29, 1836, J.F.D forwarded this letter to Morris:

I just returned from Louisville. If I am not much mistaken we shall have trouble in paying off the Northern Bank. They will I fear, refuse to take interior Kentucky paper. I have promised them $45.000-50.000 in specie at November payment.[33]

Catching up on his correspondence, James wrote Polke the same day:

Your letter enclosing the checks for $200 is rec'd. You are hereby authorized to sell any or all the lands, say 1/3 or 1/2 down and the ballance (sic) in 12 or even 18 months with 10% interest. By this means I think a higher price can be had. Money matters are increasingly hard now. My advice is to clean out on the above terms, unless you think it better to reserve some particular tracts.[34]

---

*The letter copied in the Plat Book carries the date of September 21, 1837. All of the other paper work concerning the transfer of the town lots lists dates in February of 1837. We are assuming that when the recorder copied Lanier's letter into the plat book, he changed the year from 1836 to 1837 inadvertently.

On November 2, Calvin Fletcher set out to audit the branches at Madison, Lawrenceburg and New Albany. Excerpts from his diary give some insight into the difficulties of travel and some understanding of why a transportation system was a high priority:

> Left for Madison on Nov. 2. We took passage in a long waggon (sic)- the stage could not pass in consequence of bad roads. Cold day. 6 passengers . . . dangerous crossing the Blue river-very dark. Took lanterns from E (Edinburg) but had not done 2 ms before waggon broke down. Here 6 of us laid down in a little log cabbin (sic) 14x16 and mail was carried on horse to Columbus by driver or boy. . . . (In) the morning we traveled on foote (sic) to Columbus and had breakfast at Irwins. No stage came and on the 4 I procured a horse . . . & rode with stuffed saddlebags to Madison. I went aboard (the mail boat to Louisville) . . .The boat was all life and bustle on the river. Every body going to a warmer southern climate. . . I had to take the floor with divers(e) others as all the births (sic) were filled. We arrived at L. about two in the morning. At 5 we left the boat for the Gault House a new and splendid hotel.[35]

While Fletcher was battling the elements, JFD was battling the Northern Bank of Kentucky. On November 2, he wrote to Morris on another subject and added: **"I hope you can let the No. Ky. Bank have $45. or 50.000 in specie as** (requested) **in my last."**[36]

On November 5, he wrote a long letter to Morris stating that Mr. Nesbitt and a Mr. Tieforo, a trustee of the Northern Bank of Lexington, Kentucky had visited Madison. They were in need of eastern funds. They agreed to pay par plus one-half percent and would take $50.000 to $100.000 at that rate. They needed the money before December 1, and would not guarantee the rate after that date.

He reminded Morris that the Kentucky bank was expecting $45,000 or $50,000 in silver on November 25. He complained that Secretary Woodbury had undercut them by advising Tieforo that the Indiana state bank had a great amount of specie and the Kentucky banks could get a supply from the Indiana bank. Lanier warned that **"we may have trouble paying the transfer drafts at Louisville. Kentucky money is scarce and getting more so as the banks in that state are now drawing in and putting nothing out."**

Lanier closed the letter by stating that Indiana could not rely on the Cincinnati banks as they were low and had transfers of their own to make. The matter was completely in Morris' hands.[37] Because of the urgent nature of the business, he sent the letter by special messenger.

Lanier wrote to Morris confirming the deal on November 17. Politics was never far from his heart and he commented on the election results:

> . . . Your waggon (sic) has not yet made its appearance. As soon as it does arrive I will go with it to Louisville. Accounts this morning give Pennsylvania, Maryland, Delaware, Virginia and Connecticut to Harrison. Also Ky. by a small majority. The majority in Virginia is said to be about 1,000 only. Illinois as far as heard from is favorable. Ch. for 100.000 to N. Br. of Ky. is (credited) by this to you and with 1/2 pr.[38]

Polke was actively selling their land. By November 9 he had made several sales and reported to Lanier. On the 18, James replied. He was very happy that Polke had collected U.S. Bank notes in the transactions. **"Your letter of the 9th came here last night. I am glad you have made the sales named and wish you to retain the U. S. Notes for us, at least the $2500 that you name."**

He then gave instructions on how to fill out the deeds. He also advised Polke about another loan     **"If you can not raise money to pay off your note, we will try to accommodate you as desired."** As an afterthought he pens a Post Script to the letter.

> Perhaps the best plan will be to place the whole $2500 to my credit in the Branch at Indianapolis and request B.F. Morris to hold the U.S. Notes for me and I will (write) a check for $1720 for sale of deed and the ballance (sic) on your note. Please advise me of the day that you make the deposite (sic)[39]

On November 24, there is further correspondence to Morris about the Louisville deal. Ever frugal, Lanier comments on the high rate the steamboat charged for carrying the silver.

> Mr. Sharp (?) is yet at Cincinnati. I made arrangement Louisville by which he can dispose of $20.000 eastern check at 1/2 per.     The steamboat . . . charged me $27 for . . . silver being at the rate of $1. per hundred. I remonstrated but to no purpose. As yet we have rec'd no part of the last installment (of federal surplus distribution) **nor are we likely to.**[40]

James did not make the November bank board meeting. Elisabeth was sick and the dread of a miscarriage lurked over the house. They must not lose this baby. She and Drusilla were sure the baby was a boy. James kept informed of the doctor's whereabouts day and night. He worked at home, spending more time in church than in the bank.

At the quarterly meeting held in November 1836, the balance sheet of the bank still did not reflect trouble. For the quarter ending October 31, 1836, the bank system as a whole showed a quarterly profit of $105.572.38 and a surplus of $126.431.31. The directors decided to take a profit while they could. The average dividend was slightly more than five percent The Madison and Indianapolis Branches led the pack and received dividends of 5 1/2% each.[41]

Still looking for fresh capital, the board approved the requests of the branches at Vincennes, Richmond, Evansville and Lafayette to increase their stock by $40,000 each.[42]

There were definite signs that the economy was turning sour. No bank stock sold to out of state investors. Suspended debt, (defaulted loans) had become such a problem that the board required that each branch report them in detail. Even with Merrill and Lanier absent, the board took strong action to limit discounts.[43]

The Legislature balked at the state bank's attempt to control the state purse. The economy confused and concerned them. They passed a law requiring that "visitors," with no ties to the bank, periodically audit the branches. The board was not afraid of the outsiders. The minutes made it clear that these independent "visitors" be given access to every record and the reason for every decision made by branch boards of directors.[44]

The last order of business was to approve the salaries of the branch officers. JFD, as president of the Madison Branch; and as a reflection of his day to day involvement in the operations, received $1,000.00 per year. John Sering, the cashier, earned $1,400.00. In contrast, the presidents at Evansville, Vincennes, Lafayette, and Richmond received no salary. The others collected between $200.00 and $400.00 annually.

The cashier at Indianapolis matched John Sering's salary, and a teller earned $1,000.00. The other cashiers received between $150.00 and $1,000 with the Lawrenceburg, Richmond, and Terre Haute branches each having an additional employee paid between $200. and $500.00 annually.[45]

JFD worried that the Democrats would drag the country deeper into the financial morass when. Van Buren won the election. Harrison's loss was difficult for Lanier to accept. The split Whig ticket caused the defeat. James was sure that if the Whigs had rallied behind Harrison, they could have won the White House.

The unsettled conditions increased through the winter of 1836-1837. Individuals were seeing what Merrill and Lanier had forecast months earlier. Credit was constricting. Implementation of the Specie Circular was causing great difficulties among all banks. Hoosiers were becoming disenchanted with the progress of the internal improvement projects. Contracts had become political jewels. There were few results despite great amounts of money being paid to contractors. Even confidence in Indiana state bank notes was faltering.

Lanier and Polke received a proposition from John Barron Niles concerning 525 acres of northern Indiana land. They had paid $4.00 per acre for the land. Given the state of the currency, Polke suggested asking $4.00, but taking less if necessary. He also sent a full listing of the lands the two owned in partnership, adding an ominous explanation:

> . . . (here) is a full statement of our business which I thought might be necessary to be preserved in case that either of us should not live to a final disposition and settlement of this land action.[46]

James was not ready to surrender. On Christmas Eve he wrote Polke from Madison that he thought the land was worth $4.00 per acre and it would serve no purpose to take less.[47]

Polke was not the only pessimist. That same month, Fletcher wrote to Senator Tipton summing up the tumultuous state of affairs:

> the full operation of the (Specie) Circular has commenced- our canal hands here refuse to take any of our state paper except such as is on our branch that they can go and draw the specie-our pecuniary prospects look gloomy.[48]

# Parents of James Franklin Doughty Lanier

**Drusilla Doughty Lanier**

**Alexander Chalmers Lanier**

These sketches are in a metal double folding frame and undoubtedly had a prominent place on James' dresser or nightstand

**James F. D. Lanier**

**Elisabeth Gardner Lanier**

These are thought to be wedding pictures

Images courtesy of
Indiana Department of Natural Resources
Division of Museums and Historic Sites

Photographs of paintings of JFD Lanier's children are rare. Below are some of those that survive.

Alexander C. Lanier

Drusilla Ann Lanier and one of her children

Drusilla Ann Lanier later in life

Charles Laner and his dog

Katherine Lanier

JFD Lanier at about the time he
moved to New York City

Charles Lanier as a successful
financier

Sidney Lanier

Drusilla Lanier Cravens. It is
through her and Charles'
efforts that the mansion was
deeded to the state of Indiana

**Lanier Mansion Circa 1856**

**Lanier Mansion after 1998 restoration**

Images courtesy of
Indiana Department of Natural Resources
Division of Museums and Historic Sites

# 12.
## "I must get out of this scrape the best way I can"
—JFD Lanier January 21, 1837

*The year 1837 would provide a stern test of the free enter-prise system in a representative democracy. The economic situation became so volatile that many banks and bankers did not survive. The year would test James Lanier's courage, confidence, and fiscal skills as never before. The Second State Bank of Indiana teetered on the edge of bankruptcy; if it fell it would take the state, and James Lanier, into the abyss with it.*

The Laniers were expecting the middle of January, and James stayed in Madison. Elisabeth had stayed in her room since the episode in November, and the entire routine of the house revolved around her needs and wishes.

Drusilla was becoming more feeble. Her excess weight, and advancing age attacked her back and knees. She moved to a downstairs room, but once a day climbed the stairs to check on Elisabeth. She retired early each evening exhausted, only to lie awake most of the night. Drusilla did not complain; her memories kept her company.

So frequently did the doctor visit the Lanier house during December and January that the cook routinely set an extra place for him at the dinner table. Patients searching for the doctor often stopped at the Lanier house before inquiring at his office.

The Northern Bank of Kentucky deal continued to squeeze Lanier. Nesbitt was demanding the remaining payments in specie. Lanier warned the Indianapolis branch:

**January 10, 1837**

You are charged with amt. paid Northern branch Ky. Louisville $72.252.35.
I went to Louisville by land on Thursday last. Crossed the river at Jeffersonville tho peril of life. Nesbitt held on to your promise of $50.000 in specie on this last payment and forced me an approval that it shall come from us. They want it I could not avoid it. As he had us in his power. In case this is extracted you must help us out with it.[1]

One week later Elisabeth began a long difficult labor. The weeks in bed had drained her strength and stamina. James ordered someone to stay with her at all times. The maid kept clean sheets in readiness. Hot water continually bubbled on the stove.

On January 19, the child was born. Elisabeth and Drusilla were right; it was a boy. They named him Charles.[2] Drusilla climbed the stairs, mindless of the pain. As she held her grandson for Elisabeth to see, both women whispered prayers of thanksgiving. The Dragon of Death ran from the Lanier home, chased by the cries of a baby.

James returned to work. For the first few days, a constant stream of friends stopped in to congratulate him. He did not discourage the interruptions. On January 21 he wrote Morris again. Some of Lanier's frustration leaked out in his correspondence:

Yours of the 17th inst. rec'd. Nesbitt is a real dog. Let me get clear of him once then hands off. I must get out of this scrape the best way I can.[3]

At the February 1837 meeting of the Indiana state bank board, the directors felt pressured by the constant clamor for more credit. The prevailing opinion among the citizenry was that the bank should loan money to keep the state, and the citizens, out of trouble.[4]

Elisabeth had recovered from the birth without problems, so James attended the bank board meeting. Reporting for the committee on the state of the bank, he tried to strike a balance. Despite his problems with Nesbitt, the balance sheet showed that the condition of the bank had not deteriorated since the previous November. Perhaps the worst was past. Lanier's report stated:

> **"the present condition (of the State Bank of Indiana) is such as to give increased confidence in its usefulness and the ability, skill, and fidelity with which its operations are conducted. Its means are ample to meet almost every possible emergency"[5]**

The balance sheet looked healthy. On 11/19/36:

| | |
|---|---|
| Specie on hand equaled | $ 1.075.084.53. |
| Discounts equaled | $ 3.063.104.82. |
| Circulation was | $ 1.934.070.00 |

The balance sheet dated 1/7/37 listed specie on hand at $1.236.164.35.

| | |
|---|---|
| By 2/4/37 the specie had dropped to | $ 1.212.372.33 |
| The discounts had risen to | $ 4.074.855.00 |
| and circulation stood at | $ 2.337.425.00 |

The branches listed the following suspended debt:

| | |
|---|---|
| Ft. Wayne | $ 2.400. |
| Madison | $ 200. |
| Bedford | $ 10.150. |
| Vincennes | $ 1.191. |
| Richmond | $ 2.648. |
| Lawrenceburg | $ 1.200.[6] |

James tried to point out early signs of weakness. The drop in specie on hand between January 7 and February 4 was a concern. The amount of suspended debt also clouded the balance sheet. He pleaded with the branches to reduce their suspended debt.

Reports from the West and South warned that many banks were perilously close to bankruptcy. The most disturbing aspect of the report to most board members was the fact that the dividend was down to an average of three percent.[7]

The situation confused some board members. Was the bank in good shape or not? Was Lanier really concerned about the economic situation or was he only attempting to persuade everyone to be conservative to protect his private purse?

Lanier was himself uncertain. On the way home he mulled over the problem and decided to talk to the directors individually, hoping to bring them all into his camp or at least dissuade the weak branches from being drawn down the path to calamity.

Despite the confusing financial picture throughout the United States, Secretary of the Treasury Woodbury felt it was his lawful duty to pay the third installment of the surplus funds. Confusion turned to chaos. Rather than use the additional funds to strengthen weak reserves, most banks immediately increased their loans. Fueled by increased credit, prices continued to rise.

Life outside the bank continued. Winter melt and spring rains turned roads into rivers, and fields into ponds. In the nicest homes in Madison and Indianapolis, every family member risked maiming of the most graphic description if they failed to use the boot scraper or did not remove dripping garments before entering the house. Spring brought warm weather and the promise of new life. It was time to show off a wobbly legged colt or a suckling calf. Kittens and puppies hid in children's bed clothes until their yapping or staining banished them to the yard.

In April, James and ten other men were appointed to the Education Board. There was a good mixture of older men for steady guidance and young men with fresh ideas and energy.

---

EDUCATION CONVENTION
FOR JEFFERSON COUNTY

The undersigned take the liberty to invite the friends of education in Jefferson County, to meet in Convention at Madison, on Saturday the 20th of May next.

It is hoped that teachers and all others interested in the cause, will endeavor to attend this meeting, and also to be at Madison as early in the day as practicable, that the convention may have time for its deliberations.

An Address will be delivered by Prof. Harney, of South Hanover College, at 2 o'clock P.M.

| | |
|---|---|
| J.H. Harney | Noble Butler |
| Charles K. Thompson | L.H. Thompson |
| W.M. Dunn | Wm. Twining |
| John Sering | JFD Lanier |
| Jeremiah Sullivan | Victor King |
| John King | |

April 26, 1837

**This notice appeared in the Madison papers in April 1837.**

128

William McKee Dunn was one of the new voices. James liked the young man. He was the son of Williamson Dunn from New Albany, a bank board member and friend.

The inflated economy suddenly sprung a leak. During March and April the thin skin of fiscal health fell away, revealing advanced stages of rot. By April 1837, over 250 federal Deposit Banks had failed. Jackson was still the opposition's favorite whipping boy. In a footnote to some regular banking transactions, Sering wrote Morris:"Well hasn't General Jackson turned the world upside down at last."[8]

Every day news reached Madison of another bank failure in the western states. James became increasingly worried. Could the state bank survive both the worsening economy and the pressure to make more loans? He felt that the branches at Indianapolis, Fort Wayne, New Albany, Evansville, Richmond, and of course Madison would make the tough decisions. Lawrenceburg and Lafayette would not. If the Bedford, Vincennes and Terre Haute branches caved in to loan pressures, failure was certain He wrote another round of letters to fellow directors trying to strengthen defenses against new loan requests.

Nothing, not even the difficulties of the state bank, interfered with the ritual of spring house cleaning. Throughout Madison, winter blankets, draperies, and bed hangings blossomed in the yards and on porches, as commonplace as the early flowers that splashed the hillsides. Women carefully cleaned and dried the bed linens before packing them away for the summer. The "whomp, whomp, whomp" of carpet being thrashed echoed throughout town. Wives harnessed weak husbands and slow-footed sons to the task of scrubbing walls and floors to a bright shine.

Elisabeth claimed James scheduled the bank meetings so that the directors would miss spring cleaning. In the spring of 1837, James would rather have scrubbed floors than go to Indianapolis. As he climbed the hill north of Madison, the mist that hung on the river was raising its veil on a bright new day. James hoped it was a good omen.

It was not to be. The May 1837 meeting of the state bank board opened with confusion and ended with consternation. After being assigned to the committees, the directors discussed the massive bank failures throughout the West. The U.S. Treasury, caught in the financial crisis, had called in deposits at a frightening rate. Woodbury was demanding specie. Gold was flowing from the western banks like life blood from a dying man. Businesses were failing and defaulting on loans. The nation was suddenly slithering into a disastrous depression.

The state bank's position, which Lanier called "ample to meet almost every possible emergency" just three months previous, was now precarious. Jacksonians on the bank board still clung to the belief that independent banks protected the nation from a general collapse. Only when reminded that the Indiana state bank had $1,200,000.00 deposited in failed banks did they begin to understand.[9]

These funds were to pay federal drafts against the Indiana state bank. Now the funds were unrecoverable, and the bank was still liable for the treasury demands. The payments would drain specie from the bank vaults. Lanier stated the situation as a resolution.

> Whereas the rapid withdrawals of United States deposits and the confusion that now prevails in the money market renders it very hazardous for the Branches to continue their discounts to the same extent heretofore,
>
> Therefore resolved that the Branches be directed to bring down their discounts to twice the capital paid in before the first of August next.
>
> Resolved further that the branches are earnestly recommended to give a preference in their discounts to such notes or bills that will be punctually paid at maturity.
>
> Resolved further that each Branch ought to require at least one-fifth of the gross sum of their discounts to be paid every ninety days.[10]

Amid the easy credit atmosphere of the last few months, these were unprecedented restrictions on the branch banks. There was no dissent on the board. The liberal board members sat in terrified silence.

The board recessed at 6:00 P.M. contemplating if this measure was enough to protect the bank from outside forces. The larger eastern banks were still open and everyone hoped that strong action could keep the state bank solvent. About 6:30 P.M. messengers from Lawrenceburg and Madison reached Samuel Merrill with the news that all the banks in the East, along with the Cincinnati banks, had suspended specie payment. Desperate Cincinnati residents had bought up all the Indiana paper they could, and rushed to Lawrenceburg to exchange it for specie.[11]

When the Lawrenceburg branch realized what was happening, they locked their doors against the mob. After the streets cleared, they dispatched a messenger to Indianapolis. By the time the rush reached Madison, the bank had already closed for the day. Sering, hearing the specie demands in the streets and shops, sent a messenger that arrived soon after the one from Lawrenceburg.[12]

This turn of events seriously threatened not only the Indiana state bank, but commerce throughout the state. The state treasury, and with it all of state government, was in jeopardy. Merrill rounded up all of the bank directors and invited the governor and state treasurer to participate in an extraordinary session that lasted far into the night.[13]

The debate centered on the suggestion that the Indiana state bank follow the lead of other banks and suspend specie payments. Some argued that it violated the bank charter requiring payment in specie upon demand. The proponents of the resolution argued that the charter clause was to protect the people of Indiana from loss. The current demands for specie came from outside the state and those demands would deprive Indiana citizens of their specie. The suspension would actually carry out the spirit of the charter and protect the people of Indiana from loss.

Another member suggested the legislature be called into special session to approve the move. This proved impractical, as time was critical. Some directors felt that individual branches should be free to act on their own. Others argued that the bank had to act as a unit in order to save the institution and the state.

Many directors faced financial ruin if the bank collapsed. Voices grew loud and fists pounded the table. The directors knew that they were personally liable for any action taken. They were individually responsible and cumulatively guilty if brought to court. They did not reach a decision before the adjourned for the night. The argument spilled outside the meeting hall, and was continued in whispers along the dark, deserted streets of Indianapolis.

Lanier rose on May 18, 1837, to deliver a stark proposal to the assembled bankers. The stilted language did not lessen the impact of the message:

> Whereas it has come to the information of this institution that an entire suspension of specie payment has taken place by the banks in the cities of New York, Philadelphia, including the(old) Bank of the United States, Baltimore and Cincinnati;

and whereas the banks in these cities are heavily indebted to the Branches of the State Bank of Indiana;

and whereas the safety of the institution, and the interests of the State, being so large a stockholder therein, and of the people of the State require that the large amount of specie now in the vaults of the Branches be retained from being drawn out to other states and other banks

Therefore resolved: That it is the opinion of the Board of Directors of the State Bank of Indiana that it becomes the painful necessity of each Branch of the State bank to suspend for the present specie payment until the resumption of the same by other banking institutions of the U.S., except in the cases of private deposits made with the understanding of payment in specie, and of pensioners, who should always be paid in specie.[14]

As Lanier's voice trailed off, a silence filled the room as each man contemplated the seriousness of the proposal. As if from one mind, ten voices filled the room with a chorus of calamity. They argued each point again. One by one the objectors fell silent until only two remained. In the end the resolution passed 9 to 2. The two dissenters were John Law from Vincennes, and John Mitchell from Evansville.[15] Riders were dispatched immediately to all the branches to save what specie remained in the vaults.

Calvin Fletcher proposed that Lanier be appointed as an agent for the state bank to proceed as soon as practical to Washington. There he would meet with Woodbury and make the most favorable arrangements possible with the federal government. The motion passed unanimously.[16]

Lanier needed one more resolution passed so that he could deal effectively with the Secretary Woodbury. He proposed that all deposits of public funds made after the suspension of specie be put in a special deposit account at each branch. These special deposits could only be paid out in the specific currency received. They were payable only as a counter draft of the treasurer of the U.S. at the branch receiving the deposits. The bank would report these deposits to the secretary of the treasury weekly. The exhausted board readily agreed.[17]

Once they dealt with the crisis, Merrill insisted that the board continue with routine business. The report of the state of the bank belied the truth. Profits for the quarter ending April 30 totaled $182.982.48. The Madison branch led the pack with profits of $25.004.50. Lawrenceburg followed closely with

$24.882.38. The dividend stood at three percent, unchanged from the previous period. The Surplus Fund totaled $252.066.80[18]

The interest due on the federal deposits for the period 6/30/36 through 7/29/36 equaled $2.171.38. The means (assets) of the bank as of 4/31/37 were $7.687.711.34. This included $1.227.303.82 in specie. The liabilities totaled $5.556.093.06 of which $1.427.887.87 belonged to the Treasurer of the U.S. Subtracting the value of the capital stock ($1.824.921.88) from the balance gave a net profit for the state bank of $306.816.40.[19] A disinterested board heard and approved the report. The figures were only paper profits of a pasteboard institution in grave danger of collapsing.

The directors had to tell the people. The merchants must be warned. Lucius Scott proposed the following address:

To the People of Indiana

A state of things has burst upon us as unexpected as overwhelming. The intelligence reached us by express from the Ohio River last evening that all of the banks in New York, Philadelphia (including the United States Bank) Baltimore, and Cincinnati had suspended specie payment. These banks are indebted to ours about a million of dollars principally placed with them to meet the transfer drafts of the government. We can not rely upon present aid from them and can only depend upon our own resources. Our bank paper will be drawn out from the very banks that are indebted to us and which cannot pay us. Agents are already among us and our gold and silver would soon leave the State by waggon (sic) loads. All the East including Cincinnati have stopped (specie payment) and all the south including Louisville have done so too or will soon follow. Under this state of things how long could our banks sustain themselves? The citizens of those states would draw from us every dollar of our specie and what then would sustain our currency?

Your money, fellow citizens, and the money of the state is in our vaults and we are solemnly bound to protect it. The banks that have suspended are not broken. They have been compelled to yield to circumstances not within their control, and we trust will soon resume their payments. Our only alternative was to follow their example in self defence (sic). The duty was painful but forced upon us by circumstances over which we had no control. But there is no cause for alarm. Our specie is ample, being upwards of a million in our vaults; and we pledge ourselves to resume specie payment the hour we learn that neighboring banks have done so.

We earnestly recommend to our fellow citizens to make no sacrifices of our paper- they may rely with the utmost confidence on every dollar being redeemed. Each Branch will freely receive each other's paper. We hope for a speedy resumption of specie payment in other states. On this we are determined to hold our institution in immediate readiness.[20]

The Indianapolis papers immediately published the notice, or the important parts of it. Sam Merrill wrote a letter to Secretary Woodbury explaining why the action was necessary, and dispatched it with JFD. With Lanier at his side, Merrill then addressed the citizens from the steps of the Marion County Courthouse, explaining the bank's actions.[21]

JFD held a quick meeting with Merrill and Ray. As a good faith gesture; Lanier would take $80,000 in gold to the secretary of the treasury. Lanier gathered what gold the Indianapolis branch could spare and headed for Madison to fill out the amount.

On the trip to Madison, James planned for the future. He did not dwell on disaster as others might have. He reviewed his options with the goal of saving the Indiana state bank. The suspension would protect the bank's specie from the public. The next task was to defend the vaults from the federal government. Lanier's mission was to offer a small tribute in an effort to save the treasury. It would be a dangerous journey, but if successful would be a master stroke.

All of the bank directors must have been mulling over their personal situation. Most had obtained ample wealth by their association with the bank, and had borrowed from it and invested to one degree or another. Calvin Fletcher wrote in his diary on May 20, 1837:

> I am sensible that I ought to commence a system of retrenchment in all my expenditures - all my business. I believe I have fortitude to accomplish so necessary an object. More disastrous news has arrived as to our national and individual pecuniary affairs. . . . I learn that there scarcely will be a solvent merchant in (New York City) by the first of June. News has arrived that the Banks of Louisville and all the Kentucky banks have suspended. My own debts to be paid this summer greatly alarm me. . . . I am in my own mind prepared for the worst. I have no mortification to indure (sic) by surrendering up all I have to my creditors. . . . I am as well prepared in my own mind to be a poor as a rich man.[22]

David Wallace was the announced Whig candidate for governor. He did not want to risk angering any section of the state and proclaimed the state was strong enough to complete all of the internal improvement projects.[23]

The Democrats were in disarray. They could not take advantage of the fiscal crisis because it was a national problem, and the blame fell at Van Buren's feet. Since there was no strong Democratic candidate for governor, Gamaiel Taylor stepped into the void. Announcing his candidacy in May 1837, he warned that the state had overextended itself. He favored classification of the internal improvement projects in an effort to make sense of the chaos. The most promising projects gained priority. He was a champion of free education and proposed that the surplus funds be used to finance the long delayed common schools.[24] Lanier could not disagree with "Uncle Gam's" logic. He was sure the Madison & Indianapolis Railroad fell in the first rank of projects. When John Dumont entered the race, Taylor withdrew, feeling that Dumont had a much broader base of support.[25] Dumont adopted most of Taylor's platform. James was sorry to see Taylor bow out.

# 13.
## "I suffered not a little anxiety . . ."
### JFD Lanier, May 1837

*To transport large amounts of money on public conveyance was fretful at any time. No matter how often he had carried cash between Indianapolis and Madison, James was aware of the risk. The trip to Washington was an especially dangerous undertaking.*

Banks were closing all across the country, and specie was the only sound currency universally accepted. The coins were completely untraceable. There was no way to mark or catalogue the gold coins that James carried. JFD would become a target for every cut- purse and picaroon between Indianapolis and Washington if they knew the contents of the strongboxes. In his autobiography, Lanier minimizes the dangers of the trip stating only:

I went up the Ohio River in a steamboat to Wheeling, and thence by stage, chartered for the purpose, alone across the mountains to Frederick, at that time the western terminus of the Baltimore and Ohio railroad, and 61 miles west of Baltimore. I suffered not a little anxiety on account of the treasure I carried more than 300 miles through a wild and comparatively uninhabited region, and was not a little relieved on reaching the safe conduct of a railroad.[1]

Gold coins made up the entire payment since it would have taken 16 silver coins for every gold coin. The weight and volume of silver would have been prohibitive. As it was, eighty thousand dollars in gold coins weighed about 298 pounds. The iron strapped trunks used to transport the treasure increased the total weight to well over 300 pounds. Even with the coins divided between two chests, it took a strong man to carry each one. It is very surprising that JFD transported the gold without escort, but he did. The state bank reimbursed him $268.20 for his trip. There were no others reimbursed.[2]

It is not difficult to trace the route of the trip. From Indianapolis James took a stage or private wagon to Madison. It normally took three days to complete the trip. He arrived in Madison Saturday evening, exhausted. Once in Madison, with the gold safely in the bank vault, JFD rested. Gold from the Madison branch brought the total to $80,000. JFD secured boat accommodations and left for Cincinnati on Monday, May 29. He changed boats at Cincinnati, taking the packet to Wheeling, Virginia.

The riverboat trip was fairly safe. In the spring, when the water was high, and river travel brisk, the cost for a cabin and meals was about ten dollars. James took a cabin on an upper deck as was his custom. Upper deck cabins boasted luxurious furnishings and were safer. It would be more difficult for a thief to reach a cabin on an upper deck, and almost impossible to lug the heavy trunks to the water level undetected. Stevedores carried the chests to Lanier's cabin where he could guard them. For an extra dollar or two, he had his meals served in his stateroom. James was a regular on the boats, with a reputation for being private. It was not unusual that he stayed in his cabin for the entire trip

The distance between Madison and Wheeling was about 450 miles and took three days. There were few navigation dams on the Ohio River in 1837. Floating snags, transitory sandbars, and other obstructions were common hazards. The packets moved slowly at night with a double watch on the bow. James' treasure was most vulnerable at night. He slept fitfully behind a double locked door, a pistol close at hand.

At Wheeling, the dangerous segment of the trip began. This

was much more hazardous than the Indianapolis-Madison stage run because Lanier was not familiar with the coach drivers, the way stations, the overnight accommodations, or the route. The stage used the National Road from Wheeling to Frederick, Maryland. The scheduled stages ran from Wheeling to Washington in 30 hours. Lanier's chartered coach would make the run more quickly. Freight wagons, stages, and settlers heading west clogged the road. Droves of cattle, hogs and sheep never allowed the dust to settle.

From Wheeling the road ran northeast through Pennsylvania. The road wound through the woods to Scenery Hill for an overnight stop. James paid for a private room at the inn, and requested that the trunks be carried up the narrow stairway. He again took his meals in his room and double locked the door and window. By now it was obvious that he carried something of great value in the trunks. He hoped that the innkeeper and stage driver were honest, and that his secret was safe with them.

At first light the trip continued. The road dipped south into northern Maryland toward Cumberland. Once into Maryland the mountainous terrain made for slow going and rough riding. Hostlers changed teams often as the torturous upgrades stained the horses' muscles and the downgrades shocked their bones and joints as they braced to slow the heavy coach. The rocking of the coach and the jolting of the wheels as they bounced from hillock to chuckhole precluded sleep;even for a bone-weary traveler. The gold chests cramped the inside of the coach. JFD did not want them on top of the coach where they might fall off and split open; or in the boot, unseen.

JFD ate while the drivers changed teams. He stayed within sight of the strongboxes. The varied quality of the food and its preparation, and the speed with which he gulped it down, undoubtedly contributed to his anxiety.

From Cumberland, Maryland the coach climbed through Rocky Gap and descended in the shadow of Break Neck Hill. The hand straps were little defense against brain scrambling encounters with the roof or the crushing jolts to the tailbone. James never dwelled on disaster in any circumstance, and so it was on this trip. That did not prevent his heart from leaping into his throat each time the coach slowed for an unexpected reason, or a passerby hailed the coachman in a friendly exchange.

The road followed the Maryland-Pennsylvania border and

met the Potomac River at Hancock. It ran along side the river to Big Spring and then turned straight east toward Hagerstown. The last stretch of the trip was a comparatively flat stretch from Hagerstown south to Frederick.

Lanier's fear did not slacken. It was obvious that he had no escort. Each mile brought a greater likelihood that someone knew he was traveling with a treasure.

James felt immense relief upon reaching Frederick, Maryland. Fatigue almost overwhelmed him, but he fought off sleep until the railroad assumed responsibility for the strongboxes. James did not protest the extra fee for the railroad guards. The train roadbed was silky smooth in comparison to the highway. The rhythmic swaying was a welcome relief; the temptation to nap overpowering.

When he finally reached Washington, James delivered the gold directly to Levi Woodbury. Woodbury expressed his thanks for the gold, and his amazement at the feat James had accomplished. The secretary commented that the state bank of Indiana was the only bank in the country that had attempted to pay any portion of its indebtedness in specie.[3]

The two bankers had a long discussion about the financial situation in the West, and the condition of the federal treasury. JFD explained in detail the condition of Indiana's bank. He explained the resolutions of the state bank board and the reasons behind them. Impressed by the Indiana bank's efforts, Woodbury promised that the bank could retain the government deposits at the current two percent rate until regular disbursements occurred.

JFD Lanier also impressed Woodbury. He had known the banker only through the stubborn correspondence dealing with James' efforts to have the Madison branch declared the federal depository. In addition to being tenacious, James displayed a crisp understanding of banking unusual for a westerner. His bold feat backed his words. The secretary asked James to be the federal Pension Agent for a portion of the western states. The secretary agreed to make all federal payments in the state with Indiana bank notes, without discount.[4]

Although the two men had serious political differences, they shared the common goal of strengthening the economic power of the United States. James discussed the philosophy of the new "economic empire" with Woodbury. Those who agreed with the

139

theory felt the United States could build an empire greater that the world had ever seen. An empire based, not on a Monarchy or military power, but on a strong democracy. A revived, refined, improved democracy that had its roots in the old Grecian Democracy This empire would gain its strength from a strong economic system.

But, this theory had many detractors, both in and out of government. The current fiscal panic had fed those opponents. They felt the grand experiment in representative government was on the verge of failure because it could not sustain a strong economy. James dismissed these naysayers out of hand. Woodbury, who agreed with Lanier, but was surrounded by the whiners of Washington, felt encouraged by the westerner's conviction.

The meeting with Woodbury could not have gone better. State bank notes would pay not only the pension payments, but the active military payrolls, and the U.S. mail expenses. This private agreement would allow the state bank to liquidate its federal deposits in a controlled manner that would stabilize the bank. It would allow the bank to display strength and fiscal responsibility that was so important in the chaotic market. Woodbury had affirmed the solid standing of the Second State Bank of Indiana at a time when most banks in the West were bankrupt. It was a priceless endorsement.

The fact that he had carried off the dangerous transfer of gold added to James' euphoria. He checked into a hotel, took a long bath, and rested. He spent a few days taking in the sights of the nation's capital. JFD had in the back of his mind building a glorious house on the land he owned along the Ohio River, so he probably took particular notice of the finer houses and furnishings that graced Washington. He likely compared what he saw with the residences he had already studied in New Orleans, Natchez, and other cities of the South.

After a few days, he retraced his tracks. This time the setting sun drew him toward home. The National Road was just as rough and desolate, but had lost much of its hostility. James stomach tolerated the primitive meals and his bones ached less on the return trip The way station hostlers remembered him. The innkeeper at Scenery Hill gave him the same room, and remarked at his improved appetite.

The transfer of specie from Indiana proved unnecessary. Just before recessing in July, Congress rescinded the Specie Circular. The action proved to be much too little, much too late. Specie payment did not resume. The country dropped deeper into depression. A worried President Van Buren called the Congress into special session in August.

By the time Congress convened, Secretary Woodbury reported that in only six of the deposit banks were funds available to the Treasury. Five others were able to partially meet the Treasury drafts. The remaining seventy-four deposit banks were unable to forward any funds to the Treasury Department. He stated that of a $33,700,000 balance the Treasury Department carried on its books, $28,000,000 went to the states in the surplus distributions; and $5,000,000 was in suspended banks. This left only a $700,000 balance.

Van Buren proposed that all revenue collection and payment dispersals be made through the Treasury Department. The crisis forced him to admit that the private bank system that Democrats had insisted could replace the National Bank, was now defunct.

When the Indiana state bank board convened in August of 1837, John Sering represented Madison. The situation with the federal deposits had eased somewhat. In May the state bank had held $1,338,000 in federal funds. By July 22, that figure was down to $901,000. The need to hoard specie was still strong. To save additional specie, the board decided to pay federal pensions in notes, unless the pensioner specifically asked for coin.[5]

The suspension was never absolute. The state bank did refuse to pay specie to out-of-state-banks, or brokers, but not to Hoosiers. It was true that cashiers tried to discourage specie payments by promoting the convenience of notes, but if pressed, they would always shell out coins to local citizens. The bank continued the other banking functions, and always furnished New York exchange for its customers at a one percent premium.[6]

Not all branches complied with the mandates of the board. The branches at Lafayette, New Albany, and Richmond still loaned large sums to insurance companies and savings institutions. This practice was putting bank capital at double risk. Some branches were paying more than their fair share of the public works debts. The board directed the fund commissioners to spread their demands more equitably between branches. Some branches had made little headway in reducing their discounts to the prescribed limits.[7]

141

Each meeting brought hope and confidence that specie payments would soon resume. The board repeatedly cautioned the branches to keep the circulation of notes to a minimum and to keep specie reserves high in preparation for immediate resumption. Many branches were complying. The bank system had reduced its discounts by almost $455,000, and its circulation by $139,000 in the previous quarter. The Madison branch had led the way by reducing its discounts by $74,000 and its circulation by $94,000.[8]

Only Lafayette had increased its discounts, but Evansville, Vincennes, Ft. Wayne, and Lafayette had increased circulation. This concerned conservative members of the state board. The suspension damaged public confidence in the bank. They reasoned that increased circulation lowered the value of the notes, and the bank's ability to redeem them. If resumption of specie payment caused a run on the bank, the bank would collapse, taking the fragile state economy with it.

To bring the branches in line, the board adopted several proposals introduced by Sam Merrill. Any branch that "should refuse or neglect to comply" with any legal order or direction of the state bank board must show cause why it should not be suspended. The board instructed all branches to reduce the level of circulation to the capital paid in to the branch.[9] Finally, the board instructed the chief cashier to contact other bankers in an effort to set up another national meeting on the resumption of specie payments.[10]

These decrees did not worry local board members. The state bank board had stronger vocal cords than muscles. Too often they had threatened strong action only to assign perpetual committee investigations that ended recommending no action.

Many local board members were businessmen wishing to feed the fires of inflation. Almost all members had large loans from the branches and resisted any effort to constrict credit. They exhibited the classic 'debtor mentality' that plagued most banking operations in the West. They did as they pleased while the board in Indianapolis huffed and puffed ineffectively. Some had basic philosophical differences with the state board and honestly felt the board took the wrong approach to solving fiscal problems.

A few state directors were puppets of the local boards and had little or no control. These local branches cloaked their rebellion by insisting that local conditions dictated actions contrary to the bank board decrees. How could a group of men in Indianapolis possibly know of the economic conditions in Lawrenceburg or Evansville? Most state directors had some influence over their branch boards, however. Calvin Fletcher, for instance, had great influence over the Indianapolis branch, and Hugh McCulloch controlled the Fort Wayne Branch.

None exhibited the domination exercised by JFD. Using logic, vision, or force of character, James could steer the branch board at Madison along any course he desired.

Lanier believed in the vision of a new empire. It became a touchstone of his policies. Inflation and depression were temporary situations to be endured and solved. They did not alter the vision. They could not deter the country from its destiny of being the new empire. Because of his station in life, James felt he had an obligation to help build the empire, and provide the benefits to all citizens.

James did not lose sight of the vision, but his immediate problem was the worsening economic situation. On August 29, 1837, Lanier wrote to Polke expressing an interest in a September land sale if Polke felt there are any bargains available. In the same letter Lanier predicted hard times ahead and he asked Polke what he would pay for the land they held jointly.[11] JFD wanted to dump over priced land in anticipation of a deepening recession, but was looking for good tracts that might be purchased at bargain prices during the economic down-turn. His father had taught him how to make money during a panic. Courage replaced capital in a recession.

James was adamant about keeping his legal skills honed. He argued the Dearborn Salt Lick Case on behalf of the State, and on September 23, 1837, wrote to Governor Noble concerning payment for his work. James stated that he would not directly argue the case if it went to the Supreme Court, but had contracted Stevens for the task **"in case it goes there."**[12]

The fiscal situation was never far from James' mind and he ended the letter to Noble by stating:

> **Matters look rather dark in Washington. If they stop the payment of the 4 (th) instal(l)ment to the states and compel the deposite (sic) banks to pay what they owe over the mountains it will bear very hard on us of the west There seems to be a settled determination to break down the State banks.**[13]

143

James was masterful at keeping many irons in the fire, and when he received Polke's appraisal of the land they held jointly, he offered to pay all the loan balances on the land, and buy Polke out for $750. He explained that he would be in Indianapolis for the bank board meeting on November 25, and they could consummate the deal.[14]

At the November 1837 bank board meeting, the federal deposits were still a concern. The federal balance had been declining, but the payment plan worried the board. They hoped eastern paper would pay the debt. Merrill and Fitch went to Washington to see if they could strike a deal with Secretary Woodbury.[15]

To put the bank in the best fiscal health to meet the eventual resumption, the board directed branches to reduce their discounts to 2 1/4 times their capital. They mandated a further reduction, by June of 1838, to twice the capital paid.[16]

The citizens seemed to be adjusting to the lack of specie. Only one man, John Brooks, had sued the branches protesting the suspension of specie payments. Brooks, a broker, had sued both the Lawrenceburg and Indianapolis branches. The board minutes noted "It is gratifying to know that the farming and trading interests in the state have sustained the bank with great unanimity"[17] Despite all of the problems, the bank seemed to be prospering. If a recession was coming, the directors wanted to get their money while the balance sheet still appeared healthy. They declared a dividend of from eleven percent at Madison to six percent at Ft. Wayne.

The board authorized the drawing of plans and specifications for a new bank building to house the offices of the state bank. They wanted to dispel rumors of the bank's poor condition, and proclaim their faith in the future. They also wanted a solid investment to protect their money.

With little specie available, there was no currency in circulation below ten dollars. This was hurting small businesses, reducing their ability to make a profit and repay loans. Some enterprising individuals were writing personal checks for small amounts. Instead of cashing these checks, the merchants kept them in circulation as a kind of 'underground currency'.

While the state board called this practice 'inexpedient and improper,' they realized that people needed a low denomination circulating medium. The board decided to issue notes in one dollar increments between $5.00 and $10.00, but not to issue notes of less than $5.00. They instructed the president and cashier to make the necessary arrangements.[18]

The small denomination notes did not answer all of the problems. The law regulating the amount of currency the bank could issue was based on free flowing specie. Without specie, money was extremely tight. Lack of currency to repay loans accounted for much of the suspended debt. The legislature would not vote to increase bank note issue, compounding the problem. With a public revolt against the bank so close at hand, the bank board determined that the charter did not prohibit the bank from issuing a temporary note in place of specie. Thus the "Post Note" was born. The board members approved post notes in denominations of $20, $50, $100. and $500. They also authorized the president to procure a supply of post notes not to exceed 1/4 of the capital stock sold at each branch. Post notes were redeemable soon after specie payments resumed.[19]

There were disturbing reports that the Indianapolis branch was being unfair in dealing with some of its customers. The board formed a select committee to look into the allegations and report at the next meeting.[20]

The Legislature convened in the late fall. The construction of internal improvements was not proceeding as scheduled, and was costing much more than expected. During the first year, work on internal improvements across the state cost $3,827,000. The state had made no provision to pay interest on the borrowed money, so had to take out loans to pay the interest. During 1837, $1.6 million more was expended. Politicians demanded that multiple routes be surveyed for the same project. Officials would not approve routes, however, so there was little or no revenue being generated from land sales. Concerned legislators asked Jesse Williams, State Engineer, for an honest estimate of the cost of completing all of the improvements planned in the Mammoth Internal Improvements Bill.[21]

Just in time for the legislative session, on December 1, 1837, a new hotel opened on Washington Street, just west of Meridian. Called the Washington Hotel, it contained "87 elegantly filled up rooms."[22] It contained a large dining room measuring 75 by 40 feet. The hotel immediately became the unofficial headquarters of the Whigs. Lanier made it his base of operations when he was in town.

David Wallace succeeded Noah Noble in the Governor's chair and was inaugurated on December 6, 1837. This ensured that the Whig policies would continue. Lanier and Wallace had several things in common. David's father, Andrew, had contracted to supply Harrison's army during the War of 1812, and had several dealings with James' father. Harrison had acquired a West Point appointment for David Wallace in 1817, and David later studied law with Miles C. Eggleston.[23] James looked forward to a smooth administration led by Wallace, and to continued personal influence with the new governor.

# 14.
## "I would make any sacrifice before I would do an unjust act"
—JFD Lanier July 27, 1838

*The new year of 1838 would test Lanier's strength and character. The depression continued unabated. The internal improvements program in the state began to unravel. James would face personal loss.*

State engineer Jesse Williams did not give the legislature the estimate they asked for until early in 1838. He estimated that the total cost of the internal improvements would be 23 million dollars. The interest alone would total more than one million dollars per year. Williams suggested that the Madison and Indianapolis Railroad be abandoned.[1]

The report stunned the legislature. The original estimate, just two years earlier, had been only ten million dollars. What had gone wrong with the internal improvements plan? Governor Wallace remained positive, assuring everyone that there was plenty of money available. He chose to ignore the credit constriction that had seized the country, hoping his calm approach would quiet critics. Wallace's stance did not mollify the lawmakers. They immediately began assigning blame. Dr. Coe came

147

under mounting criticism, and was soon dismissed. The Legislature placed the financial operation under Milton Stapp and Lucius Scott. To promote responsible management, they required each man to provide a $100,000 bond.[2]

As the pressures of inflation and the subsequent tightening of credit became more acute, the state bank became a target. The branches at Lafayette, Indianapolis and Lawrenceburg were accused of favoritism, malfeasance, and fraud. Using the skills he had learned as a lawyer and prosecuting attorney, Lanier worked to resolve the problems. In closed bank board meetings he evoked honor, logic, and finally shame to correct poor fiscal practices. When these failed, he threatened stiff sanctions or even indictment against violators. He insisted the bank had to solve its own problems to survive. Legislative intervention would prove the bank had failed. The specter of the First State Bank loomed large.

The board assigned investigative committees. They excused individual transgressions. They delayed hostile judgments. This attitude frustrated James Lanier. How could these men bring dishonor on their profession? They must be fiscal leaders in a time of turmoil. Just as lawyers dare not break the law, or politicians betray the public trust, bankers must not borrow excessively or squander a customer's money. Most bank directors believed in abstract honor and corporate integrity, but could not recognize individual incompetence or fraud. The reputation of the bank continued to slide. Since the bank board was notoriously slow to act, accusers appealed to the legislature. The legislature appointed a committee to look into the charges.[3]

James felt the fiscal pressures personally. Inflation, coupled with poor shipping weather in Madison, increased his stress. He kept a calm public face, but internally he was boiling. The legislature was debating whether to stop work on the M & I Railroad. Lanier visited his friends in the legislature. He cajoled and chided, pleaded and persuaded. He called in past favors, and promised future accommodation. JFD pointed out to all that would listen that the railroad would open the central cornucopia of Indiana. Hundreds of farmers would benefit and the capitol city would have instant access to the nation. The legislators opposed to the railroad pointed to the fact that the Ohio River was low and frozen. River traffic would not resume until spring rains re-energized the river. It made no sense to build a railroad to a dry port.

Most of the lawmakers had nothing against the rail line. It was strictly a matter of money. Merrill had been right. Internal improvements were costing too much money. The Madison cut was the most expensive single segment of the entire system. The bridge over the Muscatatuck River at Vernon was also a huge financial drain. The M & I siphoned precious funds from more promising projects in other districts. It had to be stopped.

The fate of the rail line was not JFD's only worry. His mother was failing. Drusilla never left her bed, and it was clear to everyone she was dying. James' heart never received the message and he refused to discuss the topic. He stoically talked with his mother about the future while each thought they were hiding the truth from the other. Drusilla died just short of her sixtieth birthday.

DIED-In this city, on the 8th instant, Mrs. Drusilla Lanier, mother of JFD Lanier, Esq.
Madison, Feb. 14, 1838

JFD suffered a personal tragedy when his mother died.

She had been a source of silent strength for James all of his life. Drusilla had taught James the importance of honor, dignity, and responsibility. She had insisted on his education, even if it meant more work for herself. Mother and son had worked shoulder to shoulder to maintain a home while Alex was off at war. Even after his return, James and Drusilla had toiled unflaggedly as they watched the strength seep from their husband and father.

It was Drusilla, denied more children herself, that had nursed Elisabeth through all of the birthings. It was Drusilla that had cared for the family members as they lay afflicted with a myriad of maladies that hovered over the house. It was Drusilla that supplied the strength to both James and Elisabeth when little John James died. As stricken as she had been by the accident, it was Drusilla that had shielded Alex from his father's wrath.

James deeply mourned his mother, and visited Third Street Cemetery more often after her death than ever before. He did not feel the cold that gripped Madison and froze the river that February. The loneliness shut out all other feeling.

His friends rallied around JFD. Milton Stapp and Gameliel

Taylor once again provided solid comfort. Jeremiah Sullivan had been serving an interim appointment to the Indiana Supreme Court since March 1837. Governor Wallace nominated him to a full seven year term.[4] Despite his confirmation battle, Judge Sullivan took time to return to Madison to console James.

Once again he found the best cure for melancholy was to bury himself in work. The legislature, while investigating the problems at Lafayette, Indianapolis, and Lawrenceburg, sent thirty-eight interrogatories to the branches. At the February meeting, the bank board stalled, unable to condemn one of its own. They claimed the questions were perplexing and the answers provided by the branches confusing. The board approved a motion by Lucius Scott, to study the problem further.[5]

The situation was not confusing to JFD. He had heard enough. The stalling exhausted his patience and calm demeanor. He offered a resolution proclaiming that cashiers not be allowed to enter into any other business while employed by the branches. The cashiers, he argued, were the highest paid employees of the bank and did not need additional income. He also moved that no officer or director of the bank or branches be allowed to serve as an officer of an insurance company or savings institution. It was a clear conflict of interest. The success of the bank depended upon its reputation, and the board must not let any action of its principal officers tarnish that reputation.

Finally he attacked what he felt was the root of the problem at Lafayette. J. S. Hanna had been a figurehead as president of the Lafayette branch. He did no work, and received no pay. His involvement seemed limited to receiving loans from the branch. James' thoughts crystallized as he developed the resolution. His proposal stated:

> . . . the Board consider it the duty of J.S. Hanna, President of the Lafayette Branch on his return home to go into the Branch (by virtue of his office as President) and attend to and direct the business and concerns thereof and attend to the interest of the Branch in all its general operations, the same being his duty as such President.[6]

As they did whenever crisis threatened, the board depended on Lanier's guidance. All motions passed unanimously.[7]

On January 26, 1838, a robbery had taken place at the Vincennes branch. Most of the $2,690.00 in specie stolen belonged to the Terre Haute branch. The committee looking into the robbery reported:

> The committee has it on good authority that the (banking) house is entirely insecure, and the funds in great danger; having no vaults in the room, the specie is kept in kegs and boxes under the counter. We believe all the other branches either have or are preparing good safe vaults . . .[8]

The board resolved that the branch at Vincennes should take immediate steps to erect a good vault. Until the branch completed the vault, they should "employ some suitable person or persons as a private watch to stay in the room of nights"[9]

Other action reflected the uncertain fiscal situation. The state treasurer was demanding the bank advance the fourth disbursement of federal funds. Most directors felt the payment would never be made, but did not want to voice their doubts publicly and risk further economic chaos.

Inflation remained unchecked. The board passed toothless suggestions on to the branches. They cautioned that the suspended debt was still too high and that bank directors possessed too many "slow pay" loans.

Lanier suggested reducing federal payments to the minimum required. This would reduce the drain of reserves.[10] In a final move to curtail spending, James proposed that it was unnecessary to have an agent in New York. The Indiana state bank agent in New York had been Dr. Isaac Coe. This resolution eased Dr. Coe out of his position and distanced the bank from the controversy surrounding him.[11]

The news was not all black, however. There was a decrease in discounts, and notes due other banks. There was an increase in specie held, bills of exchange, and Indiana deposits. It appeared that the policies of the board were taking effect. The directors were optimistic on matters that directly affected their pocketbooks, and since the bank was still making a profit, they declared a dividend ranging between three and four percent.[12]

Isaac Dunn, from Lawrenceburg, proposed that since the surplus fund had a large balance, that a dividend from that fund be declared also. He argued that this would put additional funds into circulation. Lanier, Merrill, Fletcher and McCulloch were able to make a strong case that a large balance in the surplus

151

fund was critical to the health of the bank. Dunn's proposal lost. To satisfy Dunn and his followers, the board gave state- appointed directors the discretion of increasing the stock of the bank not to exceed $30,000.00 per branch, if it was "expedient and safe."[13]

James had another plan. It would stimulate the economy, relieve the legislature of a serious problem, and insure continuation of the M & I Railroad all at the same time. He proposed that the bank support internal improvements by allowing the branches to loan the state, on her bonds, any amount the fund commissioners desired, up to $30,000.00 per branch. The state would pay the bank the going rate of six percent interest. The loans must meet strict guidelines so that the fiscal position of the bank was not in jeopardy.[14] Each branch could pick whatever project they wanted to fund. After this resolution passed, the legislature never seriously discussed abandoning the M & I Railroad.

Six months earlier, James Ray, Cashier of the Indiana state bank, accepted the task of organizing a national conference on specie resumption. He reported that the conference was set for March in New York City. The bank board was overjoyed at the news. They voted to send a representative, and instructed the delegate to vote for the earliest date proposed for resumption. Sam Merrill asked Lanier to represent the Indiana State Bank.[15]

JFD was proud to represent Indiana. This was an important conference. James met with banking friends from New York, New Orleans and other cities. He renewed his acquaintance with Levi Woodbury. He met the banking legend Albert Gallatin. He wrote about the conference:

> **I attended the convention as a representative of our bank. In the debates that took place I earnestly favored the proposition for immediate resumption. The position I took greatly pleased the venerable Albert Gallatin, who, aged as he was, was the leading spirit of the convention, and who was much gratified in finding himself earnestly supported from a quarter from which he had not expected aid. He took occasion to thank me personally and warmly for the grounds I took. I recollect my interviews with him on this occasion with great pleasure.[16]**

Mr. Gallatin took an active role, urging resumption. He told the convention that the Bank of England had forwarded £1,000,000 to eastern banks with the promise of £1,000,000 more to aid in the resumption of specie payments. The U.S. foreign debt has been re-negotiated and conditions were "eminently propitious" for resumption.[17]

Of course the shipment of sterling to the U.S. had not been a charitable gesture toward England's former children. The Bank of England had damaged itself by raising interest rates and drawing investment away from the United States. The resulting panic had led to a suspension of specie payments. English investors received interest payments in worthless state paper that clogged the vaults of The Bank of England. English bankers hoped that, by encouraging a return to specie, Americans would pay English debts with a currency that had value.

During the meeting Lanier had repeatedly voted for immediate resumption of specie payments. Other western states, allied with southern bankers, continually vetoed the plan The earliest date the convention could settle on was January 1, 1839.[18]

When the bank board convened in May, Lanier was absent. Once again the roads were impassable. There was no representative from Madison. The 1839 resumption date disappointed the board, but they were afraid to go forward without the neighboring states. Perhaps Ohio and Kentucky would break with the western collation. The board directed President Merrill to meet with representatives of those banks to see if they would agree to an earlier resumption.[19]

The board formally approved the schedule of repayment of the federal debt proposed by Lanier at the preceding meeting. The bank would repay the $372,624.00 debt in three quarterly installments of $124,208 each. The branches would forward the first payment July 1, 1838.[20]

Reflecting the uncertain state of fiscal affairs, the federal pension disbursements were in disarray. The list of those qualified to receive U.S. pension payments was several months old. The U.S. treasurer normally sent updated lists each month or each quarter. Concerned that the lists were outdated, the board decided to discontinue payments.[21] Of course being able to loan out the federal money for a month or two while the problem was solved, pleased the bankers.

Closer to home, inflation fever continued to afflict many branches. Branches still approved "slow pay" to officers. Many branch offices believed that a reduction in loans would increase the depression, not heal it. The state directors, deeply divided on the issue, did nothing.

The state treasurer relentlessly pressed the bank for the $286,751 anticipated as the fourth federal surplus distribution. The board had other plans for the money. They passed a resolution whereby each branch could sell up to $40,000 in additional stock.[22] For the first time, balances in the surplus fund would provide the necessary reserves. This action allowed the bank to raise stock levels without obtaining legislative approval. To pay the state share of the new stock, the board pledged the anticipated federal surplus funds. The conservative board members inserted a provision stipulating that bank directors were not eligible for loans of money generated by this sale.[23]

This was a shrewd move. The bank was making more money available for loans, and was technically advancing the federal funds as requested. It was using the funds to benefit the bank rather than giving them to the state treasurer to spend at his discretion. Using the surplus fund as a reserve would stifle other, inflationary, plans for the money. The plan also put a curb on internal loans to branch officers.

The bank board took other steps to cool the inflationary fires. Once again the board warned the branches to prepare for immediate resumption of specie payments by reducing bank notes in circulation, and collecting specie in their vaults. A resolution passed instructing branches to reduce their discounts to 1 1/2 times the paid in capital, and to set targets for the prompt repayment of 20 or 25% of the loans. The plea to branch officers to reduce their personal loans was becoming a standard request.[24]

In other business, the banking committee reported that a total of $103,360 worth of post notes were in circulation.. The committee reminded branches to redeem all the post notes shortly after specie payments resumed. True to form, the select committee reported the robbery at Vincennes would take more study; there was conflicting testimony.[25]

The directors could not avoid a discussion of the bank's dirty linen. Hugh McCulloch's select committee addressed the charges lodged against several branches. The charges against the Indianapolis branch proved to be groundless. The committee cautioned all branches to adhere to the rule that bills of exchange were payable only at the place of issue, not at the place of sale.[26]

At Lawrenceburg the committee found that "the branch has been greatly misrepresented and slandered and it does not appear she has been guilty of any intentional violation of the Charter." It did caution against poor banking practices, however, and did recommend some immediate steps to remove the appearance of unethical practices.[27]

The situation at the Lafayette branch was more serious, however. Branch officers often consummated loans without the full contingent of directors present, and without informing the absent directors. The committee uncovered at least one improper loan. Various tricks of bookkeeping masked the impropriety. Double charging for bills of exchange was uncovered. The Lafayette cashier took $500.00 in notes from the till, substituting his personal check. He then counted the check as cash. This amounted to mis-appropriation of 1/2 year's salary.[28]

The committee reminded the board that the charter held all branches liable for the criminal malfeasance of any branch. The committee rebuked the Lafayette branch and proposed that the cashier be terminated. Although the committee could find no evidence of wrongdoing by the president, it recommended that the branch president devote full time to the banking operation.[29]

Finally, the committee suggested that President. Merrill investigate the situation and that the board consider suspending the branch at its next session if operations had not improved. Had JFD been present, he would have been furious. The board was taking no stronger action against Mr. Hanna and the branch than reaffirming the resolution he had championed three months earlier.

Commerce and politics moved forward despite the problems with the bank and internal improvements. Polke made a counter offer for the land he and Lanier owned. Polke wanted to use his interest in the Lanier lands to become a part of a group purchasing land for the Town of Winamac. Early in July James turned down Polke's offer stating that he could get $1000 for his share of the land.

Lanier left Madison for New York City later in the month. Polke fumed at Lanier's refusal to sell. His angry reply followed James to New York.

On July 27, Lanier wrote a long letter to Polke. He felt Polke **"has not taken a right view of the case"** and restated the situation as he understood it. Polke's accusations distressed James who wrote **"I would make any sacrifice before I would do an unjust act."** The success of the Porterville Land Company encouraged James to become an active member of Winamac group. In the same letter he stated: **"give me an interest in the town (as I may be able to do it some service) and I will pay off the balance unpaid on account of the joint lands."**[30]

By the summer of 1838, many eastern banks bolstered by English sterling, had resumed specie payments. The Indiana bank directors had repeatedly promised to resume at the earliest possible date. Most Hoosiers anticipated that the bank board would approve resumption at the August 1838 meeting.

Many speculators outside Indiana were also anticipating a resumption. They were busy collecting bank notes, planning to be first in line when payment resumed. Only the branch of issue could redeem notes for specie, so branches did a bit of wildcatting by exchanging notes and paying local demands in distant branch notes to blunt the rush. On August 10, Sering sent Madison branch notes to Indianapolis. He commented on the fact that everyone was anticipating a resumption of specie payment.

> We have (paid) a very large amount this week on our public works and I chose to send our notes to you rather than circulate them here. I would thank you to use them in a way that they would not be returned to us out of the common course of business. These specie times[31]

When the board met later in the month, Benjamin Hubbs represented Madison. The bank was doing well according to the committee on the state of the bank. The bank met the repayment schedule for the federal debt. It appeared that there was more than enough specie in the vaults to meet the anticipated demand. Most branches had finally heeded the board's instructions. Discounts had decreased by $212,689.00, while stock had increased by $194,481.00.[32]

Optimism ruled. It appeared that the constriction of credit was hurting commerce and the branches could, "in perfect safety" increase lending to 1 3/4 times the paid in stock. The board also recommended a "liberal policy toward the community at large . . ." It suggested affording them "every facility due prudence will permit . . ."[33] The phrasing of the resolution gave the branches wide leeway in interpreting the board's intention.

Several members were still nervous about resuming. Many "foreign" banks were not stable. Inflation was taking its toll on the weak banks. Many bank notes carried heavy discounts. Notes on some Mississippi banks, if accepted at all, carried discounts of thirty-five percent During good economic times the notes carried a discount of only four and one-half percent.

The proponents of resumption argued that the condition of foreign paper was of little concern. Branches should always exercise caution when dealing with foreign paper. Public pressure, and the arguments for resumption, won the day. The bank board voted to immediately resume full specie payments.[34] In this confident mood, the board approved the sale of stock for the 12th and 13th branches, at South Bend and Michigan City respectively.[35]

Only one dark cloud lurked on the horizon. As a result of his investigation, President Merrill issued a 'sine facia' or 'show cause' order against the Lafayette Branch. This was the first step toward suspension. The board began a "full and patient" hearing of the charges.[36]

At the conclusion of the hearing, the board determined the charges were true, but agonized over the remedy. They knew they had to protect the institution so that "the shafts which malice and envy, as well as political aspirants, may hurl at it may fall harmless at its base." However, some felt that "forbearance, even to the point where forbearance ceases to be a virtue, seems to your committee to be the preferable course." They had great empathy for James White, the young cashier at Lafayette. As individuals they could "freely and cheerfully forgive all his aberrations from the path of rectitude and duty".[37]

In the end the board determined it held "a station of high responsibility and the public looks to it for the performance of its duty without favor or partiality." They recommended that Mr. White be removed from office, but that no criminal charges be brought against him. They determined he had not acted "with corrupt intent." Even with this tolerant treatment, the board had not heard the last of James White.[38]

August 1838, was an important month for many reasons. Three major events directly affected James Lanier. The M & I Railroad laid down the first tracks. The dream of convenient travel between Indianapolis and Madison was reinforced with the steel of reality.[39]

On August fifth the Indian land agreement expired. The Indians were reluctant to leave, but settlers were pushing into the reserved land. Skirmishes were occurring with frightening regu-

157

larity. Governor Wallace visited the northern part of the state and became concerned. Senator Tipton realized that the Indians must leave. Wallace gave Tipton the authority to carry out the removal.[40] On August twenty-first, John Tipton began rounding them up for the trip to Kansas. Eight hundred Indians began the trip west. This marked the end for the free roaming Native Americans in Indiana.[41]

On August twenty-fifth James assumed the role of federal Pension Agent. He wrote to Morris:

> **The undersigned having been appointed the pension agent for the State of Indiana has to request that you will by the earliest conveyance forward to me the books and papers connected with your agency particularly the book listing the pension names with date of last payment with such remarks in the same as may be necessary to fully understand the situation of each case. Please advise such pensioners as may apply your counter that on or after the 28th Sept. They will be paid this branch only.**
>
> **Very Respectfully,**
> **James F.D. Lanier[42]**

Summer was coming to an end, and James hoped it would also mark an end to the fiscal crisis. The designation of pension agent was a plum for James. It could increase his power and his purse.

On September sixth the Indian tribes refused to continue their retreat west until they received sufficient supplies. Six days later Tipton distributed $5,000 worth of goods among the Indians. The trek resumed; and on September 16, Tipton turned the tribes over to William Polke at Danville, Illinois.[43] Polke started them on the long trail to Kansas within two days. With the removal of the Indians, Hoosiers claimed the last vestiges of "wilderness" stripped away.

The fall of 1838 held promise for Hoosiers. The Indian threat retreated into history. The first killing frost promised not only brilliant displays of color, but more importantly, an end to the insect invasion. Mosquito netting disappeared from beds allowing cool breezes to bathe sleepers. Farmers cleaned grain bins and root cellars in anticipation of the harvest.

The harvest fulfilled the promise of the soil. Cool nights and pleasant days invigorated the spirit and enlivened the pace. Households across the state repeated the biannual ritual of cleaning. Summer items went into storage and winter trappings reappeared. The leavings of flies, roaches and other insects disappeared under lye soap and polish. Men repaired fireplace flues in anticipation of heavy service. Wood piles grew in length and height.

In the pork houses of Madison, workers cleaned holding pens and scrubbed butchering tables in anticipation of the slaughtering season. Farmers rounded up their hogs and headed to town. Hogs that escaped the death march began to appear on the streets of Madison to challenge the dog packs for survival. Enterprising young men chased down the hogs that soon ended up in backyard smoke houses.

Having the pension agent located in the southeastern corner of the state was proving difficult for the pensioners. It did not take long for their complaints to reach Washington. The problem forced JFD to rescind his order that all pension disbursements be made in Madison. The temporary use of federal funds was not worth the hassle. On October tenth he wrote Morris:

**Morris Sir;**

**I am requested by the Commissioners on Pensions to ascertain whether your branch will undertake as heretofore to pay the pensioners in your branch district.**
**Owing to the inconvenience it subjects many of the pensioners, the War Department is very desirous that you continue your agency as heretofore.**[44]

159

# 15.
## "We are as completely cornered as ever a set of men were . . ."
— JFD Lanier Oct. 11, 1839

*To the casual observer the disastrous depression was over. The seeds of economic recovery began to sprout. They would die of root rot however, as the economy took a turn for the worse, and Hoosiers once again fought for their economic lives.*

The progressive men in Madison had been attempting to incorporate Madison for some time. Many citizens opposed the move because it meant higher taxes and more control. Lanier was not eager to pay additional taxes, but knew the area needed specific laws and local control. In the fall of 1838, a majority of voters agreed with this logic and Madison finally incorporated. Moody Parks became the town's first Mayor late in November.

That same month, JFD made a proposal at the bank board meeting that would prove a lifesaver for both the struggling Indiana farmers and the bank. He reasoned that the health of the Indiana economy depended, not on the speculators, but on the farmers. He proposed that where possible "in the utmost safety, and in the exportation of the produce of the soil," the branches be allowed to increase their discounts to 2 1/4 times the capital collected.. To qualify for the discounts, the branches had to agree that all discounts over 1 3/4 be made on debts that will be paid in cash within six months.[1]

This plan loaned money to farmers specifically for the shipment and sale of farm products. The loans would help the Indiana farmers compete in the marketplace, and would be repaid from the profits of the sale. They were "quick pay" loans and were relatively safe for the banks.

At this meeting Lanier also brought two problems to the attention of the board. It did not appear that the fourth installment payment would be forthcoming from the Federal government. He proposed that the bank accept $294,000.00 ($286,751.48 + $7,248.52 in accrued interest) in state bonds to cover the funds advanced to the state in anticipation of the fourth installment. This was risky because the state securities were suspect, but there was no better alternative.[2]

The second problem was internal. Bank directors and officers were still not keeping current on their loan payments despite many warnings from the board and attempts to limit the loans. James wanted a strong stand taken on directors that were in arrears. Once again, JFD reminded the other directors that the character of the bank officers reflected on the bank itself. The opposition press was already hammering the bank on the loan issue. He feared that the citizens and the legislature would take punitive action against the bank if the loans remained unpaid.[3]

Calvin Fletcher also condemned the errant directors, noting that a renewal or extension of a loan was not an accommodation of law and was not mandatory. Renewals were only with mutual consent of both parties. If the branches did not want to extend loans, they were under no legal obligation to do so.[4]

Lanier proposed that the phrases in the Bank Charter "who shall be in arrears"; "who shall fail in business"; and "who shall become otherwise disqualified "apply to bank officers just as they did to other borrowers. The proposal passed 11-1. Only Hugh McCulloch voted no.[5]

On the whole, the condition of the bank appeared encouraging. Calvin Fletcher was among the majority of directors who felt the situation was improving. The branches had repaid the federal debt on schedule. Profits were on the rebound. Several branches were selling stock at a brisk pace. The board permitted the Madison branch to sell an additional $30,000 in stocks.[6] Most delegates left the meeting in a cheerful mood despite James' admonitions.[7]

Later in the month Lanier rejoiced at word that the Indians had reached Kansas, and William Polke would soon return to resume his position as JFD's agent. The trip had been arduous. Only 640 had survived of the almost 800 that had started.[8]

The Internal Improvements Act was starting to bear fruit, at least for Madison. Construction crews completed seventeen miles of the Madison and Indianapolis Railroad from Madison to Graham. A violent storm at sea wrecked the first engine purchased by the M & I, but the railroad borrowed a small engine from Louisville for the inaugural trip. It rode a barge up the Ohio River to Madison. The cut remained unfinished, so the "Elkhorn" rode up the Madison hill in a wagon.[9] Passengers rode up the hill in a gaily decorated omnibus. JFD crowded on one of the passenger cars for the initial run. The *Indianapolis News* of Nov. 25, 1838 described the event:

> The little engine, the Elkhorn, pulled out of North Madison with all the load it could possibly tote. The coach and boxcars — the latter built for carrying hogs — overflowed with passengers. Those not permitted to ride stood by and cheered or ran along the track yelling encouragement to the engineer. He could move his heavy train but slowly, although it is a matter of record that the Elkhorn did get going at 8 miles per hour.

Despite the success of the Elkhorn, the fiscal situation was deteriorating. Internal improvements had gobbled up another $1,863,000. In January of 1839, Caleb Smith, a fund commissioner, would report that internal improvements cost $5,000,000 to date. The interest due was $193,000.[10] Under extreme pressure from state officials, the state bank advanced the interest payment.

Governor Wallace changed his tune. "If this condition does not startle us, it should certainly awaken us," he stated in an address to the legislature on December 4, 1838. The governor's plan for solving the fiscal crisis shows the confidence he had in the state bank. He suggested that the state borrow additional funds, invest them in the bank, and pay off the debts from the interest.[11]

Wallace did not know the true condition of the bank. Capital for loans was scarce. Confidence in bank notes was waning.

There were as many as 5,000 workers toiling on the railroad, and in the Madison cut. State bank notes made up the bulk of the payroll. As soon as they received payment, workers marched to the bank and demanded specie for the notes.[12]

One of the new legislature's most contentious issues would be selecting a new senator. Tipton was not running for reelection. He was in ill health and longed to return to Indiana. A crowd of politicians sought to replace him. Milton Stapp entered the race. In addition to Stapp, Governor Noble, Thomas Blake, Tilghman Howard, Charles Dewey, and John Dupont all sought the seat. After six days and 36 ballots the battle narrowed to Noble and Blake. To break the stalemate, a compromise candidate, Albert S. White entered the contest and was promptly elected.[13]

Lanier took little interest in the political battle. He was fighting to save the bank. James desperately needed to get his branch notes out of Madison and in circulation in other parts of the state. Although he would not have appreciated the accusation, James was practicing simple "wildcat banking." On Christmas Day, 1838, he sent a bundle of bank notes to Indianapolis with this letter:

> By Mr. Marshall we send $10.000 our notes for which we ask you to send us that amount your notes or other Cin. Ind or Ky notes. Such is the state of matters with us on the river that we can not put out our own notes. If you choose to send yours we could put them where you would not be embarrassed thereby. I hope you can aid us. Please send it by first safe conveyance as we are much in want of the money. If Judge Sullivan is not coming in soon some other person (will do).[14]

After sending the letter, James closed up the bank and went home. Alex was home from school, so the whole family would celebrate Christmas together. Charles was almost two and was his father's treasure. The girls talked amongst themselves about how badly their parents spoiled Charles. When Alex tried to joke about it in front of James, his father failed to see the humor in the comment and froze Alex with a glare.

On January 19, 1839, the *Louisville Courier Journal* reported that JFD Lanier arrived at the Galt House. He most certainly could be in town on bank business, but the paper also reported that a shipment of 1500 railroad bars had arrived on the Morovian, bound for Madison, Indiana. Perhaps even at this early stage of railroad construction, James monitored the quality of the rails used by the M & I.

In February the Legislature attempted to solve some of the Internal Improvement problems. They abolished the Board of Internal Improvements set up in 1836. In its place they established a new three man board.. Noah Noble, Milton Stapp and Lucius Scott made up the board.[15] Finally the internal improvements problem was in competent hands.

The February bank board meeting was hopeful. The board decided to circulate branch notes far from home, and thus control demands for specie. The nation's economy seemed to be on solid footing once again. Trade was expanding and Lanier proposed that another agent for the bank be established in New York. The agent would be beneficial for both the bank and Indiana merchants. It appears that Lanier's earlier insistence that a New York agent was unnecessary was only an excuse to sever Coe's connection with the bank. The full board tabled the motion until branch bank boards of directors could vote on the idea.[16]

It had been four years since the first issue of bank notes, and the notes were wearing thin. The board destroyed increasing quantities at each meeting. It was also prudent to change the design slightly to foil counterfeiting. They ordered new printing plates for note denominations of $5.00 and $10.00. The notes were to be payable on demand, and were to be printed on "first rate bank paper, as good as can be purchased in the United States."[17]

There was great pressure on the fund commissioners to raise enough money for all of the projects. They had to compete with internal improvement bond peddlers from Illinois, Pennsylvania, Michigan and other states. Available capital dried up, or demanded ever increasing rates of interest. The value of the bonds continued to fall. The bank held Internal Improvement Bonds as collateral for money the bank had loaned the state.

Most previous internal improvement fund commissioners had overstepped the bounds of prudent financial dealings in an attempt to satisfy the needs. Nevertheless, the legislature still targeted Coe as the sole scapegoat. Opposing papers vilified or praised Coe depending upon their politics. Even his friend Calvin Fletcher admitted that Dr. Coe acted "with a zeal not prudent."[18] Threats of indictments filled the legislative journals.

As James rode the stage to the February 1839 bank board

meeting, he mulled over the situation. It was true the financial situation in Indiana and the U.S. appeared to be improving, but he saw some major problems and feared a downturn. Lanier also worried the bank would collapse from internal cancer. The legislature had the bank under a microscope, and the improving fiscal situation fostered loose banking practices.

Even though they had discharged him as the State Bank Agent, Coe's friends on the bank board jumped to his defense and passed the following resolution:

> The Directors of the State Bank of Indiana in session at Indianapolis deem this an appropriate time to express their estimation of the character and services of one of our public functionaries with whom in the course of the operation of this institution they have had opportunities of business acquaintance which have not been generally possessed. And therefore, as this may be the only occasion offering a fit opportunity of expressing it this Board unites in testifying to the financial Skill, the unbending integrity, and the zealous faithfulness of Dr. Isaac Coe as Fund Commissioner of the State of Indiana.[19]

Several facts lead to the conclusion that Dr. Coe was being cast as a scapegoat for the internal improvements mess. Lucius Scott, a fund commissioner who knew Coe's record, offered the resolution. There is no record of opposition by Samuel Merrill who drove out deception in the First State Bank. There was no voice of protest raised by Calvin Fletcher, whose religious beliefs would allow no brooking of Christian values. There was no outcry by JFD. They must have all felt, as Fletcher did, that Coe was a good man caught by politics. A confusing resolution also passed the board. Perhaps they were trying to ward off an attack by James White.

> That this Board, considering the unfortunate circumstances of James White, late Cashier of the Lafayette Branch Bank, think proper so far to rescind the censure of the Board, that it shall no longer stand as an objection to his employment in banks or any other trust to which he may be called.
>
> Resolved that under the circumstances that have occurred it does not appear best that Mr. White should at this time be appointed to office in the Lafayette Branch.[20]

Lanier acted on his fears of internal collapse. He warned that all actions of the bank officers must be above reproach, and that no in-house disagreements be made public. He chastised the president of the Lawrenceburg branch for the language of a letter he sent to Merrill. He criticized the Lafayette branch for accepting too many foreign bank notes. His committee directed that by April 1, all discounts over one and one-half times the paid capital had to be in notes of less than six months duration. In addition, by June first, all discounts were to total no more than twice the capital.[21]

When the new Internal Improvements Board met toward the end of March, they faced a long list of problems. Not only did they have to make sense of the confusing issues, the legislature threw another stumbling block in their path. A bill passed which mandated that only $1,500,000 be spent during 1839. However contracts were already in force that totaled $3,414,000.[22]

Even though he expected it, the passing of his friend Senator John Tipton on April 6 deeply saddened Lanier. He remembered once again how insignificant the problems of the world were. He comforted Spier and resolved to help the boy whenever he could. JFD made several suggestions to Spier on exactly how to handle his father's estate. The boy was not receptive and felt that he could handle matters himself. There was no need for Lanier to interfere. Spier's attitude stung JFD.

Spring announced the invasion of the nuisances. Mosquitoes, nourished to the size of teacups in the sloughs and backwaters of the river, attacked the town. Chiggers and head lice followed in successive waves. The poisons of ivy, oak and sumac blossomed on the exposed skin of anyone bold enough to disturb their habitat. Nettles and heat rashes fought for space on beleaguered bodies. Poultices, mud packs and salves appeared like battle ribbons.

Alex returned home from Indiana University. He was not doing well, and did not think the professors were competent. He was not learning what he needed. The frontier school was a waste of time. James quizzed Alex in detail on what he had learned and the methods of the professors.

JFD felt that Alex had never accepted the responsibilities and obligations required of an oldest son. Alex never worked as hard as James remembered working. Alex never showed the proper respect for the responsible people in the community. He seemed impervious to his father's instruction or corrective wrath. James had hoped that Indiana University would change his son. It did not.

166

Progress on the M & I Railroad was slow. Funds were running out and it did not appear that the fund commissioners could raise additional cash. In an effort to relieve the state of further expense, the legislature leased the line to David Branham. The lease ran from April 1, 1839, to May 1, 1840. The company would pay the state sixty percent of the gross profits. John G. Sering became conductor. His salary was $700.00 per year plus board. [23] This caused a rift between Lanier and Sering. James felt that the branch cashier had to devote full time to bank business. He received a good salary for his efforts. Sering countered that his clerk could handle the daily business, and that he could consult on any problems each evening. James cited the bank board prohibition against the branch cashier holding an outside job. When the argument became heated, Sering reminded Lanier that the cashier was an elected office, and the president could not fire him.

Train operatons differed from today's practices. Passengers did not purchase tickets. They signed up the night before they were to leave. The conductor checked passengers off a list on the waybill when they arrived the next morning. The train normally left Madison at 6:00 A.M. If a listed passenger was late, however, the train would wait. For most people the train would wait five minutes. For other people, such as JFD Lanier, the Bright brothers, Joseph Marshall, or Judge Sullivan, the train would wait up to thirty minutes.[24]

The legislature felt the bank was the one bright spot in the fiscal picture and approved issuing 1.5 million dollars more in Second State Bank Bonds. The board decided that Merrill should sell the bonds personally. Merrill went to New York in April. Inexperienced in selling bonds, he called on Dr. Coe for help. Coe suggested the Morris Canal and Banking Company. Nicholas Biddle, the well-respected banker, was a partner in the operation, and Coe himself was on the company board. In such a position, Coe could protect Indiana's interest. The bond repayment schedule required 10 monthly installments starting in September 1839.[25]

On April 17, Lanier wrote to the Indianapolis Branch suggesting that the two branches could each lend the state $50,000 in August to continue construction of the railroad. He made the same proposal to Governor Noble:

It is quite possible that our Br. and that at Indianapolis after the first of Aug. can each advance 50,000$ to the State temporarily at 6 per cnt. in order to put a portion more of our road under contract. I have written B.F.Morris on the Subject See him and J. M. Ray and talk with them.[26]

John Woodburn was one of the wealthiest men in Madison. His Virginia salt mines were some of the largest in the country. In the days before refrigeration, salting was the best method of preserving meat. The numerous packing houses along the Ohio river used salt by the ton every day. Woodburn also owned the ships that hauled the salt, and the pork bellies to the plantations in the South. Mr. Woodburn had increased his fortune by judicious land purchases in Madison He was well respected and completely trustworthy. James never had misgivings about suggesting that the Indianapolis branch give Woodburn a loan.

The correspondence is missing, but in April of 1839 Woodburn was evidently having difficulty paying off the note and asked the cashier in Indianapolis to do something Lanier felt was unethical. On April 23, 1839, Lanier wrote an indignant reply to Morris.

Your letter of the 20th is received. I feel much provoked that Woodburn should ask any such request on paper where my name is (involved) I ask no such thing. If he can not meet the paper I have endorsed for him I will. He is as good for the money as any man in the state but I do not approve any such way of doing business. We grant no such requests here, excepting in one particular case where Woodburn was involved and if we get forgiveness for that it will be the last. Should you see(clear) to grant his request I acquiesce and consent to in each case but I have written him to meet payment which I hope he will do. It will of course not be very (easy) for me to pay Woodburn's paper . . . but I will do it if he will not.[27]

Polke was again selling Lanier land in the north. On April 18, he wrote to JFD about a proposed land deal.. Polke commented that Spier was running into difficulty with his father's affairs. James answered on April 25.:

You may sell my interest in the Winnamac lands at such fair profit as you may think best. Also the other land named at the rate named vis $5.00 per acre. Tipton does not act wisely in not wishing aid in the management of his father's estate. The court can regulate this at pleasure by requiring large and good security. I do not wish to write him unless at his request.[28]

The report on the state of the bank in May of 1839 showed that it was still in good condition. Several branches were selling more stock. The net profit for the quarter was $171,600.00. The bank still held $133,000 in federal funds. The board encouraged the branches to pay it off as quickly as possible. The usual reminder to use Eastern notes to keep the bank's specie intact went to the branches.[29]

The problems were minimal. Lanier reported that the Fund Commissioners had not yet responded to the inquiry about the six percent bonds. He also requested that Mr. Fitch look into the problems between the Lawrenceburg branch and several other branches. The branch directors were still not paying promptly on their loans. Lanier felt the directors would pay little heed to the board until it assessed a strong penalty. Fourteen months after the robbery at Vincennes there was still disagreement on who was responsible for the funds lost.[30]

Lanier reintroduced his proposal for a bank agent in New York City. Mason Fitch proposed an agent also be established in New Orleans. Both men proposed extensive rules and procedures that would govern the agents' actions.[31]

The railroad continued building. In early June a second section of the line from Graham to Vernon, opened. The one way fare from Madison to Vernon was 37¢. The next section of 5.8 miles to Queensville was under construction.[32] The design of the bridge over sand creek at Scipio neared completion.

By August the state was in fiscal turmoil once again. All work on internal improvements had stopped. Workers went unpaid, and contractors lost thousands of dollars they had advanced on the faith of the state. A letter from former governor Hendricks, now the contractor on the Madison & Indianapolis Railroad to Governor Wallace summed up the situation throughout the state. It is obvious from this letter that the $100,000 advance from the Madison and Indianapolis branches promised for August first, was not forthcoming.

8/2/(18)39

Dear Sir

Our estimate for July is now ready. Mr. Lanier says that he can not pay us more than five hundred of it. Not until within two days had we any indication of such a danger. . . . Our borrowed money alone is $900. Great effort in (the) making to draw off men to the Ky. Works. If we can not meet our

169

men with money as usual & the word no money gets out, although I believe we have their confidence decidedly, yet most certainly they will leave us and our line-Kentucky is from twenty five to thirty three per cent above us in wages, hands badly wanted-Please Gov. let us hear from you before the—?— etc. & etc. Without money sir, you know we can not go on.

Most respectfully,
W Hendricks & Son[33]

The bank board meeting in August proceeded amid gloom. Net profit for the quarter was down to $82,500. The collapse of the internal improvements financing was choking the bank. The bank had advanced the state $771,200 for internal improvements. The total owed the bank by the state was $1,061,000. It was impossible for the state to repay the money. The bank still owed the Federal government $48,600. The directors thought that balance was paid. The Lawrenceburg branch had decided to hold the final payment against a run on the branch when the fiscal crisis became evident.[34]

The Internal Improvements Fund Commissioners admitted they overspent the fund. There was no money to continue work, much less to pay interest on the bonds. They also admitted it was unlikely they could raise funds in the near future.[35]

The internal cancer was still alive. Mr. Fitch's committee, appointed to look into the continuing problems at Lawrenceburg, reported that the branch rescinded the letter critical of Samuel Merrill.[36]

Another charge proved more serious. The practice of purchasing local bills of exchange drawn on fictitious companies, and payable at distant branches was "purely fractious, and a mere cover for usury. . . . such a practice is directly calculated to draw upon our institution the censure of the legislature and the odium of the community."[37]

To Lanier's disgust, the bank board seemed incapable of solving problems. After months of study, the board could not fix blame for the robbery at Vincennes. The board ordered the Vincennes and Terre Haute branches to share the loss equally.[38]

The branches had decreased circulation during the last quarter by $187,900, but still had $3,647,000 outstanding. As the condition of the bank became apparent, the once sterling reputation of the Indiana State Bank rusted. Eastern banks demanded

170

specie for Indiana notes. The crisis had already forced the branches to pay out $47,200 in specie.[39]

Alarmed at the turn of events, some members pointed fingers of blame, while others rung their hands in despair. In the end they turned to their financial rock. They appointed Lanier chairman of a select committee to investigate "the present and perspective state of the branches." The committee was to devise some plan of action for the "protection and relief of the community."[40]

Lanier was worried, but not beaten. He drove his committee late into the night. They sifted information and called upon directors for information or clarification. They reported back to the board before the close of the meeting.

The report was bleak. It began with a litany of crises. "The aspects of pecuniary matters . . . are anything but flattering and will require great care and circumspection on the part of the branches to weather the storm." The report stated the sale of all American stocks in London depressed. Until the market improved, there was little hope of selling either State Bank of Indiana stocks or internal improvement bonds overseas.[41]

Lanier's committee reiterated the state indebtedness to the bank, and proclaimed that repayment "now lies dead and unavailable." There would be no payment made by the state until at least November or December 1839, and even then, the payment would be small. There was great concern that the bankruptcy of the state would pull the bank down also.[42]

The report went on to explain that the bank's note circulation level relied on repayment by the state, and since this was not now possible, redemption of the notes required specie payments. The committee expected a great rush for specie in the next three months. The river branches were at greatest risk of a call for specie, and would require help from the interior branches.[43]

The Lafayette Branch had been rash in advancing the state an additional $140,000 and in borrowing another $23,000. from the Morris Canal and Banking Company. Morris C&B was already late in payments to the fund commissioners for stock they had purchased, and was a very bad risk. This loan was due soon. As a consequence, the Lafayette branch was about to go belly-up.[44] Lanier's report summed up the situation: "This sudden and unexpected turn in our affairs will very much embarrass the branches and the citizens of the state."[45]

JFD would not throw in the towel. The board gratefully adopted the ideas he proposed to relieve the problem. The board instructed the Lafayette branch to discontinue loans and consolidate her means to fend off a run on the branch. They restricted credit at all branches to 1 1/4 paid capitol unless it was for "prompt paper" of less than a six month term.[46]

In addition the board required the river branches (Madison, Lawrenceburg, New Albany, and Evansville) to keep at least one-third of their total loans in bona fide bills of exchange with terms of less than four months. During the next three months the president and cashier received the authority to call on any branch to help the Lafayette Branch, or any other branch that found itself in immediate danger of closing.[47]

Finally, Merrill, or "some member of the board" was to travel east to purchase bank paper to blunt an external demand for specie. The board voted to "clothe (the representative) with such power and authority as may be necessary for him to affect the object desired." Merrill, Fitch and Lanier made up a committee to determine the exact course of action that would save the bank. The board adjourned. They had done all they could to prevent the bank from being sucked into the morass created by the internal improvements debacle.[48]

JFD declined the offer to go East. He felt the situation was so volatile at Madison that he must stay home. James wrote to Merrill on August twenty sixth, giving detailed instructions. The Morris Canal and Banking Company were the root of the problem. Not only had they not paid for two million dollars of internal improvement stock they purchased; they had reneged on the payment of one million dollars worth of bank stock they had purchased in April. He went on to state:

> It is not necessary for me to go to NY as Fitch and yourself can go. I hope the Morris C&B can meet the Sept. payments promised the bank. If not the Fund Commissioners ought to raise the funds to meet the drafts that the banks have already paid. If they (FC) can not, and I think they can, then you and Fitch must try to raise money to meet them. Some of the banks or brokers can lend you for 60 days money enough for that object at some rate or other If money can be had to keep us going until Nov. 1, then the Legislature might be called upon to issue Treasury Notes . . . [49]

Lanier further suggested the U.S. Bank in Philadelphia (still run by Biddle) might lend the money and proposed a rate of 6 or

8 percent for six or eight months. JFD thought Merrill should attempt to secure between $200,000 and $300,000, spreading it between two or three lending institutions. The rate of interest did not concern JFD. Biddle was a major stockholder in the Morris Canal and Banking Company. Surely, as a gentleman, he would fulfill his moral obligation to at least pay the interest on any loan that was necessary.[50]

In the midst of this financial crisis, James was still aware of family needs. He sent Alex off to Yale. Money was tight, but education was paramount. He remembered the sacrifices his parents had made for his education. Alex knew this was his last chance. He had to succeed. His father might believe the professors were inept once, but not a second time.

Before Merrill and Fitch accomplished their mission, the situation became critical at Madison. Everyone was demanding specie. The bankers searched the dark corners of the vault for every last coin. Lanier wrote to Morris on September 13, 1839, pleading for help:

> We have our hands full I assure you. We have not currency enough to meet the current demand at our counter. We have paid out in silver this week $18.000 all to the (railroad) Co. They get in our notes at the rate of $1.500 per day. What is to be the end of matters I can not say. I have just sent a special messenger (Mr. Jenning's son) for our balance there. (When) Samuel returns I wish you to let us have three or four thousand dollars in currency. We shall (soon) have that amount replaced by the branch in Michigan City as they have promised to do so. We can not get a (word) from Merrill Fitch or anyone else. What are they doing?[51]

This was as close as the Madison branch had ever been to closing. Lanier kept a calm public face, but he could scarcely take a relaxed breath. He could not sleep at night so he decided he might as well work. Perhaps he could find an answer. Candles flickered late in the back offices of the bank. Most passersby marveled at JFD's industriousness. A few, who knew of the fiscal crisis, guessed the truth. Critics added to the public's anxiety by loudly forecasting a locking of the vault.

James never surrendered. He confronted those that had overdue loans requesting immediate payment. He requested those bank officers with loans prepay if possible. New loans were out of the question, but he promised applicants to consider them the next time the board met. He would not give a date for the next loan committee meeting.

He convinced himself that this crisis would be short-lived, but did not like the long term outlook for the bank. Loan capital would remain scarce, making dividends minimal. If the bank was not making money it could not loan money. Without a solution the bank and the state would die of capital starvation.

Looking beyond the immediate problem, James knew the M. & I. could be severely affected. There must be a way to proceed with the construction, even if money was tight . On September 17, he wrote to the governor suggesting the right-of- way be reduced from 24 to 16 feet. This would significantly reduce the cost of land purchase as well as clearing and grading.[52]

He knew that a change in the White House was the only permanent solution to the country's fiscal problems. He spoke for the Republican cause, and lent his name and money to the campaign.

James was able to keep his priorities straight even in crisis. He took time to endorse a plea from Judge Eggleston to Governor Noble to spare the life of Michael Brennan. Brennan, convicted of murder in Jennings County, was to hang on October 20,1839. On October 9, Judge Eggleston pleaded for commutation of the sentence because of the boy's age and the fact there were no eyewitnesses to the crime. The boy had little time. JFD, John Sering and two other men laid aside their troubles long enough to endorse the Judge's recommendation. There were other letters urging commutation, and Governor Noble heeded the requests, commuting the sentence to life in prison.[53]

The situation at the Madison Branch was desperate by October 11. James fought like a trapped badger. He wrote to Mr. Ray, the Chief Cashier of the Bank:

**This has been a hard day for us. The trust company in Cincinnati has drawn on us for $13.000 and the Louisville Savings for 6.000$ in notes which I have got a few days time(to send) if not silver must be sent . . . We are as completely cornered as ever a set of men were, we have no foreign funds whatever and but little domestic. $9.000 specie was yesterday drawn from New Albany & 13.000 from Lawrenceburg . . . If the branch in your place can lend us . . . we will pay them interest (on) 60 days. I hope they can do it. Will you see for us? Will you please let me know when the State Board meets.[54]**

FOR THE INDIANA
REPUBLICAN.
PUBLIC MEETING.
We, the undersigned citizens of Jefferson County, (Indiana) feeling a deep interest in the welfare of our common country, and especially in the selection of a suitable person as Chief Magistrate of the U.S. as one of the means of promoting this welfare; and viewing the alarming course pursued by the present incumbent of that office and the dangerous, pernicious, and unconstitutional doctrines advance, and attempted to be put in force, by him, in several of his leading acts, particularly in his several Veto Messages, in relation to the Maysville Turnpike, and Bank of the U. States; his refusing his assent to various appropriations for the Internal Improvement of the country—his attach upon the purity and independence of the Judiciary and congress—his wavering and dubious policies as to domestic manufactures; and various other subjects too numerous to mention here, do hereby unite in a call for a public meeting of our citizens, at the Court house in Madison at one o'clock on Satur-

day the 22d day of September inst. for the purpose of expressing their sentiments on the above subjects.

Sept. 4, 1839.

| | |
|---|---|
| James Tilton | James H. Cravens |
| John Bennett | D. Blackmore |
| John H. Bowen | James Emerson |
| Joseph G. Marshall | John Craig |
| Alexander Jamison | Henry McBride |
| John Griffin | James A. Taylor |
| Samuel Jamison | James Hill |
| J.C. Pogue | W. Brewning |
| John Bice | John Wildman |
| Jessee Whitehead | Evan Milos |
| C.P.J. Arinn | Milton Stapp |
| James Bristow | Nathaniel Driggs |
| Thomas Wise | Stephen S. Harding |
| Levi Poston | Joseph Troxell |
| B. Wilber | F.C. Hoyt |
| John McClelland | Solomon Dovennish |
| Charles Woodard | A. Foster |
| M. Kennedy | S. Andrews |
| J.M. Millan | R. Craig |
| W. H. Stratton | John Thomas |
| Oliver Lewis | David Carr |
| Mathew Ralson | JFD Lanier |
| J.J. Vail | Thomas Brown |
| Joseph Oglesby | Campbell Kinnear |
| W.G. Anderson | George Kennedy |
| Wm. Randell | John Sheets |
| J.M. Brainwell | D. Whitaker |
| H. Watts | .H. King |
| Wm. Dutton | John H. Moore |
| James Knight | James S. Smith |
| Ralph Griffin | Wm. Hutchinson |

JFD joined an attack on the Administration, hoping to build support for the Whigs.

Like a summer rainstorm, the bank crisis suddenly vanished. Madison no longer needed the Indianapolis funds by the time they arrived. Lanier returned the funds to Indianapolis on the 18th:

Yours of the 17th rec'd. The (crisis) having for the present left us, we have no occasion to use the $5.000 draft on the Franklin, consequently I herewith endorse it to you thanking as much as if we had used it The banks have all suspended in Kentucky. We have not. Up to close of bank hours today we have met all demands but should a big one come we should take that course into consideration. One chap came from Cincinnati Monday with $1.200 our notes. I told him we had not fully decided as to what course we should pursue. Desired him to wait to the next dy but to accommodate him I must give him a check on NY at 4 percent and. which he very quickly took having some notion what our determination might be the next day. (Everyone) sleeps well at night now.[55]

Perhaps the immediate crisis was over, and everyone was sleeping better. Perhaps he did not need to borrow money and pay interest to keep the branch solvent; but JFD had endangered his own funds in the rescue. He needed a reserve. On October eighteenth, he sent Polke a short note: **"Sir, will you please send me the amount rec'd by you for the sale of my land as I am much in want of the money."**[56] The same day, he wrote to J.B. Niles, searching for the overdue payment:

Will you please inform me whether Judge Polke has left any money in your hands for me or made any arrangement by which I am to get any. The Judge sold some land of mine the money which I think he advised me would be placed in your hands.[57]

James went to Cincinnati to try to collect some money. On the twenty-fifth, he wrote to General Orr, the president of the Lawrenceburg branch:

I was up at Cincinnati yesterday. The banks there talk of resuming within 30 days from the date of suspension. If they do not, they have to be wound up under their Laws. The N. York banks still all hold out . . . for political effect. On the river here not yet suspension. We pay no demands from Brokers and Banks but do all home calls. I shall expect to meet you at the State Board. If B. McCarty has not yet paid to you $300 for me will you do me the favor to employ someone to to go down and get it of him and I will pay the messenger.[58]

The crisis might be over, but business was at a standstill. Where once they transferred thousands of dollars between branches daily, now it was down to a pittance. On November 15,1839, the transfers totaled thirteen dollars and fifty cents.

The state bank was under attack from several quarters. The citizens were up in arms, and the Legislature took their cue from the voters. Sam Merrill fought back in his annual report to the Legislature dated October 31:

The failure of the $1,000,000 of extra capital (the bonds sold in N.Y. that never were paid for) is making money scarce and depressing prices. The Bank has had to curtail its loans to the extent of $730,000 in 30 days. It has too many useless officers and directors. State regulations also hamper the actions of the Bank. We would open the Thirteenth, Fourteenth, and Fifteenth branches, but the state can not get capital for its part of the stock. Politicians are injuring the Bank by catering to its enemies. In many cases worthless directors get on the bank boards only to insure to themselves a loan from the Bank. Long time loans ought to be avoided, especially to merchants and speculators. The state has made a net profit on its bank stock of $391,334.[59]

Merrill did not say it, but in normal times, without the internal improvements fiasco, $391,000 would have been enough to pay for all the expenses of state government.

Passenger cars ordered by the M & I in flush times were now ready for service. Their luxurious decor seemed ludicrous at a time when most families were happy to just have food on the table. An article in the November 3, 1839, *Indianapolis Journal* describes the cars:

The passenger cars intended for the Madison and Indianapolis Railroad are splendid specimens of workmanship and reflect great credit upon the mechanical skill of our artisans. The painting of the cars is also a neat and tasty piece of work. On the inside is an imitation of mahogany and curled maple. They are calculated to contain 100 passengers each and are furnished with elegant cushioned seats. It will be a pretty sight to see them flying past the countryside at 30 miles per hour.

# 16.
## "... the credit of the State is gone forever..."
— State Bank Board Minutes, November 1839

*The country continued in the grasp of the depression. It had stretched on for several years, and there were forecasts that the country would never recover. James Lanier disagreed completely. He felt that with a change in the presidency, and the right fiscal policy the country would prosper. The next few months did not strengthen Lanier's assumption as the Second State Bank of Indiana continued to struggle, although most of its pain was self inflicted.*

The bank board met in its new building near the corner of Kentucky Avenue and West Streets for the first time in November of 1839.[1] The building contained extra space for rent, and the additional income was welcomed. The new surroundings cheered the group momentarily, but then they returned to the serious problems confronting the bank.

As bad as the situation had been in August, it was worse by November. The Lawrenceburg and Lafayette branches were on the edge of collapse. Lawrenceburg still owed the U.S. Treasurer $47,000 and the payment was overdue. The branch had liabilities totaling $377,000 against available means of only $58,000. Lafayette was in much the same situation with debts of $387,500 and assets of but $83,500.[2]

The board once again turned to Lanier to untangle the Gordian knot of fiscal misadventures. As it had numerous times in the past, JFD's committee laid down strict rules for the two wayward branches. The board again ordered the Lafayette branch to reduce their loans as quickly as possible. It ordered the Lawrenceburg branch to accept no new debt, and to call in its outstanding loans without delay. The branch was not to increase circulation under any circumstance or pretext. The board ordered the branch to immediately withdraw deposits in the Urbana, Ohio bank.[3]

To add to the state bank's woes Milton Stapp, writing for the fund commissioners, requested that the bank pay the interest on the Internal Improvement Bonds due bond holders in January 1840. Governor Wallace, and State Treasurer N.B. Palmer, as well as William Brown, the Secretary of State, supported Stapp's request. Stapp promised to repay the money from the sale of bonds. The interest amounted to $209,000, with Stapp estimating the pending revenue at $304,000.[4]

Lanier wrestled with the question all the way to Indianapolis. He very much wanted to believe the promises of his friend Milton. The honor of the state and every Hoosier was at stake.

After much debate, the bank board felt they had no choice but to make the interest payments. One board member argued that if they refused, "the credit of the State is gone forever, and every door of hope for the future will be effectively closed."[5] Publicly the board hoped the fund commissioners could repay the money by April 1. Privately, many members felt the prospects for repayment were dim.

The board knew another political storm was brewing over internal improvements and they wanted to steer the bank into the lee. Paying the interest on the bonds would deflect criticism away from the bank. James voted with the board. To meet the interest payments, the board pulled whatever specie the branches could afford, loaded it in wagons and sent it east. Because the Ohio river remained frozen, the guarded shipment traveled over the National Road.[6]

When the internal improvements problems reached scandalous proportions, Lucius Scott did not attend the November

179

bank board meeting. His term on the board expired on December 31, 1839, and he did not expect to be re-appointed. With the governor, state treasurer, and secretary of state all supporting the fund commissioners' request, Scott felt there was no need for him to suffer through the November meeting.

Lanier was in a quandary. Should he sell his Internal Improvement Bonds, or stay the course? How would the public perceive his actions? Not only were internal improvement securities in a shambles, construction costs for the projects had exploded. With all the construction proceeding at the same time, labor and supplies were in high demand. Projects competed with each other. Premiums as well as bribes were commonplace. The once shining dreams of "avenues of future glory for Indiana" had become slippery, empty canal beds that oozed corruption and failure all across the state.

As JFD had noted on October 18, most of the banks in surrounding states had suspended specie payment. All branches were under extreme pressure to pay specie. The border banks were particularly vulnerable. The crush could be deadly. On November 13, the board voted the sternest set of measures ever adopted.

They voted to suspend specie payments on out of state requests. They set down criteria that allowed individual branches to suspend Indiana payments, but hoped to avoid this drastic step.[7] This time there was no gnashing of teeth; no conference with the governor or state treasurer; no published position paper; no speeches explaining to the public the need for the drastic step; just a resolution buried in the board minutes.

The board did what it could to dam the red ink that ran from its books faster than water through the unfinished canals. They suspended authority to issue post notes. They ordered "long paper"(long term loans) in "slow hands" (delinquent in payment) curtailed. The board condemned "foreign" debt. Finally, they strongly discouraged loans for land and speculation.[8]

The board endorsed JFD's plan of purchasing short term bills of exchange once again. The branches would direct all their energies toward carrying Indiana pork, wheat, flour and manufactured products to market. They could not loan over 2 1/2 times the capital paid, and must limit future loans to short term business paper. For the first time, the state debt to the branch became a liability against that ceiling. The Lawrenceburg and

Lafayette branches were so close to failure that they could not participate in this program.[9]

Years later, Hugh McCulloch would comment that this strategy saved the Indiana state bank. The short term loans turned over so quickly, that with capital of only about two million dollars; loans approached 10 to 15 million dollars per year. An added advantage of the loans was that they were very safe.[10]

As bad as the situation was, the directors still declared a dividend of between three and five percent. The board did not allow the Lafayette and Lawrenceburg branches to claim a dividend. This prohibition hurt those branch directors more than all the stinging rhetoric and dire threats.[11]

Returning from the bank board meeting, James immediately carried out the mandate of the board against a borrower with extremely "slow hands." Griffin Treadway had borrowed money from the Madison branch to purchase land in northern Indiana. Treadway failed to make payments. James gave J.B.Niles detailed instructions on how to proceed with a suit against Treadway.[12]

The bank board had forecast correctly. The citizens were distraught over the handling of the internal improvements. The state had sold $3,000,000 in bonds and was strangling on a debt of $13,000,000. There was nothing to show for the debt except a few half dug canals and short stretches of track. European bankers, led by the House of Rothschild, threatened to destroy Indiana's credit far into the twentieth century.[13]

The voters elected a Democrat majority in the Indiana House of Representatives. The Senate held on to a slight Republican majority, but the remaining Republicans needed to show their anger.[14] Stung by Merrill's report, and fresh from a whipping by the electorate, the legislature acted to protect its collective hide. The House of Representatives called for seventeen separate investigations. The Senate, not to be outdone, requested eighteen different studies of the problem.[15]

The black brush of blame painted everyone. One representative who pushed incessantly to punish the state bank was a new member from Tippecanoe County, Mr. James White. The same James White that the bank board had fired, and then tried to mollify in February. It had not worked. He and his cronies succeeded in passing a Joint Resolution that would have removed Merrill, Calvin Fletcher and Robert Morrison from the bank board. The motion passed the House 51-47 but the Senate tabled it indefinitely. The votes were strictly along party lines. It appeared that the bank was becoming a valuable chip in political poker.

The Legislature issued $1.2 million dollars in "State Treasury Notes" to pay contractors for work performed on internal improvements. Critics of the notes claimed they violated the U. S. Constitution that prohibited states from issuing bills of credit.[16] Some newspaper wags insisted these were not bills of credit because the state had no credit. With only the dubious credit of the state to back them, merchants heavily discounted these treasury notes from the beginning.

During the February 1840 bank board meeting, the legislature was still in session. The fiscal situation still looked grim. The board further distanced itself from the internal improvements board, the fund commissioners, and the legislature, by directing the branches not to loan any more money for internal improvements.[17] The bank board was very reluctant to accept the treasury notes.

The board made every effort to increase the safety of the bank. Discounts dropped to 1 1/4 the capital stock paid in or due from the state. Twenty percent of all loans were due every 90 days. From one-third to one fourth of all branch loans were mandated for prompt bills of exchange only. Borrowers had to demonstrate a "pride and duty" to repay the loans. Current borrowers that could not pay off ten percent of their loan, could not obtain a new loan. The board ordered foreclosed property sold immediately. They wanted new bank stock sold aggressively.[18]

The board was happy that Lawrenceburg no longer owed the federal government. The character of several Lawrenceburg branch board members was still an open question, however, so the board established a committee to look into the problems at the branch again.[19]

The Legislature finally adjourned, and the *Indianapolis Journal* wrote this epitaph on February 20, 1840:

> This body, after a stormy, protracted, and useless session of eighty-five days, has at last adjourned, and may heaven for all time save us from such another.

On April 2, James wrote to Niles, sending a deed in Griffin Treadway's name. He instructed Niles to give the deed to Treadway if Treadway paid the $1500 owed on the property. Treadway owed JFD about $5700 on several other pieces of land. Lanier was willing to continue the loans on those parcels, at eight or ten percent interest, if Treadway gave Niles "good additional security for the whole debt."[20]

Since flood waters constantly jeopardized the old Third Street Cemetery, Madison established a new burial ground above the flood plain. James purchased a large lot far up the hill on the north side of the cemetery. He planned the burial design just as carefully as he planned his other projects. His parents would lie on the east side of the plot. Drusilla would be uphill, or north of Alex. Uncle James, the doctor, rested in that line, down hill next his brother.

In the next row west would be James' family. He left a space for Elisabeth on the north end of the row. John James was carefully re-buried in the next plot. The plot furthest down the hill, on the southern edge of the lot, James reserved for himself. In this manner all of the children could rest eternally protected between father and mother. The women would be the farthest uphill protected forever from the ravages of floods.

JFD did not attend the May 1840 meeting of the board. Jesse Whitehead from Madison sat in James' stead. Problems kept appearing. In addition to Lawrenceburg, the Michigan City branch was now faltering.[21]

Sam Merrill headed a committee that looked into the difficulties. The committee found that the Lawrenceburg Branch had paid little attention to the instructions issued by the bank board in February. Their suspended debt and discounts were much too high. Director's loan payments were not current. The branch had made new loans contrary to the board's explicit instructions. To add insult to injury, most of the new loans were to directors and shareholders.[22] The branch was thumbing its nose at the board; betting they would back down once again. The fact that JFD was not at the May meeting was a welcome surprise to the violators.

Merrill's committee recommended strong action for the board:

1. Any dividend paid Lawrenceburg stockholders be retained to reduce the stockholder debt.
2. Dismiss the president and cashier.
3. Limit branch loans to 4 months duration.

4. Remove any branch director that did not repay his loans in regular installments.[23]

The Lawrenceburg directors guessed right. The full board was not willing to take such drastic action. They decided that the cashier should reduce his debt "at an early day, or face dismissal by the branch board."[24] Evidently board members did not want another James White roaming the halls of the legislature.

The board struck down the recommendation to remove directors that did not promptly pay on their loans. The motion hit too close to home. They argued that only the branch board or the legislature had the authority to remove branch board members. In a show of responsibility, William Tate, a state appointed director for Lawrenceburg, resigned because his loans were under protest (overdue).[25] It was refreshing to know that not all the directors at Lawrenceburg held the bank directors in contempt.

Buell, one of the bank directors appointed by the legislature, was a member of Merrill's committee. He was unhappy with the committee findings and submitted a formal dissent to the report.[26]

The problems at Michigan City were as serious as those at Lawrenceburg. Hugh McCulloch investigated those problems. Directors were withdrawing specie from the South Bend branch for their own use. The normal drain of specie was a serious problem without branch directors adding to it. Public discovery of the withdrawals would undermine the credibility of the whole state banking system. McCulloch recommended that the guilty directors be censured.[27]

A number of Michigan City branch directors had overdrawn their accounts with the direct knowledge of the president and cashier. In other instances, directors had written checks and obtained cash, when there was no money in their account to cover the checks. The cashier had held the checks for a considerable length of time and counted the checks as cash.[28]

This same infraction had caused James White's dismissal. This time the board decided that Sam Merrill should visit Michigan City and investigate the situation.[29] This was typical of the state bank board. They consistently refused to take strong action against violators. They either declared such action the responsibility of the branch boards, or sent Sam Merrill to do their dirty work.

184

Although the suspended debt reached $391,500, most of the branches declared a four or five percent dividend. The directors applied the state dividend against the state debt to the branch.[30] The board also required directors that had overdue bank loans to apply dividends to the loans.[31]

With every fiscal transaction of the state under investigation from several quarters, many branch officers were running for cover. They were making political marriages they hoped would protect them from financial ruin or from the prison yard at Jeffersonville.

The state directors worried about these political alliances. They felt it was extremely important to remain non-partisan. Decisions must remain free of party politics if the bank was to survive. They adopted a resolution reinforcing this view.[32]

The Fort Wayne and Lawrenceburg branches had defied the board and withheld interest payments on the Internal Improvement Bonds. They argued that the financial condition of the branch had precluded paying interest on an account that was in arrears. Although many on the board agreed with the actions, they were afraid to further anger the legislature. The board ordered the interest paid, claiming that the integrity and honor of the state, and the bank was at stake.[33]

When Whitehead reported the results of the meeting to Lanier, James questioned him closely on the actual resolutions and who had said what and voted for various proposals. He then excused himself and retreated to his private office.

The spineless bank board so infuriated him that he could not concentrate on bank business. He took a walk along the river. Despite the tragedy that the river symbolized, James liked to walk along its banks. The water had a calming effect. It continued to roll to the sea, promising continuity in the future, giving stability to catastrophe and change. He would work his way out of these problems, just as he had solved earlier dilemmas.

# 17.
## "It is rumored that Lanier is opposed to specie payment . . ."
— Calvin Fletcher, November 9, 1840

*The next 18 months were full of change. The depression continued unabated. James Lanier decided to make a symbolic statement of his faith in the country in hopes it would set an example for recovery. The electorate decided to make a statement of their own at the ballot box. They turned out those who they thought were responsible for the long panic. Both efforts pleased James.*

Alex came home from his first year at Yale. He was in the general studies curriculum and had not yet declared a major. His grades were barely passing, but he convinced his father that was not too bad. There were many adjustments to make. It was his first year, and he was far from home. The life style at New Haven was completely different from Madison. Many of Alex's classmates failed. Yale was a very difficult school. A "C" or "D" there was as good as an "A" or "B" at Indiana University. There was so much to learn. Education had changed drastically since JFD had attended Transylvania. Alex argued that it was really quite an accomplishment that the dean had invited him back for the fall semester.

James' oldest daughter was still keeping regular company with William McKee Dunn. The boy was ambitious, and discouraged talk of marriage until he had finished college and could support a wife. Elisabeth sometimes confided in her mother that he might never be ready for marriage.

While Elisabeth worried about the progress of the courtship, James stewed about the progress of the railroad. In June the state leased the M & I to a different set of contractors. John Sering became a principal.[1] This arrangement was less offensive to JFD. The new position would keep Sering in Madison where he could attend to his banking chores. Since James was a principal in several ventures, he could not deny Sering the same arrangement.

The state was to receive seventy-one percent of the gross earnings of the line. The company set freight rates realizing the line had to pay expenses and make a profit while capturing only twenty-nine percent of the gross income. The high payment required by the state doomed the agreement from the outset. For the twenty-three mile run from Madison to Vernon, the cost of general freight was 16¢ per hundred pounds. Bulky items, such as furniture, garnered 20¢ per hundred-weight. Salt, whiskey or pork cost 45¢ per barrel. A barrel of flour brought in 25¢, but lard cost only 7¢ per keg.[2] The train left Madison about 9:00 A.M. and arrived in Vernon at 10:30. The return trip left Vernon at 3:00 P.M. and arrived it Madison two hours later.[3]

Sam Merrill concentrated on bank problems. On August 10, 1840, just prior to the quarterly board meeting, he wrote to Internal Improvements Fund Commissioners, Stapp and Scott. He had received correspondence from the Morris Bank and Canal Company stating they would not pay the installment due for the Internal Improvement Bonds. He requested that the commissioners obtain some security from the Morris Bank, or have them return the bonds. Merrill impatiently wrote again on August 13 commenting "common honesty would require them (Morris Bank & Canal Company) to return the bonds if they can not pay for the bonds or sell them."[4]

Whitehead again represented the Madison branch at the board meeting.[5] The board requested that Merrill, Fitch, or Lanier go east, to resolve the Morris Bank problem in person.[6] Only the Madison, Richmond, Indianapolis, Bedford, and Terre Haute branches had reduced their discounts to 1 1/4 the paid stock as mandated by the board in February. The suspended debt had increased from $367,573 in April to $392,111 by July 30, 1840.[7]

Most board members felt resumption would take place by February of 1841. Because of the poor fiscal situation of the state government, they expected a rush for specie. The board once again admonished all branches to take definite steps to reduce their loans and suspended debt.[8]

The new contractors for the Madison & Indianapolis Railroad did not last. On August 22, 1840, the *Madison Courier* stated:

> The partnership existing between Butt and Sering in the contract with the Commissioner of the M. & I. railroad for the transportation of freight and passengers on said road dissolved by mutual consent. Sering will be responsible for debts due the firm and all business will henceforth be conducted by him.

The 1840 election was one of the most contentious battles ever waged in Indiana. Libel flourished as every candidate sought to smear his opponent with the deadly tar of internal improvements. Everyone in power from the governor to the county prosecutors attracted blame for the mess and defended themselves against accusations of profiting mightily from the fiasco.

On the national level, James worked tirelessly for his friend General Harrison, who was now the sole candidate for the Whigs. The party recaptured its old name in an attempt to lure back supporters. Political observers felt the Whigs had substituted their best vote producer for their most able statesmen, Clay and Webster. Lanier was optimistic that the general was the one man that could break the Democrats strangle hold on the White House. He was desperate for a Harrison win that would set the economy back on track. Locally James was less partisan. He backed those he thought offered the best solution to the fiscal crisis, regardless of party affiliation.

In 1840, Henry Ward Beecher accepted an appointment to fill the pulpit of the Second Presbyterian Church in Indianapolis. He quickly became a favorite of Sam Merrill, and the president of the bank introduced him to Lanier. Beecher was an outspoken abolitionist with an unshakable moral code. His quest for equality included education for women, and he found an ally in James. Catherine Beecher, one of Henry Ward's daughters, opened a school for young ladies in Cincinnati. Although there is no solid record, there is some evidence that JFD sent at least one of his daughters to her school.

By the November meeting of the bank board, a Legislative report on the bank vindicated Merrill but embarrassed officers of the institution who could feel that emotion. It showed that of a total of $2,339,819 in outstanding loans, board members or officer loans accounted for $1,338,599.[9] When the report became public, the Democratic press filled column after column with scorn and accusations against the bank. The papers hoped the attack would seal the election for the Democrats.

The stinging public criticism prodded the board into action. They chose to focus their wrath on the Lawrenceburg branch. Members who had defended Lawrenceburg three months earlier, heaped scorn on the branch. They directed the president to issue a sine facia against the Lawrenceburg branch, requiring it to prove why the directors should not bar and shutter the branch. It further mandated the branch stop making loans until the directors reduced the total debt to 1 1/4 the paid in stock. The only loans allowed were bona fide bills of exchange having a life of not over four months, drawn on produce shipped, and negotiated with a person that had no current liabilities with the branch.[10]

Merrill proposed that the numerous loans, or "accommodation papers" afforded the directors of various branches be significantly reduced. Scalded by the *Indianapolis Journal* and other Democratic papers, the board quickly agreed.[11] Lanier, who returned to the bank board after an absence of two meetings, felt vindicated, but disgusted that it had taken outside intervention to solve problems he had complained about for years. Public exposure of private problems had seriously wounded the bank. It need not have happened if they had acted on his complaints months ago.

Lanier attacked the South Bend branch as being grossly mismanaged. Taking advantage of the board's mood, he proposed strong measures against the branch He forced the same restrictions on South Bend as were put upon Lawrenceburg. He accused one of the branch directors of being in league with a known criminal. JFD thundered that the branch was not safe while the crooked director held office.[12]

The condition of the other branches had improved. Several branches still held discounts exceeding 1 1/4 of paid stock, but the excess was only $18,450.00. This was down from $319,000 the previous quarter.[13]

Most people awaited the resumption of specie payment with the fervor of the Second Coming. The board urged Merrill to maintain contact with the other states. Lanier was in favor of maintaining the suspension. He was afraid that if the Democrats prevailed in the election, the fiscal situation would deteriorate. James saw the widespread fiscal problems as an indictment of the Democrats that the electorate could not miss. JFD wanted resumption to be a reward for turning out the Democrats. Calvin Fletcher opposed this reasoning and wrote in his diary on November 9, 1840:

> It is rumored that Lanier is opposed to specie payment, and has used his influence with banks in other states. This I dislike. I am for resuming specie payments let either party prevail. The community will not indulge the makers of such evidence of debt to withhold payment. It is wrong. I shall go for specie payment.

The Panic of 1837 had been long and devastating. The entire country wavered for several years on the brink of collapse. A large majority of people had lost hope and then faith. There was a growing belief that, if the representative democracy form of government could not sustain a strong economy, it would fail.

James disagreed. His father had instilled within him the dream of the founding fathers: the idea that all could prosper under the new democracy. Alex had added his own ideas. Merchant princes and entrepreneurs would lead the new democracy, not landed lords. James lived that dream. He had an obligation and a responsibility to support the empire that democracy was building in the U.S. — the only empire that had been build without being continually reinforced with blood. What better way to honor that dream than to build solid evidence that it could happen.

For several years Lanier had planned to build a mansion. He originally planned to use the river lot for commercial development, but decided to build his house there when the continued depression discouraged commercial ventures. The neighborhood teemed with activity. Steamboats kept the river in front of the site alive with lights and sounds 24 hours a day. West of the property was the large pork house owned by Lanier and Milton Stapp. To the East was a group of warehouses, and immediately north of the property was an iron foundry.

There were newer forms of American architecture budding on the east coast, but James chose Greek Revival architecture, the architecture of Jefferson. Greek Revival architecture was the symbolic architecture of the American democracy.[14]

He would build the finest house west of the Allegheny Mountains and north of New Orleans. The house would be solid and strong to weather the storms of the future; just as the government would weather this storm or anything the future might bring. The metaphor would be unequivocal.

It was hazardous to build now; the financial crisis had depleted James' private purse. Lanier decided he would not become a target for critics of the bank by applying for a loan in this crisis period. He would pay cash for each stick of wood, each pane of glass and each brick, even if it took several years to complete the house. He would show maverick bank directors that progress was possible without fiscal irresponsibility.

JFD picked a young architect trained in the East. Francis Costigan was ten years younger than JFD, and had plied his trade as a carpenter-builder in Baltimore. Wishing to expand his knowledge he became an apprentice draftsman and studied architecture. Although he constructed buildings in Madison, Louisville, and Indianapolis, the Lanier Mansion was his finest work, and became his signature piece.

Costigan and Elizabeth contributed ideas to the design, but this was James' house. He insisted that the grand scale not be compromised in either the house or the gardens. He approved every detail. He demanded perfection. Francis Costigan did much of the detailed plaster work himself because other workers could not meet J.F.D's rigid expectations. In the end, the work satisfied James. His house had no equal in the western United States. Money fluctuations continued during the four year construction period, but James sacrificed other plans to keep the building on schedule.

Immersed in building plans, Lanier received some good news. The campaign against the state bank and the Whigs fell short. With all the ballots finally counted, the Whigs won the top two spots. William Henry Harrison carried Indiana by 13,000 votes while Judge Samuel Bigger gained the Governor's Office with a 9,000 vote margin. Lanier was ecstatic. Finally Harrison had received his due. Finally the Whigs broke the Democratic choke-hold on the national economy.

As Harrison traveled to Washington for his inauguration, he stopped unannounced in Madison. James was at the landing preparing to journey to Cincinnati when he discovered that the president was aboard the incoming mail boat.[15] James chest swelled with pride as he saw his old friend and realized he was soon to be President of the United States. The surprise meeting also pleased William Henry who readily accepted James' dinner invitation. The Madison Banner reported that Harrison spent several hours at a hotel dining room, amongst a throng of supporters.[16] He then retired to the Lanier house to spend the night. After the invited guests left, James and the President reminisced until a full scuttle of coal was reduced to glowing clinkers.

Bigger's inauguration took place on December 9, 1840. In his speech he set the current expense toward internal improvements at $6 million. To finish the projects would take $14 million more. In his diary, Calvin Fletcher roundly criticized all involved with internal improvements.

> . . . a reckless board of internal improvement of some 6 or 8 members from each part of the state bucking each other by agreeing if Expenditures and works not called for should be made in his section of the state the other would agree to equally useless improvements in some other portion of the State. So mad (excited) with expectation was the community that the mechanic left his shop & turned merchant & the farmer left his farm to buy and sell on credit. Everything from the borrowing of millions to carry on these improvements to the shirt that the laborer wore on his back was on a credit. Even the interest that fell due on the loans made to the state was on a credit except that made for Bank capital which was paid as it fell due.[17]

Fletcher made a good point. Through all the chaos, inflation, extended borrowing, and defaults, the bank remained a solid, trusted institution.

JFD spent the last three weeks of December in Indianapolis. He attended Bigger's inauguration and stayed to celebrate Christmas. He, Fletcher, Merrill, and Orr met to discuss the specie situation and to develop their strategy for the legislative session.[18]

Calvin Fletcher felt discouraged. He did not share Lanier's optimism about Harrison's Administration. On Christmas Day he wrote: ". . . a very general distress. More than 1/2 of the active businessmen and promising politicians 4 years ago are insolvent on the limits."[19]

# 18.
## "... his improper connections with brokers, shavers and swindlers ..."
— Legislative Report, 1841

*The year started out with promise and happy celebrations, but as time progressed, predictions of prosperity did not materialize. All of James Lanier's wealth could not shield him from tragedy again during the next few years.*

In January of 1841, Sam Merrill attended a bank conference in Louisville, representing the Indiana State Bank. The conference elected him presiding officer. Representatives from banks in all parts of the West and South attended. There was much talk about resuming specie payments, but since the banks in New Orleans were not willing to agree, no action ensued. It was the general feeling, that if the harvest proved good and crops brought a fair price, the resulting financial improvement would allow resumption in the fall.[1]

The legislature was still stinging from the internal improvements mess. The indictment of Dr, Coe did not cool their blood, so they continued to cast about for another whipping boy. Milton Stapp was the newest target. Stapp had served his country honorably at the Battle of Thames; had served in the Legislative and Executive branches of state government; and as a lawyer had sworn an oath to uphold the law. None of that mattered. Although the legislature cleared him of criminal malfeasance, it characterized Stapp as being duped by Dr. Coe. The report castigated him for his ineptitude and naiveté:

> Not what has he (Stapp) done wrong, but what in his whole business has he correctly done? His complicated negotiations with Sherwood, Danforth, Dodge, Robinson (wildcat bankers of New York and Ohio), and others, his loans of State Property to sustain tottering swindling shops, his ante dated letters and receipts, his negligence and confusion in business, his improper connections with brokers, Shavers and swindlers, are facts too glaring to be denied, too grossly wrong to admit to palliation, and too palpably indefensive to invite attack.[2]

Not content with vilifying Stapp, the foes of the bank pushed through a bill demanding another investigation. The legislature appointed Nathan B. Palmer, a six-term Democrat State Treasurer, to carry out the examination.[3] Lanier did not worry. Palmer was an old friend from Madison whom he had once supported for election. Lanier felt Palmer was fair, honest, and knowledgeable.

After having heard nothing of the Treadway situation for several months, James wrote a sharply toned letter to Niles on January 29, 1841. He asked for at least a receipt for the deed that he had sent, and suggested that if Treadway did not pay, the land be sold under a lien. James suggested a local lawyer to handle the problem if Niles was too busy.[4]

The new year found the Ohio River frozen and Madison stranded again. The ice broke up allowing James to journey south in February to check on "safe banks" and to purchase eastern notes and bills of exchange. James took his wife and daughter Elisabeth. The cold winter had been hard on Mrs. Lanier, and the New Orleans' climate would help her. They also needed to do last minute shopping. Elisabeth's wedding to William McKee Dunn was to be March 11.

Since he was in the South, Lanier missed the February 1841 bank board meeting. The main topic of discussion was the resumption of specie payments. The board planned to resume on July 1, 1841, at the latest, provided that Illinois, Ohio, and Kentucky did likewise.[5]

The bank board refused to issue notes of less than five dollars because it violated the bank charter. They felt the charter took precedence over the law recently passed by the legislature.[6] Later in the meeting the board reversed itself after they confirmed that the legislature had amended the bank charter to permit temporary notes of less than $5.00. The board instructed Merrill and the cashier to have the notes printed.[7]

Merrill offered several resolutions severely restricting the operations at Lawrenceburg. The members passed the resolutions over the strenuous objections of the branch representative. The other branches' fiscal health showed much improved over the previous quarter.[8]

When Lanier returned to Madison, three letters from Niles awaited him. Niles suggested that they take Treadway to court and get an order to sell the land at a sheriff's sale. In a letter dated March 8, 1841, JFD agreed and suggested a $10.00 per acre selling price. He also suggested that Niles take possession of the land if Treadway would relinquish it peacefully. He ends the letter by stating: **"I am very desirous of closing my matter with this SKUNK as soon as possible."**[9]

The Lanier-Dunn wedding was a grand affair, with many of James' friends in attendance. William Dunn was from a good family, he graduated from Indiana State College in 1832, and from Yale in 1835. Having been admitted to the bar in 1837, he already had a thriving law practice.[10] Although the Dunns were outspoken and independent, James approved his oldest daughter's choice. Alexander, 20, was two years older than Elisabeth, and not married. If James felt disappointment in his oldest son, he did not share it with anyone.

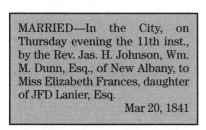

MARRIED—In the City, on Thursday evening the 11th inst., by the Rev. Jas. H. Johnson, Wm. M. Dunn, Esq., of New Albany, to Miss Elizabeth Frances, daughter of JFD Lanier, Esq.

Mar 20, 1841

The *Madison Courier* carried this happy announcement

Sam Merrill attended the wedding and discussed business conditions in the South with JFD. On March 24, Merrill answered a letter from former governor Noble.[11] Noble raised the fear that the bank branches would not pay the dividend on the shares of bank stock owned by the state. He was counting on the dividend to help defray state expenses. Merrill's letter was long and detailed:

> Yours of the 5th inst, reached here during my absence from home, but a copy was forwarded to me at Madison. Lanier thinks the branches will not refuse to pay over the dividends and I have never thought they would refuse but as a last resort.

Merrill then reverses himself stating that Lawrenceburg can not pay a dividend in May and other branches are hard pressed to come up with the money:

> . . . while such extraordinary revolutions in finance are in progress but you may rely on our only yielding to inevitable necessity. Situated as you are you will be able at an early day to see what we ought to do in self defense and when nothing better is presented to us, we must go with the current.

The remainder of the letter relays JFD's evaluation of various banks and the Appalachicola Land Company in Mississippi. Merrill also gives Noble some instructions on how do dispose of various securities.

More bad news reached Madison in April. William Henry Harrison, having reached the pinnacle of success, did not live to enjoy the honor. On March 4, 1841, he died from pneumonia. The news shocked JFD. He read and reread the details of his friend's death, his mind unable to absorb what his eyes read. Whatever economic advice Lanier had given Harrison as the coals dwindled in his fireplace that night, whatever cabinet appointments James had suggested, went to the grave with William Henry. On April 17, James headed a committee to plan an appropriate tribute to the fallen leader.[12]

Vice President Tyler took over the vacated office, but was ineffective. He did not follow the Whig party line. He attempted to be as independent as Jackson had been, and only succeeded in splitting the Whigs. The Democrats seized the opportunity, blocking all of Tyler's legislation. The arguing disgusted Lanier who was a master of political accommodation.

Once again JFD was absent when the May 1841 meeting of the bank board came to order. There was great discouragement that neighboring states were not willing to resume specie payments. Reluctantly the board decided they would have to postpone resumption.[13]

The Lafayette branch now took center stage as the problem child. Records revealed no reduction in accommodation loans to stockholders and branch board members as previously directed. Because of the "embarrassed position" of the branch,

196

any dividend would apply to the outstanding loans of the stockholders.[14]

If the penal system in Indiana was "a moth on the treasury" in 1830, the internal improvements system was a voracious monster, gobbling up all of the state's available capital. The bank held state securities totaling about $366,000 plus interest. Because of the fiscal condition of the state, the bonds were worth about sixty percent of their face value. This large, apparently uncollectable debt, forced the board to reduce discounts and accept only prompt paper with a term of not over eight months. They also mandated that twenty percent of outstanding debt be paid every four months. After much discussion the board directed the branches to collect all possible suspended debt.[15]

Although the Lawrenceburg branch was still delinquent, the vote to suspend branch operation lost.[16] It was once again apparent that the state board had no backbone to uphold, nor teeth to enforce its mandates. Even when faced with public condemnation, branches could defy the board without fear of serious consequence.

On the other hand, those branches that followed the state board policies, such as the one at Madison, remained healthy and strong. They not only provided their customers with needed capital, but they continued to return a sizable dividend to their stockholders. It was these branches, and the individuals that ran them, that gained the Second State Bank of Indiana the reputation of the strongest bank in the West.

The Vernon to Queensville section of the Madison & Indianapolis Railroad opened on June 1, 1841. The state had spent $1,624,292.00 on the project and was running out of funds.[17] There were only enough funds left to finish the Madison Cut. The cut was critical to the success of the rail line. Without direct access to the Ohio River, the railroad would lose much of its efficiency. While not involved directly, James often visited the work site and talked to Alexander Williamson, the chief construction engineer on the project.

The workers lived in tents close to the right-of-way. Some hardworking men had installed wood slab floors. Most gang foremen had hammered together slab huts. Narrow paths meandered between the dwellings. A policeman in "Irish Hollow" could wander for days in search of a crook. The doctor always received exact directions to a patient.

Finally the crews removed the last wagon-load of rock, and spiked the last rail in place. The town held a grand party to celebrate the completion of the cut. They saluted Williamson and the 2,000, mostly Irish, laborers. The speeches were short, and the dances were long. The whiskey outlasted the food, and the drinkers outlived the darkness.

Until a special engine arrived to pull loaded cars up the grade, the railroad employed an eight horse hitch. Cars were lowered by gravity to the waiting river steamers.[18] The state took control of the railroad in June of 1841. The prospects of the line looked good, and the legislature decided that the state might as well gain all the profit

The state was unable to meet the interest payments on the Internal Improvement Bonds due July 1, 1841, and legally defaulted. Despite pleas by Fund Commissioner Noah Noble and State Treasurer Dunn, the bank could not pay the interest. Noble and Dunn went East to try to sell state seven percent bonds but got few takers.

Lanier was back on the attack at the August 1841, bank board meeting. A letter strongly criticizing the Lawernceburg branch had been delivered to the state board. The charges were serious, and could damage the entire system if substantiated. The best JFD could do was to get another committee appointed to look into these new allegations.[19]

The key locks that protected the vaults at the various branches worried JFD. The locks were proving to be undependable. On one of his trips to New York City, he had seen the new "combination" locks demonstrated, and believed them to be far superior to the key systems. He proposed that all branches adopt the policy of having someone "sleep in close proximity to the vaults each night" until they installed "the Patent Combination Lock sold by Mr. Cornell Althouse, 443 Broadway, New York City."[20]

Lanier harped on the fact that Lawrenceburg, Lafayette, South Bend and Fort Wayne continued to have too many bills in circulation. He also bemoaned the large amount of suspended debt. His manner remained civil, but his words cut deeply. His eyes bored into each board member in turn, forcing each to nod in agreement, or turn away. His committee recommended that all efforts be directed toward reducing these two liabilities.

James proposed the unthinkable. The bank should disregard

profits during the next several months until liabilities were under control. No one could protest. Lanier held the largest block of state bank stock, so if he was willing to forego a profit, the others could only silently wince. He held up the Holy Grail of specie resumption, and confidently predicted that specie payment resumption by early in 1842. The state bank must be ready.[21]

The wheels of Justice moved slowly in the wilderness of northern Indiana. It was not until October 5, 1841, that it appeared the Treadway matter was coming to a head. James wrote that day praising Niles for his efforts. **"I am really pleased to know that I am about to get through with that man Treadway."** He once again expressed his wish to get $10.00 per acre for the land.[22]

The election in the Fall of 1841 saw the demise of the Whigs in the Indiana legislature. The voters elected Jesse Bright to represent Jefferson County. Both Jesse and Michael Bright were rabid Democrats. Michael could separate business and politics, and shared several business interests with Lanier. Jesse took politics more seriously. He counted as friends only those who regularly fed the Rooster.

For James the election took second billing. Elisabeth informed James that if all went well he would be a grandfather in the summer. James was ecstatic.

The pressure was on the bank branches again as stories of the possible resumption spread throughout the state. To prepare for resumption, people were exchanging notes from remote branches for those closer to home. The bankers, on the other hand, tried to keep these notes in circulation to ease the coming crunch. Lanier wrote to Morris on October 2, 1841:

> **It was my intention not to send home any small notes but the notes of other branches are crowding on us so fast that we must do so.**[23]

By November of 1841, the investigation of Lawrenceburg was complete. It found that Daniel Major, Branch President, and state board representative, had converted $2500 of bank funds for his own use. He recalled a Bill of Exchange worth $2,450 endorsed by Thomas Guard (Major's in-law); and refused to press collection of a long outstanding note for $1800.00 endorsed by his father in law.[24]

Lanier rose to address the board. His voice was calm and his

199

manner deliberate. Those who knew James heard an unfamiliar hardness in his voice. They saw a cold, dangerous light in his eyes. He looked directly at the Lawrenceburg representative as he recited the sins. As he proposed the immediate suspension of the branch, JFD could have been a judge pronouncing the death sentence.

Major's friends on the board weakly proposed another committee be appointed to look further into the matter. This was the first actual suspension. There were legal, ethical and moral considerations they argued. Suspension of Lawrenceburg damaged the reputation of the entire system, they forecast. Lanier answered each point and turned away each challenge with the cold logic of a prosecutor who knew he had an open and shut case.

The board was under James' spell as completely as any jury ever had been. They defeated the attempt to form another committee, and passed the resolution for suspension of the branch.[25] Pressing the attack against miscreants, Lanier now criticized the directors of the South Bend branch for excessive loans. The condition of the branch was precarious. JFD proposed that they be prohibited from making any new loans or discounts or from even purchasing any bills of exchange. He demanded the local board call in the debts as soon as possible; make all efforts to collect suspended debt; and reduce circulation. In a move that never failed to get local directors' attention, Lanier proposed that no dividend be paid at the branch. It was a desperate prescription aimed at saving a patient's life. The board agreed to all the proposals.[26]

Again the board discussed specie resumption.. All agreed that lack of specie circulation caused a wide range of problems. Lack of confidence in the bank, and in the government; an open defiance of the law; and a disregard for contracts were but a few examples cited. Lack of specie payments fomented a general demoralization of the country. "A sound circulating medium is as important to the community as fresh air is to the sick or convalescent" offered one board member. John Law was adamant that the best tonic for all the fiscal ills was quick and decisive resumption.[27]

Some board members wanted to resume specie payment immediately, whether other states did or not. Some even suggested that individual branches resume payment if the branch boards decided to do so.

Others argued it would be fiscal suicide for a branch to resume payments alone. People from all over the state, even from out of state, would flock to the branch and suck every last shekel from the vaults. The state bank had to act in concert. Others argued that Indiana could not resume alone. There would be a rush to the Indiana bank counters that would make the Great Migration look like a stragglers' parade. Indiana needed at least Ohio and Kentucky to go along. After a long and heated discussion, those favoring resumption in concert with other states won.. To get the vote, they had to agree to a definite date for resumption. The directors appointed Morris, Law and Lanier to contact other states.[28]

The board discussed the state debt in detail and decided to apply every political pressure possible to persuade the legislature to pay the debts. One tactic suggested was to promise resumption when the state paid her debts. Another would have credited interest earned on state owned bank shares against the state debt. The proposals had strong political implications. Those opposed wanted time to evaluate the question. The board voted to refer the question back to the individual branch boards.[29]

As had been proven so many times in the past, approval of sanctions was easy. Enforcement was almost impossible. Once away from Lanier's damning accusations, Major fought back. "Immediate" suspension of the Lawrenceburg branch took months.

A bill before the legislature proposed lowering the appraisal value of land sold by Sheriff's sale. In a letter to J.B. Niles dated December 11, 1841, James gave some instruction about land in Marshall County he had purchased from John Walker and then sold to James Falconer. He adds:

> It will be well to have the Treadway land sold soon as the present Legislature will put the appraisement lien to 2/3 or 3/4.[30]

On December 12 Lanier pens another request for bank notes from distant branches in an effort to maintain the circulation.:

> Morris:
> Can you send us some Indiana paper? Mr. Chapman wrote me that he had sent a package of Bank notes to your care for us. Can you find a safe opportunity to send them . . .[31]

201

On January 11, 1842, just before leaving for the South, Lanier wrote Morris again:

**We are greatly in want of the back up of money in your vaults sent by the branch at South Bend for us. You will much oblige me by getting it a safe conveyance by first chance.**[32]

Toward the end of January 1842, James took his entire family to New Orleans. It was becoming a ritual to visit the South during the worst of the Madison winter. The climate seemed to help Elisabeth's worsening consumption. JFD checked out the health of several southern banks, and exchanged southern currency while the children enjoyed the boat trip and the big city. In a letter to Alexander at Yale, dated Feb. 24, 1842, Drusilla relayed the joys of the trip. At 17 Drusilla was old enough to understand the problems of a financial panic and relayed them to her brother. She seems little worried for her own well being, however, having faith that her 'pa' will set things right:

We returned from New Orleans Thursday after three weeks absence and spent in the most agreable (sic) manner you can possibly imagin (sic). I never enjoyed myself so much before nor do I expect to soon again. We expected to be gon(sic) four r five weeks, at the least but we changed our minds after we had been in New Orleans several days. We went down on the Grey Eagle which is the largest and finest boat on the river. We left Louisville Saturday noon and arrived in New O the next Saturday at one oclo . . . the weather was just warm enough to make it comfortable though we slept with our windows raised and we used ice in our water all the time and had the musquto(sic) bars up . . . we boarded at the St. Charles Exchange where Pa met a number of his acquaintances and which added to our pleasure.

There is nothing new in Madison except that the gentlemen that whose(sic) family were living in all the luxury and comfort of life have not money to go to market now. Pa says that since he returned that had he known, that money was so scarce or would have been that he would have remained at home. He said yesterday that he was very much afraid that he could not keep you at New Haven indeed he says that he can not if we do not curtail our family expences. (sic) So we have dismissed our white girl and keep but Lindy and a little Black girl we have taken to raise.[33]

Things had gotten much worse while JFD was in the South, so James changed his strategy. On February 21, JFD wrote Morris:

**You will much oblige us by laying up all of the notes of this branch which you now have in hand or may hereafter get, as we are desirous of getting in all we can. Please advise us from time to time of the amount you have.**[34]

Earlier the plan was to disperse the notes, but still oblige the solid borrowers. The new plan was to withdraw notes from circulation to keep the bank sound. Banking in that period was not for the weak at heart or the indecisive manager.

Another distressing letter greeted Lanier when he got home. James discovered that Niles had not sold the Treadway land and it came under the provisions of the new law. He wrote a stinging letter to Niles:

> I have greatly to regret that the property has not been sold before the late law took effect. I . . . gave particular instruction to avoid it. After all my trouble and expense I am worse off than when I began. The appraisement is most outrageous as Treadway was to give me but $12 per acre for the prairie and 3$ for the worst land during the highest prices.[35]

As bleak as the fiscal picture was, James would not let work on the house slacken. The family had moved to a house James had acquired on the corner of Second and Elm. The turmoil and dirt from building precluded staying in the house next to the construction site. Each day James made his way to the work site to check on progress.

The new house sat on the "second bank" safe from any possible flood. It was just west of the old house, almost adjacent to the shed and a summer kitchen. James could not decide what to do with the present dwelling. It certainly was an intrusion on his mansion, but he could rent it, and this was not a time to eliminate income sources.

The conservatory was another concern. James had his heart set on a formal garden between the river and the mansion. He had seen drawings of modern glass conservatories and wanted to build one to complement the garden. He agonized over the cost. He might have to delay the conservatory and the gardens..

The work never progressed fast enough to suit JFD, so Costigan was reluctant to admit that the new house would not be ready until the Spring of 1844. Lanier's calm surprised him. Secretly the news relieved James. Perhaps by then, the fiscal situation would improve.

Nathan Palmer released his report in May 1842. It was exhaustive. The report pleased JFD. It highlighted all of the weak areas James had previously crusaded against. Some board members grumbled privately that Lanier and Palmer collaborated. It was generally favorable to the management of the bank. Palmer singled out Lawrenceburg for criticism. "It (the Lawrenceburg branch) appears to be under the control of those who used the institution with an eye to their individual interest too much scheming and favoritism ending in a large amount of suspended debt."[36] JFD could not have said it better himself.

Palmer found that a major problem was the citizen's loss of confidence in the bank. Litigation tied up about $750,000 of bank loans. This plus the loss from advances to the Internal Improvements Fund had seriously crippled the bank. Palmer did ferret out one thief that Lanier had missed: Aaron Fontaine, the cashier at Terre Haute had embezzled $9,500. Fontaine fled to Texas before Palmer filed charges.[37]

The 1842 Legislature, deciding it could not hang the bank, moved to put the internal improvements nightmare in the history books. They voted to contract private companies to finish the internal improvement projects. To any company willing to undertake the work, the state would sign over all the property of the state connected with the improvements.[38]

Another portion of the rambling act provided that a state agent be appointed to take charge of the state's affairs in the East. The first agent appointed was Michael G. Bright.[39] Before he went east, Bright spent almost a year trying to sort out internal improvements fact from fraud. The senate formed a separate investigative committee headed by Senator Joseph C. Eggleston of Switzerland County.[40]

JFD sent Jesse Whitehead to represent Madison at the February 1842 meeting of the board.[41] Without Lanier, the report that the conditions at South Bend and Lawrenceburg were improving, and that the directors had seen the error of their ways, went unchallenged.[42]

The suspended debt owed the bank was still a major problem, totaling $542,900.[43] The committee on the state of the bank was appalled at the failure of the branches to reduce circulation in direct contradiction of a board order at the last meeting. The committee wrote in the minutes:

> Branches seem to be asleep, and folding their arms in conscious security while they are standing on the verge of a volcano which threatens ere long to engulf us all in one common destruction[44]

The committee made their point. The board dictated that

any branch that did not reduce its circulation to prescribed levels by April 30, 1842, would incur the direct and unqualified censure of the Board.[45] The Evansville branch was in serious trouble, having a state debt due the branch of $104,486; outstanding state bonds totaling $19,000 and suspended debt equaling $19,000. Efforts to solve the problem over the last quarter had fallen short. The board instructed the branch to reduce their circulation by $20,000. by April 30.[46] They also decided that the reduction in circulation be accompanied by an increase in specie. They hoped to heal the balance sheet by treating both ends of the problem.

The bank was still reluctant to accept State Treasury Notes. This caused much confusion and consternation when cashiers turned customers away at the bank counters. It was one more evidence to the legislature that the bank was not responsive. In February, the board finally caved in to the inevitable. They decided to accept State Treasury Notes, specie, or Indiana Bank Notes as payment for the various state debts. As discounted as Treasury Notes were, they were better than nothing.[47] The decision also kept the legislative wolves from the bank's door.

By May of 1842 it was evident that the branches had listened to the board. They greatly reduced circulation.. The branches at Fort Wayne, Evansville, and Vincennes had reduced circulation as low as possible. Poor business conditions prevented further recall of notes at these branches.[48]

The board applied the state's quarterly dividend to her loans. They allowed the Lafayette, Bedford, Evansville, and South Bend branches a dividend of 2 1/2 per cent. The other branches awarded a dividend of 3 percent.[49] The directors requested a full report on the condition of the sinking fund, and a plan for repayment of the debt it owned the bank. Nathan B. Palmer had taken over as Agent for the Sinking Fund.[50] JFD was confident Palmer would set the fund in order.

Under pressure from the Legislature, the board resolved to resume specie payment on or before June 15. 1842.[51] The branches needed to retrieve bank paper from Cincinnati before announcing specie resumption. It was Lanier's opinion that some branches would have to make sacrifices, but the bank would survive.[52]

Lanier was in Cincinnati in May, and missed the board meeting. He found a locksmith there that handled "combination" locks for banks. Cincinnati bankers insisted the Canal Bank was close to bankruptcy. The Canal Bank was a stalwart bank in New Orleans, if it was failing, resumption was impossible. He wrote to Morris on the 19th:

> **I found now $12,000 of our notes there (Cincinnati) I think there is not a very large amount of Inda. money in cinti. We have bad reports about the New Orleans Canal Bank.** [53]

The state was not prospering in the railroad business, so a group of investors proposed purchasing the Madison and Indianapolis rail line under the terms of the 1842 law allowing disposal of internal improvements. The talks with the state continued for several months. JFD followed the talks with great interest.

On June 14, Elisabeth delivered the first Lanier grandson.[54] In the Lanier family tradition he was named for his paternal grandfather, James Lanier Dunn. Grandpa James was beside himself with happiness. He visited his grandson as often as time, distance and Elisabeth would allow. It surprised his friends that this normally introspective and quiet man would talk incessantly about his namesake. James reveled in being a grandfather.

In July, a request came to Governor Bigger to pardon Michael Brennan. After considering the case and the evidence presented at the trial, Bigger decided Brennan had acted in self defense, and granted the pardon.[55] He set March 1, 1843, as Brennan's release date. The man who came within ten days of death walked out a free man. He was eternally grateful to those who, engulfed in crushing problems, realized that life was more important than money, and took the time to speak in his defense.

JFD was still doing business with Judge Polke. He wrote Polke in August of 1842 for an opinion on some land along the Tippecanoe River, and on a tract in Kosciusko County. Lanier liked to get ahead of the crowd and often purchased land before the county organized. He asked Polke where he should pay taxes as Kosciusko County was, as yet, unorganized.[56]

James made another trip to Cincinnati in August. Upon his return he wrote to Niles asking if Treadway has paid any rent or has paid anything on the mortgage. He asked Niles to pay the taxes if Treadway had not.[57]

206

Lanier decided to put his land in the North under the plow. He might as well obtain income from the land while he waited for land prices to improve. On one of his trips east, JFD found a man to farm his land. In his August letter he introduced John Vanderverihen to Niles. Vanderverihen, from Cherry Valley, New York, was **"very industrious and honest."** JFD asked Niles to advance John money if he needed it and to send an accounting to Madison for reimbursement. He then gave Niles some detailed instructions on land deals he wanted consummated including: **"Please use some care in making out deeds for me for the Treadway land."**[58]

Although he had once suggested the legislature might authorize "Treasury Notes," they now worried JFD He studied the pros and cons of the notes closely. On August 21, 1842, he wrote to Morris stating that to his complete satisfaction the issuing of the treasury notes was unconstitutional. He cautioned however **"It is best to say nothing about it."**[59] He must have feared a citizen's revolt if they found out that the legislature had compounded the financial problem rather than solved it by issuing the treasury notes.

Little James became ill in October. He could not seem to shake the illness. JFD undoubtedly did all of the things grandfathers have done through the ages. He visited the boy often to cheer him up and to check on his care. He quizzed his daughter. He questioned the doctor closely. He prayed. He begged. He cajoled. Nothing helped.

On November 3, 1842, James Lanier Dunn died.[60] It was a terrible blow to lose his first grandson and namesake. James was devastated. His 42nd birthday passed without celebration.

Slowly the bank worked its magic. Work once again healed Lanier. The fiscal problems demanded all of his attention. Demand for currency was draining the bank vaults. By December the bank was back at the practice of "wildcatting." On December 29, James wrote to Morris:

> By Sam Sering I send package of our notes $10,000 hoping that the Michigan City Br. has sent that amount of their notes to be exchanged with us.[61]

# 19.
## "A robbery of a most daring and successful character . . ."
— Madison Banner March 2, 1844

*The next two years would bring a glimpse of a new career for James Lanier. It would also provide one of the sternest tests of his professional and personal integrity.*

It took months for the lawyers, accountants and politicians to struggle through the litter of paperwork and the babel of arguments surrounding the internal improvements debacle. The Cohen Brothers failed owing over $300,000. They gave the state a portfolio of worthless stocks, bonds, and mortgages including a sperm oil and candle factory in New York. The Bank of Western New York, and the Erie County Bank (New York) were both founded using Indiana Internal Improvement Bonds as collateral for incorporation. They both went under paying less than 35¢ on the dollar.[1]

The Morris Canal and Banking Company and J.D. Beers and Company were major debtors accounting for several million dollars in losses between them. Dr. Coe was on the board of directors of both these companies. Nicholas Biddle was a major stockholder in Morris Canal and Banking.[2] All of these compa-

nies sold and resold Indiana bonds until the trail was so complicated that an Indiana coon dog could not follow the track. Still,
Michael Bright persevered. Still, Senator Eggleston led his state
senate investigating committee through the fiscal swamp.

It was amid this climate of profound confusion that James
Lanier and others on the bank board worked to keep the state
bank of Indiana solvent. The wild fluctuations of inflation and
recession, of jubilation and dismay, beat like waves on a shore.
The trick was to anticipate the ebb and flow so that the undertow was not crushing. It was a difficult struggle, but a struggle
that James loved.

Michael Bright's first report to the Governor came in December 1842. There was no good news. The words were etched
in the deepest black of doom and the figures reflected the
abysmal red of failure. Bright concluded that the state had issued in aggregate, $15,000,000 worth of bonds. From these
bonds the state had collected $8,593,000 in cash, and held
$4,000,000 in securities, most of them worthless. The balance,
over $2,400,000, was unaccounted for. Bright reported the funds
embezzled by those associated with the internal improvements
fund.[3] Coe and Stapp were the prime suspects. The legislature
produced reams of accusations and promised lawsuits.

The Madison and Indianapolis rail line cost the state
$1,624,291.93 and the bill was still rising. The state operation of
the line had been unsuccessful. The administration still hoped
to realize some gain from the railroad, so contracted with a new
group to run the operations. Under the agreement, the state retained ownership for the first 28 miles north of Madison. The
contractor would pay the state a yearly rent of about $1100.
After 1846 the contractor and the state would share in the revenue of the line based upon the percentage of track built by
each.[4] The legislature told the contractors to find an alternate
route to the river, and abandon the incline. Under this arrangement the Madison and Indianapolis railroad re-organized on
June 17,1842. John Brough became president, and John Cravens
vice president.[5] Brough was from Ohio with strong political connections in that state. The legislature hoped an outsider could
make the line profitable. Brough's first order of business was to
find a better route to the river.

The state deeded the unimproved right-of-way to the company. The company could purchase the state portion of the road

209

at any time by depositing with the state treasurer state bonds equal to the amount the state had expended on the line.[6] John Brough immediately began designing and constructing a route out of the valley. It would run along the face of a hill west of Madison and involved at least one tunnel. The plan was ill-conceived and the cost excessive. The idea became known as "Brough's Folly." The project drove the company into bankruptcy.

The electorate once again decried the incompetence of their elected officials. The administration began looking desperately for a buyer. A group of investors from Madison stepped forward. Although savaged by detractors in the legislature and the press, Milton Stapp led the negotiations on behalf of the state. There is no record of who negotiated the deal for the investors. JFD wanted desperately to see the rail line become a success as did N. B. Palmer. They both became actively involved. Michael Bright played a major role in saving the railroad. In 1848 the line's newest engine became the "M.G. Bright."[7]

The law stated that investors could purchase internal improvements outright if they paid the state the amount the state had paid for construction.[8] There was no prohibition against payment with state bonds. At the time of the negotiations, the bonds were worth about 37 cents on the dollar. The investors balked at the $600,000 price tag. The final agreement stated that the investors would pay the state $200,000 in cash in four years.[9]

The investors accepted some serious risk. Floods had ruined canals, and could do almost as much damage to railroads. Wrecks were commonplace on rail lines and could close a track for weeks. To be a financial success, the line had to reach Indianapolis. The new group needed money to finish construction. In the throes of Indiana's internal improvement problems, fresh cash and willing investors were scarce.

The state negotiators and investors concluded the deal in February of 1843. N.B. Palmer became president of the line. [10] JFD joined the board of directors. Lanier was in his element. As when he started with the bank ten years earlier, James worked hard to learn the business. With a skill learned in the court room, and honed on the state bank board, he bent the M & I board to his will.

Under the leadership of Palmer and Lanier, the Madison and Indianapolis Railroad began to prosper. The income from February 20, 1843, to Feb. 1, 1844 totaled $24,385.[11] The expenses totaled $12,960 or $36.00 per day in operating expenses including the pay of eighteen full time employees.[12] In addition, repair and maintenance on the line cost another $7,000.00. The board reserved $6,500 dollars for a new engine. The balance of the profits they used to retire debt and pay dividends.[13]

JFD was a master at balancing several enterprises. He remained deeply involved in the bank as well as land speculation in northern Indiana. All through the winter of 1842 and spring of 1843 James corresponded with J.B. Niles on various land matters. The Treadway problem continued to plague him. The only real hold James had on Griffin Treadway was a title bond worth $150-$200.

In May of 1843, James finally devised a plan to rid himself of Treadway. He explained the plan to Niles in a long letter. Griffin Treadway has a brother, identified only as R. Treadway in the correspondence.[14]

James held a judgment in Jefferson County against a Mr. Goodman. Mr. Goodman held a judgment against R. Treadway. To satisfy his debt to James, Goodman was willing to sign over R. Treadway's judgment. Griffin Treadway was a co-signer to his brother's debt. If R. Treadway could not pay his debt, the burden would fall to Griffin. James proposed taking Treadway's land to satisfy the debt and to release the bond he held against Griffin.

James took his annual trip to the South in February. He took a large amount of southern bank paper collected from all of the branches and redeemed it at face value at the southern bank counters. He was a well known and respected figure in the South and dined in the private residences of many of the bankers, exchanging fiscal observations and forecasts over wine before dinner and brandy after dinner.

The bank board meetings in February and May of 1843 were uneventful. The financial situation in the state was improving, and the branches and directors worked in harmony. The board glossed over problems with the wayward branches.

In August 1843, JFD became a grandfather again. Elisabeth named her second child William McKee Dunn Jr.[15] James was happy but much more subdued. He loved the little boy, but was afraid to become too attached to him for fear that some curse would envelop him.

The railroad opened the first depot in Madison on the Ohio River, between West and Mulberry streets, in 1843. It was 150 feet long, and 50 feet wide.[16] The depot swarmed with workers and allowed for the rapid transfer of cargo between rail cars and packet ships. It did not take an active imagination to realize that Madison was on the threshold of an economic boom.

In the summer of 1843 the Indianapolis branch, in a complicated transaction with the Bedford branch, issued some currency signed by Thomas Sharpe, a deputy cashier at Indianapolis. This upset Sam Merrill. The Bank Charter required that all notes be signed by the branch cashier, not a deputy cashier. At the August meeting, Merrill persuaded the board to void the deal between Bedford and Indianapolis. It also declared the bills signed by the deputy cashier to be improper and asked that they be recalled.[17]

Calvin Fletcher, representing the Indianapolis branch, was furious. He argued that the board had repeatedly turned a blind eye to the most flagrant misappropriation of funds, but now was cracking down on a minor infraction. He felt that Merrill led the attack against Indianapolis because the branch had refused to loan him $1500. Fletcher further speculated that Merrill was attempting to make new friends because he would need influence with the Democrats for re-election in the spring.[18]

Fletcher was right. The board was not consistent in its penalties. The Lawrenceburg branch, for all its transgressions, did not suffer suspension until Novem-

**PROTECTION**

The Protection Insurance Company of Hartford, Connecticut, continues to insure all kinds of property, against loss or damage by fire or water, on favorable terms. As the Company expect to merit the confidence of the public, by pursuing the most liberal and just course in all its business, I would refer for character of the Company to the following persons to whom losses have been paid at Madison,

| | | |
|---|---|---|
| Martin Picquet, received | | $6,070,00 |
| JFD Lanier, | " | 800 00 |
| C.G.Core | " | 200 00 |
| Polleys & Butler | | |
| Pitcher & Vanbrunt | " | 1,654 50 |
| A.W. Pitcher, | " | 1,500 00 |

E.G. WHITNEY, Agent.
Madison, Indiana
Dec. 2d 1843

**Men sought out Lanier as business associates because of his unblemished record of success. His endorsement, either political or financial, was gold in the vault. E.G. Whitney, Madison agent for The Protection Insurance Company of Hartford Connecticut tried to capture some of that gold by portraying JFD as a happy customer.**

ber of 1843. Political judgments were ruling the board. Political loyalties previously left in the hallway outside the meeting room became invited guests. Long time friends argued with one another. Financial alliances dissolved in favor of political ones.

Lanier, who reveled in private political maneuvering, but despised public political dog fights, attended fewer meetings. He had other interests. Construction on his house was progressing rapidly. The M & I was at a critical juncture.

If Merrill had been wooing votes, it did him no good. In January of 1844, Samuel Merrill's ten year reign as president of the Second Indiana State Bank came to an end. The vote in the legislature was strictly along party lines. A Democrat replaced a Whig. Judge Morrison, a good party man, became the new president.[19]

The election loss had a serious financial effect on Sam Merrill. He had used his position to obtain many loans. While not so delinquent as many officers, he had exceeded his credit limit. No longer bank president, Merrill was a poor risk. He wrote his brother on January 17, 1844: "I must have much trouble for two or three years with my debts, but as the prospect for improvement of the times are much more favorable, I hope to get along"[20]

Fletcher gave grudging praise to Merrill. He felt Samuel was very hardworking and was usually right in theory and principal. When Merrill's own interests or popularity were at stake, however, Calvin thought the president was excessively self serving.[21] Whatever his contemporaries thought of Merrill, history certainly gives him high marks for being one of the prime reasons that the Second State Bank of Indiana was successful.

Fletcher was very unhappy with Judge Morrison. He had argued before the judge in court, and did not think his rulings outstanding. He felt the judge had no background in banking and felt Morrison was completely unfit for the job. Calvin did promise to support Morrison if he was right, but vowed to oppose him whenever he was wrong.[22]

Later in January, Isaac Dunn from Lawrenceburg tried to stir up trouble for the bank by stating publicly that its paper was worthless. Merrill took up the fight. Charges and accusations flew between the two antagonists. Dunn sued Merrill for libel, and Merrill sued Dunn for perjury. After two years of haranguing, both sides withdrew their charges and the dispute died a quiet death. The incident serves to illustrate how the bank had become meal for the political mill.

James found reasons to miss the contentious bank board meetings and send substitutes. He would run the Madison branch with a clean honest hand and avoid controversy. The economic situation was beginning to heal. This was no time to be poking the wound.

Drusilla was 19 years old. Love had overcome John Cravens' awe of JFD and the young man had been earnestly courting Drusilla for some months. James and Elisabeth were happy with the match. John's father was a doctor and the family were longtime residents of Madison. James advised the couple to wait and be married in the new house, but understood their impatience.

> MARRIED.—On the 1st. inst. by the Rev. Mr. Curtis, *Mr. John Robert Cravens*, to *Miss Drusilla A. Lanier*, daughter of Jas. F.D. Lanier, Esq., both of this city.
> Feb. 3, 1844

This announcement appeared in the *Madison Banner* after Drusilla's wedding.

After the wedding, the house seemed very empty without the energetic Drusilla swishing along the hallways.

In the spring of 1844 the state indicted Dr. Coe. It did not come to trial until the fall. Calvin Fletcher acted as defense council for his long time friend. Fletcher stated in his diary that this would be the last case he would try.[23] He wanted to devote more time to farming. Delays and postponements filled the court records.

All of the investigations of internal improvement fraud, while cleansing the wound, did not silence the infuriated Hoosier electorate. Citizens felt a double outrage. First, state agents stole millions of dollars that should have financed the internal improvements. Then, the faltering projects were "stolen" by financiers who paid ten cents on the dollar for state property. The arrangement did relieve the state of crushing financial obligations, however, so the politicians hunkered down to wait out the verbal storm.

James took the steamboat to Cincinnati on February 27. He wanted to visit several banks, and to do some shopping for the house. He planned to return on the packet the next day. Early on the 28th, a man who had often acted as a bank messenger appeared at James' breakfast table. The messenger asked to speak

214

to James privately on a matter of utmost urgency. James led the way back to his room and the two men talked in front of the freshly stoked fireplace.

The previous night the Madison branch bank had been robbed. The man who slept in the bank came late and had found the inner doors open. He contacted Mr. Sering at once, who had determined that money was missing. Sering immediately dispatched the messenger who traveled most of the night to find Mr. Lanier.

James had the man repeat his story, more to gather his own wits than to garner more details. As the messenger talked, James began to pack his suitcase. His mind raced, but he asked few questions. JFD settled his bill but arranged for the messenger to use the room to rest. He wrote notes to men he had planned to meet that day, and had them delivered. Lanier then talked to some police officers about the robbery. He arrived early at the wharf to board the Madison packet.

Although the trip seemed to take twice as long as normal, James reverted to his old habit of using travel time to plan his actions. He pondered. He made lists. He wrote letters. The robbery unnerved James. He prided himself on running the bank under the strictest rules, and strongest security. He looked upon other robberies as the result of a lax operation. JFD had advised all of the branches to obtain the new keyless combination locks. He had been too slow in ordering them for the Madison branch.

He knew his enemies on the bank board would attack him because of the robbery. He decided that rather than hide, he would attack. He would authorize a reward ad for the same newspaper issue that reported the theft. He hoped avarice would spur honesty and good intentions.

Immediately upon arriving in Madison he had a long private discussion with John Sering. He asked for details of the break-in and viewed the locks. He interviewed the night man and tried to determine how the crooks knew when he would be absent. Both the night watchman and Sering seemed halting and nervous under Lanier's cross examination. James could not detect any deliberate evasion in their answers, however.

On March 1, 1844, James sent a note to Indianapolis by special messenger.[24] It read in part: **"You are . . . advised of the robbery of this branch by false keys on Monday night last** between the hours of 7 and 10 O'clock, and $27.370 abstracted therefrom."

The letter went on to describe the currency taken, and gave some instruction on how to handle bills of the same denomination credited to the Madison Branch. A final sentence stated **"Please do not mention out of doors what you are doing"**

The robbery was the main topic of conversation for weeks afterwards, and every stranger in town drew at least a small degree of suspicion. The fact that no break-in occurred gave life to rumors that it was an inside job. James easily proved he was in Cincinnati at the time of the robbery. Although no one of standing in Madison would admit to harboring the slightest suspicion of James, there were those who would relish his downfall. No one was as successful as JFD without gaining enemies or exciting feelings of envy and jealousy.

The river rats and stevedores were under no social code of silence. Even the young boiler monkeys and roustabouts realized Lanier could have supplied the keys for duplication and arranged to be out of town for the actual robbery. Who really knew how much Lanier had lost in the last panic? That new house he was building was a castle. No one hoped to see better in their lifetime. Lanier lived in high fashion. Perhaps he needed the money to maintain his lifestyle. JFD felt considerable embarrassment and discomfort. He knew the town was alive with rumors. He had to do something to still them.

Lanier made the apprehension of the robber his prime responsibility in the ensuing months. He used the contacts and techniques gained as a prosecuting attorney. He again questioned John Sering and the night guard at the bank. Since law enforcement was scarce at Madison, he brought in detectives from Cincinnati and made several trips to Cincinnati to consult with them. The problem continued to eat at Lanier. He financed several trips to New Orleans.

James wondered about John Sering's involvement in the robbery, and immediately dismissed the thought. Still, the old man was sick and was not as attentive to business as he should be. He was keeper of the keys He did have opportunity. James even questioned if the recent slack business was due to the cashier's inattention. Doubt nagged in the back recesses of JFD's mind. He became increasingly unhappy with John Sering's behavior and began pressuring Sering to resign.

## Madison
### Saturday Morning, March 2, 1844

Bank Robbery.— A robbery of a most daring and successful character was committed in this city on Monday night last. The Branch Bank was entered and robbed of $27,370, in bills of this and various other branches of the State Bank. The deed was done between the hours of 7 and 11 o'clock last night. The money and thief or thieves are missing, and we are not aware that the slightest suspicion is entertained as to the person who committed the robbery. There seems as yet no possible clue that can lead in the remotest degree to his discovery. It was a bold trick and must have been executed in a most prompt and masterly manner. It is evident, we think, that it was done by an old and experienced burglar, well supplied with implements of his trade; and it seems probable likewise that he had been sometime on the watch and mastering his plans for the accomplishment of the robbery. He must have known the officers of the bank, the hour of their leaving it; and also that the young man who slept in the bank was absent on the evening of the robbery, and would not probably return until a late hour. He must have had a good knowledge of the size and make of the locks on the alley door, the bank parlor door, the external and internal doors of the vault, and on the safe within the vault; for all those it is said were unlocked and opened in the usual manner without violence and without chisel or crow-bar. As it is probable that little, if any, of the money taken, can be identified, the robber may succeed in getting the whole in circulation without detection. It is useless to speculate as to the probable thief; but we feel a strong conviction that he belongs to the same band, or perhaps is the same person, who committed the former depredations in this city; and that tho same hand that broke into the dwelling of Dr. Watts some time ago and more recently Mr. Wharton's, is the one that abstracted the money from the bank vault, having become emboldened by frequent visits and better acquaintance with the town, to make this grand effort

—See the advertisement

## 3,000 Dollars Reward
### Daring Robbery

The Madison branch Bank was entered on the night of the 27th ult. between the hours of 7 and 11 o'clock, by some daring villain or villains who must have been well provided with skeleton keys and abstracted from the safe in the vault $27,370 dollars. Two thousand dollars rewards is hereby offered for the recovery of the money and one thousand dollars for the arrest and conviction of the thief or thieves.

By order of the Board.

John Sering, Cash'r

Madison March 2, 1844.

## MADISON
### SATURDAY MORNING, MARCH 2, 1844

The RailRoad.—The Board of Directors of the Madison and Indianapolis Rail Road Company have been in session the past week.

The Board declared a dividend of eight per cent on the capital stock, out of the nett proceeds of the Road for the past year. But we understand that no money will be paid out on this dividend, but the amounts will be carried to the credit of the stockholders on the stock accounts, with a view of appropriating the money to the payments for Iron, for the further extension of the Road.

In addition to the dividend declared, an amount equal to two per cent. on the stock was set apart, out of the nett proceeds, as a surplus fund for the future disposition of the Board; making ten per ct. as the nett proceeds of the Road for the past year

The rest of the state heard about the robbery in the March 2, issue of the *Madison Courier*. It was the lead article under the Madison news. The reward notice appeared in the same paper. It was little consolation to James that the *Banner* carried the good news about the railroad stock.

217

Sering refused, feeling that to resign at this time would lead people to believe him connected with the robbery. Sering admitted that he was not as sharp as he had been in the past, but it was the sickness he had suffered over the last few months. He needed a long rest. He proposed going to Logansport. When he returned, he would be as good as new. James argued that the bank could not survive without a cashier for an extended period. Sering still balked, and the discussion became heated. John Sering's face grew red, and his breath came in short gasps as he reminded Lanier that the cashier was an elected position and the president could not remove him.

Seeing the old man's distress, James calmed down and tried to reassure Sering his reputation and his position were safe. He patiently explained the problem of running the bank without a cashier, using examples of Sering's own importance to the operation. The discussion ended with an agreement that John would take a short vacation to Logansport, and if he had not recovered in a reasonable period, a resignation would be forthcoming.

JFD tried to convince himself it had nothing to do with the robbery, but business took another down-turn. Foreclosure notices filled the paper. In June JFD was forced to begin foreclosure against his brother-in-law and fellow Mason, John Sheets. Ann Sheets was too proud to protest to her sister. It would have met with little success. Elisabeth had no influence in James' business affairs.

The railroad, too, developed problems. Palmer left the presidency of the M&I after less than 18 months. Lanier saw an opportunity to put Sam Merrill's talents to work. On June 14, 1844, he wrote Merrill urging him to take the Presidency of the Madison and Indianapolis Railroad. JFD was a major stockholder in the road and assured Merrill that **"this is the wish of the Stockholders here . . . This offer in the end will be a good one."**[25]

John Sering, although he had promised to take a vacation in the North, kept procrastinating. Despite assurances from Lanier that the bank could run without him for a few months, there was always some pressing business that only he could accomplish.

JFD was growing impatient. He wanted the robbery solved, and the problem with the cashier solved. Both were detrimental to the bank. Lanier wrote in the June 14 letter to Sam Merrill: **"Mr. Sering has not yet resigned nor is it now certain that** he will. If he does, it will be after a contemplated (trip) to the northern part of the state."

During 1844 the fiscal health of the country and the state showed steady improvement. Despite a constant undercurrent of political wrangling at bank board meetings, dividends ranged between ten and twelve percent for the year. The Madison robbery did not stir as much interest as James had feared. The general opinion seemed to be that Lanier was handling it as well as possible. It was the practice of the board to keep all robberies away from public scrutiny.

Alex was home from New Haven. His father put him to work in the firm of Ross and Lanier, a commission house dealing in flour.

In early July the robbery investigation yielded results. On July 8, Lanier wrote to Indianapolis: **"I have just brought up the robber from New Orleans, but did not get the money. We have evidence to convict. The money (has) not been found."**[26]

Sering finally decided to go North about the same time. On August 2, 1844, the name of "S. Moore" first shows up as cashier of the Madison branch.[27] John Sering's name never again appears on any bank documents.

> **BANK ROBBER**
>
> Mr. Lanier, the President of the Branch Bank in this city, returned from New Orleans on Saturday night last in the company with police officer O Neal; of Cincinnati. That officer had in his custody the notorious *David Root*, whom he arrested in New Orleans on a charge of robbing the Madison Bank in February last. This personage is well known to the police officers at New Orleans, Louisville, and Cincinnati as a bold and daring offender. We forebear to give a detailed history of him as he stands committed to prison for trial; and it is deemed prudent, for the present, to withhold the publication of the circumstances which fastened suspicion upon him, and led to his arrest.
>
> Officers Saffin and ONeal of Cincinnati, deserve great credit for their ingenuity in finding out who the offender is, and bringing him to justice—officer ONeil in particular, as he has visited New Orleans three times in pursuit of this man, and only captured him on the third visit. Besides the loss of the stolen money (no part of which has been recovered,) the Bank has been great expense in pursuit of this individual.

**This article appeared in the *Madison Republican Banner* on July 10, 1844**

# 20.
## "Mr. Sering is too sick to travel to the trial . . ."
— JFD Lanier testimony Fall 1844

*Even though he never recovered the money from the robbery, the trial of David Root was important to James Lanier. It proved that he would not let crimes against the bank go unpunished despite the cost, and it restored confidence in the state bank, especially the Madison branch. Likewise it restored the citizens' confidence in JFD Lanier.*

The *Madison Banner* of September 25, 1844, reported that the term of the Jefferson Circuit Court began on the previous Monday and would run for at least three weeks. The Grand Jury delivered a true bill against David Root and the trial commenced.

It was not unusual for the prosecution to hire outside lawyers. Those who had an interest in a case often paid for additional attorneys. Lanier saw to it that the prosecutor, John Dumont, had all the help he needed. Joseph G. Marshall, William Hendricks, M.G. Bright, and Courtland Cushing all aided the state. William Hendricks was a major stockholder in the Madison branch of the bank. Courtland Cushing served on the church board with JFD.

Jesse Bright was the only attorney defending David Root.[1] There was no concern that brothers were on opposing sides of the trial. The Judge in the case was the Honorable Miles C. Eggleston.

The amount of space each competing newspaper gave the trial, and what they chose to report, illustrates their loyalties, and political leanings.. The *Republican Banner* printed the testimony almost word for word, but evidently left out Mr. Root's final statement to the court. The *Banner* presented the trial as an "open and shut case." The *Madison Courier*, on the other hand, barely mentioned the trial.

Richard Holloway was a key witness for the prosecution. The defense objected to Mr. Holloway on the grounds that he stood convicted of burglary, sentenced to eight years in the Ohio Penitentiary. The prosecution presented a full pardon for Mr. Holloway from Ohio Governor Bartley, dated October 18, 1844. Judge Eggleston ruled that the pardon restored the witness' veracity.

Mr. Holloway testified that he had been friends with Root and another man named Buell while living in Cincinnati. The two men bragged that they were the best bank robbers in the U.S. They talked about having keys to banks at Dayton, Portsmouth, and Columbus, Ohio as well as the Northern Bank of Kentucky at Lexington. They explained that they had already made one attempt on the Madison, Indiana bank, but one key was faulty. Mr. Holloway and Mr. Root went to Lexington in the summer of 1843 to rob the Northern Bank. While there, police arrested Mr. Root for passing counterfeit money. He escaped from jail, but suffered an ankle injury that caused him a permanent limp.

After Mr. Holloway's arrest, he told Officer Jesse O'Neal of the Cincinnati police about Root's and Buell's plans to rob the Madison bank. Evidently the Cincinnati police never passed on this warning to bank officials or the sheriff in Madison.

Holloway testified that he did not know of the bank robbery until recently, and that the authorities promised nothing in return for his testimony. He learned of the pardon only a few days before the trial. Other testimony depicted Holloway as a good man from a respectable family in Cincinnati. Root and Buell led Holloway into his evil ways

The next witness was a Mr. Warmsly who stated that he saw Root and two suspicious looking men in Kentucky across from

Madison for several days before the robbery. Warmsly described their boat as a "handsome skiff, painted pale green, yellow and white with perhaps a narrow black stripe along the stanchions." Mr. Warmsly noted that Mr. Root appeared to be "wearing whiskers" at the time, but he was positive that the accused was the man he saw. Other witnesses stated that Warmsley had a "peculiar faculty for remembering countenances."

Four additional witnesses living varying distances down river corroborated Mr. Warmsly's testimony, describing Root and the skiff in detail. One of them identified Root and stated that he appeared to limp as he walked. Two witnesses testified that they saw the skiff described as belonging to Root heading down river on the morning after the Madison bank was robbed. The next witness for the prosecution was Cincinnati police officer Jesse O'Neal., who corroborated Mr. Holloway's warning of the bank robbery. Officer O'Neal stated that an informant named Vines contacted him and officer Saffin. Vines had a letter from Root corroborating what Holloway had told O'Neal.

Armed with this information, O'Neal contacted Mr. Lanier. Lanier sent O'Neal and Vines to New Orleans to find Root. They discovered Root in the workhouse, charged as a "rogue." Officer O'Neal attempted to get Root released. The New Orleans authorities would not release their prisoner.

O'Neal went back to Cincinnati, but returned to New Orleans in an effort to have Root released. Still the authorities would not budge. After meeting with Mr. Lanier, O'Neal and Vines went back to New Orleans. A few days later Lanier followed, armed with a letter from the Governor of Indiana. The letter, and Mr. Lanier's influence in New Orleans, did the trick. The authorities released Root.

Root and Vines went to a small house on "the lake." O'Neal, hidden in the house, heard Vines ask Root about where he stayed in Madison. Root said he was too smart to stay at a hotel, but said he stayed aboard a boat on the Kentucky side of the river. His description of the boat matched the one given by Mr. Warmsly and the others. Root told Vines he had stayed in Madison two days, but would not admit to robbing the bank.

Officer O'Neal arrested Root the next day. O'Neal and Lanier brought Root back to Madison on the steamboat "St. Louis". Officer O'Neal stated that Root was often talkative on the trip north. He wanted to know what the penalty for the robbery would be, and when told ten years in prison, stated, "It would be good wages if I had the money."

Root talked about other criminals, crimes, burglary devices and illegal schemes. He named many men who were "of that stripe." Root also commented that his son was in college in Ohio. Officer O'Neal testified that he knew for a fact that Root's son was in the workhouse in New Orleans. Officer O'Neal concluded his testimony by stating that Mr. Lanier had paid all the expenses for the manhunt. He (O'Neal) expected nothing more than what the Bank Directors might give him for his trouble.

JFD then took the stand. He stated that the last time he was present at the bank prior to the robbery was on February 26 about 2:00 P.M. He left Madison for Cincinnati on the mail boat about 4 o'clock on the 27th, the day of the robbery. The first he heard of the robbery was Wednesday morning when a messenger arrived with the news. Lanier said he immediately notified the Cincinnati police and posted a notice in the Cincinnati paper.

JFD testified that Mr. Sering determined the exact amount stolen to be $27,105 James described the locking system at the bank in detail. He admitted that the locking system was not as good as a combination lock. He explained that Mr. Sering kept all the keys to the bank, and that there was no duplicate key to the outside door of the bank. Mr. Lanier testified that he had received a letter from Mr. Sering stating that he was in Logansport and too sick to travel to the trial.

JFD then reiterated much of Mr. Vines' and Officer O'Neal's testimony as to what occurred in the weeks and months after the robbery, and the apprehension of Root in New Orleans. Mr. Root and Mr. Lanier had several conversations on the riverboat returning to Madison. Root told Lanier that he had been to Madison only once in the company of Officer Saffin to advise the police on some counterfeit bills of the Madison Bank. At one point Root told Lanier that he could prove he was on "The Ben Franklin" going through the canal at Louisville at the hour of the robbery. He stated that he had left the "Ben Franklin" at Milliken's Bend near Vicksburg.

The next prosecution witness was the Reverend Gamaliel Taylor. He testified that he saw Root in Madison in August or September of 1843, sitting with Mrs. Hackett on the porch of her millinery shop. The shop was on the same lot as John Sering's

223

house. Under cross examination Taylor admitted he did not see Root too well and it was only his "impression" that Root was the man at Mrs. Hackett's.

D.D. Jones, a printer took the witness stand. Mr. Jones positively identified Root as the man who came to him in the summer or autumn of 1843 to settle up a bill for Mrs. Hackett. Mr. Jones had the impression that Root was a clergyman and that Root and Mrs. Hackett were going away together.

Mr. Gurdy was the last prosecution witness. Arrested for drunkenness, he shared the jail with Root.. The witness testified that Root asked him if he would swear to a lie to prove an alibi. Gurdy decided to humor Root out of curiosity. Root sent him a note. Gurdy identified a note he received from Root. The prosecutor entered the note as evidence. It read:

> The Bank was robbed on the 27th Feb. at 8 o'clock in the evening. I left Cincinnati on board the boat the Dr. Franklin on the 25th Feb.-got to Louisville the same night. You came aboard the same night with my friend Major Neil. You both took deck passages for Smithland and- you called at Root's stateroom with Maj. Neil often-for both played checkers with me. Root came down below and talked with Neil. Root was alone in his room and Neil slept with him one night - his son, a young man was on the boat - the boat left Louisville 11 or 12 o'clock the 26th - got through the canal 3 or 4 o'clock - wooded that evening the 26th about dusk near Salt River - we left at Smithland. Such facts as you know you can state.

The prosecution rested its case and the defense began. Mr. Rivington, the clerk on the steamboat "Dr. Franklin", took the stand. He stated that the boat left Cincinnati on February 25 at 11:00 A.M. Mr. Root, or a man closely resembling him, was on the boat with a young man. He could not read the name in the passenger book, but the boy's last name was "Powers." The "Dr. Franklin" left Louisville on the 26th at half past 5. Mr. Rivington stated that he did not know Root previously.

Mr. Rivington saw Root in the Madison jail and Root recognized him as the clerk on the "Franklin". Root told some stories of what happened on the boat that he would not have known if he had not been there. Mr. Rivington said the stories were true and he especially remembered Root because he and the boy left the boat at Milliken's Bend without paying for their passage.

The defense called another witness who had measured the boot print outside the bank window. It was a size 7. He testified that Root's boots were larger than size 7. The defense then called

Mr. Russell Lathrop. He testified that he hid under Root's cot in jail during a conversation between Vines and Root. Vines suggested that Root take Lanier down to the river and show him where the money was. Root could then escape. Root said he could not show Lanier where the money was because he did not have it.

Lathrop further testified that Vines said he knew Root was innocent but had testified against him to get even for some past wrong. Vines asked how Root had known about the keys and other details he transmitted in the letters. Root said he had guessed. Under cross examination Lathrop admitted being offered twenty dollars to testify against Vines, but he refused the money.

In an effort to refute Lathrop's statements, Governor Hendricks and JFD took the stand. They testified that they heard Vines say he would have one more meeting with Root and try to convince him by all statements he could make, true and untrue, to tell him where the money was. This was the meeting Mr. Lathrop overheard.

After deliberating for a day, the jury found David Root guilty. Judge Eggleston sentenced him to six years in the state prison at Jeffersonville and fined him $1,000.

Only after the trial, on October 12, 1844, did the *Madison Courier* comment on the proceedings:

> David Root, the man brought here from New Orleans and imprisoned, charged with robbing the Madison Branch Bank in February last, was tried in the Jefferson Circuit Court last week. The trial occupied four or five days, and was concluded about 5 o'clock on Saturday evening; when after a very able and impartial charge by Judge Eggleston, the Jury retired, and after an absence of 24 hours, returned into court with a verdict against the prisoner, sentencing him to 6 years imprisonment in the penitentiary, and a fine of $1,000. The evidence was, mostly if not altogether, of a circumstantial nature.

> On Thursday the prisoner, by permission, made a speech in Court, in which he, in a most solemn manner, protested his innocence of the robbery, reviewed the evidence of the trial, and read a paper, which he wished given to Mr. Lanier, containing directions by which that gentleman might obtain evidence to show that he, the prisoner, was elsewhere at the time of the robbery, &c.

On November 6, just days after the trial ended, the *Banner* reported that branch directors held an election. The board reelected James F.D. Lanier president and elected J.M. Moore the new cashier. Both votes were unanimous. The bank never recovered the money.

# 21.
## "... sweating and snakeroot were recommended ..."
old pioneer remedy for a fever

*In the late fall of 1844, the massive house neared completion. The family reveled in the spaciousness of their new home. James and Elisabeth explained to the children new strict rules of conduct for living in the house. The men that helped move in the furniture spread the story of the elegant furnishings from Irish Gulch to the riverfront. James considered the house a fine birthday present to himself.*

After talking with men privileged to tour the house, the publisher of the *Madison Banner* prevailed upon James for a tour. He reported his observations in the November 27,1844 issue of the paper:

> We learn that many gentlemen both from Cincinnati and Louisville, who have been out in our place and examined this building, have said that in point of architectural beauty and workmanship, it surpasses anything in those cities; and several gentlemen from eastern cities have also acknowledged that they have seen nothing there superior to it.

JFD planned a garden for the land between the mansion and

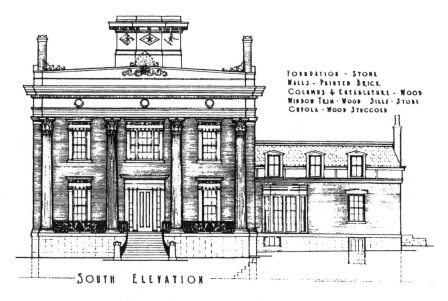

FOUNDATION - STONE
WALLS - PAINTED BRICK
COLUMNS & ENTABLATURE - WOOD
WINDOW TRIM - WOOD  SILLS - STONE
CUPOLA - WOOD STUCCOED

SOUTH  ELEVATION

Credit: Historical American Building Survey, Library of Congress

the river. The garden and a high wooden fence all around the property would improve the view from the mansion, but would not keep out the smells, sounds, smoke, and soot of an active commercial riverfront. The *Banner* continued:

> The form is a rectangle, 54 by 67 feet having a cellar 12 feet deep under the whole, with walls 2 feet thick; the part under the kitchen is 15 feet deep and arched with brick to prevent alike the penetration of heat in summer and cold in winter. On the south front a basement of cut stone 7 feet high and extending around the whole building.

As was the common practice in eastern cities, the first floor rose about six feet above the street level. This afforded some separation from the dust and traffic noise and offered a better view of the street. A wing on the east side of the structure housed the main kitchen. Lanier left the old house on the corner standing. He planned to rent it. An outbuilding stood between the mansion and the older house. It served as a summer kitchen and carriage house.

Four thirty foot fluted columns that featured capitals with both a Greek and Roman influence dominated the south or river side of the house. They were typical of Costigan's work. Three small round windows placed just below the roof line provided

227

natural light to the third story bedrooms. Large carved anthemion leaves (a Greek floral design) decorated the roof parapets at the center of each wall and on all four corners. Costigan repeated this anthemion leaf in wrought iron grille work and railings. The design is a signature of the Lanier Mansion.

Brick fired on the site was the primary building material. The soil of Indiana has a high clay and shale content, and the firing of bricks on building sites was common into the late 1800's. Stone masons fashioned the foundation, the window and door frames, and the ornately carved window and door capitals from locally quarried limestone. A detailed decoration on the stone foundation exemplifies the fact that Lanier meant for this house to be second to none. The foundation stone was decorated with a series of exact hammer marks called "bush milling." The process was very time-consuming and very expensive. The decoration can be seen today on the southwest corner of the house.

Large windows that flooded rooms with natural light were an important design element during this period. The windows in the Lanier Mansion are massive. The first floor windows on the south side of the house measure 8 1/2 feet tall by 4 feet wide. The double hung sash allows easy access to the outside patio. The Lanier children often escaped through the open sashes despite admonitions from their parents. The windows would have also provided an excellent method of removing all of the furniture from downstairs rooms during the extensive spring and fall cleaning sessions.

The remaining windows on the first floor, and all windows on the second floor, consist of double hung sashes measuring about 7' 6"x4' 0". They provide ample natural light to all the rooms. Shutters blocked out the hot summer sun, heavy rain or pelting hail that assaulted the house.

The interior layout of the mansion is a textbook example of the best design elements used in the mid 19th century. A central hall runs the full length from north to south on all floors. A central hall was critical to provide for the free flow of healthful air throughout the house. All rooms leading off this hall had doors that blocked the frigid winter drafts that swarmed through the house.

On the first floor, four rooms lead off the hall. On the west side of the structure are two "best" parlors. The rooms became one large room by opening the pocket doors between them.

These rooms are ornate, and were furnished in deep carpeting of a bold pattern. Bright wallpaper covered the walls. In the winter, heavy drapery not only added to the lush feeling of the rooms, but also provided an effective shield against the harsh wind. Decorative cornices and ceiling molding add elegance to each room. Balance and symmetry were critical to Costigan. Two large false doors on the interior walls of the best parlors balanced the large windows on the exterior walls.

There is a fireplace on the west wall in each room, each with a black marble mantel and decorative facings surrounding the firebox.. These provided the main source of heat, although the large candle chandeliers added considerable warmth when lit.. The 14 1/2 foot ceilings provide ample area for the heat to lodge, however, so the best parlors were never exceedingly warm in the winter. Large, gilt framed mirrors over the fireplace mantels doubled the grandeur of the room and reflected the candle flame, providing maximum light.

Furniture was normally lined up against the walls of a room so it did not present tripping hazards to someone entering a dark room. People pulled chairs into convenient conversation circles once the room was lit and occupied. They were always set back against the wall before extinguishing the last flickering light. Heaven protect the child that left a chair or stool in the middle of a darkened room.

The furniture had a definite southern influence. Elisabeth's early years among the gentry of Kentucky strongly influenced her taste. James added those elements that had most impressed him during his travels through Mississippi and Louisiana. Sofas and settees became popular with women in the 1830's, and Elisabeth picked one of the latest style. Men preferred high backed chairs. Men never sat on the same piece of furniture with another person..

A piano was a recognized sign of opulence, whether anyone in the house played or not. A piano graced the best parlor of the Lanier mansion. The fact that Elisabeth played was a bonus. Lanier designed the double parlors to entertain royalty from Europe, or American politicians and industrial leaders of the highest rank. It served its purpose well.

The family seldom used the best parlors when there was no company present. They used instead the room in the southeast corner of the first floor across the hall from the best parlor. it was at once the family parlor, sitting room and library. It is small, relaxing and friendly. A deep carpet covered the floor. The walls glowed when the sunlight or candle light reflected from the wallpaper. The furniture was less formal. The chairs retained the indentations of comfortable habitation. The family often pulled the curtains aside so they could enjoy the view of the river and garden.. The fireplace in the family sitting room was the least pretentious, but the one most used.

This was the room that Elizabeth heard Charles' lessons recited; where Drusilla would practice her needlework; where Alex could read the latest poem from the new macabre poet Edgar Allen Poe and scare the younger children. Sometimes when James was away, the family would eat in this room. Elisabeth accepted the informalities of "second china" plates balanced on knees; of dunking a cookie in a glass of milk; of using your fingers instead of your fork, in the family parlor. The children marveled how much keener their mother's eyesight, how much quicker their father's disapproving glare, how much more proper the servants' actions were in every room except this one.

This room was the children's favorite. They had the attention of father and mother, under a code of conduct that was not stifling. Secretly, as they grew older, the children might occasionally enjoy the strict table manners insisted upon in the formal dining room, or the stiff decorum of the best parlors, but here in the family parlor they could gossip, or wrestle, or relax.

The formal dining room occupied the northeast corner of the first floor. A serving hall ran from the dining room to the kitchen. A formal dining room marked the ultimate social status. A solid, non-portable dining table was an enviable possession. In most homes, even of the upper classes, a parlor or hallway became a dining room, using temporary tables.

The omnipresent fireplace with large mantel dominated one wall of the dining room. A small serving table hugged another. There was a small closet in one wall that housed the silverware, table linen, and china. JFD selected the silverware and had his name engraved on the handle. Elisabeth kept the key to this dining room vault. She counted each item out of and back in to the vault. Friends teased that she kept better account of her silver than JFD did of his.

The table rested directly beneath the chandelier. Its light reflected off the fine china and glassware and from the highly polished beeswax finish on the table. A scenic wallpaper would have been most appropriate in this room. Heavy velvet drapes hid the windows. During meals a felt baize rug that intercepted any dropped crumbs, grease, or bones protected the carpet. Servants removed this cloth immediately after dinner, so guests could appreciate the full affect of the fine carpet.

Formal dinners were a production. Many started as early as two in the afternoon and continued for several hours. The table settings were a geometric masterpiece. Each plate, each knife, each glass, was set with Pythagorean precision. The Laniers had several fine tablecloths. They were of double French damask ironed, but never folded, before being put on the table. Men and women sat on opposite sides of the table. The host sat at the head, and the hostess at the foot.

Chafing dishes kept the food warm on a sideboard. Serving customs came and went. At times, servants dished the food at the guest's request. The "French or Russian method," in which the diners passed the serving dishes, was the fashion for a time. It never gained great popularity in the highest circles because it interrupted conversation, caused some awkwardness in serving, and increased the chances for spills. JFD was a strong temperance supporter, but he grew his own grapes and was quite knowledgeable about their propagation and fermentation. He often served wine at his dinners.

Servants removed the table cloth after the dessert and before serving the fruit, nuts, and final wine. The table, burnished to a deep luster with a beeswax polish, reflected not only the candlelight and fine stemware, but the jewels and fine clothing of the ladies. After dinner the guests often retired to the best parlors. The pocket doors between the parlors provided privacy for each group as the men and women separated.

The centerpiece of the hallway of the Lanier mansion is a beautiful staircase that spirals, like an elegant chambered nautilus, to the floors above. It terminates in a glass skylight that bathes the stairs in light during the day. In the evening, as candle light filtered up the staircase, the skylight appeared to be a huge glowing lantern when viewed from the upper decks of passing river steamers. The cantilever design of the stairway gives the impression that it is floating in the center of the house. The stairway was practical as well as picturesque. It provided a vent for the all important air movement that cooled the house in summer and purged the house of "unhealthy air" in all seasons.

In most households of the time, even those owned by the "upper middle class," the parlor served the double purpose of a bed chamber. Another measure of the opulence of the Lanier home is the inclusion of private sleeping quarters for the family. Large families did not often enjoy individual privacy. When designing the mansion, James ensured ample privacy by mandating large bedrooms that could double as sitting rooms. Each bedroom has its own fireplace.

The second floor contains the "best" bedchambers. JFD and Elizabeth occupied the room on the southeast corner. It was farthest from the clatter of First street and had a good view of the formal garden and river. This room was also the first to warm up as the window panes magnified the rays of the morning sun. By the time the summer heat reached blast furnace temperatures, the sun's target was the west side of the house. The "best" bedchamber connected to a small "morning room" in the south center of the second floor. Elisabeth often took her breakfast in this room, and issued the servants orders for the day from here. It was not unusual for the lady of the house to stay on the second floor until the early afternoon. Elisabeth had a perfect sanctuary from which she could conduct the household business, or retreat from the cares of the day. The bedroom in the southwest corner of the second floor belonged to the oldest daughter living at home. At times Elisabeth commandeered it as a guest room.

James wanted his house to stand out in every way, so designed two closets to serve the second floor. This feature set his house far above the norm.

The central room at the north end of the second floor, was the same size as Elisabeth's morning room and served as James' office when he worked at home. The large bedrooms that flanked the office belonged to the children. Charles occupied one of these rooms; the girls occupied the other. An inside passage parallel to the hall connects the east side bedrooms. A door from this passageway leads to the trunk room. An identical passageway on the other side of the hall connects the west bedrooms. Maids used these passages as access to the rooms. Charles could use the passage to spy on his sisters. The girls could listen to their parents' muted conversations. Being caught in these passageways led to the severest punishment.

James planned ample room for servants. The third floor of the mansion contains four large rooms used as additional servants' quarters, or male guest bedrooms. Alex probably slept in one of these rooms when he came home, moving any servants out.

If the Laniers had a live-in cook, she occupied the best third floor room. Other live-in or indentured servants shared a room. The ceilings are over six feet, but appear to be low when compared to the rooms on the lower levels. Several small round windows lighted the rooms.The third floor hallway served as a sitting room for the servants.

Most often, children slept in their parents' bedroom until they were several years old. The master bedroom is of ample size to permit a child's bed. The morning room allowed two children to be in close proximity to Elizabeth if family sickness developed.

James, Elisabeth, and architect Francis Costigan attempted to match the elegance of the interior with a beautiful exterior. The north side of the house that abutted First Street offered little opportunity for improvement. Workmen constructed a high wooden fence to block the visual rabble.

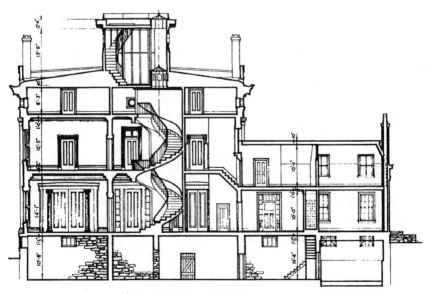

TRANSVERSE SECTION

Credit: Historical American Building Survey, Library of Congress

The south side of the house offered an escape from the crush of commerce. They concentrated the landscaping efforts here. An expanse of open ground about 300 yards long sloped down toward the boat landings on the Ohio River. Ohio Street, heavily used road that serviced the steamboats cut across the property from east to west, just above the wharf. Building the house on the second level afforded an added benefit. The family had an unobstructed view of the gardens, and could look over the tops of most boats for a clear view of the river and the Kentucky shoreline.

James was raising fruit trees long before he built the house. In a letter to John Tipton dated September 19, 1835, he stated: **"I have laid up for you a fine parcel of Peach stones also Sundry other seeds shrubs &c. which will be sent out on my return from Lawrenceburgh Court."[1]**

JFD had seen many formal gardens in his travels, and wanted one of his own. He fought nature all of his life. He forded raging streams, traveled through overpowering forests, and battled swarms of insects for the very ground he occupied. This garden would be a formal garden using precision and geometry to proclaim victory over nature.

The first 200 yards between the house and the river were ideal for the purpose. James personally superintended the details of the garden. It is a fine example of a "gentleman's garden." The center section of the garden follows the Greek Revival mandate for order and symmetry. It is exactly twice the size of the first floor of the house. Each section is twice the size of a first floor room. Flowers for cutting, watermelon vines, strawberry and blueberry plants fill some of the beds. Fruit trees fill other spaces. Boxwood bushes outlined each bed. Lanier tried to introduce exotic plants to the Ohio River Valley and discussed his efforts with friends in Cincinnati. The gardens were open to the public during the day, and many people considered a walk through Mr. Lanier's garden a highlight of their trip to Madison. The distinguished visitors to the house marveled at the garden also. Henry Ward Beecher visited the house on more than one occasion. Standing on the portico of the Lanier house looking down on the violets that covered the first terrace he supposedly expressed the impulsive desire to lie down and roll among the darlings of spring.[2]

Between the formal gardens and the river were a small vineyard and several outbuildings. These utilitarian structures formed a buffer between the gardens and the industry along the river front.

As elegant and advanced as the Lanier house was, life was still difficult. Dirt and grime invaded every crevice despite the best defensive efforts. Just walking to the store could be an adventure. There was no safe haven from disaster. Illness did not consult a bank book before striking.

Although the north-south streets leading from the river were the major commercial thoroughfares, First Street was also filled with animals, wagons, and pedestrians. Droves of pigs on their last journey squealed past the house. Wagons loaded with processed pork bound for the wharves rumbled in the opposite direction. Four and six horse teams clogged the street pulling wagons loaded with salt, logs, lumber, wheat and corn. Vendors with loaded push carts, or knapsacks hawked their wares.

"Fresh chickens"

"Fresh vegetables-corn, beans, cucumbers-all fresh"

"Goose feathers and the finest down in Indiana, refresh your quilts and pillows now"

The churned dust seldom settled on First Street during the long summer days. Constant traffic whipped the clay streets into a sticky morass during winter thaws and spring rains. Snow and ice made for treacherous travel in the winter. Without organized snow removal efforts, tracks stayed in new fallen snow. Traffic turned these ruts into ice.

The crush of humanity and commerce generated a great deal of trash and litter. Roving pigs, dogs, and a legion of smaller wild and domestic animals grew fat on the refuse. In this respect Madison was no different from the cosmopolitan cities of the East. In New York City, trash collection began in the early 1800's, but other cities were not as progressive.[3] As late as 1840, most people in Boston did not set trash out until the collectors were in sight in deference to the wandering animal packs.[4] In the city of Washington not only pigs, but cows roamed the streets.[5] In some cities of the South, turkey buzzards laid claim to the garbage.[6]

The inky black darkness of the frontier, and lack of sidewalks made night time travel an adventure, if not downright dangerous. Garbage eating pigs and dog packs took control of the streets. Street lamps were non-existent. The feeble glow of candles, or later gas lights, that leaked out of houses did little to light the way. Even progressive New Yorkers lit the street lamps only on moonless nights.[7] Washington lit street lamps only in the winter.[8]

However, the master of the house welcomed the heavy traffic of commerce that flowed past the north side of his mansion. Elisabeth took for granted the dust and grime that hitchhiked into the house.

Fleas and lice were little more than a nuisance. Horse flies and mosquitoes became devilish in the quiet isolation of a bed chamber, and called for the most ingenious defenses. Window screens were years in the future, so mosquito netting was common around cribs and beds. Placing bed legs in a pan of water effectively stopped an army of crawling insects, but provided a haven for mosquitoes.

Like most wives of the era, Elisabeth controlled the household operations. She vowed that the new house would keep its luster. It was no easy task. It required planning, financing, intelligence, and personnel management skills that would rival those of a small business today.

James and Elisabeth relied heavily on servants to help with the huge house. While staying with them on one occasion, Sam Merrill wrote to his wife that James and Elisabeth often complained of sickness. Merrill opinionated that they would feel better if they did more work themselves and relied less on servants.[9]

When finances became tight, it was necessary to curtail the staff. This occurred at least once, according to a letter from Drusilla to Alex. It certainly threw a larger burden on the family.

It was not unusual for wealthy families to have indentured servants. Indentured servants could be black or white. They became indignant if compared to the slaves of the South. These servants were bound to a person for a specific period of time. They would perform labor for room and board. At the end of the indenture period they were free to leave. Many immigrants obtained passage from Europe and a safe place to survive while learning the language and customs of their new country by indenturing themselves.

Another ready source of labor was orphans and wards of the court. In exchange for labor, the children received room, board, and often home schooling. No doubt many of these children suffered ill treatment. It is equally true that many households, such as the Laniers', treated these children very well and gave them an opportunity to make something of themselves. There is at least one documented instance where James' mother arranged with the court for a servant.[10]

A cook, while the most important of the household staff, was the most difficult to train and keep. The Laniers insisted on the customs, manners and protocol common in the East or South, but unheard of in the frontier west. To train a cook and staff to prepare and present the most cosmopolitan dinners was a constant chore. More than one cook left the house in tears or exasperation. More than one employer backed away from demands when a cook threatened to leave hours before an important dinner party.

The maids, when employed, served Elisabeth, watched and entertained the small children, and kept the house clean. It was an exhausting battle. Tables, light fixtures and mirrors became the targets of choice for flying insects. Wood and coal soot left an oily film on walls, ceilings and fabrics. No matter how careful a person was, several varieties of dung, mixed with the mud of the season, found its way onto the carpets. Dust floated through the open windows and settled like a gray lace on every surface.

Twice a year Elisabeth would marshal her forces and attack. Elisabeth drafted the coachman and children for the battle. If James was like most men, he retreated to obscurity, suggesting that Elisabeth do the cleaning during the spring and fall bank board meetings Perhaps he allowed her to hire additional help for the chore. Even a banker would see the gain in providing extra funds for the task if he escaped..

Spring cleaning required removal of all of the furniture. The large windows on the first floor would make convenient portals. The strips of carpet would be untacked, removed and pounded like a fire bell. A light matting, or painted canvas floor covering would replace the carpet. Some floors remained bare for the summer months. The workers removed, cleaned and stored the heavy drapes. Some were rehung, tied back against the window frames. Light gauze curtains blocked the view of passersby, but not the breezes of summer. Women and girls stretched "mosquito bars," a light fabric, across the lower half of windows. Men and boys cleaned chimney flues and fireplaces. A decorative screen hid the fireplace opening.

Elisabeth directed that blankets, quilts, and heavy bed drapings be cleaned, dried, and folded neatly away in trunks salted with camphor or cedar chips to repel insects. Gauze-like mosquito netting replaced the bed hangings. She insisted the heavy cotton sheets, so snug on a winter night, be washed and boiled, dried in the warm spring sun, and packed away.

The older girls polished windows to invisibility. Table tops and other wood surfaces reflected a sheen seldom seen outside the cabinet shop. All of the dishes, glasses, and silverware glistened with new-in-the-box-perfection. The lamps and candelabras glinted from a liberal application of elbow grease. Elisabeth closely supervised the cleaning of the wallpaper. She wanted the soot, but not the gilt removed. The whole house showed with renewed sparkle and smelled of fresh lilac and rose when James arrived home from Indianapolis.

In the fall, Elisabeth reversed the process. She had the summer curtains washed and tucked away, and the heavy wrappings of winter reinstalled. The house once again glowed, but the work proceeded with less ardor. People did not anticipate winter with enthusiasm.

Illness and disease, pestilence and plague, even death, became well known, if unwelcome, visitors to each family. In large families illnesses spread easily from one family member to another. It was not unusual that some member of the family was always sick. Doctors were scarce and overworked. They kept very busy treating the most serious illnesses. For the most part, mothers and grandmothers prescribed the medicines:

> For fevers, sweating and snakeroot were recommended with a purge of white walnut bark peeled upward, sassafras, dogwood, willow, or a glass of pearlash and water. The breaking out in eruptive fevers such as Measles was hastened by the use of sheep dung tea. For pleurisy, if no bleeder was at hand, catnip or penny royal or butterfly weed tea, and applications of boiled hot nettles, or brimstone, sulfur and eggs.[11]

With such treatments, it is not a wonder that so many died, but that so many survived.

The fear of fire was omnipresent. Unused rooms remained dark. Adults prepared the candles in the kitchen each evening. They cleaned the wax gutters on the candle holders, and trimmed the wicks. At dusk, they brought candles into the occupied rooms.. As the family moved from one room to another, adults carried the candles. Children seldom carried lighted candles. Adults always escorted children to bed, and took the candles away after making sure the children were safely in bed. Bedroom doors remained open so that the faint glow of the candles, and the murmur of voices could reassure a small child in a large bed, inundated in darkness.

# 22.

## "... no longer be worthy of their respect and confidence."
### — Legislative Joint Resolution January 13, 1845

*The next two years would bring another round of personal sorrow and financial suffering for James Lanier, but once again he would conquer his problems and strengthen his financial foundation. As with many great men, adversity seemed to bring out the best in the Madison banker.*

The one project that remained a millstone around the neck of Indiana was the Wabash and Erie Canal. The canal opened from Lake Erie to Lafayette in 1843 and it appeared that at least part of the dream of cheap transportation would be realized. The bondholders, who had received no interest in three years, dusted off their coupons and expected to begin collecting their due. Disappointment replaced anticipation. The revenue for 1843 and 1844 did not pay for operating expenses; much less repay interest or principal.[1]

Creditors from the eastern seaboard, and even from across the ocean, demanded the Indiana legislature pay the overdue principal and interest. Not the least of those creditors was the House of Rothschild, The influential family had offices in both

240

### Branch Bank
Madison, Jan. 10, 1845.

The public have already been informed that on the night of the 26th February last, the vault of this bank was entered and robbed of the sum of $27,000, of which robbery one David Root was convicted at the last September term of the Circuit Court in this county.

About $24,000 of the money stolen was in notes of the Branch of the denominations of $20, $50, and $100. Of these, perhaps there was a few thousand dollars of new plate, dated in 1843, but the principal portion consisted of notes of old dates which had been for some time in circulation, and had been laid away to be canceled. They were mostly signed by S. Merrill, President of the State Bank, and John Sering, Cashier of the Branch. A small amount may have been signed by M. Stapp, Cashier.

No part of the stolen money has yet been recovered, and we are inclined to think that no part of it has been put in circulation; and as the Bank has withdrawn from circulation nearly the whole amount of its issues of the denominations named, (except the note referred to as stolen) we are induced to caution the public, in order that persons offering $20, $50, or $100 notes of this branch, may be scrutinized.

At the time of the robbery there was in circulation 8,000 dollars of $20's, dated Sept. 4, 1843, of the notes of this Branch; and as no part of these were in Bank they could not have been stolen: they are excepted from this notice.

A reward of five thousand dollars will be paid for the recovery of the stolen money, or in that proportion for any part of it.

JFD Lanier, *Pres't.*

Editors throughout the United States may promote the course of justice by giving the above notice an insertion.

The fact that the money from the robbery was never recovered still concerned Lanier. He ran this article in the *Madison Banner* on January 10, 1845.

England and France and were "the bankers of Europe"[2] The state's credit faltered. The value of state bonds and banknotes dropped.

Hoosiers became outraged and frightened. Politicians blustered, threatening grave harm to all those (except themselves) who were to blame. The Legislature issued a Joint resolution on January 13, 1845, which read in part:

> We regard the slightest breech of plighted faith, public or private, as an evidence of a want of that moral principle upon which all obligations depend: that when any State in this Union shall refuse to recognize her great seal as the sufficient evidence of her obligation she shall have forfeited her station in the sisterhood of States and will no longer be worthy of their respect and confidence.[3]

The legislature directed the governor to send the resolution to all of the other states. Lanier appreciated the strong words, but wondered privately if they had the courage to take the forceful action necessary.

The federal government refused to help states struggling with internal improvements. In March 1845 President Tyler vetoed a bill that contained money for repair of the National Road, the only artery of commerce that served Indianapolis. The *Indianapolis Sentinel* complained bitterly:

> Money enough is fooled away every year on West Point Academy to finish the Road without difficulty. But that is a mill for the manufacture of aristocrats, whether we have a military road or not.[4]

Early in 1831, residents of Madison formed a fire fighting brigade to protect the city from that ever-present danger. As the town grew, a more efficient response was necessary. The Fairplay Volunteer Fire Company Number 1 organized in 1841. In addition to housing firefighting gear, the firehouse became a social center, hosting dances and meetings. In March of 1845, the fire company would face its sternest test.

The night of March 19, 1845, was clear and very cold in Madison. There was very little wind, but those that ventured out wrapped their faces in a heavy muffler and those that stayed indoors piled extra logs on the fire. The First Presbyterian Church sat on the south side of Main Cross Street about half way between Mulberry and West Streets. About midnight the pealing of the church bells woke most Madison residents. Those rushing to their windows thought the bells signaled the opening of hell.

242

Bright columns of flame shot above the church spire.[5] Outlying farmers noticed a crimson glow that appeared to singe the very edge of Heaven.

Volunteers rushed to assist the fire brigade. Men formed bucket lines from every water source. Others stationed themselves on the roofs of nearby buildings to extinguish glowing sparks and embers. The inferno created its own wind that spiraled burning ash high into the sky before sprinkling it at the devil's whim across the roofs of Madison. Water sources quickly dried up and rooftop guardians could not keep up with the rain of fire.

Before fire fighters controlled the conflagration it destroyed the heart of the business district. Thankfully no one died, but damage estimates ranged between $50,000 and $75,000.[6] It was one of the most devastating fires in Madison's history. The Madison branch bank building survived, and in the next few weeks become the hub of the rebuilding effort. Loan requests inundated the bank. The directors were as understanding as possible in making funds available for those hardworking merchants that wished to start again.

After the fire, criticism of the fire brigade surfaced. Grumblings surfaced about insufficient training and poor equipment. Another disastrous fire would wipe out the town. Influential merchants began talking of the need for another fire company.

Soon after the fire, Alexander came home a graduate of Yale University. Never mind that he never declared a major course of study; that he graduated with a very low grade average in the general studies curriculum. He did garner a diploma.

He had no definite plan. He stayed at home weighing options and awaiting opportunities. He enjoyed horticulture more than business and spent most of his time in the gardens. James decided it was best to put his son to meaningful work, and if he liked horticulture, what better place for him than on his father's farms. On April 7, 1845, he wrote this letter of introduction to J. B. Niles:

> Permit me to introduce my son AC Lanier. He visits your part of the state with some views of occupying my land in your county. He may need your kind advice occasionally. Will you please hand to him the deed for the Treadway land also the proper deed from Treadway for the 80 acre tract purchased of him for which you hold the Title Bond.[7]

243

Evidently J.F.D's grand plan against Treadway had not worked. Treadway was still a skunk. No harm in letting Alex have a go at him. If Alex could bring in the Treadway land he would rise immeasurably in his father's eyes.

If JFD's activity with the state bank was on the wane, he more than made up for it with the time he spent on the Madison and Indianapolis Railroad. Public opinion was changing about the railroad. Most people looked upon it favorably. There was a constant argument as to which city would benefit most when the line opened from Madison to Indianapolis, but all agreed that both places would boom.

Even the *Indianapolis Sentinel* urged investment in the line.[8] It was clear that the National Road would never support extensive commerce, and the railroad looked more promising every day. Although most people praised the railroad, few were willing to put their money where their mouths were. Repeated efforts to sell stock were unsuccessful.

A tax appeared to be the best option for raising funds.. A referendum proposed a three year tax of 1%. Proponents proclaimed: "Railroads are to commerce what the genial sun of spring is to the growing corn of the husbandman."[9] Despite admiring the eloquence, The *Sentinel*, true to its Democratic roots, opposed the tax. The tax carried in Indianapolis, but the rural vote dealt it a death blow.[10]

Unable to raise capital close to home, and rebuffed by the taxpayers; James turned to the financial capitals of the country. Surely these intelligent businessmen could see the future of the railroad. The *Sentinel* reported in June of 1845:

> The R.R. Company has positively obtained $35,000 from N.Y. capitalists and $15,000 from Philadelphia. The company we understand has also obtained $20,000 in cash and $20,000 in land from other sources so that it now seems certain that the grading and bridging of the whole road will be finished in about a year. This is good news for Central Indiana.[11]

The railroad was doing a good business. The *Sentinel* reported that in a typical week in October of 1845 the line carried 253 passengers into Madison, and 175 people north. The outbound waybill from Madison listed 201,115 lb. of general merchandise, 970 bbls. of salt, 35 bbls. of whiskey, 18 bbls of tar and oil, 9 bbls of molasses and 131/2 bbls of beer. In addition the locomotive hauled 13 kegs of powder, 120 bushels of stone coal, and 12,000 shingles. Ten plows and two threshing machines reached the farmers to the North over the rails.[12]

The trains heading into Madison were not empty. In addition to the passengers, they carried 9830 bu. of wheat, 252 bu. of flax seed, 90 bu. corn, 115 bu. apples, and 80 bu. of rye. The cars transported 853 bbls. of flour, 96 bbls. of pork, four hundred twenty kegs of lard, 20 cords of wood, 20,000 barrel staves and 11,250 ft. of lumber.[13]

On October 24,1845, John Sering passed away in Logansport.[14] The paper listed no cause of death.. There is no indication in the brief notice whether he returned to Madison after the trial. A street and subdivision in Madison bear his name. Local history reflects a noteworthy citizen.

On November 14, 1845, JFD was riding "the cars" to Indianapolis to attend a bank board meeting. John Mitchell, the bank board representative from Evansville, was riding beside JFD. Mitchell enjoyed the train trips, and regularly took a boat to Madison and the train north. There was no direct route from Evansville to Indianapolis. This route was a great improvement over riding horseback or coach. For James, even though the tracks terminated at Columbus, it was still better than the old stage trips. It gave him an opportunity to check the operation, and the pace of construction.

The train had left Scipio and was just south of Columbus. JFD and Mitchell may have been discussing bank business or the great change that the railroad had made. Lanier might have been explaining that even though the freight figures were impressive, unless the line reached Indianapolis, the railroad would fail.

Suddenly a violent rocking of the car jolted the two bankers. Metal screeched as the wheels dug into the rails. John Lodge, the long time conductor, started forward to investigate the problem. As he was passing between cars, they left the tracks. The cars crushed him as they tipped down the embankment.[15]

Glass shattered and wood splintered as the heavy car slid to a stop. The impact threw James out of his seat. He landed awkwardly on the floor. He gingerly got to his feet and brushed the glass shards from his clothes. He suffered cuts and bruises, but only slight injury. John Mitchell also sustained cuts and bruises, but he too escaped serious injury.[16] James crawled outside to survey the damage and confer with Lodge. The sight of his friend's body mangled under the cars stunned JFD.

John Lodge and James Lanier had been friends for many years, ever since the days that Lodge was part owner of the *Madison Banner*. The two men shared the same political ideology and had sat together on many political committees. It was with James' encouragement and blessing that Lodge had become the M&I conductor. Lanier canceled his trip to the bank board meeting and accompanied his friend's body back to Madison.

It was not the first wreck on the M & I, nor would it be the last. Critics renewed their efforts to discredit the line. In the end, investigators declared the wreck unavoidable. The rail line compensated the injured and repaired the tracks. Although physically badly shaken by the wreck, JFD's confidence in the railroad remained strong.

James' oldest daughter Elisabeth was due to have another child at the end of November. She hoped that the baby would be born on his forty-fifth birthday, and employed every tactic she knew to delay the birth once it became imminent. The baby arrived on November 21, despite her efforts.[17] JFD did not mind, and little Charles Norwood Dunn banished the gloom of John Lodge's death.

James continued his land dealings in the North and corresponded with Niles on various matters. The correspondence is less voluminous than in the past. Perhaps JFD was allowing Alex to handle most of his business, but no correspondence between father and son survives.

On January 1, 1846, the Washington Fire Company Number 2 organized in Madison. The company planned a new modern fire house. Several wealthy men in town joined the fire company to ensure protection of their property. Charles Shrewsbury, who owned the Palmetto Flour Mills and other businesses, was one. JFD was another. So many wealthy men in Madison joined the brigade that it became known as "Silk Stocking Fire Company." It is almost certain that Charles and James did not participate in hose and ladder practice, but it is just as certain that they furnished most of the capital for the firehouse and equipment. The firehouse is still in use.

In another move to proclaim its progressive stature, Madison contracted with Thomas J. Goodman and his Clifton Water Company to supply water to the town. The company immediately mapped routes, purchased supplies, and began trenching.

Late in January of 1846, James made a trip east. He spent some time in Washington, and New York City. He visited the banking house of Winslow and Perkins on Wall Street. The Madison branch bank had done business with the two bankers in the past. Perkins was from Ohio, and was well known in financial institutions in Cincinnati before relocating in the East. The three bankers discussed the condition of the economy and the prospect of selling western stocks.

Meanwhile, Coe's trial finally began in January 1846. Calvin Fletcher worked oratorical magic, and the trial ended in a hung jury.[18] The trial fed the fires of unrest, and the politicians took up the question of the Wabash and Erie Canal in the Legislature. A House Ways and Means Committee report in 1846 stated:

> Humiliating as was the task, candor and a sense of justice require that we should acknowledge our liabilities and assert our willingness to discharge them as soon as our resources could be rendered available.[19]

General Joseph Lane exclaimed in the Senate that he would cut cordwood rather than see his state dishonored. U.S. Senator Hannegan of Covington stormed that "I would sooner part with my last cent and divide my last crumb of bread than sully the honor and fame of Indiana."[20]

Words did not pay the bills. Despite the loud protestations, the politicians did not vote increased taxes to pay off the canal debt. They knew the voters revenge would be swift and deadly. The "temporary currency" aimed at solving the problem had been a dismal failure. The State Treasury Notes, Bank Script, and Canal Script all lost value of between forty and sixty per cent.[21] Even though the state bank attempted to divorce itself from these notes, its paper suffered also.[22]

Indiana's bond holders were politically powerful and doggedly determined. They hired Charles Butler, an attorney from New York to press their case. Butler had performed a similar service for holders of Michigan bonds and achieved impressive results.[23]

Butler convinced the Indiana General Assembly that the only way to obtain full repayment of principal and interest on the canal bonds was to complete the Wabash and Erie to the Ohio River. He estimated that this would cost at least $2,225,000.[24] He proposed that new canal bonds paying 5% interest be issued. The state would pay 2 1/2 per cent. The law stipulated that canal revenue pay the remaining 21/2 percent.[25] The law was long and complicated, and in the end unworkable.

James held considerable state stock in his private portfolio and followed the debate closely. The situation concerned Lanier, but he felt the legislature would never renege on the state debts. If an investor was patient, profits would eventually come.

Soon after the first of the year Elisabeth became ill. The weather aggravated the problem, and she did not recover as she had in the past.. James hired a nurse and other servants to tend to her and to take every burden off her shoulders. He kept the doctor on immediate call. He cajoled Elisabeth to keep fighting until spring. Warm weather would work its magic on her weary body and the bright spring flowers would cheer her heart.

James cautioned the children to keep quiet while in the house. A slammed door or a barking dog brought immediate sanction. James ordered the streets around the mansion filled with straw to dampen the sound of the groaning wheels and steel shod hooves. Teamsters, recognizing the universal sign of illness, slowed the wagons, and tried to muffle the harness chains. Vendors bypassed First Street between Vine and Elm, hoping customers would seek them out.

James' eyes saw that Elisabeth was losing the battle, but the message probably never got through to his heart. No doubt they planned their next trip to New Orleans in an attempt to shield each other from the truth.

Work did not help as it had in the past. He stayed by her bedside. On Tuesday night, April 14, the doctor sent out a call for Elisabeth and Drusilla. They and the other children met in the family living room. Alexander and the eldest daughters took turns sitting the vigil with their father.

Seldom did Elisabeth speak now, drifting in and out of consciousness, the tortured breathing welcome only because it proved life. Then on the morning of April 15, the rattle in Elisabeth's throat ceased.[26] For an instant James hoped the fever had broken. But he knew.

Once more up the hill to the cemetery he rode. The grave on the north end of the family plot awaited. The two women James cherished were now beyond his reach. John James could be with his mother once again.

James moped around the house. He barked at the servants and stormed at the children. He could not concentrate. His mind

248

turned inward and drifted back to the happy times. The children still at home turned to their oldest sisters when it became apparent that their father was not responding to them.

JFD tried the old cure-all of work, but with mixed results. The economy was improving and the bank was becoming stable. There were few crises that needed his special attention. Sam Merrill tried to interest James in the problems of the railroad, but was cut short and told to handle things himself.

The fact was that Merrill did not feel as comfortable running the railroad as he did the state bank. He would not run out on his friend, but he was pessimistic about the future of the railroad. On April 26, 1846, he wrote to his brother David:

> My troubles before I thought at the time to be sufficient but this doing a big business with limited means seems now the hardest of all. We must increase machinery, keep up repairs and tend the road and no allowances for failure in anything. We no (sic) so little of railroads in the west. I do not like to run away, but I should have very little objection to being turned out that they might see whether management by other hands might lead to better results. If we can borrow some money this summer, the road can be finished in the winter, but if we can not, which now appears doubtful, there is great danger of a shipwreck of our credit. Mr. Lanier here lost his wife ten days ago. She was a very fine woman and the family are much distressed.[27]

JFD did not attend the May 1846 bank board meeting. False profits filled most branch bank ledgers for the months preceding May of 1846. High dividends were the rule until Fletcher and other conservatives finally reached the conscience of the liberals. The board agreed to continue contributing to the surplus fund until it equaled the suspended debt. The board also decided to put a realistic value on the bank real property to give the balance sheet credibility.

Lanier spent more time in the East. He investigated purchasing rails from various foundries in Pennsylvania. He called at the Baldwin Locomotive Works. He explored funding in New York and Philadelphia. Distance from Indiana and the house dulled the memory and scabbed the wounds.

Alex had come home when it appeared his mother would die, and was reluctant to return to the North. He left some unfinished business. On May 30, JFD wrote a short letter to Niles: "**I enclose you a check for Mr. Van. 49$ (atty charge $12) My son will be at home (north) in a few days he shall im-**

**mediately attend to the __ __ matter. I regret his negligence therein.**"[28] What had Alex done now?

During June the long and contentious verbal struggle between the U.S. and Mexico broke into open warfare. Mexico could not stand in the path of U.S. "Manifest Destiny." War fever ran high in Madison and two companies of volunteers immediately formed. The Federal government was slower to react than Indiana, and made no immediate arrangements to equip, feed or house the troops. JFD offered the funds of the Madison branch of the state bank to provide for the troops until they joined Federal service, but Governor Whitcomb had made other arrangements to provision the troops, so turned down Lanier's offer.[29] The Madison boys appreciated the effort and marched off to war knowing that Madison fully supported them.

The Madison and Indianapolis Railroad reached another crisis. Construction costs devoured the eastern money, but still no locomotives reached the Capital city. Without money to proceed, the promise that seemed so close at hand was slipping away. Merrill had all but given up, but James was not a quitter. He had to try one more time. Would the well be dry? He took Margaret with him to New York. She went for a vacation; he went to save his dying dream.

JFD once again visited the banking house of Winslow & Perkins. The far ranging fiscal operations of the company impressed the Madison banker. They would be a proper representative for his efforts to raise capital for the railroad.

While her father and Richard Winslow talked business, Mr. Winslow's son, James, showed Margaret the sights of New York. She loved Madison, and was impressed with the hustle and bustle of Cincinnati, but New York filled her with an excitement she had never known. It left her short of breath and full of excitement. Even after leaving the city the feeling stayed with her.

JFD attended some of the dinner parties with Margaret. At most of these, Winslow arranged a dinner companion for James. Miss Mary McClure visiting from Carlisle Pennsylvania was his companion at one of the parties. James tolerated these parties as business necessities, and was always gracious and gentlemanly. That her father actually seemed to enjoy himself with Mary McClure surprised Margaret. He did not associate with her and James Winslow, and seemed disappointed when reminded that it was time to leave.

250

James was doing his task well. The *Sentinel* reprinted an article from the *New York Globe;*

One of the most promising railroad stocks in the country is the Madison and Indianapolis-its business is increasing at the rate of one hundred per cent per annum. The receipts thus far for this year have been equal to $100,000 for the year, which would yield a dividend of 20 per cent on its capital stock.[30]

The second week of August, 1846, the *Madison Banner* reported first hand on Lanier's success.

It is with pleasure that we are authorized to say that the Madison and Indianapolis railroad Company through its agent JFD Lanier of this city has succeeded in negotiating in the City of New York a loan of $100,000 on favorable terms. This will enable the company to complete the road to Indianapolis by the 1st of March next; and when completed it will be of great benefit to the people and no doubt highly profitable to the stockholders. This they deserve as they took hold of it with energy in a dark and trying hour in the history of Indiana. We are informed that Mr. Lanier was very much indebted for his success to the credit and exertions of Messers. Winslow and Perkins, a highly respectable and responsible firm in Wall Street New York. They took the pains to look into the condition and prospects of the company and became satisfied of its entire security and good management and that its stock must prove at an early period very profitable.[31]

JFD returned to Madison reinvigorated. The spark was back in his eyes, and the spring returned to his step. Most important of all, resolute confidence again filled his voice. Once again, when fear and doubt paralyzed others, James' decisive action saved the day. He accepted the congratulations of the board of directors of the railroad, and of Sam Merrill, who once again looked upon his friend with awe and wonder.

Margaret seemed invigorated also. She related to her friends every detail of her trip. James Winslow was in every story. Her polite letter to James, thanking him for being her escort, drew an immediate answer.

On August 17, 1846, Lanier wrote a short letter to Niles. Some good news and some bad.

**If the Bank has bought the Treadway farm I may make some arrangement to buy it. My son-in- law Mr. Dunn will be out this fall and will attend to it and other things in the north.**[32]

The good news was that Treadway may have finally vacated the land. The bad news was, that Alex had given up the North.

251

This forced JFD to send William McKee Dunn to tend to his affairs

While his business interest was back, JFD hated to enter the house. He saw too many ghosts and relived too many dead dreams. James worked long hours and went home only to sleep.

On September 1, 1846, the railroad reached Franklin, 65.5 miles from Madison.[33] About twenty miles remained to Indianapolis. Most people now believed the tracks would reach the capital. Offers of land bombarded officers and board members of the line while they determined the exact location of the Indianapolis terminal.

Troubles still awaited the railroad, however. November 4 dawned without a sun in Madison.. Black clouds rolled in from the West absorbing the dim morning light. Old-timers predicted a "turkey drownder." By 8:00 A.M. rain washed in unremitting sheets across the town. Streets became sluiceways. Horses slipped and slid in the mud. Those that fell had to be unhitched before they could stand. Drivers abandoned loaded wagons and fled to higher ground.

Most people stayed home plugging leaks and watching the river. Some business continued. The branch bank board of directors met and reelected JFD president.[34] The railroad also had a schedule to meet and rain would not halt their efforts. As the rain continued, Crooked Creek rose at a frightening rate. The culvert under the railroad could not handle the torrent.

A lake that formed behind the culvert backed Crooked Creek into Irish Hollow. A deadly undertow developed that swept people off their feet and moved houses off foundations. By the time the rain stopped and the water drained away, eleven people succumbed to the raging waters. The men that built the railroad became its victims. Critics once again attacked the railroad for installing an undersized culvert.[35]

Although pleased at his re-election as President of the Madison branch, James efforts centered on helping those that suffered in the flood. Neither the bank nor the railroad occupied his mind for long. JFD's thoughts dwelled on New York City. He made several trips east in the fall of 1846, and each time Margaret tagged along. It became increasingly difficult for her to leave the east coast, except when James Winslow found a reason to return with the Laniers.

In November of 1846, Dr. Coe again stood trial and the case again ended in a hung jury. Fletcher tried to get the prosecutor to drop the case, but was refused. The state had to have a conviction to quiet the citizen's outrage

Also that month, the skies over the Bank begin to darken. Fletcher noted that his long-time conservative ally, Fitch was turning liberal and voting for what was good for him and his branch, not necessarily what was good for the bank. Judge Morrison reported that the Michigan City branch directors were not holding regular meetings, and that stockholders had piled up $39,000 in personal debt. In addition, 900 shares of branch stock, close to half the total, were sold to three Illinois men. One of the three, a Mr. Taylor, moved to Indiana. He soon became president of the branch.

In the case of the Michigan City branch, the endless investigations proved beneficial. McCulloch reported in February of 1847 that the men were all of good character and sound judgment, and that they should prove to be a good influence on the branch and the bank. Still, some on the state board worried that these outsiders favored high instant profits instead of modest profits and long term stability.

# 23.
## "Hurrah for the railroad."
— Indianapolis Journal October 1847

*The state legislature would dispatch James Lanier on a mission to save Indiana. In the process JFD would discover a transportation system that would unlock the treasure of the western U.S. and mark him as one of the earliest American empire builders.*

The rescue plan for the Wabash and Erie Canal was not successful. Butler returned to the Legislature demanding changes in the law. The outstanding debt against Indiana was now about eight million dollars. Including interest, the total reached to twelve million dollars.[1]

The 1847 Legislature completely revised the statute. The state would issue new bonds for one-half of the outstanding debt. Indiana would be liable for these bonds. The state would turn over title of the canal to the investors as payment for the other half of the debt. The investors could operate the canal and retain all of the revenue. The legislature encouraged investors to invest more money to finish the canal to Evansville.[2] Surely they would feel proud to be owners of the longest canal in the U.S. and would invest additional capital.

Grumbling about investors "stealing" the Madison & Indianapolis Railroad ceased. Compared to the Wabash & Erie settlement, the railroad deal looked very lucrative for the state. The electorate was hoarse from complaining about the internal improvements. They were as happy as the legislators to put these disasters behind them.

Few Hoosiers realized the risks of the Wabash and Erie plan. If the stockholders acted in concert to reject the plan, it would ruin the credit of the state. The most immediate problem facing the legislature was: Who could they trust to travel to the capitals of Europe, exchange the bonds, and not rob the state blind? The messenger would have a great opportunity to accept bribes, alter bonds, or doctor the books. The legislature, burned repeatedly by entrusting Indiana's fortune and future to men of mediocre ability and questionable integrity, worked to pick the right man. They had to pick a man of unimpeachable moral character who was a first rate salesman.

The General Assembly rejected most politicians out of hand. None of them knew the intricacies of international finance. All members of recent legislatures carried the indelible stain of incompetence. In the minds of legislators, many on the bank board were equally inept. Merrill and Morrison were too political to gain a consensus. Calvin Fletcher and Hugh McCulloch had little or no fiscal experience outside Indiana.

All agreed that James Franklin Doughty Lanier would be the perfect envoy. He owned canal stock. He had a sterling record of raising eastern capital for the M. & I. against daunting odds. He had, most argued, the best fiscal brain in the state. Most importantly, Lanier was honest and trustworthy. Never had the Lanier name been tinged with scandal. Never did JFD use his position at the bank to procure excess loans or delay repayment. While well known as a strong Whig, James was never blind or deaf to Indiana Democrats. Few could remember when he did not promote the interest of Indiana above personal or political gain.

James was happy to help Indiana out of a fiscal crisis for a second time. The trip would have to wait until summer, however; he had family obligations. Margaret had accepted James Winslow's proposal of marriage and wanted the wedding in the mansion. She saw the wedding ceremony as an opportunity to wipe the dark shadow of her mother's funeral from the double parlors and to replace it with the shine and joy of a wedding. JFD agreed, and the entire family set to the task of breathing life back into the house. In addition, Drusilla was expecting her second child in May, and James wanted to be present.

An anecdote about the wedding survives:

> On the morning of the wedding day, bridal cake, such as only a bride to be would order, was sent from the confectioners by a boy half grown. Margaret herself answered the knock on the north door of the breakfast room, and perhaps dazzled the messenger boy with her comeliness for he dropped the cake from the glass stand enthroning it; and with all its bridal adornment it lay in fragments at their feet. A wave of horror swept over the boy, but the amiable Miss Lanier-Mrs. Winslow of after years said: 'Never mind here's the money run back and have another made just like it. I won't tell anybody and don't you.' To his dying day the boy, grown to manhood and age, told this as the greatest glory of the Lanier name.[3]

Despite whether the cake story is true or not, the wedding was beautiful as all weddings are; the bride was radiant, as all brides are. JFD was doubly happy. Not only was young James a fine man, but he also shared JFD's fascination for investment banking. The house sparkled from the massive pier mirrors to the gleaming candelabra. Joyous music rolled up from the first floor through the third floor skylight. James danced nimbly with his daughter. More than one guest remarked that they could not remember the house so beautiful as it was on that March 18, 1847.[4]

James had promised to take his oldest daughter to New Orleans. They left a month after the wedding. Elisabeth enjoyed shopping and JFD visited the various banking houses, cashing bills of exchange and reviewing the conditions of the banks. It was not the same as when he and his wife were there, but he was conditioning himself to live without her. He accepted invitations to several dinner parties. His daughter made an enjoyable companion, but he sometimes wished it was Mary McClure on his arm.

In April of 1847 Dr. Coe's third trial commenced. This time the jury acquitted him of all charges. [5] The evidence against Dr. Coe appeared to be damning, but Fletcher was successful in convincing the jury that the real culprits were the politicians who pork barreled the internal improvements projects. The citi-

256

zens of central Indiana had lost interest in retribution for Internal Improvements mistakes.

Drusilla delivered a healthy boy on May 25. James was still reluctant to have a child named after him, so Drusilla named her son Robert Cravens. Mother and daughter appeared to be doing fine, so JFD continued his plans to leave for Europe.

James began his trek to Europe by first visiting Philadelphia where he conferred with Nicholas Biddle. He obtained letters of introduction and insights on the European bankers. Mary McClure's father became a merchant in Philadelphia about this time so James may have seen her there on this trip. James then went on to New York City, where he met with James Winslow and gathered more information. He sailed for England on June 21.[6]

JFD must have been glad to get away. Madison was depressing. Margaret's wedding had been a welcome distraction, but James still saw reminders of Elisabeth everywhere in the house. The trip to Europe, among other advantages, would bring new opportunities, new sights, new experiences. In addition to helping Indiana, James might discover some trade opportunities that could benefit his personal bank account.

He was aware of the effect the repeal of the British Corn laws would have on central Indiana and the railroad, but missed the grandiose prediction made by the editor of the *Sentinel* on June 27. It was one of the few *Sentinel* editorials that James would have agreed with:

> The repeal of the British Corn laws . . . is almost as much a matter of rejoicing to the people of the Western states as to the starving people of Britain themselves. Give us now but a just modification of our own tariff and a long vista of prosperity opens to our view, unsurpassed in the annals of the world.

Lanier carried millions of dollars worth of State of Indiana bond certificates, completely executed except for dates of issue, amounts and names of stockholders. They were blank checks to the wealth of Indiana. To a lesser man they would have been an overwhelming temptation.

James set up an office in the Bank of England and began to sell the Indiana plan to the European stockholders.[7] He was in almost daily contact with the likes of Sir J. Horsley Palmer, Governor of the Bank of England, and Baron N.M. Rothschild of London. Palmer was a friend to America. He believed in the country, and felt that the Bank of England could benefit from America's prosperity. He took James under his wing. Not only did he arrange for offices in the great bank itself, he provided additional introductions and, more importantly, current backgrounds on all of the financiers of the Continent. During the next four months James visited Baron James Rothschild in Paris, and Mr. Labouchere of the banking house of Hope and Company in Amsterdam.[8]

He went across Europe in search of outstanding bonds and, according to his autobiography, was able to **"get up nearly all the outstanding bonds, and was in this way instrumental in placing the credit of the state on the firm basis upon which it has ever since rested."**[9]

Europe impressed James, and James impressed Europe. He was not the stereotype American braggart that talked down to Europeans. He was quiet. He listened; he complimented; he asked searching questions. Truly interested in what they felt, he absorbed what they could teach him.

JFD invoked his credo to treat his client's problem as his own. He listened to their complaints. He shared their doubts. He complimented their financial systems and mentally filed ideas that would help him back home.

The financiers liked JFD Lanier. He was a kindred spirit. He was a stockholder, not a salesman. He was a banker, and a good one. The success of the Indiana State Bank had preceded him across the ocean. He was coming to them. He was not afraid to meet on their home ground. Above all he was quiet, honest, confident, and gracious. The bankers paid him the ultimate compliment by inviting him to their homes.[10] At dinner parties James exhibited manners and social graces befitting European blood. Some people left the parties impressed, but perhaps secretly disappointed that the American had not committed some social faux pas.

Labouchere's ancestors had been Huguenots driven from France for the same reason as the Laniers.[11] Shared tribulations sparked a close friendship. JFD absorbed the business history of Holland and learned the details of both it's rise and decline. He observed the extensive canal system gouged across the country. He enjoyed the canals of Amsterdam, and the fine houses that lined the banks of the Gentleman's Canal.

James marveled at the engineering feats of the Dutch, and

the massive dikes that kept the sea from inundating the western half of the country. He came to understand why Holland's canal system was successful. The canals were actually drainage ditches, constantly collecting ground water from farmland that was below sea level. The canals transported the water to the sea. Indiana's canals required filling from a near-by water source, usually a river. This required expensive and vulnerable feeder dam systems.

Holland's landscape was generally flat and sloped to the sea, providing natural water flow. In Indiana the topography was rolling. This necessitated an expensive system of locks. The experience in Holland reinforced James' doubts that a viable canal system could survive in Indiana.

It was becoming increasingly apparent that the royal robe alone could no longer control the destiny of a nation. Sovereign decrees needed the backing of a strong industrial base. The trip reassured James that an industrial empire could flourish in a democracy. Commerce and industry could guide government; it was not necessary for government to lead commerce. The friends gained on this first trip to England and Europe would last a lifetime and would benefit James throughout his career. Lanier shared firesides with the real empire builders of Europe.

England, too, had a canal system cut across her face, yet railroads seemed to be stitching the cuts closed, sewing together the hubs of business. The topography in England resembled that in Indiana more closely than the topography of Holland. English canals solidified James' conviction that canals would not survive in Indiana..

Seeing the development of railroads in Europe and England was like a trip into the future for Lanier. The railroads were much advanced over the ones in America. They were solid, and dependable. Larger engines were pulling bigger loads farther, faster.

Shipping farm produce to market before it spoiled was a prime concern for farmers throughout the western United States. The gait of a team of horses or mules forever limited the speed of canal travel. The speed of railroad travel in England seemed unlimited. Railroad engines were on the drawing boards that could pull a string of cars as fast as 50 miles per hour.

Critics of railroads in the U.S. warned that maintenance of tracks and roadbeds would swallow up all profits. European railroads dispelled this fear. Heavy rail and solid tie and roadbed systems stood up under heavy loads and faster speeds. England was about the size of Illinois, somewhat larger than Indiana. If railroads were successful in England, they could be successful in Indiana. If successful in Indiana, why not in the vast expanse of the West? The speed of railroads would shrink distance and time.

No matter how he admired the railroads, Lanier was true to his mission. James was careful as he questioned the operation of the rail lines, turning each weakness to an advantage for the canal system he was trying to sell.

Lanier included himself as a canal investor when he admitted that they had little choice. It was either approve of the new financing plan and hope that the canal would become profitable, or get out and lose all of the money they had poured into the project. Most investors took the lesser of the two evils, and accepted the new stock. They even promised the additional capital needed to finish the works. James must have been very persuasive. The Rothschilds had lost considerable money, and distrusted American investments.

Even as James was selling the Wabash and Erie Canal abroad, a deadly shadow cloaked its future. On October 1, 1847, an engine rolled into Indianapolis, coming all the way from Madison. Towns all along the line held celebrations that extolled the railroad's bright future. Henry Ward Beecher put the historic trip back to Madison in perspective:

> On a wood-car rigged up with boards across from side to side went I forth. The car was no car at all, a mere extempore wood-box used sometimes without seats for hogs, but with seats for men, of which class I (ah me misserable) happened to be one. And so at 11 at night I arrived at Madison not over proud in the glory of riding on the first train that ever went from Indianapolis to Madison.[12]

The *Sentinel* was unconcerned about the uncomfortable ride. The editor was looking on the bright side. On October 6 he wrote: "The change is so great, although but a few days have intervened; the times so wonderfully altered that business flows upon us without parallel"[13]

Despite Beecher's complaints, the *Indianapolis Journal* extolled: "All passenger cars on the road have been brought into requisition and the demand of the traveling public not fully met at that." The price of wheat at Indianapolis rose from 43¢ to 73¢

per bushel in just three weeks and the *Journal* proclaimed "Hurrah for the railroad."[14] It could have added "Hurrah for James Lanier" who had done more for the success of the line than any other single individual.

At that moment James was facing bleak fall weather in Europe. Cold rains, and sea-washed gales assaulted the shores. Stone houses stored the cold and added their own frost that permeated the interior walls. No manner of conflagration in the immense fireplaces could banish the rime.

Lanier despised the cold and feared the train of diseases that followed in its wake. After successfully completing his work, and a round of farewell dinners, he sailed west. Writing to Merrill he stated that he would sail on the Caledonia from Liverpool on October 19, and would arrive in New York on November 2. He expected to leave for Madison between November 7 and 10.[15]

The Atlantic Ocean can be rough and rolling in late October. The weather was miserable. James stayed in his cabin reviewing his months on the continent, counting the days until landfall.

Lanier wrote a letter to Governor Whitcomb upon his arrival in New York proclaiming the success of his trip, and promising a full report when he returned to Indianapolis. James stayed in New York a few days to recover from the voyage. Winslow had saved newspaper articles and letters from Margaret describing the completion of the Madison & Indianapolis Railroad. This news greatly pleased Lanier and he tested his theory of railroad development for the West on James Winslow. He stopped in Philadelphia where he consulted with Biddle. Of course he had several opportunities to escort Mary McClure to dinner. Did she miss him as much as he had missed her, or was it his imagination?

JFD decided to travel as far west as he could on the railroad to judge how advanced rail transportation was in the U.S. Once he reached Wheeling Virginia, he booked passage on a packet for Madison. James had hoped to make it home for the birth of Elisabeth's child, but missed it by just a few days. Frances Elisabeth Dunn was born December 6.[16] Despite the proliferation of grandchildren, JFD brought all of them special gifts from the continent. Christmas at grandpa's house was always special, but Christmas of 1847 was one of the best. He brought a christening dress from Europe for Frances Elisabeth, and memorable gifts for the entire family.

Less than a month after he returned from Europe, the Ohio River flooded, stalling commerce. The high water mark reached 63.6 feet on December 17.[17] The water lapped at the gardens of the mansion. Torrential run-off heavily damaged locks and canal banks. The flood seemed a final exclamation mark to the advantages of rail travel.

# 24.
## "This is annihilating time and space."
— Madison Daily Tribune, November 22,1851

*The next few years would bring unprecedented prosperity and then unprecedented decline to Madison. The town would also lose its most famous entrepreneur and booster.*

The success of the Madison & Indianapolis line spawned new ventures Other rail lines were building, but were not yet completed. Led by Lanier, and eager to take full advantage of their monopoly of high speed travel, the railroad directors applied for charters for spur lines. Construction on the Shelbyville Lateral Railroad began. The spur line joined the M & I at Edinburg. The directors planned extensions from Shelbyville to Rushville and from Shelbyville to Knightstown.[1]

Friends knew James Lanier as a man of action. While others on the bank board had puzzled and delayed, he had discovered the root of a problem and immediately prescribed a cure. He was quick to recognize a business opportunity and to capitalize on it. He surprised even his closest associates and family, however, when, upon his return from Europe he announced his plans to wed Mary McClure. On January 20, 1848, the wedding took place in Madison at the home of Dr. A. Hays, and the couple moved into the mansion.[2]

James was about 20 years older than Mary. A paunch foreshadowed a pot belly, but he was in excellent shape for a man nearing fifty. He stood erect and held his head high. His eyes were deep-set, the pupils hard and cold. He was clean shaven and although his hairline was beginning to recede, his hair remained deep black. His mouth turned down at the corners in a perpetual frown during business meetings. Only Mary and his grandchildren could guarantee a smile. The creases that appeared in the corners of his eyes pulled his mouth into a smile and his eyes twinkled.

Their age difference mattered little to Mary. James was intelligent, powerful, and virile. His voice commanded attention, and his eyes held undiminished fire. They could still penetrate to a mans soul; still burn the fight from an adversary.

Undoubtedly, James' marriage became a favorite topic of conversation from Irish Hollow to Slabtown along the docks. Although most would have denied it, secretly, the men coveted James' choice, and the women envied Mary.

JFD refused to acknowledge the gossip the wedding precipitated. His skin may have softened, but his jaw remained rigid. He had been a target of backwater whispers for so long, for so many false reasons, that he was immune.

When they moved into the house, the newlyweds occupied the southwest bedroom. James could not, and Mary would not, sleep in the room that had been Elisabeth's domain. Mary Lanier, 16, the oldest daughter at home happily claimed the bedroom.

James spent more time in New York. It was a combination of the influence of his new wife, and the lure of one of the financial capitals of the world. He managed to make it back to Madison for a grand party in the Shrewsbury House in early April. Newspaper reports stated that champagne "was all the rage" at the party. The Governors of Indiana, Kentucky and Ohio attended the gala.

In 1848 the Ohio legislature mandated that the Ohio banks refuse foreign paper after June 1.[3] They ordered all transactions with out-of-state banks conducted with specie. This action shocked and worried the Indiana State Bank Board of Directors. Merchants must curtail trade with Ohio immediately or the

264

specie drain will be intolerable. Either course would seriously injure Indiana commerce.

JFD seldom attended bank board meetings. Times were good and running the bank provided few challenges. He was absent in May when the board sent a delegate to meet with the Ohio bankers. The two banking organizations reached an agreement allowing Indiana bank notes to be redeemed beyond June 1.

Mary had a free hand to redecorate the house. She chose furniture from New York, the east coast, and New Orleans. She gave the older pieces, all displaying Elisabeth's southern influence, either to the children, or to others. New paint and wallpapers completed the make-over of the first floor. Mary had a gas generator installed in the yard which served gasoliers throughout the house. No more sputtering candles; no more smoky wicks.

The railroad was a success. Samuel Merrill did not agree with the stockholders in New York that the profits should go toward dividends and expansion. He wanted the money set aside for repairs and maintenance. The stockholders in New York pushed Merrill to find a better route out of Madison and eliminate the incline. They increasingly interfered with the day to day operation of the line, and eventually sent their own man, H.R. Hall to act as superintendent. He and Merrill clashed on a daily basis. At a board of directors' meeting in New York, Merrill presented a sixteen point bill of charges against Hall.[4] Failing to obtain backing from the board, Samuel Merrill resigned as president. On August 1, 1848, he wrote a long letter to Lanier, justifying his conduct.[5] As was Lanier's custom, the reply was short and business-like. He stated that there were no charges against Merrill, and that the new president would need his advice and expertise.[6]

Despite Merrill's concerns, the railroad brought the long rolling thunder of success to Madison. The M. & I. outgrew the original depot. The railroad paid $20,000.00 for a square block on the Ohio River between Vine and Mill streets.[7] This was immediately west of JFD's home. Now he could watch the cars load and unload from his bedroom window. The freight depot was 346 feet long and 63 feet wide. Freight doors ran the full length of the building on both sides. Warehouse workers could unload a full train before the engine boiler cooled.

In the Fall of 1848, William McKee Dunn won a seat in the Indiana House of Representatives.[8] James helped his son-in-law with the election, but there was no doubt that Dunn won the voters over with his strong views and common sense.

Pork processing led the commercial parade. By 1852 there would be 14 pork houses in town. There were also numerous secondary businesses that dealt with pork by-products; bristles for brushes; lard for cooking; hides for several uses. Perhaps there were even some sow's ears for purses.

Milling was also big business as dependable steam took over for fickle water power. Four large mills vied for the grain that flowed south on the M. & I. The milling industry too had its auxiliary businesses. Madison taverns proudly featured home town brews for their Irish and German customers. Feed mills took their share of grain to sustain the large population of horses necessary to support commerce.

Riverboat construction began in Madison as early as the 1830's. Far from competing with boats, the railroad increased the need for river packets. The slips at the Madison Marine Railway Boat Building Company sang as barge after barge glided into the water. Warehouses, foundries, sawmills, and wagon works were the warp and woof of Madison's economic fabric. Carpenter shops, tanneries, pottery kilns, dry goods and grocery stores gave the fabric body and color.

The discovery of gold in California relieved the chronic shortage of specie, and good economic times sluiced across the country. Indiana was no exception. The state bank sustained good profits, that did not go unnoticed. Those favoring a "free" banking system become more vociferous. Calvin Fletcher suggested to Governor Wright, that economic conditions now warranted some plan to honestly retire the state internal improvements debt.[9]

In November the Madison & Indianapolis Railroad accepted delivery of a new cog wheel engine, the M.G. Bright, to take advantage of expanded business.[10] James was in New York and missed the maiden trip of the new engine. J.N. Perkins had passed away. James took advantage of the situation by proposing that he and Winslow form a partnership.

Mary could not accompany her husband to New York at the end of 1848 because she was expecting their first child. She took to her bed soon after Christmas. January 1849 was a banner month for JFD. The new banking house of Winslow & Lanier opened its doors for business on the first, and later that month Mary presented James with his ninth child and sixth daughter. They named her Jean.[11] JFD was as happy as if she were his first born. James felt young and vibrant.

Jean received more love, affection, and worldly goods than she could fathom. The older children teased their father about spoiling her and reminded him how strict he had been with them. He was so happy he did not scowl, but entered into the humor.

In 1849 the Madison and Indianapolis Railroad built a passenger station just north of the freight depot. James could wait for the departure whistle before leaving his house to board the train. The mournful train whistles, the packet boat pipes, and the foundry hammers that kept the beat for the commercial symphony, lulled James to sleep. He was the conductor of that symphony and he never tired of its music.

Both joy and tragedy visited James during the summer of 1849. Drusilla gave birth to her third son, and this time, over her father's objections, named him James Lanier Cravens.[12] Drusilla and Mary spent time together, comparing the growth of their two children. James did not seem to mind playing the role of father and grandfather to two children born only months apart.

Elisabeth's son, Charles, contracted an illness that confounded the doctor. Despite using several courses of treatment, the child did not respond. The entire family attended church on Sunday, June 30, as they prayed for the life of the child, and gathered to support Elisabeth. That evening the boy died.[13] Not prepared for the death, the Dunns did not have a cemetery plot. JFD was glad to give them one of the Lanier gravesites.[14]

The pressing business of the railroad gave Lanier the challenge he needed to recover from the grief. The spur rail line to Shelbyville opened amid much celebration. Some farmers along the tracks complained that the engine whistles were causing their cows to go dry. Others that cinders threatened to set fire to their haystacks. However, none of the complainers turned down the increased milk and grain prices the noisy engine brought.

Despite the care and attention, Jean did not thrive. In November she died.[15] James hated the trek to Springdale Cemetery. He stoically supported Mary as she wept over the tiny casket. His heart all but burst as the ground closed over yet another Lanier.

James and Mary spent most of their time in New York City. She to return to the cosmopolitan life; he to learn the new business, and escape Madison. Only to himself would he admit that whenever he was in town, the sorrow of Spingdale Cemetery suffocated him like a shroud.

New Wharves &c.
Messrs. JFD Lanier and John Woodburn have already commenced the work of grading and filling in some three hundred and seventy feet of their property, on the bank of the river, for the purpose of making wharves, &c., commencing at the railroad wharf and extending up the river as far as Cherry Lane. When this work is completed, Madison will have the most extensive wharf of any city on the banks of the Ohio.
May 14, 1850

The *Banner* of May 14, 1850, carried the news of Woodburn's and Lanier's wharf.

In mid-summer of 1850, their feud long since patched up, JFD and John Woodburn constructed a large wharf on the west end of town, near the rail line. The wharf was 370 feet long. The city of Madison had constructed a wharf for passaenger boats on the east end of town.Woodburn and Lanier built their wharf for cargo, anticipating the opening of additional spur lines. Lanier's railroad carried the produce of Indiana to Madison. After being transferred to Woodburn's and Lanier's wharf, Woodburn's boats hauled it away.

By August of 1850 the tracks were complete to Rushville and Knightstown. The citizens had never imagined such prosperity. The big steam engines truly pulled a revolution up the track.. The *Rushville Whig* could only marvel:

"Our merchants opened goods in the evening which were shipped from Madison in the morning. Our farmers can unload wheat here in the evening and the next day it can be carried to the Ohio River. A new era in business is about to commence in Rush County."[16]

The railroads were thriving, but the state bank was under attack. As the state bank charter neared the end of its term, opponents turned up the heat. They discounted the benefits of the bank.

"Free banking" was the rallying cry. Privately most state bank directors conceded that the bank would die when its charter expired. Many directors were positioning themselves to become part of the new system.

The *Courier* of June 27 carried the familiar Democratic attack on the State Bank. Half-truths and exaggerations were more important tools to publishers than ink and paper. This indirect attack is as close as anyone ever came to publicly criticizing Lanier.

James was among those planning for the "free banks." He did not agree with the criticism of the state bank, but realized he could not stop the avalanche of change. JFD. did not intend to take an active role in Indiana's free banks, but could see no reason why he could not benefit from investment in the institution

The August 15,1850, issue of the *Madison Courier* reported that David Root succumbed to cholera at the state prison in Jeffersonville. He died only one month before he completed his sentence. While admitting Root was a man of bad character, the paper claimed the jury convicted him despite "nothing positively was proven against him and notwithstanding he had most positively proved an alibi"

The paper went on to state that on his death bed Root:

> . . . freely confessed to a number of forgeries and crimes and implicated as to being connected with him in his forgery transactions a person who at present is a resident of this city, and who is now reputed to be worth one hundred thousand dollars! He, (Root) however most earnestly and solemnly denied having ever had anything whatever to do with the Madison bank robbery, or of knowing anything about it directly or indirectly. As we have already said, he freely acknowledged to many other crimes but, with a full knowledge that death would soon claim him as a victim, he asserted to the last that he was suffering the penalties of a crime of which he was entirely innocent. The confessions were made to his physician, Dr. W.F. Collum, and from all the attending circumstances his statements are believed to be true.

In another section of the paper, the *Courier* continued its constant feud with the *Banner:*

> The *Banner* this morning doubted whether any one but the thief or thieves know whether the money stolen from the bank for which David Root was convicted was in circulation or not. It is usual with all banks to number and to keep a correct memorandum of all issues; and we think the *Banner* folk are satisfied by this time that the Bank officers do know that the notes stolen have not been put into circulation. We are (not privilege) to the secrets of the bank, but have seen enough evidence to satisfy us that bank officers know **all about this** . . .

James silently fumed over the article but passed it off as politics. This was just another attempt to discredit the state bank, which was again struggling. By August 1850 the situation with the Ohio banks had deteriorated. The bank board decided to pull out more than $200,000 the Indiana state bank had in the Ohio Trust Company.[17]

Although he spent most of his time in New York, Lanier had not resigned from the bank board and attended the November 1850 meeting. The board declared a five percent dividend and one per cent for the sinking fund.[18] Business was good and the problems were few.

Madison continued to prosper. New businesses sprung up. Land prices soared.. It seemed to many residents that the tracks were never empty; that the soot from the engine smoke stacks never settled. Every week brought new shipping records. The

December 2 issue of the *Banner* reported "A single train arrived with 1,365 hogs. Twenty eight double cars." Still the railroad could not keep up with the demand. Farmers around Knightstown were impatient because there were 4,000 hogs in the vicinity and no cars available.

The citizens of Madison would not limit their travel options to the river boats or railroad. Both were expensive and overcrowded. There was a need for a good road system. For years the Michigan Road had been a primary route, but there were many other pikes laced across the country. Weather was the major destroyer of roads. Stone filled some mud holes, but could be washed out and ground away. Corduroy construction bridged the major sink holes, but winter and spring travel still ranged from adventuresome to disastrous. Planking seemed to provide a safe dependable roadbed. The materials were plentiful and sturdy. Farmers would gladly pay to travel on a good plank road. In the late 1840's and early 1850's, plank roads across southern Indiana and Northern Kentucky attracted the interest and capital of many Madison residents.

The Madison Street Committee struggled with mud and dust as well as excess traffic. Vendors appropriated street corners and set up shop, often blocking a lane. Teamsters abandoned their wagons in the middle of the street and went into a tavern. The water company crew dug up the streets. A street crew kept busy cleaning ditches and graveling, but to no avail.

The Madison water system was in place, but the town had expanded beyond the original plans. New citizens clamored for water service. The town purchased the system from Goodman, confident that expansion would make it profitable.

By 1851, when JFD was making plans to leave the city, Madison was bursting with importance. The town fathers were discussing a gas lighting system for the streets. There were two daily papers published in town, while Indianapolis could only muster two weeklies. In April an event occurred that best illustrated the importance of Madison.

Miss Jenny Lind, the "Swedish Nightingale," and the most famous female singer of the era, visited Madison. It was one of only eighteen cities on her American tour. The local promoters of the appearance promised P.T. Barnum $5,000 as a guarantee. George Phillips converted his pork house into a music hall.[19] At least 10 steamboats lined the wharf from Walnut street, past the

Lanier mansion, to the depot. People flocked from all corners of the state and from many of the surrounding states as well.

Tickets bought at auction averaged $7.00 each, more that a week's wages for most men.[20] Jenny Lind's voice carried clearly through the rough weatherboarding of the pork house, so standing spaces around the outside of the hall sold for one dollar each.[21] Surely any members of the Lanier family that were in Madison at the time purchased tickets to the once in a lifetime event.

The concert was not a financial success, but Mr. Barnum forgave the loss.[22] Papers across the country wrote stories of Jenny Lind's appearance in a pork house. Those stories ensured a full house at each of the remaining stops on the tour. Not all those that saw the concert in Madison thought Jenny Lind was the greatest singer they had ever heard. In a letter to his son Algernon, Judge Sullivan stated:

> Did you hear Jenny Lind? We all (Charlotte and Mrs. S. included) heard her. The girls were charmed, but your ma and myself thought we had heard better singing and seen prettier girls.[23]

Mary became pregnant again. JFD demanded that the doctor leave a list of his whereabouts at his office at all times. James insisted that Mary stay in bed during her entire term. They compromised, and she spent most of the time in the day room on the second floor. James prayed for a safe pregnancy and wished for a boy.

His wish came true and his prayers answered.[24] James Lanier Jr. came into the world with his mother's beautiful hair, but with his father's double chin. Also in 1851, Drusilla had her fourth child, a boy named Alexander.[25] James was happy his father's name survived to another generation. On August 2, 1851, Elisabeth bore her fifth child, a boy named Lanier Dunn.[26] If the fact that James became a father, and twice a grandfather in the same year embarrassed him, he did not show it. He must have been proud his children were carrying on the tradition of large families.

In his diary Calvin Fletcher happily noted in May 1851, that "Lanier from Madison and all the old delegates are present-Pleasant meeting."[27] It is the last board meeting that James would attend.

In November, with wife and son safe and healthy, JFD made

**JFD Lanier, Esq.**

We understand that his active and enterprising citizen of Madison, who has long been officially connected with the Branch Bank in this place, is soon to take up his permanent residence in the city of New York. In parting with one so universally esteemed for his many good qualities, we hope we may be pardoned for indulging in a few reflections, which the occasion suggests.

Our first acquaintance with Mr. L., commenced about the year 1824, at which time he was one of the principal lawyers of this city, and had an extensive practice in this and the adjoining counties, as well as in the Supreme Court of the State. At that period and for several years afterwards, he was officially connected with the General Assembly of Indiana, and subsequently held the office of Prosecuting Attorney in this Circuit. After the formation of the Bank, he soon acquired distinction as one of the best financiers in the West, and in 1847 went to Europe where, in his negotiations with the foreign holders of Indiana bonds, he aided largely in the adjustment of our State debt and the restoration of our State credit. Soon after his return to this country he became connected with one of the most substantial Banking houses in the city of New York, where, by his experience, and his knowledge of the capacities, as well as the wants of the West, he has contributed greatly to the establishment of western credit, especially in furnishing and obtaining facilities for the commencement and completion of many of the important rail-way lines in this and the adjoining States. The constantly increasing business of the house with which he is connected in New York, requires his removal to that city, and while we rejoice in his success, we cannot but regret that Madison is to be deprived of so worthy and so useful a citizen.

Nov. 15, 1851

The *Banner* printed a glowing tribute to JFD

273

public his plans to permanently move to New York City. All of James' friends lamented his decision, but admitted that there are many more opportunities on the east coast. They admired his fortitude in starting a new business in a new city at his age

It appeared that Alexander was going with his father. He disbanded his partnership with L.M. Ross. Shortly afterwards, however, Alex entered business with JFD's old friend Michael Bright. Was this just a normal business change? It was not unusual for businesses to dissolve and new ventures to immediately open. Was the timing just a coincidence, or did James squash his son's plans? Did he forbid Alex from moving east with him? Did JFD go so far as to arrange that his old friend take Alex in?

JFD identified what he saw as a fundamental economic change building on the east coast and would sweep across the country. The western migration cried for the cheap goods. The need now was for a transportation system that would link buyer and seller. James knew how to supply the transportation system. Now was the time to act on his idea. It was difficult to leave his family and his successes in Madison, but if he did not act immediately, the opportunity would be lost forever.

As Lanier began his new business with Richard Winslow, he discovered two problems. Poor construction methods plagued all of the rail lines in the West. Many were leftovers from state internal improvements efforts. They all consisted of light flat iron bar rails laid on longitudinal sills that could not support heavy loads or high speeds. In addition, they were all financial and operational disasters. His first job would be to persuade the rail line owners to upgrade the tracks and re-engineer the routes. His second task would be to convince investors that the rail lines were a good investment. He began this second effort even before he left Madison, by writing pamphlets and articles for newspapers extolling the benefits of a modern rail transportation system.

Madison did not begin its decline because James Lanier left town, nor did James leave town because he could foresee the town faltering. The two events were simultaneous, but happened for different reasons. James moved to New York because it was the financial capital of the country, and the best place to carry on his new business. Madison began to decline because the railroad was so successful.

274

The very tracks that brought Madison its success would steal away its prosperity. With the success of the Madison and Indianapolis Railroad, requests for charters deluged the General Assembly. By 1852 trains were running from Indianapolis to Terre Haute, Muncie, and Noblesville. Tracks stretched from the capital city east toward Bellfontaine, Ohio and south to Jeffersonville and Cincinnati.

The *Madison Daily Tribune* was a relatively new paper in town. On November 22,1851 it printed this editorial:

> "Before the railroad era, it required two weeks and often three to drive hogs from Hendricks County to Madison. A drove of hogs loaded on the cars at Bellville on Thursday (A.M.) was landed in North Madison the same afternoon. This is annihilating time and space."

Friends considered this article a nice birthday tribute to JFD. He probably appreciated it as much as the *Banner* story.

Arguments for additional rail lines were convincing. Grain shipped to Vicksburg and New Orleans via Jeffersonville would not have to travel around the treacherous Falls of the Ohio. Corn shipped to the eastern markets could avoid a twelve hour boat trip if they went directly to Cincinnati. Despite intense lobbying by the agents of the M & I railroad, the legislature readily approved new lines.

The extremes of weather, a drought in the summer of 1854 and a hard freeze the following winter combined to close the river at Madison. Shipping ceased for sixty-three days in the winter of 1855–56 and forty-nine days the next winter. By the winter of 1855–56 hog butchering in Madison dropped to half of the record year 1852–53.

Despite the larger and better equipped fire brigades, disastrous fires added to the troubles. The Magnolia Mill burned in 1854 and the Madison Marine Railroad Shipyard in 1856. The Palmetto Mill burned in 1858. A vibrant Madison of 1848 would have been hard pressed to recover. A depressed Madison of 1858 stood no chance. Fewer trains stood on the sidetracks. Grain bins and storehouses stood half empty. Weeds grew between the cobblestones on the wharf. Store fronts stood mute. Madison withered.

# 25.
## "We not unfrequently negotiated a million of bonds daily."
— JFD Lanier 1853

*In the first four years of his new business, Lanier would be more successful than he had imagined. New York investors would purchase western stocks and bonds at an unprecedented rate. Winslow Lanier & Company would be instrumental in transforming New York City into the center for American railroad investment.*

James and Mary had spent much of their time in New York City before finally moving there. They lived in a hotel that was close to Margaret and James Winslow. Most of the downtown businesses were rebuilt after the fire in December 1835. The major buildings used brick construction with cast-iron facades. Not only were they more fire resistant, they gave an appearance of wealth and stability. Lanier liked the new construction.

Once they made the decision to move, James and Mary began looking for a suitable house. They first found a house at 11 East 17th Street. The couple lived there until sometime in 1853.[1] James and Margaret Winslow lived at 52 Tenth Street, in the Washington Square area. JFD wanted to be close to his daughter, so they began looking in that area. It would afford a chance for him and his son-in-law to converse on business matters. It would also allow Margaret and Mary to socialize and become close friends.

A city complex, including a produce market, a court building and a fire station, stood on the triangle formed by West Tenth Street, Sixth and Greenwich Avenues.[2] Justice in the courtroom was swift and final. Condemned men traveled only a few blocks to Washington Square, the site of public executions which included a pauper's cemetery.[3]

New York City's population was expanding rapidly during the first quarter of the 19th Century. Tenements were crowding the Battery Park area. Businessmen slowly moved north away from the rabble. In 1826 the city fathers decided there was a better future for Washington Square. They relocated the graves, and planted trees and grass, transforming the execution grounds into an inviting park.[4] It quickly became the focal point of a prosperous residential area. The newly popular Greek Revival architecture sprouted around the park. By the time Lanier was looking for a home, the development had spread north to Tenth Street and beyond.

James purchased a four story townhouse at 54 Tenth Street.[5] The typical townhouse was approximately 25 feet wide, with a hall running the full length of each floor. The main entrance was three or four steps down from the street, with the first floor being three to four feet below street level. The front room was normally the family parlor and the room to the rear was the kitchen and laundry room. A door screened the family parlor from guests as they climbed the interior staircase to the second level.

The second level also contained two rooms, a front formal parlor and a formal dining room. Pocket doors separated the rooms. A dumbwaiter lifted food from the kitchen to the dining room.

The upper levels contained two bedrooms each. The front room was normally the master bedroom and the back bedroom was for the youngest children. The fourth level contained additional bedrooms and perhaps servants' quarters. While less than half the size of the Madison house, Mary was very happy. This was their house. She did not have to share the dwelling with ghosts and memories. She set about making it a haven for James.

James led his family back to the Presbyterian Church after

attending the Episcopalian chuch for some years. Henry Ward Beecher had accepted the pulpit of the Plymouth Church in Brooklyn, in late 1847.[6] He welcomed his old friend, and they reminisced about their years in Indiana. Beecher's stories of his ride on the Madison and Indianapolis hog cars in 1847 became more colorful with each telling. Although he visited Beecher's church on occasion, Lanier became a member of the Presbyterian church at University Place and Tenth Street.

Two more grandchildren arrived in 1853. Drusilla had her fifth son, William Jackson Cravens on June 3, and Elisabeth had another girl, Mary Louise, on September 21.[7]

Winslow, Lanier & Company retained the offices of Winslow Perkins at 52 Wall Street, in the heart of the commercial district. JFD enjoyed the carriage ride to work, marveling at the level of activity at all hours of the day. New Orleans, the other major port and commercial city James was familiar with, was slow and quiet in comparison. Southerners had a more deliberate, aristocratic attitude. While Lanier appreciated the genteel, courtly manners of the South, the slow pace of business frustrated him. He was eager to start his new career. His own energy and urgency matched that which flowed through the streets around him.

"Exchanges" were the most efficient method of doing business in large cities. They grew from the need of buyer and seller to get together. It was time consuming and often fruitless to visit a client's office on the chance he might be there. More often then not he was out looking for business and both businessmen missed an opportunity. Other methods of bringing businessmen together developed. The most common of these were the "exchanges."

At first exchanges were informal locations where buyers and sellers would meet. By 1850 the institution of exchanges had become commonplace. Bankers and brokers devoted the morning to office work and record keeping. After lunch, the banker or broker, as well as buyers would go to a known location where they would exchange information and buy or sell commodities. There were cotton exchanges in the South, tobacco exchanges in the Southeast, and livestock exchanges in the West. St. Louis had a large fur exchange. New York City boasted a large stock and bond exchange on Wall Street.

Winslow, Lanier & Company offices bordered the stock and bond exchange. JFD and other members of the firm would spend at least part of almost every afternoon at the exchange. James was at first intimidated by the lack of privacy and organized chaos of the exchange, but it did not take long to adapt to the business practice.

Lanier's decision to concentrate on selling stocks for western ventures, especially railroads, was new, and therefore risky. Many western investments had not proven profitable, and some were unmitigated disasters. Still the entrepreneur that enters a market just before the rush, or that has an edge, is the one that gains the most profit. James felt the timing for railroad and western investments was perfect. In addition he did have an important edge. His trip to Europe, and his association with the M & I, gave him unparalleled knowledge of railroad construction techniques and equipment. Familiarity with the people and projects of the West allowed him to sift the profitable ventures from the worthless schemes.

On January 1, 1849, when Winslow and Lanier established their business, only about 9,000 miles of track existed in the United States.[8] The, western states north of the Ohio River accounted for only 650 miles of that total:

Ohio
    Little Miami                       84 miles
    Mansfield & Sandusky     56 miles
    Mad River                    102 miles
Indiana
    Madison & Indianapolis   56 miles
Michigan
    Michigan Central         146 miles
    Michigan Southern      70 miles
    Erie & Kalamazoo       33 miles
    Detroit & Pontiac       25 miles
Illinois
    Sangamon & Morgan    53 miles[9]

JFD was undaunted. He knew that properly engineered and constructed railroads could be a success. While others felt the sparse population in the West would not support rail construction, Lanier bet his future that rail construction would encourage western migration. He knew profits would follow.

James planned a two pronged effort. First he published a

flood of pamphlets and newspaper articles praising the benefits of proper rail construction. He aimed these pamphlets at future customers and investors. His second effort was to confront rail line executives. Winslow, Lanier would guarantee the sale of the rail bonds if the railroad conformed to the highest design and construction standards.[10]

One of the first New York financiers that JFD took a liking to was Junius Morgan. Morgan was one of only a score of millionaires in the country, having inherited that sum from his father in 1847. Although from different backgrounds, the men had similar ideas. Both realized that the United States was a debtor nation, dependent upon foreign capital for development. As the largest emerging market in the world, the United States offered great opportunities for European investors. Both Morgan and Lanier courted the continental coin with little competition; there was plenty to go around. Both men had boys of the same age. John Pierpont Morgan and Charles Lanier became lifelong friends.

JFD continued his business contacts in the West. They allowed him to keep abreast of business conditions and in touch with decision makers. One of these contacts was Sam Merrill. Lanier's insistence that friendship and business remain separated surfaces in his answer to Merrill's request for a loan. In the spring of 1851, Sam Merrill wrote to Lanier requesting a loan. Lanier replied on July 4, 1851, that a loan was not possible:

**Dear Sir;**
**I have delayed answering your letter to see what can be done for you.**
**It is impossible to make a loan here on securities out West, or indeed out of the city.**
**Money can be had on Bond and Mortgage at 6 per cent. We have tried repeatedly to make loans for people in Ohio at 10 per cent on the most (underrated) mortgage. As to our own money we only lend on call when we have a supply on hand in order to be bringing interest and to have it when we can realize it on a day's notice to use in our business.**
**My own money is all locked up. I have rather to be a borrower myself. It would really give me pleasure to serve you in any way that I can.**
**If I was out at home I could help you to a temporary loan if that would (serve) you.**
**The idea abroad is that money is so plentiful in New York that it can easily be had. This is a mistake. It can only be had on the best local security.**
**Yours truly,**
**JFD Lanier[11]**

Did James refuse his old friend because money was truly not available, or was Merrill a poor risk as Calvin Fletcher had proclaimed years earlier?

It soon became evident to investors that Winslow, Lanier and Company would only sell the bonds of well constructed and properly managed railroads. The brokers continued to give their customers service after the sale, urging the rail lines to continually upgrade. Buyers returned to Winslow, Lanier for additional stocks, confident of a safe, profitable investment. Lanier's friendships with European bankers bore fruit also, as they preferred to purchase stock from a friend.

Winslow, Lanier floated bonds for the Little Miami; Columbus & Xenia; Cleveland, Columbus & Cincinnati; and Cleveland, Painsville and Ashtabula railroads in quick succession. They sold to private investors, institutional investors and to other banking houses who then resold the stocks. Winslow, Lanier sold the Little Miami Railroad bonds by sealed bid. This was another first initiated by Winslow, Lanier & Co.

Government securities sold in that fashion, but not railroad securities.[12] To protect themselves, the brokers probably submitted a base bid that would ensure making a profit.

James plan was more successful than he ever imagined. The brokers took on additional clerks to keep track of the sales. With willing investors on their doorstep, Winslow and Lanier found they could dictate construction and operating standards to rail lines wishing stocks sold. James discovered another profit center. Sometimes the directors of a line allowed Winslow, Lanier to purchase the proper rails to comply with the bankers' standards. Winslow Lanier was happy to oblige, charging a large commission.[13] Once again, by making the cause of his clients his cause, JFD was not only making friends, but making money.

The stockholders were so happy with the services of Winslow, Lanier that they often turned to James to represent them in disputes with the rail lines. In pursuit of a better product and increased dividends for its clients, Winslow and Lanier often gave advice on financial matters, presided over reorganization or proposed policies aimed at helping their clients.

In more than one instance, stockholders elected or appointed Richard Winslow or James Lanier to the board of directors of a rail line. These were very unusual steps for bankers to take at the time.[14] As with the Second Indiana State Bank and

$1.000.000 LITTLE MIAMI RAILROAD COMPANY SIX PERCENT FIRST MORTGAGE BONDS FOR SALE.

Office of Winslow Lanier & Co.,
No. 52 Wall St. June 18, 1853

The Little Miami Railroad Company offer for sale One Million of their six per Per Cent Bonds with their Coupons, Interest and Principal payable in New York, the former half yearly, 1st November and 1st May,

They are in sums of $1,000 each, payable the first day of May 1863.

These bonds are issued under express authority of the Legislature of the State of Ohio; and are part of the $1,500,000 loan authorized to be issued by a vote of the Stockholders for the purpose of raising means to make a double track; the greatly increased and increasing business of the Road make this absolutely necessary.

The Little Miami Railroad is eighty-four miles commencing at the City of Cincinnati and terminating at Springfield.; is now in complete running order; has cost including equipments, stations, station houses &c up to this date $2,708,109.19.

This Company owns stock in the Columbus and Xenia Railroad Company to the amount of $386,000 which now commands a premium of 20 per cent. also in the Hillsborough to the amount of $11,716.

The receipts of the Road have been as follows:

| For the year ending Dec. 1, 1844 | $18,632.26 |
| For the year ending Dec. 1, 1845 | $43,327.58 |
| For the year ending Dec. 1, 1846 | $116,052.02 |
| For the year ending Dec. 1, 1857 | $221,139.52 |
| For the year ending Dec. 1, 1848 | $280,085.78 |
| For the year ending Dec. 1, 1849 | $321,398,82 |
| For the year ending Dec. 1, 1850 | $405,597.24 |
| For the year ending Dec. 1, 1851 | .$487,845.89 |
| For the year ending Dec. 1, 1852 | .$526,746.35 |

The receipts from Dec. 1 to May 1,

| (the last five months) | $260,051.27 |
| For the same time the year before | $172,281.18 |
| Increase in 5 months | $ 87,770..09 |

The position of this road being the most natural, shortest, and most usually traveled route from Cincinnati and the vast country south and west of it, to the northern cities, must make it one of the most important and profitable lines in the country.

An inspection of a map will show its connections to be many and important. This road operated the Columbus and Xenia Road and runs in connection with the Cleveland and Columbus Road, in fact they are now run as one line, greatly to the advantage of all.

Regular annual 10 per cent dividends, have been declared since December 1847, with an extra dividend of 5 per cent in 1851. In 1852 two cash dividends , each 10 per cent were made.

| The present surplus and reserve fund amounted to | $98,546.18. |
| The mortgage covers the entire line of Road costing to date | $2,708,109.19 |
| To be expended on double track etc. | 1,500,000.00 |
| Value of security. | $4,208,109.19 |

The security for the payment of these Bonds is of the most ample character, being a first and only mortgage or deed of trust (excepting one of $100,000 to the city of Cincinnati) on the Company's Road, Stations, Franchises, Net Income &c., to JFD Lanier Esq. of this City, in trust for the Bondholders, with ample power to take possession of the Road, its real and personal estate, franchises &c., and to sell the same to the highest bidder for cash; if default be made in the payment of interest or principal. Its mortgage is for $1,500,000 and can not be increased.

The stock owned by the Road in the Columbus and Xenia and Hillsborough Railways will much more than pay off the $100,00 prior lien to the city of Cincinnati and all other debts of the Company excepting this loan of $1,500,000.

Sealed proposals will be received for any sum not less than $1,000. until Thursday the 1st of September next at 3:0 P.M.

Proposals will be addressed to WINSLOW LANIER & Co. agents of the Company, 52 wall St. New York, endorsed, "Proposals for the Little Miami Railroad Bonds."

One-half of the purchase money will be required to be paid at the time of accepting the bids, the residue in thirty and sixty days. Any purchaser will be at liberty to pay up in full at once.

Interest on the Bonds will run from the day of payment.

The above $1,000,000 will be sold absolutely, and without reserve to the highest bidder.

For any further information apply at the office.

WINSLOW, LANIER & Co.

This advertisement in the *New York Daily Times* in June 1853 is typical of those inserted by Winslow Lanier & Co. It shows the great detail the company used to assure customers that the bonds they offered were safe. It also shows the control over the railroad companies that Winslow, Lanier & Co. demanded if they were to sell the lines' bonds. Winslow Lanier & Co. and the Little Miami Railroad had cooperated before. They two trusted each other.

the Madison and Indianapolis Railroad, James wielded great power.

Lanier's desire to serve both his bond purchasing clients as well as the railroads that issued the bonds, made the company the first full service banking firm. Winslow, Lanier acted as the agent for interest payments on the bonds they sold as well as transfer agents when bonds changed hands.

Often cities and counties would pledge funds if a rail line would agree to serve their area. It was a guarantee of growth and success. The internal improvements disasters made municipal bonds risky. Winslow, Lanier & Company was the first banking house in New York City to sell city and county bonds issued for construction of railroads. Richard Winslow was familiar with the municipalities of Ohio, and Lanier with those of Indiana. Using their combined knowledge, they backed the strongest bonds. This strategy led to another unqualified success. Lanier states that at one time **"we paid the interest on fifty different classes of securities."**[15]

The volume of business was staggering. Lanier writes in his autobiography

> **We not unfrequently negotiated a million of bonds daily. The aggregate for the year was enormous. We were without competitors for a business we had created, and consequently made money very rapidly. The commissions for the negotiations of bonds averaged at first five percent. . . . Our business soon became so great that it was a question with us, no so much what we would undertake, as what we would reject. We not unfrequently took on our own account, an entire issue of important lines.[16]**

This statement is not an exaggeration. On June 24, 1853,

**COLUMBUS AND XENIA RAILROAD COMPANY-TRANSFER NOTICE-** On and after the 25th instant a register of Transfers of Stock of the COLUMBUS AND XENIA RAILROAD COMPANY will be opened at the office of the undersigned in this city.

Holders of certificates issued at the Home Office in Columbus desirous of having them placed on the books in New York , will surrender the same to S.E. Wright, treasurer of the Company in Columbus, requesting to be transferred to the books here, and proper certificates will be sent them.

WINSLOW, LANIER & CO., No. 52 Wall St.

This transfer notice appeared in the *New York Daily Times* on June 18, 1853.

Winslow, Lanier & Company ran one dividend notice in the *New York Daily Times* that listed 38 different bonds. The notice included one for the Second Indiana State Bank, one for the State of California, seven for various city bonds issued for railroads, fifteen for counties supporting railroad bonds,and the bonds for several townships in seven Ohio counties that also supported railroads. Finally there were bonds for eight railroads in Indiana and Ohio. This was only one call for dividend payments, there were many others throughout the year.

Although James was a personal friend of all the major financial barons, he kept a low profile. Lanier continued his earlier practice of working diligently for his clients while deflecting attention away from himself. Consequently he never gained great public attention as did his contemporaries; Jay Cooke, Junius Morgan or Commodore Vanderbuilt. James preferred the anonymity.

Winslow, and Lanier's contributions to the banking and railroad businesses did not go unnoticed, however. Banking historians give the pair their due. Vincent P. Carosso, in the book *Investment Banking in America-A History*, states that:

> Of all the private banks that existed in the United States before the Civil War, Winslow, Lanier and Company probably came closer than any other to providing clients with most of the investment banking services commonly associated with the great banking houses of the latter part of the nineteith and early twentieth centuries. This firm, probably more than any other, contributed substantially toward making New York City the principal center of American railroad finance.[17]

James was very proud of his success, and in a candid moment passes on his satisfaction:

> **The uniform success of the enterprises in behalf of which we acted was something remarkable, and has since been a source of great satisfaction. I feel that investors, as well as the country at large, have been greatly benefited by my labors. The interest on almost all of the securities brought out by us has been regularly paid, while , in not a few instances there has been an enormous profit upon the prices paid. Our house was the first to bring out county and city securities issued for the construction of railroads. These securities were instrumental in the construction of an immense extent of line, which, but for them , could not have been built, while they have proved a most excellent investment. In no instance, I believe, have the**

counties and cities, the bonds of which we negotiated, made default either in principal or interest.[18]

James Lanier could always see into the future. Once again, he was able to sense a fiscal panic before it burst upon the country. By 1853, foreign investors held over twenty-five percent of all American railroad bonds. Europe required large sums of money to fight the Crimean War. Responding to higher interest rates, European investors withdrew capital from America at a time when American railroads desperately needed it.

JFD and Junius Morgan probably talked about the looming crisis. In 1854, Junius moved to England and joined George Peabody. The banking house of Morgan and Peabody functioned as a link between British investors and the American borrowers. Such a link was critical during the rising financial panic. John Pierpont Morgan, was only 17 at the time.

JFD also saw a new and disturbing trend developing in the railroad business. Individuals purchased controlling interest in rail lines and consolidated them into networks. They then controlled these networks for their personal gain. Commodore Vanderbilt, a New York City neighbor of Lanier, was one of this new breed of business giants. Vanderbilt dismissed James' objections as old fashioned and parochial.

Because he disliked the new trends in railroad financing, Lanier decided to enter the banking business so that he would have closer control over his money, and could carefully pick investments. Short term investments like bills of exchange had seen him through the 1837 Panic, and short term would see him through this one. Beyond the panic, JFD saw the dawn of a new banking era. An era where bankers and financiers would control the building of the American Empire. His innovation had been instrumental in building a large railroad dominion. Now he wanted to influence the entire spectrum of American industry. Consequently, at the close of 1854, Winslow, Lanier and Company changed from a brokerage house into a full service banking institution.

# 26.
## "A period of great general depression and discouragement . . ."
JFD Lanier 1857

*Over the next few years Winslow, Lanier & Company would reflect the country's economic situation. Uncertainty was the watchword. It would sink to the point of temporary closing, but rebound to gain strength and stability.*

The transition from brokerage house to a full scale banking house was minor. Winslow, Lanier & Company already provided many services that a banking house would normally offer, now they began taking deposits and discounting. The change allowed the company to readily diversify.

JFD was back in the business that he knew best and loved most. He could pick and choose his fiscal ventures. Of course the firm continued to be fiscal and stock transfer agents for the rail lines whose stocks they had previously sold.[1] This provided a steady income base.

The city was unbearable in the summer. There was no relief, day or night from the steaming heat. The cobblestone streets and the brick buildings soaked up heat during the day and gave it off at night. The summers were more oppressive than they had ever been in Madison. James needed relief. Several friends had built homes along the shore of Staten Island. In the summer of 1854 he joined them, selling his house at 58 Tenth Street.[2] The new house was a large house, continually cooled by the off-shore breezes. Travel in the winter proved difficult, however, so James brought his family back to the city in the spring of 1855. He moved back to the old neighborhood at 54 Tenth Street. He kept the Staten Island house for several years as a summer retreat.

Business dealing required that JFD maintain contact with the political and economic climate in Indiana. The second state bank charter was due to expire. Throughout the country, the Democrats pressed for "free banks." Democrat candidates for office made free banking a cornerstone of their campaigns. The Democrat Press hounded state legislatures for a "free banking system." Indiana was no different from other states. Democrats insisted that the state get out of the banking business, and that stock in the new bank be sold on a first-come first-served basis.

The state bank forces were not willing to give up without a fight, however. They had some powerful facts to support the state bank. In 1855 the stock of the state bank was worth about $75. with a par value of $50. The state owned roughly $1,000,000 in stock. The surplus fund contained another $1,000,000 that accrued to the state. The state still owed a bonded debt of $1,390,000. on its bank stock, but the current value of stock made that a paper debt.[3] Many legislators, even some Democrats, understood the value of the bank, but few would stand in the path of public pressure. Most common people still did not understand banking, and continued to feel that bankers were somehow stealing their money. The Democratic Press fed this misconception, and the push for a free bank intensified.

Bank directors had another effective tool that some were not afraid to use — money. Money could buy influence by either fair means or foul. Selected state bank directors met in Madison in the summer of 1854 to hear a proposal to bribe members of the legislature to renew the current bank charter. They anticipated it would cost about $200,000 in bribes to swing the deal. Encouraged by the lack of opposition at the Madison meeting, General D.E. Taylor, president of the Michigan City branch, and Judge Thomas Smith, attorney for the New Albany branch introduced the idea at the regular August meeting of the bank board. They proposed offering each key member of the state legislature

287

$10,000. J.M. Ray, long-time secretary of the board, squelched the idea by flatly refusing to take part in the scheme and threatening to expose the conspirators.[4]

Thwarted in their efforts to re-charter the old bank, Judge Smith and his cronies developed a new tactic. They publicly supported the free bank. Through his political influence, and perhaps with a few well-placed bribes, Judge Smith secured the appointment to write the new bank bill. The bill contained many of the clauses of the old charter, but was cloaked in new clauses that conformed to the new constitution and appeared to allow for free and open selling of bank shares. The bill provided for commissioners who were responsible for selling bank stock. The measure passed the Senate on a vote of 27-22, and then passed the House of Representatives. Governor Wright vetoed the bill, citing several serious flaws, but the Senate overrode the veto by a 30-20 vote.[5]

Judge Smith succeeded in having himself appointed a commissioner. W. C. Depauw was another. All of the commissioners were judges or politicians. The commissioners earned payment for their efforts by selling the bank locations to interested parties.[6] The commissioners appointed sub-commissioners in several locations to actually sell the stock in the new bank. Michael Bright became a sub-commissioner for Madison.

Section 79 of the law contained the stock subscription language. It reduced the amount of surplus stock allowed, and prohibited corporations from owning stock. Citizens living in the branch bank district received preference when purchasing stock. The books for stock subscription were to open between 9:00 A.M. and noon on the appointed day.[7] This innocent clause gave Judge Smith and his followers all of the control they needed. By appointing sub-commissioners they trusted, and carefully explaining the rules of opening the subscription books, Smith had complete control over the bank shares.

At Indianapolis, W.H. Talbott, and John S. Spann opened the books at 11:50 A.M. Mr. Talbott had a list of subscribers already prepared. It took him ten minutes to copy the list into the subscription book, and the office closed. In Madison the subscription books never opened to the public. Bright took 1200 shares, and his friends the other 600. Bright also purchased large blocks of shares at Rushville, Logansport, and Lawrenceburg.[8] Evidently there were no local residents interested in the stock.

At Evansville, the original sub-commissioners would not follow W.C. DePauw's instructions, so he forced them to resign, delaying the subscriptions until he found new sub-commissioners. DePauw gained controlling interest in the Indianapolis and Bedford branches.[9]

In almost all instances, those purchasing bank stock did so strictly as a short term investment. In many cases, the directors or presidents of the Second State Bank purchased shares in the new bank, and were back in business in the old bank buildings. Michael Bright sold his shares in the Madison branch to James Lanier for a premium of $14,000. At Vincennes, 1300 shares, a controlling interest, was sold back to directors of the old bank at a handsome gain. At Evansville, Mr. Rathbone, of the old bank, purchased 1200 of the 2,000 shares in the new bank. He paid a $10,500 premium for the privilege. At Terre Haute, the owners of the old bank brought a controlling interest in the new one for an extra $10,000. At Fort Wayne, old state bank directors purchased enough shares in the new bank to gain control. At Richmond, new stockholders sold to old bank interests at a premium.[10]

The Democratic newspapers, and those individuals that had cried for a "free bank' took no offense at the double dealing surrounding the subscription of stock. They seemed to believe that the stock distribution was fair because Democrats had benefited. Could it be that the Indianapolis Sentinel relaxed its vigil on the state's purse because Austin Brown, the editor, obtained 500 shares in the Indianapolis branch?[11] Whatever the circumstances, James Lanier once again became involved in banking in Indiana. W.G. Wharton became president of the Madison branch.

While firmly reestablishing himself in the commerce of Indiana, James did not neglect the New York business or political scene. JFD always felt politics was an integral part of business success, and it was an avocation he enjoyed. James found that like business, politics was more intense in New York than in Indiana.

Thurlow Weed was the influential New York Whig boss. Although he held many of the same beliefs that James espoused, the two men were never close. JFD abhorred the strong-armed tactics employed by Weed. Weed flaunted his power, using it openly for his own gains. Lanier preferred to exercise his power quietly, and by always benefiting a person or idea in addition to himself. Another Whig, William Seward, former governor and now senator representing New York, was more palatable to Lanier, but still the banker questioned Seward's motives and moral fiber. The Whigs seemed to be losing popular support in New York. James blamed it on the Whig leadership, but there seemed no alternative.

The situation was no better on the national level. After electing Zachary Taylor president in 1848, the Whigs lost in 1852, with Daniel Webster at the head of the ticket. The party began a precipitous slide from power. With the Whigs losing favor and constituents, alternative parties began to emerge.

The Know Nothings, and Free Soilers were just two of the groups that claimed many former Whigs. James worried about the strength of the Know Nothings. They were essentially a secret society that hated Catholics in particular, and foreigners in general. They showed surprising strength by capturing the Mayor's offices in Washington and Philadelphia while sweeping the legislature and governor's office in Massachusetts. Only the strong forces of Seward and Weed kept the Know Nothings out of Albany.[12]

The problems in politics, and business foreshadowing a depression lost meaning as James Lanier endured another personal tragedy. In July 1855, his youngest son, four year old James Lanier succumbed to illness.[13] Devastated, Mary spent months in seclusion. The curse seemed to be still haunting JFD. He would not have a namesake son. The death hammered JFD's resilient spirit. The Laniers had no cemetery plot, and were so devastated they could not cope with that detail. Richard Winslow told James he could use the mausoleum Winslow had purchased in Greenwood Cemetery in Brooklyn until JFD made other arrangements.[14]

By 1855 the Know Nothings exposed their true colors, and they began to lose favor. A new coalition was on the rise to face the Democrats. They called themselves Republicans, and put forward General John C. Fremont as their presidential candidate in 1856. The Republicans championed many of the popular stands of the Whigs, Free Soilers and Know Nothings, while ignoring or denouncing the more radical ideas. Although a newcomer to politics, Fremont gave a good accounting of himself, and encouraged the new party. Reinvigorated, James contemplated a more active role in politics.

In 1855, Drusilla had her sixth child and first girl. James was happy for his daughter, and pleased that Drusilla named the child Elisabeth Gardner Cravens.[15] On March 20, 1856, Elisabeth had her seventh and final child. They named the boy George Marshall Dunn.[16] Still mourning the loss of their own son, Mary and James may not have looked forward to seeing the baby for the first time, but Elisabeth was so happy, and the baby so cute that he won over his grandparents' hearts.

Business once again helped James recover. The money supply was constricting and interest rates were rising. Lanier evaluated business ventures with an increasingly skeptical eye. He refused loans with increasing frequency. Any loans he approved carried stringent conditions.

Bankruptcies became more numerous. Business reorganizations to stave off bankruptcy more common. Banks became victims as often as failed businesses. JFD had been through all this before. He reduced the ratio of capital to loans. He shortened the loan periods. He increased the reserve funds. Still the signs of an economic panic continued to intensify like a far off tidal wave that promised to engulf everything in its path. There was little Winslow and Lanier could do but brace for the onslaught.

In 1857, Richard Winslow's health began to fail. He had lived in Connecticut for many years, renting rooms during the week in New York City, but retreating to his country home for quiet and rest on the weekends. Now he spent more time in Connecticut than in the city, trusting the business to Lanier and to his son James. The Lanier family continued on a roller coaster of emotions. On June 21, Robert and Drusilla Cravens had another boy, named Charles.[17] In September Mary, who had married John Cameron Stone the previous October, delivered a stillborn boy. The grieving family laid the child to rest in the borrowed mausoleum on September 23.[18]

Adding to Lanier's burden of more responsibility for managing the firm, was the weight of a full blown depression that hit the country by 1857. Payrolls dwindled and loan payments ceased. Businesses failed by the score. Railroad revenues dropped dramatically, driving them to the brink of bankruptcy. Many banks suspended specie payment. JFD described the situation:

> **These (railroad) earnings, owing to the embarrassments into which every kind of industry and business had fallen decreased largely for several years and in many cases proved wholly inadequate to meet even the calls for interest. Many of**

> our most valuable enterprises were forced into bankruptcy, and had to be reorganized by new adjustments of interests, and, in most cases, by large sacrifices on the part of stock and bondholders. A period of great general depression and discouragement followed one of previous confidence and hope.[19]

Railroads and other large capital industries require substantial floating debts to continue expansion. They suffered greatly during the 1857 panic. Another casualty was the Wabash & Erie Canal. It suffered not only from the depression, but from floods, and strong railroad competition. Lack of capital for the canal caused deferred maintenance, further reducing revenues in a deadly downward spiral.[20]

Several happy occasions brightened an otherwise dismal 1857 for the Lanier family. Charles graduated from Russell Military Academy in New Haven Connecticut, and joined Winslow Lanier & Company.[21] On November 7, 1857, Charles married Sarah Egleston in New York City.[22] The wedding was a beautiful affair, and the reception elegant. For a few days, JFD was able to retreat from the crush of the depression and enjoy the anticipation and optimism of a new beginning. James would not let the darkness on the horizon discourage his son. He admitted that the present looked bad, but reminded Charles that he had survived many panics. Business would revive, stronger than before. They just needed patience.

Everyone connected with Winslow, Lanier & Company needed a full measure of patience and faith within two weeks of Charles' wedding. The depression continued to deepen, and on October 20, 1857, the *Madison Courier* reported that Winslow, Lanier & Company had suspended operation. The shutdown apparently lasted less than two weeks, however, as the same paper reported on October 31, that Winslow, Lanier was again resuming payments. This was the lowest point in the company's long history.

Lanier still had a large stake in the Wabash and Erie, so suffered with the other investors. The bondholders met in London, Washington D.C. and New York City. They formed a joint committee to address the problems. The committee elected JFD chairman. They decided to petition the state legislature for relief, pleading that the legislature never met the conditions of the 1847 law, and the state had been remiss in chartering railroads that paralleled the canal. All of the major bondholders including the Rothschilds, Baring Brothers, and JFD Lanier signed the petition.[23] The legislature responded with a Joint resolution which stated:

> The General Assembly has no power under the Constitution to purchase the Wabash and Erie Canal, and be it further resolved that if the General Assembly had the power it would be impolitic, unwise, and injurious to the best interests of the people of the State to purchase said canal.[24]

James Lanier was not ready to admit defeat. He orchestrated one last effort to recoup the losses. In a letter written to all bondholders on November 26, Lanier assessed each Wabash and Erie Canal bondholder 1/4 of 1 percent of the value bonds they held to carry on the fight.[25] JFD hounded the legislature all during the 1858-59 session, to no avail. Although William McKee Dunn was a successful politician in Indiana, James was losing his influence in the state. Many of his friends in the legislature had retired or died. He lost the canal battle, but not his faith in Indiana, nor his love of the state.

James continued his close watch on happenings in Indiana, and in Madison. City of Madison bonds were presented to Winslow, Lanier & Company for payment. Lanier knew these bonds violated the Madison City Charter, and refused payment. JFD's old friend Jeremiah Sullivan represented Madison in the matter of the bogus bonds. His son, Algernon Sullivan was an attorney practicing in New York City. In November of 1859, Jerimiah wrote Algernon requesting a deposition from James Winslow on the problem.[26]

James was able to keep his family life separate from business. He was happy when Sarah announced she was pregnant, and ecstatic when she delivered a boy on June 25, 1858. The Lanier name would survive. He had serious concern when Charles insisted on naming the boy JFD the second.[27]

There was much to celebrate in the Lanier family as 1859 began. Drusilla and Robert had their eighth child, Joseph Marshall Cravens, on February 9, 1859.[28] On the political front, William McKee Dunn continued to climb the political ladder. Following the election of 1858, the Indiana legislature sent him to Congress, and he took his seat on March 4, 1859.[29]

Despite the poor economic situation, James continued to help the railroads where he could. He felt an obligation to help the companies he had helped to create and the industry he had promoted.[30] It was a responsibility not only to the companies, but to the stockholders. Lanier held stock himself in some of the lines, so he had a personal interest in their survival as well. The depression would be fleeting. Railroads represented the future of the country. He just had to keep the faith.

JFD aided many rail lines weather the storm, but the Pittsburgh, Fort Wayne and Chicago Railroad Company is the best example of his involvement. Three smaller companies joined to form the PFW&CRR. The railroad borrowed money to continue the work, but the fiscal crisis made it impossible to pay the interest on the debt. PFW&CRR stock was worth about five cents on the dollar, and foreclosure appeared inescapable.[31]

To raise cash to pay for participation in the railroad rescue, Lanier sold his stock in the Madison Bank to his old friends Calvin Fletcher and Thomas Sharp. Sharp became president, replacing W.G. Wharton.[32]

The future looked grim for the PFW&CRR. Nine different classes of bonds remained outstanding. The overdue interest on the bonds totaled several million dollars. Several first mortgages were coming due. In addition, the company owed more than two million dollars in floating debt.[33] Operating problems included poorly maintained rolling stock, and a roadbed that required significant rebuilding.

The first mortgage bondholders, which held about thirty-three percent of the bonds, met in the offices of Winslow, Lanier to discuss the situation. This group appointed a committee to proceed with the plan to save all of the investors. The committee consisted of Samuel Tilden, Louis Meyer, J. Edgar Thomson, president of the Pennsylvania Railroad, and Samuel Hanna of Fort Wayne. They elected Lanier chairman of the group.[34]

To protect the line from suits of individual investors, the PFW&CRR went into receivership under the protection of the U.S. District Court for the Northern District of Ohio. On January 17, 1860, the judge signed the court order. The committee then attempted to develop a plan that would protect the right of all stockholders, but allow the railroad to continue operating. This plan required the consent of every stockholder, which proved impossible.[35] Undaunted, the committee began work on an alternate solution.

Despite the fiscal crisis that swirled around him, James remained actively interested in politics. Lanier heard from friends in Indiana that Abraham Lincoln was a rising Republican star in the West. Lincoln intrigued Lanier. James had not met the lawyer, but remembered that Lincoln had campaigned in western Indiana in 1840 for William Henry Harrison. Lincoln and Lanier had many experiences in common. Both their fathers left Kentucky because of fraudulent land claims; both he and Lincoln were lawyers, and had lived for a time in Indiana. Both had married girls from Lexington, Kentucky. It was very possible that Elisabeth's father had been friends with the Todds; Lexington was a small close-knit town in the 1820's.

Young Republicans in New York opposed the Seward campaign for president.[36] They invited Lincoln to give a major speech in New York City. James was increasingly unhappy with the Weed-Seward coalition, and was looking for an alternative. He decided to attend. Perhaps Lincoln was the man.

Monday evening, February 27, Abraham Lincoln delivered his speech at Cooper Union. There was a heavy snowstorm in progress, and although about 1500 people came to hear the rising Republican politician, there were a number of empty seats.[37] Cooper Union was near Lanier's home, so the snowstorm did not deter him. James Lanier paid the twenty-five cent admission and settled in to hear the speech.

After being introduced, Lincoln unfolded from his chair and seemed to stretch beyond the cuffs of his rumpled suit. The simple cut of the coat reflected the western style, causing snickers through out the audience. James must have found it familiar and reassuring. Lincoln's Kentucky twang jolted many in the audience, but James found it comforting. The future president's speech was engrossing. Noise in the hall died as the sophisticated audience strained to hear every word of this awkward westerner. He argued that the founding fathers held a Republican view on the evils of slavery. He categorically dismissed the notion that slave and non-slave viewpoints could survive together. The speech ended with the words: "Let us have faith that right makes might, and in that faith let us to the end, dare to do our duty as we understand it."[38]

He had captured the crowd. Applause and cheers filled the hall. He had also captured Lanier who had found his alternative.

JFD could sense a change in the country as he entered the sixth decade of his life. The nation edged closer to the abyss of revolt. The panic of 1857 signaled the people were not happy with the fiscal management of the nation. The increased opposition to the Democrats was a warning that the political situation was deteriorating. Positions hardened on the state's rights and slavery issues. The people were no longer willing to accept compromise. Lanier decided it was time to concentrate his efforts and consolidate his holdings.

James still owned the house in Indiana, but returned infrequently for visits. The winter weather made travel too difficult, and the summers were unbearable. He contemplated turning it over to Alex. The move would save paying the taxes and upkeep. Although Alexander was the unofficial caretaker, several family members lived in the house for varying periods of time.

Before he could make a final decision, disaster struck Madison. On Monday, May 21, 1860, a strong tornado roared down the river valley, devastating parts of the town. The wind blew the roof off the passenger and freight deport of the M & I Railroad. The Star Mills and the Pearl Starch Factory also lost roofs. Three of the four chimneys at the Madison Hotel toppled. Many boats sank resulting in the loss of several lives on the river.[39]

The Lanier house was in the middle of the storm. The main structure withstood the blow, but the swirling winds took the roof off the east wing. Fortunately there were no injuries at the house. JFD instructed his eldest son to make immediate repairs, and to reinforce the house if possible to protect it from future storms. Alexander decided a mansard style roof might protect the wing against future calamities.

James probably gave his eldest son a stipend for maintaining the house. Still a bachelor, Alexander had no need for the expanse of rooms, so lived in the kitchen wing. He kept the main house ready for his father's visits. Alex still disappointed James, but in the last analysis, he could not completely abandon his eldest son. On November 18, 1861, "in consideration of natural love and affection, and of one dollar," James deeded the house to Alexander.[40]

Alex had become his own person and was making a reputation for himself in Madison. He was a man of education, wealth and leisure, whose life "flowed on like a song" He was a "citizen of social nature, civic interests and kindly heart." He often sent fruit baskets to invalids, and was fond of sharing game that he shot on hunting trips.[41]

Everyone in Madison knew the story of Alex's lost love. Sam

Sering, a childhood playmate, and Alex both fell in love with Stella Godman. Stella chose Sering over Lanier, and Alex never overcame the disappointment.

Alexander inherited the love of formal gardens from his father, spending most of his time improving them and testing exotic plant species. At some point after 1860 he had several fountains constructed throughout Madison. The fountains doubled as horse watering troughs. Townsfolk pointed to the fountains as another example of Alexander's kindness.[42] It was also, perhaps, one final act of contrition.

James did not relinquish all of his interests in Indiana. He continued to fight for the Pittsburgh Fort Wayne and Chicago Railroad. The stockholders of the PFW&C Railroad would not agree to the original plan; the only solution left to the committee was to obtain a court order to sell the railroad, and all of its assets. The court required the new owners to prepare and publish a detailed fiscal operating plan. Unhappy debt holders stalled this plan for many months with court challenges. Finally on Thursday, October 24, 1861, the line sold at auction. James Lanier purchased the PFW&CRR on behalf of himself and the committee for the sum of $2,000,000.[43] The directors elected him president of the line. Years later his son Charles became president of the PFW&CRR.[44]

James appointed Jesse Williams as the Chief Engineer for the PFW&CRR with instructions to provide an honest assessment of the condition of the system and the cost of rehabilitating it. This was the same Jesse Williams who years earlier had recommended that the Madison & Indianapolis railroad be abandoned. Despite disagreeing with Williams about the M & I, Lanier admired the honesty and ability of the engineer.

James would not let the problems of the Pittsburgh, Fort Wayne & Chicago blind him to the election. Lincoln's nomination pleased him, but he knew from disappointing experience that this was only the beginning. Nomination did not mean election. It did not surprise Lanier that Weed and Seward returned from the Chicago Convention as strong supporters of Lincoln. JFD knew they had gained important concessions. Seward was not bashful about explaining that he had a fool-proof plan for avoiding civil war. He fully expected to be running the country while the 'prairie statesman' served as a figurehead.[45]

James had heard political blunderbuss for as long as he

could remember and discounted the talk that others took as gospel. This was a critical time for the nation. He liked Lincoln's stand on principle, and had growing appreciation of his political ability. Lanier agreed that the nation his forebears had fought to establish and preserve was again in mortal danger. He felt that Lincoln was the best man to save the Union.[46] As was his custom JFD worked diligently behind the scenes to influence the outcome of the election.

The campaign was as desperate as the consequences. The pro-slavery Democrats broke from the mother party and ran John C. Breckenridge. John Bell ran as the Constitutional Union candidate. Stephen Douglas, Lincoln's old opponent from Illinois, tried to rally the northern Democrats. Remembering the Whigs failed strategy, JFD wondered if the election was headed for the House of Representatives.

October returns from elections in Pennsylvania and Indiana gave Lincoln sweeping victories. The Pennsylvania results discouraged Douglas.[47] The Indiana results encouraged Lanier. Tuesday, November 6, was election day for most of the country. New York ballots were some of the earliest counted, and the state went solidly into the Lincoln camp. The large number of electors in New York all but clinched the election.

# 27.
## "The white trash of the South spawned on Illinois"
— Wedell Phillips 1860

*Secession followed quickly on the heels of Lincoln's election. Like all other families, the Laniers faced the long desperate struggle of a civil war.*

Critics of Lincoln stepped to the forefront as soon as the election results became known. The Atlanta newspaper *Confederacy* predicted:

> Let the consequences be what they may - whether the Potomac is crimsoned in human gore, and Pennsylvania Avenue is paved ten fathoms deep with mangled bodies, or whether the last vestige of liberty is swept from the face of the American continent, the South will never submit to such humiliation and degradation as the inauguration of Abraham Lincoln.[1]

Not all the criticisms came from the South. Radical Northerners had their say. Wendell Phillips, an outspoken abolitionist who welcomed war, called Lincoln "The white trash of the South spawned on Illinois."[2]

Along with the thousands of congratulatory letters to the

new president came numerous threats and recommendations. One citizen proposed he resign at his inauguration in favor of Douglas. Another suggested that Lincoln have all his food tasted. One man offered to make a shirt of chain mail to protect the president.[3]

Southerners acted immediately on their convictions. The South Carolina Legislature voted to raise and equip 10,000 volunteers. In Louisiana $500,000 was pledged to defend secession. Not to be outdone, the Georgia Legislature approved $1,000,000 for troops and equipment.[4]

Hundreds of federal employees in the South; judges, postmasters, customs agents and others sent in their resignations. More than one-third of the 1108 regular army officers resigned. Secessionists occupied the Mint in New Orleans along with several small military garrisons and countless post offices.[5]

Many feared that Lincoln would be assassinated on his way to Washington, or even more dramatically on the steps of the Capitol during the inauguration. Some suggested that the inauguration site be changed to a more protected area. Lincoln vetoed the idea reportedly telling a friend he would rather he hanged by the neck until dead on the steps of the Capitol than buy or beg a peaceful inauguration.[6]

The problems of the country weighed heavily on James Lanier. He knew and loved the people in the South. It was hard to imagine that those old friends believed in secession. JFD believed in the political process, and was devastated that it had failed his country in its most desperate hour. Radicals on both sides had taken control of events. There seemed no solution except war. Lanier was a staunch Republican and Union advocate. He states in his autobiography:

> **In 1860, the election of Mr. Lincoln to the Presidency of the United States, an event which I earnestly desired, was followed by mutterings of the coming storm, which soon burst upon the country with resistless violence. I was too old to take to the field, but I gave whatever aid encouragement I could to the cause of the Union.[7]**

James might be willing to take to the field himself, but he would never allow Charles to go. He would gladly provide all of the time, effort and money at his disposal but not his treasured son. Other family members volunteered to fight. Elisabeth's husband, William McKee Dunn, had vowed to join the army if war

300

came. Their son, named after his father, was 17 and anxious for a fight. James understood young William's feelings. At 17 he would have gladly marched off with General Harrison. JFD toyed with giving William his father's sword.

JFD never wavered in his support even though a war could devastate Winslow. Lanier. The firm would surely lose its investments in the South. Investment capital would move toward war production and away from expansion. Unlike the majority of Northerners, he knew it would be a long, desperate war. Rebuilding after the war could take years. He dreamed of a transcontinental railroad. Now he wondered if he would live to see it happen.

There were other, more distant relatives in the South that would surely fight against the Union. His friends in Vicksburg, Natchez, and New Orleans or their sons would take up the cause. Many would die. What a waste this war would bring, but there seemed no alternative left. Along with the rest of the country, James Lanier undoubtedly prayed long and often for a peaceful solution.

Amid the turmoil and uncertainty, on February 14, 1861, Richard Winslow succumbed after a long illness. JFD felt relief that his old friend no longer suffered, but the loss deeply saddened him. Richard Winslow was more than a trusted business partner; he was James' closest friend. *The American Railroad Journal* printed a litany of Richard Winslow's accomplishments in the March 2 edition. James thought it a fitting obituary for his friend.

On March 14, 1861, Drusilla delivered her ninth child, Mary Louise.[8] James reassured his daughter that the war would be over long before her daughter was old enough to have a memory of it.

Despite prayers that must have rattled the gates of Heaven, the country moved unrestrained toward war. On Sunday, April 14, 1861, after two days of bombardment, Fort Sumter fell. The "resistless violence" had begun. The next day, Lincoln sent out the first call for volunteers to defend the Union. Both sides were unprepared. In addition to losing over 350 of its trained officers, and uncounted troops, the Union Army possessed antiquated, poorly maintained equipment. Lincoln asked individual states to raise and supply the troops for a protracted war, but the militia arsenals were empty.

In Indiana the situation was critical. Lt. Governor Oliver Morton ascended to the Governor's chair when the state legislature sent Governor Lane to the U.S. Senate. Upon inventorying the state arsenal, Morton found less than 500 small arms of various makes and caliber. All were in very poor condition. There were only eight cannon available.[9]

The state treasury was equally bare. Indiana would have to issue bonds to pay the troops and purchase equipment and supplies. With all states and the federal government attempting to raise funds, the bond market collapsed. Lanier offered his help in a letter to Governor Morton dated only five days after Lincoln's first call for help.

The original amount promised by JFD proved to be woefully inadequate and Lanier continued to advance the state money until the loans totaled $400,000.[10] This money allowed Morton to supply Indiana's troops with the best equipment available.

When the first Indiana regiments marched through Cincinnati, the Cincinnati *Commercial* stated:

**On April 26, 1861, the *Madison Courier* carried this article.**

The following letter from JFD Lanier , Esq. formerly of this city, to Governor Morton was published yesterday in Indianapolis:

$25,000 Tendered

Banking Office of Winslow, Lanier & Co.
52 Wall Street
New York, April 20, 1861.

HIS EXCELLENCY OLIVER P. MORTON.
GOVERNOR OF INDIANA
INDIANAPOLIS, INDIANA

Sir: should your State need more money to arm and equip your quota of volunteers for the defence of our country now so wantonly assailed, you can rely on my advancing her any sum not exceeding $25,000.

I have the honor to be your ob't servant

JFD Lanier

> The Governor of Indiana has out generaled the Governor of Ohio. The former has sent four admirably equipped regiments to the battlefield and has two more ready at an hour's notice.

Several days later when the other two regiments passed through town, the *Commercial* once again sang their praises: "They are armed with the new United States muskets of the most approved pattern. No Ohio troops have such arms."

The Indiana Legislature, afflicted with "War Fever," directed that $2,000,000 in bonds be sold to finance the effort. JFD was instrumental in selling all of the bonds, despite the unfavorable market.

Lanier helped in other ways. On July 23, 1861, Morton feared that the federal government could not supply the necessary rifles before Lincoln called the troops to service. He telegraphed JFD "See what you can buy 5000 rifles for at once."[11]

Charles also offered his help. Father and son decided that Charles could be of great service to Morton without donning a uniform. They offered his services to Robert Dale Owen who was representing Morton in New York City. Morton requested that Owen visit a contingent of Indiana troops at Fortress Monroe. When Owen found it impossible, he telegraphed Morton on November 12, 1861 "Can not go to Fortress Monroe without neglecting ten times as much business here. Have sent Charles Lanier instead, Have written him today"[12] Charles went immediately. Charles telegraphed the Governor on November 16, when his inspection was complete.

> I am just from Fort Monroe. The boys have been provided for by government with the exception of guns. They want 750. I will give full particulars from New York.[13]

On November 18, Charles wrote Governor Morton a long letter detailing the condition of the Indiana troops at Fortress Monroe. He also sent the Governor a bill for $54.00 for his traveling expenses.[14]

The turmoil in the country affected business. Capital dried up as investors tried to determine the future. Those who had capital to offer purchased government bonds to help fight the war.

William McKee Dunn Jr., Elisabeth's son, took a more direct role in the conflict. He joined the army soon after the outbreak of war and was commissioned a second lieutenant. He eventually joined Grant's staff. Grant is proported to have said of him:

He is as brave as Julius Caesar. Had I ordered him to a place that it was certain death to go I do not believe he would have hesitated a moment to obey the order.[15]

Life sprung anew midst the terrible killing that had begun. Sarah Lanier presented Charles with a girl, Sarah Egleston, on April 8, 1862.[16] The arrival of the granddaughter cheered JFD. She was a sign that there was still goodness in the world. The mundane tasks of life went on also. Farmers planted seed and harvested crops, driven by the need to feed a growing army. Businesses sprung up to supply the troops. To some it was a patriotic duty, to others a way to profit amid chaos.

Life continued in Madison, as well as a thousand towns along the disputed border between North and South. When Alexander discovered the main sills under the front wall of the mansion were rotting, he called in an engineer from Cincinnati. The solution was to install 18 hydraulic "presses" (jacks) under the sill. Three water pumps, fed the jacks to raise the house. The Madison *Courier* of August 12, 1861, described the results ". . . we saw the walls raised 1/2 of an inch in two minutes" With the house raised, workers installed stone sills. Stone wedges believed used in the operation can still be seen under the southwest corner of the house.

The repair of the house was interesting to JFD, and he probably loaned Alexander the money to pay for it, but his immediate concern was the disruption of Winslow, Lanier caused by the outbreak of war. He believed the drop in the market to be short-term, but it did affect cash flow, which was always minimal.

Still he pressed on with saving the Pittsburgh, Fort Wayne & Chicago Railroad. It was more important than ever to save the line now; the war effort needed every mile of track. The major stockholders had gained time with their maneuvering, but their investment was still at risk. The plan was to form a new company, but to do so required enabling legislation in the states of Pennsylvania, Ohio, Indiana and Illinois. The committee obtained the necessary legislation solely by hard work and persuasion. At a time when paying off politicians was commonplace, the committee paid not a dime to obtain the legislation needed.[17]

Investors received stock in the new company in the same amounts and classes as the old stock. The stock transfer occurred on May 1, 1862. The company required investors to forgo interest for two years, and that money paid for improvements to the line.

During this two and one-half years of uncertainty George W. Cass, the president, ran the line. He kept the trains running, and the creditors at bay. Tilden acted as the railroad's attorney and rendered invaluable service. Lanier played a vital role as detailed in the *New York Times*:

> The Chairman of the Committee was not infrequently called upon to advance, from his private funds, considerable sums in aid of the operations of the road. Such advances were, of course, repaid, but only with simple interest. The good name and financial strength of Mr., Lanier joined to his well known prudence and caution, tended to inspire great confidence in the action of the Committee in which he justly exerted great influence.[18]

At the end of the day, the Pittsburgh, Fort Wayne and Chicago Railroad survived. During 1862 the line had profits of $2,000,000. The officers plowed it all back into improvements. In 1863, aided by war traffic, the railroad netted $3,000,000.[19]

Even though many Hoosiers opposed the war,[20] everyone supported the troops. Even Mary Lanier, who had little or no direct ties with Indiana troops, sent boxes of clothing to Col. Barker's. Indiana Cavalry.[21] During the time that JFD was saving the Pittsburgh, Fort Wayne and Chicago Railroad, Indiana rallied behind her regiments. Oliver Morton became known as the "Soldier's Friend" by spending most of his time and energy providing for Indiana troops in the field. He established a State Sanitary Commission, and was in constant communication with field commanders in an effort to improve supplies, rations and living conditions.

Morton argued fiercely on behalf of Indiana troops, and was not afraid to take his case to Secretary of War Stanton, or to President Lincoln himself. When he could not visit the troops personally, he sent emissaries. The mothers and daughters left at home revered the Governor for his efforts, and the troops in the field cheered his name. Morton wanted a more active role in the war. Twice he asked Lincoln for a military command. The president refused him both times, stating that Morton was more valuable where he was.[22] History would prove Lincoln was correct.

The faction of the Democratic Party in Indiana that favored the southern cause retreated, but did not die. They secretly fomented unrest whenever possible, and openly criticized Gover-

305

nor Morton. They became known as "Copperheads" because they would strike without warning and silently retreat.

Not all of Morton's problems stemmed from Copperheads. To be valid, state bonds needed the signatures of several state officials in Indianapolis. Bonds sold in New York also had to carry the signature of the state agent. The state agent was a political appointment made by the legislature. To expedite bond sales in New York, the state agent kept a book of bonds that had been pre-signed by state government officials. To sell a state bond in New York, it needed only the state agent's signature to be valid. It was a poor procedure, but in a time when sales were critical, it was common practice.[23]

James A. Cravens was the state agent under Governor Hammond. Cravens was a Democrat from Washington County. He was no relation to Drusilla's husband. His deputy was David C. Stover.

When Col. R.N. Hudson took over as Indiana State Agent in New York City early in 1862, a routine audit uncovered a potentially disastrous problem. Scores of bonds were missing. Stover had signed them and gave them to a Mr. Samuel Hallett. Hallett sold the bonds and split the proceeds with Stover. The missing bonds totaled over $250,000.[24]

Fearing disclosure of the fraud would have a devastating effect on Indiana's and the national credit, Oakey Hall, the New York City Prosecutor, and Col. Hudson decided to keep the problem quiet while they pressed Stover and Hallett to return the fraudulent bonds. The thieves agreed to return the bonds and make full restitution, but while returning some bonds, they continued to issue others until the total outstanding reached alarming proportions.[25] When Governor Morton learned of the problem he moved for an immediate indictment of the criminals.[26] Morton probably consulted with Lanier on the issue, but there is no record of Lanier's involvement at this point. Oakey Hall persuaded the governor to wait.[27] Hall had southern sympathies, so may have enjoyed keeping a strong Union state in hot water.[28]

By May 1862, it appeared that the story was about to leak to the newspapers. Governor Morton was in Corinth Mississippi visiting Indiana troops. Jesse J. Brown, a bond commissioner, telegraphed Morton on May 21:

Stover is now in Indiana. The fraud increases in amount. I will be in Indianapolis Friday, don't be about.[29]

On May 23, Morton's secretary telegraphed:

I think you had better come here at once. Matter of importance I can't telegraph in connection with New York matter.[30]

JFD also wired Morton on May 23, informing him the story was about to break: **"An expose of the radicals will be in the paper afternoon. Names may not be given. You and Brown had better come on immediately."**[31]

J.J. Brown rushed to New York to file a criminal complaint against Stover. In the meantime Indiana Attorney General Kibby had Stover arrested and held in Indiana on a preliminary charge. It appears the move satisfied New York investors. Hudson telegraphed Morton's secretary on May 26:

After consulting with Mr. Lanier we have thought it best to wait further action until Mr. Kibby arrives here. Am getting along with the fraudulent issue pretty well and think we can save the state from all harm.[32]

The opposition press began a blistering attack. Morton telegraphed Oakey Hall asking about the charges against Stover. He also asked when Hall wanted Stover in New York.[33] Morton wanted to announce the Stover indictment.

To Morton's dismay, Hall telegraphed that he was in the country, and a grand jury would not meet until the following week. Morton wanted Stover out of town, so sent him to New York on May 28, accompanied by Kibby, and in the custody of two police officers. Morton telegraphed both Brown and Hall, instructing them not to let Stover talk to anyone. He telegraphed Brown again requesting a statement exonerating Morton be printed in *The New York Times, Tribune* and *Herald*. On May 29, the governor boarded a train for New York, as much to escape as to testify.[34]

The criticism did not diminish with the target out of town. The Democratic press accused Morton of being in league with Stover, and turning on his friend only after discovery of the plan. Morton talked with Hall, who finally agreed to write a letter to the papers taking full responsibility for delaying the prosecution of Stover and Hallett.[35]

The grand jury hearing dragged on. Morton asked that all of the laws pertaining to the issue and transfer of Indiana stocks be sent to him "be sure and get all" he instructs Holloway.[36] Finally, on June 21, the grand jury indicted Samuel Hallett[37] The action did not diminish the *Indianapolis Sentinel's* attacks on Morton, but it did give his supporters ammunition against the attacks.

About this time, the offices of the Indiana state agent moved to a building next to Winslow, Lanier & Company. This allowed close consultation with Lanier.

The situation on the battlefields also aided the Copperheads. During the summer of 1862 the Northern troops suffered a series of setbacks. The last week of August, a badly outnumbered Confederate General Robert E. Lee, whipped Brigadier General John Pope at the Second Battle of Bull Run. On August 29, Confederate Lieutenant General Kirby Smith mauled the Union forces under Major General William Nelson at Richmond, Kentucky. Indiana brigades suffered heavy casualties in both these engagements.

Union Major General Don Carlos Buell won the race to Louisville, but it did not escape Indiana residents that this gave Confederate Major General Braxton Bragg free run of the rest of Kentucky and most of Tennessee. It appeared in these tense days, punctuated by repeated calls to stem the gray flood, that the Ohio River would become the northern boundary of the Confederacy.

Hoosiers had a reputation for "splitting their ticket." Both political parties ardently courted the state in every national election because it was an important swing state. Faith in the Union cause was waning among the Indiana electorate. The majority of Hoosiers could still trace their roots to states south of the Ohio River, and many still held a strong distrust of the eastern states.

Hoosiers became bitter toward President Lincoln when he proposed the Emancipation Proclamation. They would fight to save the Union, not to free slaves.[38] Frustration mounted against generals that refused to fight or fought and lost. Fear that their sons, brothers, husbands and fathers died for naught intensified.

Copperheads under the banner of the "Peace Democracy" played on the fears and prejudices of the voters. They promised to pull Indiana troops out of the battle lines and work toward a negotiated settlement to the war.

Governor Morton's tireless efforts to provide troops and material, not only for the eastern campaigns, but also for the alarms attending the Confederate advances on Louisville, Kentucky and Cincinnati, Ohio kept him from campaigning during the off year election. This undoubtedly aided the Peace Democracy, who also counted on the fact that soldiers in the field could not vote.

In the October 1862 election, the bitter, frustrated, confused and scared Indiana electorate voted out the Union party and voted in the Peace Democracy. Neither Morton nor Lincoln was standing for reelection, but that did not save the lesser lights of the Union Party. The Peace Democracy captured the offices of the secretary of state, state auditor, state treasurer, and attorney general. They also won control of the general assembly. Since the legislature elected the U.S. senators, Peace Democrats filled these offices.

After the election it did not take long for the battle of wills to clash. On November 15, 1862, the Democracy held a "jubilee" in Cambridge City, Indiana. Crowds cheered Clement Valladigham, a southern sympathizer from Ohio, deported by Lincoln for treason. Even the name of Jefferson Davis evoked applause and cheers. Valladigham called on Governor Morton to resign.

Copperheads advanced a plan to establish the "Northwest Confederacy" made up of the states of Indiana, Ohio, and Illinois. The Northwest Confederacy would withdraw from the war and establish strong ties with the Southern Confederacy.

The Democratic State Central Committee added to the destructive rhetoric when they asked the electorate: "Will you submit to abolition . . . and allow a degraded race to share the soil consecrated to the dignity and glory of the white race?"[39] The Knights of the Golden Circle, a secret society that favored the Confederacy, spoke more directly. They talked openly of killing Governor Morton. "We can easily dispose of him when the time comes. It will be an irrepressible assassination-that is all"[40]

When the legislature opened, Peace Democrats introduced resolution after resolution favoring the Southern Confederacy. Proposals for an armistice, and for the convening of a peace conference, filled the legislative agenda.. Debate on resolutions demanding the withdrawal of the Emancipation Proclamation and declaring the military draft unconstitutional echoed through the chambers.. Opponents initiated several investigations into Governor Morton's handling of the war funds..[41]

The Indiana troops soon learned of the events at home and

rushed to the aid of "the soldier's friend." The officers of Indiana's 27th Regiment offered to come home and help Morton make examples of the treasonous legislators.[42]

Troops serving in the Army of the Cumberland responded to the Copperhead actions:

> Some day we expect to return when, we will remember and honor those who have aided us, and will visit those who have sought to defeat us with a retribution proportionate to the evil they have brought upon us and our country.[43]

The Indiana regiments at Corinth wrote:

> Beware the terrible retribution that is falling on your coadjutors in the South, which as your crime is tenfold blacker, will swiftly smite you with tenfold more horror should you persist in your damnable deeds of treason.[44]

The Peace Democracy did not expect this strong counter attack. They decided upon a public relations campaign, and offered a resolution of thanks to Major General William Rosecrans for his victory at Stones River. Rosecrans responded in a scathing letter reprinted in the Union press:

> The unscrupulous despots at our front call us 'Lincoln hirelings' and we hear that this calumny has lately been repeated at home by some of the men whose property and persons have been kept safe by our toil and blood from the ruthless hands of Kirby Smith, Bragg and Morgan. Presuming on our absence, these men talk as if we were not citizens, and speak mockingly of our patriotism. They stab in the back the most generous, truehearted men of the country, who are standing guard in front of their doors, and they prolong the war by encouraging rebels to hope for divided counsels in our homes.[45]

It was obvious that the troops were still angry. A legislative committee brought forth a resolution that praised the troops in the field and stated that the aims of the legislature and the soldiers were one in the same.[46]

By this time it was evident that the legislature had lost the confidence of the public, so they proceeded to do what damage they could before being replaced. They introduced bills that would create an executive council and a military board.[47] These bodies consisted of Democratic office holders that would strip Morton of his power. When a preliminary vote showed that the Democrats would easily pass the bills, the Republican legislators bolted the chambers and met in Madison. Left without a quorum, the legislature adjourned.

A state budget never passed, so the Democrats were certain that Morton would have to call the legislature back in session. When he did, they would pass the contested bills.

Governor Morton would not take the risk. He decided to finance state operations with loans and donations. This was a prodigious task. Not only must he meet the military obligations, but also the expenses of the state hospitals, prison, and all other institutions. One of the most important payments was the interest on state bonds. The internal improvement bonds were still outstanding as were the war bonds. The interest on these bonds was high, and default would ruin Indiana's credit into the twentieth century.

At first the Democrats laughed at Morton's plan. Then they threatened to arrest him for embezzlement. Finally they filed suit saying his actions were unconstitutional. This did not discourage Morton.. He established the Bureau of Finance that ran out of his office.

The governor began to raise money. He charged the federal government for munitions produced at the arsenal in Indianapolis; he petitioned Stanton and Lincoln for funds; he solicited counties for money; he begged bankers and other groups for loans and donations. At one point he carried a market basket full of money from a bank back to his office.[48]

Morton was collecting enough money to run the state on a pauper's budget, but not enough to cover the interest on the state bonds. The governor went east to talk to his good friend JFD Lanier.

James was not blind to the situation in Indiana. Friends in the state had kept him informed in letters. Newspapers printed a running commentary on the Hoosier troubles. Still, the magnitude of the problems, and the depth of the animosity in the state surprised him. Some of his old friends were leading the opposition. He suggested several solutions, but upon learning that Morton had exhausted those avenues, decided that the only recourse left open was to act himself. He agreed to pay the interest that was due on the bonds, and further agreed to make all interest payments until a favorable legislature could appropriate funds to repay him. JFD explained his decision in his autobiography:

311

In this emergency, Governor Morton, most anxious to preserve the honor and credit of the state applied to me to advance the funds . . . This application was made at the darkest hour of the war. I could have no security whatever and could only rely for reimbursement only on the good faith of a legislature to be chosen at a further and distant day . . . If the great contest should turn out disastrously to the cause of the Union and of freedom, I could never expect to be repaid a dollar. I felt, however, that on no account should the debt of a great state be discredited, nor the position of its chief magistrate, the ablest and most efficient of all the loyal Governors . . . be compromised or weakened. No alternative was left to me but to advance the sums required. I would not allow myself to be responsible for the consequences of a refusal of his request. If the credit of the state in such a critical period should be destroyed, that of the other states, and even the Federal government, might be so impaired as to render it impossible for them to sustain the immense burdens of the war. . . . . Another influence of very great weight with me was an ambition to maintain the credit of a State with which I had long been identified, to which I was indebted for my start in life, and for whose credit in former times I had earnestly labored. The last perhaps was the ruling motive.[49]

James' decision lifted a great burden from Morton, and the immediate crisis passed, but the constant alarms of the war were having a debilitating effect on both James and Mary. The setbacks suffered by the northern army; the strain of having relatives and friends in constant mortal danger; the never-ending attacks upon the government by "loyal" unionists; and the economic chaos all added to a feeling of hopelessness that pervaded the Lanier household. Even James, who remained a staunch supporter of Lincoln and the Union cause, felt beaten down by the constant uncertainty. In years past he could always escape to the South where warm breezes and southern hospitality renewed his spirit.

But the South he knew, and the courtly charm of the region, would never return. The only option left to him was Europe where the war was but a column in a weekly newspaper. He and Mary sailed for the continent soon after January 1, 1863. They toured London and then went on to Paris. The couple did not seem to mind the winter weather. The brisk winds brought the color back to Mary's cheeks. The fine French brandy warmed James' belly. The depravations of war faded as the orchestras played the European waltzes and the opulent ball gowns flashed around the ballrooms. Guilt about eating a full course meal while soldiers subsisted on beans and crackers vanished. Once again the music of Mary's laugh filled the room. James mouth remembered how to smile. JFD renewed friendships in the banking community, and defended Lincoln and the Union whenever the subject of the war came up in conversation.

On Saturday, January 17, they left Paris bound for Italy. The first leg of the journey was by rail, and was most enjoyable for JFD. He spent the better part of the trip comparing the French rail lines with those of America. The track ended at San Michel at the foot of the Alps. From here horse drawn sleighs would carry the travelers across the mountains.

The weather was sunny, and the wind calm. The sleighs started out about three o'clock on Sunday afternoon, planning to travel all night and reach the Italian side early the next morning. The night sky was clear and the stars never seemed so close. By 12:30 A.M. the string of sleighs reached the peak of Mont Cenis and the travelers congratulated themselves upon traversing the worst of the track. From there it was literally all downhill.[50]

Within thirty minutes the wind picked up and snow began to swirl out of the dark sky. The trail became obliterated, and even the experienced drivers appeared confused. JFD's own words best describe the situation:

> **At 3 o'clock in the morning having reached a point more than 1/2 way down, the gale became terrific, roaring like a thousand Niagaras, dashing and whirling the fine dry snow so as to darken the atmosphere.**

> **By this time the drifts had become deep and our progress was stopped. On our left was a precipice of a thousand feet or more deep. The sleigh next in front of ours was upset with the passengers, and was only prevented from going over the precipice by its lodging in the soft snow within a few feet of the edge. The conductor now came and told us we would have to sit in the sleigh where we were until daylight; that he must seek the lee of some rock with his horses to save himself and them from perishing from cold.[51]**

In his usual understated manner James states that **"this announcement was anything but agreeable to us."**[52] Between five and six in the morning they heard avalanches fall across the road in front and behind them, effectively cutting off forward progress or retreat. These avalanches **" greatly increased our** alarm as we did not know what moment another would sweep us over the precipice in its course. It was truly a night of horror."[53]

About 9:00 A.M. they continued down the mountain but the avalanche blocked their path. There was an Italian cantino, or house of refuge, about 400 yards down the trail, but the avalanche field, over 100 yards wide and fifteen to twenty feet deep, blocked their way. The passengers had to leave the sleigh and walk to the cantino.

James was the last to leave the sleigh. He started across the avalanche, but soon became bogged down, sinking past his waist into the drifts. The more he struggled the deeper he sank. The wind roared around him and took his breath away. It smothered any shouts he could muster. Thankfully, one of the party saw his plight and sent rescuers back to him. They carried him to the safe house unconscious.[54]

The storm continued for another day, during which time he recovered. He was everafter a strong supporter of the French and Italian efforts to tunnel through the Alps. Soon after, they left for the United States, with little regret about leaving Europe. More problems than James realized awaited him at home.

# 28.

## "The events of last night in Washington will strike with profound horror the whole American people."

*New York Times* April 15, 1865

*To Lanier's dismay, the war situation was no better. Lee and Jackson seemed to be everywhere, out-thinking the best generals Lincoln could find. Union loyalists anticipated a push to capture Richmond in the spring. When that did not occur, morale in the Confederacy and among their sympathizers increased. Peace Democrats, including New York Governor Horatio Seymour, and A. Oakey Hall, continued to speak out against Lincoln and the war.*

James was glad to be home and under the care of his regular physician again. He never really recovered from his ordeal in the Alps, even though he spent most of the trip home in his stateroom where he took most of his meals.

To the Laniers' dismay, the war situation was no better. Lee seemed to be everywhere, out-thinking the best generals Lincoln could find. The Union still held new Orleans. James found himself wondering how his old friends were enduring the occupation. Winter turned to spring, and anticipation of a Union push to capture Richmond this year blossomed again along with the tulips.

Governor Morton was facing another financial problem. The interest payment for the state bonds was coming due. Because of the Stover Fraud it was necessary to have a list of legitimate bondholders so that only proper bond holders be paid interest.

The state auditor, and the state agent in New York had a list of legitimate bondholders, but refused to turn it over to Morton. The new agent was John C. Walker Jr. Appointed by the Peace Democracy legislature, he was a violent enemy of Governor Morton.

Morton was in Washington and New York City almost as often as he was in Indianapolis during the spring of 1863. He talked to Stanton and Chase in Washington, and consulted Lanier in New York City. He and Lanier worked out a plan they thought would allow payment to the bondholders without compromising the legislature.

Winslow, Lanier & Company would pay the debt and sign a legal document absolving any officer of Indiana of blame. On June 20, Morton telegraphed Indiana State Treasurer Matthew L. Brett:

> Can you come here immediately. I think it's likely an arrangement can be made to pay the interest on the state debt and save the credit of state without compromising you or anyone under the decision of the supreme court. Please answer immediately to the St. Nicholas hotel.[1]

Brett refused to even discuss the matter.

The debt payment was due July 1, 1863. Lanier tried once more. Walker's father, John C. Sr. had been a Whig state senator in the 1830's, and a friend of Lanier. On June 24, JFD wrote to Walker requesting the lists. James attempted to persuade the agent to turn over the list by invoking his father's memory and loyalty to Indiana. Walker refused stating:

> ... The party or parties who unnecessarily subject her (Indiana) to the shame of such apparent confusion only insult and dishonor her. Governor Morton has his partisan politics and his selfish ambition to prompt him, and I will not lend myself to the furtherance of his acts which are revolutionary and ruinous. He has no right after the people of Indiana have taxed themselves and filled their treasury for the purpose of paying their debts, still in his obstinacy to accept as a favor the advancement of funds from individuals to save them from dishonor. Without therefore intending disrespect to you gentlemen, I must decline to render assistance to the Governor in his attempt to carry on the state gov-

ernment in defiance of law and without that legislation which the Supreme Court has decided to be essential in the premises.[2]

Winslow and Lanier offered to exonerate Walker from any legal blame in the matter, but still he refused.

At the same time Lanier was fighting this fiscal crisis, another crisis loomed. Instead of the Union Army taking the offensive, Lee once again outwitted the northern commanders and invaded the North. All available troops in the East mobilized. The army stripped New York of any soldiers that could walk as it massed to meet this latest threat. Mary was beside herself as she read accounts of the gray horde marching into Pennsylvania, straight toward Carlisle. Mary's family was originally from Carlisle, and many aunts and uncles still lived in the vicinity. She begged James to do something — to talk to his army friends and persuade them to stop Lee's marauders. She wrote to her relatives in Pennsylvania and offered them sanctuary in New York. Gaining no reply she was sure the Confederate Army intercepted the letters.

When news of the battle at Gettysburg first reached New York, Mary visited the newspaper offices waiting for news along with the wives, mothers and daughters of soldiers. The casualty list covered the walls outside the offices, from above eye level to the gutter. Cries and whimpers followed the discovery of a loved one's name on the list. Many a woman fell to their knees crying, or fainted. Her place at the wall quickly filled with another woman praying that she would not find what she came looking for.

After three agonizing days, news arrived that Lee was in retreat. Reports of General Grant's capture of Vicksburg followed news of Lee's defeat. The possibility that William McKee Dunn Jr. might be among the causalities at Vicksburg dampened Mary's elation. She studied the death and injury lists with the dread of a mother. After several days she concluded that no news was good news, and asked James to send Charles to Carlisle to see about her relatives.

JFD also rejoiced. Despite the rumor that General Morgan had led a strong raiding party into Indiana, James and his friends thought the tide had turned in favor of the Union. With Lee beaten as badly as the newspapers had stated, it was just a matter of time until Union forces captured the entire Army of Northern Virginia. After ten days without news, the euphoria evaporated. Lee had once again slipped the noose.

317

Whatever role William Mc Kee Dunn played in the capture of Vicksburg, he had an interesting part in the aftermath. Grant wrote:

> I sent Captain Wm. M. Dunn of my staff to Cairo (Illinois), the nearest point where the telegraph could be reached with a dispatch to the General in Chief.[3]

The dispatch announced the surrender of Vicksburg and Grant's plans to send Sherman against Johnston immediately, and also send troops to relieve Banks. Finally, he promised to return the Ninth Corps to Burnside. At this point, Julia Grant picked up the story:

> . . . one of General Grant's staff officers, Major (William M) Dunn arrived at Cairo, and after telegraphing the glorious news to the Secretary of War, was privately directed to come to St. Louis and escort the children and me to Vicksburg to visit General Grant.
>
> We had a pleasant sail down the Mississippi. On arriving at Vicksburg, General Grant met us with his ambulance.[4]

JFD's grandson also escorted Mrs. Grant on her return:

> Major Dunn escorted me to St. Louis and I fear I must have tried him very much, for on arriving at East St. Louis we found the river frozen over, and the passengers were carried across in omnibuses. I absolutely refused to go over in one of these huge vehicles, fearing they would break through, and so I had to walk at midnight over the frozen road nearly a mile, leading Jesse by the hand, and the young Major walked beside me.[5]

James was in much greater danger than his grandson during the second week of July. On Monday morning, July 13, on his way to his office, James reviewed his plan to open a national bank in New York. He had talked briefly to Hugh McCulloch about the idea during one of his trips to Washington. Surely the war would soon be over and now was the time to make his postwar plans. If he could entice McCulloch to join him, even as a non-operating partner, the Comptroller of the Currency's name would give the enterprise instant credibility and prestige. Of course McCulloch could have top billing, and James would do the work. He spent the day sounding out investors.

In the afternoon a rumor spread along Wall Street that rioters were setting fire to buildings in the northern part of the city. Thousands of men were purported to be rampaging the streets and burning government buildings. Although the riots were far north of Tenth Street, the mobs were moving south. James sent Charles home to reassure the women and protect their houses. By the time James started home at the end of the day, the streets teemed with police and firemen rushing north. As he neared Tenth Street he met a continual stream of people heading south away from the melee.

Charles, Sarah, and the children were already at his father's house. James had to knock loudly on the locked door and identify himself before gaining entry. Charles was on the roof watching the ever increasing glow from fires to the north.

Far from being quelled, the riot was growing. Some people contended that those against the war carefully timed and directed the riots.[6] Early in the march elaborate signs and placards appeared "The Poor Man's Blood for the Rich Man's Money" read some. "No draft and No $300 Arrangement with Us" was also a popular banner. The mob's first target was the U.S. provost marshal's office at 43rd Street and Third Avenue. They drove the provost marshal from his office, wrecking the huge drum used to draw names for the draft. Then, pouring turpentine over record books, they torched the building. The fire spread to six adjoining buildings. With barrel staves, iron bars and rocks, the mob drove the police and firemen into retreat.[7]

The mob moved south, and attacked the draft office at Broadway and Twenty Ninth Street, setting it and twelve other buildings afire. The leaders of the riot seemed only interested in destroying pro-union buildings. They led their forces toward Republican Mayor Opdyke's house. The masses had other ideas, however. They began to smash windows and loot stores along the route of the march.[8] The mob set fire to hotels, drug stores, saloons, a ferry house, and a police station. Nothing was sacred to the rabble. They torched a Methodist church, a Protestant mission house and an orphan asylum for black children.[9]

At midnight on the thirteenth, the main body of rioters attacked the home of U.S. Postmaster Abraham Wakeman. Postmaster Wakeman and his family were in Washington D.C., so the mob broke into the house, carried off everything they could lift, and torched the building.[10]

The rioters erected barricades along First Avenue from Eleventh to Fourteenth Streets and on Ninth Avenue from thirty-second to forty-third Street.[11] While not exceedingly close to either of these strong points, the Lanier house was between the two. There was a considerable number of agitators and riffraff roaming Tenth Street and the main thoroughfares in the vicinity. When the situation appeared no better on the morning of July 14, James and Charles decided to stay at home.

Loyalists accused Governor Seymour of prolonging the riots because of his anti-union sentiments. The fact was that Seymour was powerless to stop the riots. There were no state militia troops to call upon. The Governor had to ask Lincoln for federal troops to put down the riot.

Charles knew that he and his friends were the targets of the rioters, and at one point suggested that he enlist. After all, he argued, he had graduated from Russell Military School, and was young and fit.

The idea horrified Sarah and Mary, and James would not hear of it. JFD patiently explained to his son that he was more valuable where he was; that Governor Morton and General Owen depended upon Charles for special missions. Charles was doing much more in his present capacity than he could ever do in uniform. If the rabble roaming the streets did not know that, it was their problem, not Charles'. Besides, with two men in uniform, the Lanier family was giving more than their share to this war. What deterred Charles from further protests, was not his father's arguments, but the fear in James' eyes. Charles had never seen fear in his father's eyes before. He knew that JFD was not afraid for himself, but of losing his treasured son.

The draft riots continued for two more days. It became increasingly apparent that the criminal element in the city was taking control of the mob. Looting and burning became indiscriminate. The mob chased down and hung blacks. At least thirty were killed during the three day rampage. The 1500-man police force put up a valiant defense, but were overwhelmed. Scores died and several hundred suffered serious wounds.[12]

Mayor Opdyke begged for help from Governor Seymour who reluctantly called upon Lincoln for assistance. Federal troops, worn out from the Gettysburg battle began arriving, and on the 15th confronted the rabble. The first skirmish pitted 150 troops of the line against a mob of 2,000. Impressed with the bravery of Lee's soldiers, the Union troops held no esteem for these criminals and draft dodgers. After one volley in the air failed to disperse the crowd, they brought their guns to bear and fired directly into the mass of jeering rioters. The crowd broke and ran, and the uprising began to fall apart.[13]

Within a few days the city routine was back to normal with only the burned skeletons of buildings as monuments to the turmoil. On August 19 the draft resumed in New York City. Ten thousand federal troops patrolled the streets and enforced the power of the provost marshal.[14]

The crisis over, JFD returned to work. The riots did nor dissuade him from his plans, and on July 31, 1863, he wrote to Comptroller McCulloch broaching the idea of a national bank to his friend:

> **We have some thought of making a national Bk. with a million to begin on with power of increase with a view of keeping the accounts of similar institutions & bankers & others.**
>
> **If you will agree to come into our concern as we talked about & be the Prest. of the contemplated Bank we will go into it.**
>
> **The controlling interest will be held by us the residue distributed out among western associates, under the same (session laws).**
>
> **You need not in that event leave your present position for an indefinite time.**
>
> **Could I leave here I would go once to Washington to see you.**
>
> **Your servant,**
> **JFD Lanier[15]**

While McCulloch and Lanier contemplated the new bank, the stalemate surrounding the Indiana bonds continued. The state was technically in default. Thinking the bonds devalued, the state treasurer ordered Walker, the Indiana state agent in New York, to purchase $100,000 worth of bonds. He forwarded money from the state treasury for the purpose.[16] This was without legislative approval, of course. Once again Lanier went public with the problem, relying on the honesty and loyalty of the people. Few bondholders took advantage of the agent's offer, so the price remained stable.

With victories at Gettysburg and Vicksburg, the Peace Democracy suddenly lost public favor in Indiana. When there was no rush to sell Indiana bonds, State Auditor Ristine realized the game was over, and surrendered the bondholder list to Winslow, Lanier. The company promptly paid the back interest and reassured the bondholders that they would pay the interest until the Indiana General Assembly appropriated funds for the purpose. This notification, coming from a man they knew and trusted, quieted the European bankers.

Copperhead Fever broke in Indiana. The Union Party, now adopting the Republican label, regained control of the General Assembly in the fall elections. The legislature passed budget bills repaying, with interest, all of the loans negotiated by Governor Morton.

The total amount advanced by James. Lanier, "with no security whatever," was $640,000.[17] Including the money advanced at the beginning of the war, JFD Lanier advanced the State of Indiana over one million dollars from his own purse.

With that fiscal crisis passed, James decided it was safe to invest in Indiana. He, William English, and John C. New opened the First National Bank of Indianapolis with capital of $150.000.[18] JFD purchased a large block of shares and handled the bank's eastern business. Stockholders elected William English, a major power in the Democratic Party in Indiana, president of the bank. He became known as "the Great Forecloser" for his ruthless foreclosing on loans when they became delinquent. He amassed large property holdings in Indianapolis by purchasing the foreclosed property at bargain rates.[19] English resigned as president of the bank in 1877 to pursue national office. In 1880 he ran as the Democratic nominee for Vice President with Winfield Scott Hancock.

There was more good news for Lanier. The Pittsburgh, Fort Wayne and Chicago Railroad continued to prosper. In 1863 it realized a net revenue of just under $3,000,000, and in April of 1864 began paying dividends to its loyal, patient stockholders. Eventually the Pennsylvania Railroad leased the line for 999 years. The Pennsylvania railroad guaranteed full payment of all principal and interest on the debts of the PFW&C, plus paying twelve percent per year for the lease.[20]

James intended to purchase the borrowed mausoleum from the Winslow family. The only time it came to mind was when a death occurred. Distractions and grief always postponed the purchase. In March 1864, he finally made the purchase.[21]

JFD received word from Madison that Drusilla had delivered her tenth child on April 27, 1864.[22] He marveled at her ability to birth 10 children and thought that her grandmother and namesake would be proud of her. Still, she was forty years old, and childbearing was very dangerous at her age. Sarah was pregnant again too, and presented Charles with a second daughter, Fannie, on August 17, 1864.[23]

In November of 1864, Sidney Lanier, a signal corps officer in the Confederate Army, was captured, providing JFD a vivid example of how the war divided families. Sidney was signal officer aboard the blockade-runner *Lucy* when the ship was overtaken by the USS *Santiago de Cuba*. Refusing to don the English sailor costume provided, Sidney was captured and sent to the prison pen at Point Lookout Maryland.[24]

On December 22, 1864, Lanier wrote to Hugh McCulloch inviting him to his house over the holidays and stating that they were going to file the papers for the new bank the next day.[25] There is no mention in this short letter that McCulloch has acquired any interest in the bank. There is a J.N. McCulloch of Pittsburgh listed as a stockholder in the audit report of June 1866, however.[26]

Several old friends do show up on the stockholder list including Samuel Hanna of Fort Wayne and George W. Cass of Pittsburgh. Lanier held 4628 shares. This was the largest block, and amounted to over forty percent of the shares issued. Charles held 200 shares, and James Winslow 150. Leonard Winslow and John F. Winslow had 50 shares each. Winslow, Lanier and Company owned 200 shares.[27]

The war dragged on into the new year of 1865. The Confederacy, although mortally wounded, refused to die. Despite his defeat at Gettysburg, Jefferson Davis appointed Lee commander of all southern forces. Lee sent General Joseph E. Johnston to consolidate all of the troops in Georgia and the Carolinas in a final stand against Sherman to keep the blue horde out of Savannah. Lee once again became the "King of Spades" as he prepared the defenses of Richmond. He hated being on the defensive, but knew his soldiers could never mount another offensive push.

During the first days of February, hopes across the Union soared on the news that the Confederates were suing for peace. Seward and Lincoln himself were meeting with southern representatives. The secret conference was taking place aboard ship in Hampton Roads. Alexander H. Stevens, vice-president of the Confederate States of America led the Confederate delegation. Lincoln and Stevens had been friends in the Congress in 1848. The nation held its breath.

Charles and Sarah waited with James and Mary for word from the peace conference. They desperately wanted the war to end. The principles of union and equality had already carried the day. Why prolong the killing to satisfy the blood urge of a few radicals on both sides?

The nation released its breath in a cry of anguish as the results of the conference became known. The parties could not agree on terms. There would be no peace. The killing would continue. Despite the disappointment, JFD was among the majority who felt it was just a matter of time until the fighting ceased.

Sidney Lanier was still a prisoner at Fort Lookout, and was very ill with what the doctors feared was consumption.[28] JFD knew the consequences of that disease first hand, so redoubled his efforts to obtain Sidney's release. In early March his pleas were successful. Sidney was sent home on parole.[29]

Lincoln too thought the conclusion of the war was fast approaching and, in his inaugural address, set out the tasks that faced the country after the war. A few days later he assembled his new cabinet, asking JFD's old friend Hugh McCulloch to assume the post of Secretary of the Treasury. William Fessenden resigned, preferring to represent Maine in the Senate.

As the Union army pressed on relentlessly, the defenses of Richmond crumbled. The remnants of the government fled southward on Sunday, April second, hours before the rear-guard burned the abandoned war supplies in their Capital. Union General Weitzel took command of the city. Lincoln visited Richmond on April 3, walking through the crowds with only a lightly armed guard.

The North was delirious with joy. Church bells rang continually. Spontaneous celebrations broke out on every street corner. Men and women who days earlier had wept with fear now cried in joy. Churches filled with worshipers as prayers of thanksgiving stormed the gates of Heaven.

Charles, Sarah, James and Mary, like tens of thousands of New Yorkers, eagerly opened each edition of the *New York Times*, hoping each day that the headline over the left hand column would proclaim the end of the war. On Palm Sunday, April 9, their wait ended. Newsboys began hawking the news when the first editions hit the streets. Bold headlines over the first column on the first page of the *Times* proclaimed what every citizen in the North longed to hear:

The story started with a dispatch to General John Dix in New York City, from Secretary of War Stanton in Washington. Stanton proclaiming that General Lee had asked for a meeting with General Grant to discuss surrender terms. It went on to detail the dispatches between the two antagonists that lead up to the meeting at Appomatox Court House in Virginia.

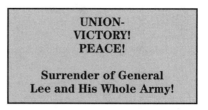

People stormed into the streets, shouting and dancing. Church bells pealed in celebration. Impromptu bands began miniature parades. The entire city turned into one big celebration ground.

The Laniers celebrated right along with everyone else. For years to come, everyone would remember where they were and what they were doing when the news came.

Churches stayed open far into the night, and the pews filled with worshipers who came to reflect and pray. The Lord had sided with the North in the battle of Armageddon, and the people poured forth their thanksgiving.

Work went undone during the next week as people talked about the war, the peace, and the future. Officially the war was not over, Sherman was still battling the remnants of the Confederate forces under Johnston, but the rebels' cause was lost. Governor Seymour declared April 20 as a day of celebration. Businesses were to close. Special committees planned ceremonies and parades across the state.

JFD participated in the spontaneous parties. Never in his sixty-five years had he seen such continued euphoria. He remembered the end of the War of 1812. Then the feeling had been one of relief, but not overwhelming joy as was the case now.

James made additional post-war plans. As he thought, his excitement grew. The South would need capital to rebuild. Factories needed extensive repairs. Entire towns needed rebuilding. Railroads would require extensive repair. He could lend his knowledge to that task. This was an opportunity on an unprecedented scale. Winslow, Lanier & Company could lead in the task of rebuilding the nation. He would contact his friends in New Orleans. If they wanted to open a national bank, he could supply the money

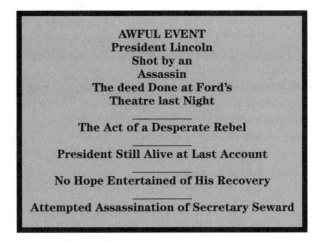

AWFUL EVENT
President Lincoln
Shot by an
Assassin
The deed Done at Ford's
Theatre last Night

The Act of a Desperate Rebel

President Still Alive at Last Account

No Hope Entertained of His Recovery

Attempted Assassination of Secretary Seward

The joy was short lived. On Saturday morning, April 15 another headline in the *Times* shattered the the jubilant anticipation of peace. Once again the news came in a War Department dispatch from Stanton to General Dix. A disbelieving nation read the news, but did not believe what they were reading.

The wounds of the president were mortal. The condition of Seward and his son Frederick was hopeless.

The president's assassin entered his box at the theater and shot him in the head at close range. The assassin struggled with a soldier who accompanied the Lincolns, but escaped by leaping from the box onto the stage. The attacker shouted "Sic semper tyrannus" as he landed on the stage. He ran out a back door of the theater.

Seward's assassin hit Frederick with a "billy," and attacked Major Clarence Seward, another son. A male nurse and State Department messenger also tried to fend off the intruder, but both suffered serious injuries. After fighting off those men, the attacker stabbed Secretary Seward three times and escaped.

Another report in the paper stated that Lincoln died at 1:00 A.M. A third story corrected that misinformation. The president was still alive at 1:30 A.M. The paper described the president's attacker as about thirty years old, five feet nine inches tall, sparsely built and of light complexion.

Soldiers carried the president to a private house across the street from the theater, where a team of doctors including Surgeon General Barnes tended to his wound. The bullet entered

326

the middle of the back of the skull and angled toward the left eye. Brain matter oozed from the wound.

The editor of the *Times* could not find the heart to comment on the tragedy, stating only:

The events of last night in Washington will strike with profound horror the whole American people. At this moment of writing we have only a partial announcement of the facts and have neither the data nor the spirit for comment

Few people went to work. They gathered in knots in the street and traded the latest rumors until solid information was delivered by the newspapers. The rumors ran from one that stated absolutely that all cabinet members were assassinated; to talk that a fresh Confederate Army had captured Washington.

As devastated as he was, JFD was sure the country would survive even this disaster. As strong as Lincoln was, he drew his strength from the people, and now that strength would reinforce the leaders that remained. Lincoln's death was a despicable act and a terrible trial for the country, but the country would survive.

Churches once again drew thousands of worshipers. One week after joyous prayers of thanksgiving inundated Heaven, desperate prayers for Lincoln's recovery beat against Heaven's gate. Most places of worship stayed open all night. The main pastors silently withdrew early in the morning to revise their sermons.

At dawn the first papers on the street declared little change in the president's condition. Churches filled to overflowing for all of their services, some people staying in their pews from the first service through the last.

The regular edition of the Easter Sunday *New York Times* reported the awful news. Once again all of the columns dealing with the tragedy carried a heavy black border. Abraham Lincoln died at 7:22 A.M. Saturday morning. He never regained consciousness.

The story continued on the first page of the paper. Attendants wrapped the body in an American flag and transported it to the White House about 9:30 A.M. A cavalry escort accompanied the hearse with other military officers walking behind the vehicle. Later, Surgeon General Barnes and Dr. Stone performed an autopsy. After embalming, the body rested in a mahogany

327

casket lined with lead. White silk lined the casket and black silk draped the outside. According to the paper, the lid of the casket bore a simple silver plate that read:

Abraham Lincoln
Sixteenth President of the United States
Born; July 12, 1809 (sic)
Died April 15, 1865

Secretary Seward would recover from his wounds. Frederick Seward suffered a fractured skull and a severe cut on his head. His condition was still grave. The male nurse was still alive, but his condition was hopeless. Major Clarence Seward was recovering.

The paper identified John Wilkes Booth as Lincoln's assassin. A hat dropped in the president's box and a spur he lost on the stage of Ford's Theater belonged to him. One story reported Booth's capture fifteen miles from Baltimore, but a later account denied the rumor. Troops blanketed the countryside around Washington in pursuit of Booth. The same article accused John Surratt of being Seward's attacker.

Contrary to the rumors of Saturday, there was no secret Confederate force marching on Washington. According to dispatches in the *New York Times*, the city was quiet. All day long church bells tolled mournfully throughout Washington.. Troops blocked all roads and rail lines in and out of the city. No one could leave. A similar blockade isolated Richmond, Virginia..

The *Times* had additional stories centered on the tragedy. Evidence implicated the Surratt family in the assassination plot. While questioning the family, military authorities decided to arrest all of them. This included Mrs. Surratt, her daughter Kate, and two nieces. Kate cried uncontrollably at the threat of jail, but Mrs. Surratt was stoic. During the questioning of the Surratts, a gentleman entered the house and after giving conflicting statements to the officers, they arrested him also. Later in the day Seward's maid identified him as Seward's attacker. His name was Louis Paine.

President Lincoln's funeral was set for April 19, in Washington. After the funeral the train carrying the president's body would take a circuitous route through the country before final internment in Springfield, Illinois. The train was to arrive in New

York City on Saturday, April 22. The nation did not want to part with their beloved president, and throngs of mourners at each stop delayed the official schedule. The body arrived in New York City on Monday, April 24 and lay in state in the Governors Room of City Hall. The casket was open for public view from 12:00 noon on Monday until 12:00 noon on Tuesday. The Laniers were probably among the many dignitaries that were ushered into the room before the doors were opened to the general public. Tens of thousands walked silently past the coffin. About 60,000 people formed a procession to accompany the casket from City Hall to the train station. James and Charles along with their wives undoubtedly rode a coach in the procession.

In the following days and weeks, the killing of John Wilkes Booth, and the trial and execution of the other conspirators filled the newspapers. It provided a constant topic of conversation in the bars and ballrooms of the country. Slowly, very slowly, the nation returned to normal. Time heals the worst of tragedies, and so it was with the death of Abraham Lincoln.

# 29.

## "... a gentleman of your distinguished and well-merited reputation ..."

— Hugh McCulloch May 29, 1865

*The war was over, and the killing stopped in the summer of 1865, but the ravages were still apparent everywhere. Hospital wards both north and south remained filled with wounded soldiers. Released prisoners still wandered home. Veterans, missing limbs or fingers or eyes, populated every street corner. The major cities in the South were uninhabitable. In the North as well as the South, unemployed soldiers roamed the cities and countryside. The warm weather heated men's tempers and boiled away their tolerance. Many cities teetered on the edge of anarchy. Police struggled to maintain order. The expense of the war went on as the federal government pledged to fulfill Lincoln's last promise: "to care for him who shall have borne the battle; for his widow, and his orphan."*

Before the year was out Drusilla had another child who she named Franklin Cravens.[1] JFD worried about remembering all of his grandchildren's names, and who belonged to whom.

Others worried about the federal finances. While not in critical condition, they were far from healthy. The national debt was about $3,000,000,000. More than half of the debt was payable in gold. Since gold was scarce, it carried a premium which had the effect of almost doubling the debt. The government, and particularly Secretary of the Treasury Hugh McCulloch, were looking for a solution. Europe had cash to spare, and interest rates were low. McCulloch's problem was how to approach European bankers after they had lost considerable money on America's internal improvements.

When McCulloch learned that JFD planned to visit Europe, it solved his problem. JFD needed a vacation. Cold winters and miserable rain and sleet of February and March never had been kind to his constitution, but he had to admit that his health was deteriorating. Whether the malady he had suffered from the winter crossing of the Alps was to blame, or whether he was just getting older, he was not sure. James could still not visit the South, so Europe was his only choice. Determined not to visit Europe in winter, JFD made plans for a summer departure.

McCulloch wrote to his friend on May 29, 1865. The letter stated in part:

> Although you are about to visit for the benefit of your health, and desire to be relieved from all cares and responsibilities, I can not permit a gentleman of your distinguished and well-merited reputation as a financier to visit Europe with out asking for him the benefit of his services in explaining to Capitalists in that country the condition of our financial affairs . . .[2]

McCullough enclosed a summary of the country's financial condition for JFD to study. Although he needed the rest, James could not refuse his old friend or turn a deaf ear to his country's call. As he studied the information, his mind began to race with possibilities. It would be a good excuse to visit his old friends and an opportunity to reward those that had stuck with him during the demise of the Wabash and Erie Canal.

After agreeing to undertake the task, he received this letter:

Department of State
Washington, 2nd June, 1865

*To the Diplomatic and Consular Agents of the United State in Europe:*

GENTLEMEN— It is my pleasing duty to introduce to you J.F.D. Lanier, Esquire, a distinguished banker of the City of New York, and a most estimable gentleman.

331

Mr. Lanier has been requested by the Secretary of the Treasury to look after the financial interests of the Government while in Europe, and he has kindly consented to do so.

I commend him to your friendly attention and consideration, and bespeak for him such facilities as may contribute to the effective discharge of the duties confided in him.

I am, gentlemen,
Your very obedient servant,

William H. Seward,
Secretary of State.[3]

The Laniers had a wonderful time in Europe. JFD hired a guide and interpreter in each country. The couple delighted in the fine old buildings and the thriving cities. Mary marveled at the beautiful Our Lady of Antwerp Cathedral in Belgium with its unfinished second tower. JFD explained the workings of the antiquated but effective windmills in Holland that provided power for everything from pumping water to grinding chalk for paint pigment. The vineyards that marched up the hillsides along the Rhine River were beautiful. Venice was a storybook city, and the palaces at Versailles and Vienna were breathtaking in their splendor.

The castles and cathedrals were ostentatious, especially when contrasted with the pauper existence of the common citizens. They were clear testimony why American colonists had revolted against the monarchy and why they insisted on a wide separation between church and state.

James enjoyed meeting his old friends, and at each opportunity spoke to the bankers about the viability of the U.S. even after the devastating war. His friends trusted him and his message impressed them. Many promised investment capital.

Several investors helped JFD set up a meeting on September 14, 1865, at Frankfurt-am-Main, Germany. Here James addressed bankers and capitalists from around Europe on the subject of the financial condition of the U.S.

He began his speech by stating that after the war the national debt was $3,000,000,000 which amounted to nineteen percent of the wealth of the loyal states. He reminded his listeners that, after the war with France, England's national debt stood at forty percent of her national wealth.[4]

He explained that between 1850 and 1860 the wealth of the United States grew at an average annual rate of 8 1/2 per cent per year.[5] Projecting that same rate of increase to 1881, the wealth of the U.S. would be $51,516,000,000. At that point the national debt, without a dime repaid, would be only six percent of the national wealth of the present states.[6]

To those skeptics who asked when the southern states would be an asset rather than a liability, JFD pointed out that they were already contributing to the national wealth. New York City already received 20,000 bales of cotton weekly from the South. The cotton, sold overseas, boosted customs revenue.[7]

James went on to explain that the above projections did not factor in the value of the unsettled western lands, totaling about 950,000,000 acres. Now that the war was over, citizens were streaming to the West, and land sales alone would garner $1,000,000,000 for the federal treasury.[8] With the burden of the war past, the industrialized eastern states could turn their production capacity to developing the West. Additional rail lines were on the drawing boards. There would be an insatiable appetite for farm implements to turn untamed grasslands into checkerboard fields of wheat and corn.

Honest estimates expected gold and silver deposits in the western territories to yield $200,000,000 annually. Other minerals, such as coal, copper, lead, gypsum and salt would add an additional $1,000,000,000 to the economy each year.[9]

To draw the figures together James gave a conservative picture of the economic future of the United States:

> **Taking the past as a basis for calculation of the future, the United States in 1880 will have a population of 60,000,000, and a National wealth of $60,000,000,000. It will then not only be able to meet the interest on the public debt, but will be able to discharge it with entire ease;-and true to our historic policy will undoubtedly do so.[10]**

Public debt was often misunderstood. Frequently owed to foreign investors, the populace did not support it. JFD was quick to explain why the United States debt was different. All classes and occupations of U.S. citizens held ninety percent of the current debt. Notes of less than $50.00 made up the majority of the debt.[11]

> **Each citizen felt himself a part of the contest and contributed to it according to his ability. No national loan has ever been so universally distributed. All, consequently, are directly interested in maintaining inviolate the public faith.[12]**

The bankers and capitalists realized that this attitude boded well for all investors, foreign and domestic. Sensing that he had won over his audience, James closed with as strong a closing argument as ever he used in court.

> Under the able and judicious administration of our affairs, the nation has started anew on career of growth and prosperity unexampled in its own history, or that of any other people. The nation has pledged its honor for the fulfilling of all its obligations. . . and no one who considers our means, our present position, or the guarantees of the past can doubt the payment of our national debt.[13]

The speech was an immediate success. Bankers asked for private meetings to learn the details of investment opportunities. Many asked that he be their agent in the United States, not only for government securities, but to pick the most promising private stocks. At Lanier's request, U. S. embassies reprinted the speech, and circulated it throughout Europe. He headed home assured that European money would follow fast on his heels.

Upon returning home he immediately reported his success to Hugh McCulloch, who arranged for a meeting with President Johnson.[14] Lanier's success encouraged the president. The foundation of the rebuilding plan centered on securing European capital, and James' efforts seemed to guarantee that investment.

Not only did he impress the government, but the newspapers gave JFD's efforts high praise. Both the Associated Press, and the *New York Times* credited Lanier with convincing the bankers of Europe that the nation's moral fiber and financial future were both strong.[15]

Lanier was so successful in appealing to German investors that the German government warned against excessive investment in the United States. *The New York Times* ran an article on January 19, 1866, that reprinted a letter from Frankfurt-am-Main:

> The Wirtenberg official paper has brought out a long article warning the excessive investment in your (U.S.) bonds; over 100,000,000 in guilders being invested in them to the detriment of other interests. But to the disappointment of the Government, your bonds next day rose 2 per cent., the liberal press taking the ground that the people could do nothing better than invest in American Securities as the safest loan offered in an age.[16]

334

The trip appeared to have only a short-term effect on James' health. Bothered only by nagging respiratory ailments for the first sixty years of his life, more serious maladies now attacked him. Combined with the chronic respiratory problems, they interfered with his business activities.

JFD spent more time at home. Charles began taking on most of the daily activities of the firm. James now handled only the business of his oldest friends and clients. Although he was an active advisor to Charles, his most important role was providing the image of strength and longevity so necessary to a banking firm. JFD still made the major decisions, and attended the important meetings, but he depended upon Charles to carry out his orders. Charles did not fail his father.

James did what he could to speed the revitalization of the South. He was instrumental in opening the Louisiana National Bank of New Orleans and became a prime stockholder. The bank was on Charles Street in the building formerly occupied by the Bank of New Orleans. James knew the building well. In addition to JFD, Charles, and James Winslow, twelve individuals who had stock in the Third National Bank of New York City also held shares in the Louisiana National Bank.[17]

Radicals condemned any northern involvement in the rebuilding of the South as treason. They ridiculed McCulloch and Lanier as "Indiana Butternut Bankers" These were not the first whispers of vitriol JFD had heard, and the criticism never penetrated his tough old hide. Investment in the South was good business, both for the country and for his pocket. The officers of the bank were old friends and competent bankers. Until they proved otherwise, he would back them.

Drusilla wrote that she was pregnant again, but admitted to having problems. Her other births had been so natural it surprised her this one was causing so much trouble. James lectured her on the trials of having children at her age, but he still worried about her health. After a long and difficult delivery, Drusilla gave birth to a girl on February 13, 1867.[18] John and Drusilla named her Margaret. Drusilla was slow to recover, and the baby did not prosper. Drusilla slowly regained her strength, but Margaret never seemed to gain much weight.

In April, Sidney Lanier made the first of several yearly trips to New York City. He wanted to re-establish ties with his northern benefactor, and investigate opportunities in New York City.

JFD and his family welcomed Sidney warmly. On April 16, 1867, he wrote his father, Robert S. Lanier a long letter.

> ... On Saturday I dined with JFD, (of Winslow Lanier, Bankers). We had only a family party, being Mr. wife, sister, Miss Anthony (don't know her connection with him), Captain Dunn (Mr. Lanier's grandson and Aide de camp to General Grant throughout the war) and last and best, little Kate, 8 year old pearly -decked, blue-eyed, broad of forehead, ... no lip, only daughter of Mr. L and present wife.
> About the time the captain came in, I happened to mention that I had been a prisoner during the war.
> "Poor fellow!" says little Katy, "and how did the rebels treat you?"
> "Rebels?" said I. "I am a rebel myself, Kate."
> "What!" She exclaimed, and lifted up he little lilies(when I say lilies I mean her hands) and peered at me suspiciously with all her blue eyes a stare "A live Reb!"
> The phrase in Katy's nursery had taken the time-honored place of bugaboos and hobgoblins and men-under-the-bed. She did not realize that I, a smooth faced slender old mortal, in all respects like a common man, should be a "live reb". She was inclined to hate me as was duty bound.

Sidney won Kate over that night, and as he left she allowed him to kiss her goodby. After the kiss she whispered to him:
"Your mustache is so much softer than papa's"
Sidney ends the letter:
I said good night amidst the most cordial invitations to make myself at home in their house.[19] JFD took an immediate liking to Sidney, and underwrote the author's first book of poems, *Tiger Lilies*, published in 1867.[20]

Little Margaret, JFD's newest granddaughter struggled for life. She did not lack for love or attention. The family consulted doctors in Cincinnati and Indianapolis. Drusilla devoted full time to caring for her baby. She slept only when Margaret slept. She seldom left the room the baby was in, and never left the house. The hot summer in Madison did not help. On August 14, after just 6 months and one day of life, Margaret died.[21] No matter how often the black wreath darkened his door, the anguish still burned in James heart.

In 1868, JFD planned another trip to Europe to relieve his worsening health. Once again Hugh McCulloch asked him to test the European money markets for further investments in America. Once again James Lanier responded to his country. Although his illness prevented extensive consultations, he was able to sell the idea of new bonds.

He had his remarks at Frankfurt-au-Main reprinted. James did confer with enough leading bankers to be convinced that they were receptive to five percent long bonds, payable in gold in New York City. This bond could replace the six percent bonds then in circulation.[22] He conveyed this information to McCulloch, and shortly thereafter the government issued the new bonds.

The European weather soothed James' pains, but he was becoming mentally tired. He did not like the way the new breed of bankers conducted business. They were ruthless. The only goal was to make money, no matter whom they ruined in the process. Clients were not important to them. JFD's creed of being diligent, and striving for respect; of making the cause of his clients his own, was passé. Concern for those of lower station seemed out of fashion; working behind the scenes for the good of all, ridiculed. He felt too old to fight any longer. He could not relinquish control of the banking house, but acted more as a corner second, allowing younger men to actually do battle in the financial ring.

Lanier took another vacation in an effort to re-invigorate himself. He re-instituted his old habit of visiting the South to escape the northern winter. He visited with Sterling Lanier, his father's first cousin, and Sidney's grandfather, but did not have time to travel to Macon, Georgia, to see Robert.[23]

Sidney visited New York again in May of 1869, and was once again well received. Writing to his father on May 4, he states:

> I found Mr. JFD and his son Charles very cordial indeed, and the former seemed very agreeably impressed with such of his kinsmen as he met while in the South.
> I breakfasted with Mr. JFD this morning and I am to meet him at the banking house tomorrow to open my business with him, after which I dine at his house. . . .[24]

James took Sidney to his favorite restaurant on May 5. The next day Sidney writes to his wife, Mary Day Lanier, recounting the evening:

> Yesterday Mr. Lanier gave me a very fine dinner at Delmonico's, where I met many of his relatives and was cordially received by them. We had most delicious wines, Chablis, Sherry, and Champagne; we had 13 courses of all manner of delicacies; we sat drank and ate 3 hours. . . . [25]

Sidney had come north for more than good wine and food, however. He was looking for business opportunities. He met with James Winslow, who owned the patent on the Bessemer Steel Process for the Eastern U.S. and wrote his father of the prospect of impressing Winslow with the

> . . . importance of our own iron properties in view of the availability of our iron for this steel process, and to suggest to him the possibility of profit in locating steel work where the south market would be commanded . . . [26]

The trip south, and the enjoyable company of Sidney could not cure the aches constantly bothering James. He found it difficult to move around and sit in meetings and to concentrate on proposals. Charles was now running the business. As reluctant as JFD was to admit it, he was little more that a figure-head. His name in gilt on the door was more important than his presence in the office.

Sidney, too, was feeling the pain of consumption (tuberculosis). During his annual trip north he sought medical help. In a letter to his father dated August 19, 1870, he indicates that Charles Lanier and others have assured him that Dr. Marcy, whom Sidney has consulted, "was one of the most skillful and reliable physicians in New York"[27]

A bond grew between James and Sidney. They talked for hours. Sidney explained his ambition to be a writer. James talked freely about his business accomplishments, something he was reluctant to discuss with his own family. With the skill of a writer, Sidney drew the accomplishments from JFD.

Sidney may have suggested that James write a book detailing his business triumphs. Some day his children would appreciate it. Besides, Sidney may have argued, James' achievements were almost a textbook for modern banking. Unless he wrote about them, there would be no record of his contributions as an empire builder, banker, and patriot. Sidney could have used the argument that because James preferred to keep in the shadows, only he knew the entire story.

Sidney's influence was persuasive. JFD decided to write a short book detailing his experiences. He addressed the foreword of the 62 page book:

There was no need to include family history in the book, the
children knew that well. He published it in 1871. More than a list
of accomplishments, James wished to leave his children a blue-
print of the moral principles that would guide them to a successful life. Putting others first was one lesson. Being more concerned with others problems than with your own was another.
Education for both sons and daughters a third. Not allowing religion or politics color your judgment was important. Patriotism
was high on James' list of values as was the idea that those in
positions of power had an obligation to help those unable to
provide for themselves.

He also believed that wives were to comfort and provide a
good home for their husbands. In return, men had an obligation
to earn a living and to take care of their wives and children. Men
should earn their keep and not depend on inheritance. Every
man had a responsibility to marry and raise a family. It still bothered JFD that Alex had not done so.

On May 11, 1870, Frances Elisabeth Dunn, James' granddaughter, and Elisabeth's eldest daughter married David Richie
McKee. She gave birth to a boy Lanier Dunn, on March 1, 1872.[28]
His first great grand child enthralled JFD. He remembered how
common infant deaths were when he was younger and marveled
that he could live long enough to see a great grand child. Surely
medicine had advanced about as far as humanly possible. Later
in the year Sarah and Charles presented James with another
grand daughter, Elisabeth Gardner Lanier.[29]

In the fall of 1871, JFD returned to Europe. This time the
government put no demands upon him. He spent time in
Switzerland and then headed back home on October 12.

In September of 1871, Sidney is once again in New York City,
and regales his wife and father with the hospitality of Charles.
He stayed until JFD returned from Europe, attending a birthday
party for Kate at Delmonico's on November 10.[30]

The now familiar pattern of travel was repeated in 1873. Sidney was in New York, and James in Europe. Sidney wrote to his
wife on September 25, 1873:

> . . . the letter of the 22nd I got at Winslow Lanier & Company this morning. I did not stay to talk to Charles(Mr. JFD is yet in Europe) knowing the load of care that must be on his mind in this great crisis.[31]

The last remark refers to the panic of 1873, which Charles was facing without the ready advice of his father. In another letter to Mary dated November 5, he describes an enjoyable evening at James Winslow's house:

> . . . last night I dined with the James Winslows who have moved to their beautiful town house for the winter. I had carried my flute by previous arrangement and after dinner, Mrs. Edward Winslow ( a lithe, fragile little blond, not long out of Vassar, young wife of Mr. James Winslow's oldest son) and I moved upon the enemy with piano and flute.

He goes on to enumerate a long list of classical and popular selections the two played.[32]

In what had become almost an annual event for him, Sidney was present at Kate's birthday party. She was 16 and the milestone party occurred at James Winslow's house. Less than a year later, on September 25, 1874, Sidney reported to his wife that James Winslow was dead after a short illness.[33]

JFD's health deteriorated markedly during the summer of 1876. Sidney writes to his father from West Chester, Pennsylvania on August 7:

> . . . I made an application for a loan to Mr. Lanier and yesterday received an answer refusing it. He was just. . . leaving for a prolonged absence: had given up all matters of business in consequence of ill health etc. etc. The letter was written by another person and stated that Mr. Lanier had long ago abandoned all attempts to write.[34]

Lanier's son-in-law, Judge Advocate General William McKee Dunn, appears to take over as Sidney's sponsor in 1877. On June 28, Sidney writes to his father:

> It would take a long letter to tell you the pleasant things that General and Mrs. Dunn said to us and did for us; and we feel that their friendship has become a genuine new possession for our lives. General Dunn says there is no doubt Mr. Sherman will offer me something- and I want to hear from him.[35]

It disappointed Dunn that the government offered Sidney a low level job, but advised him take it as an entry level position. He continued to use his political connections to secure Sidney a consulate appointment.[36]

In July 1877, JFD decides to reprint his book, and commissions Sidney to write a genealogy appendix. Sidney agreed to please James, but his heart was not in it.[37] A month later, on August 16, Sidney writes his wife "I saw Mr. Lanier and General Dunn this morning, and have my hands full of work for a couple of days. Mr. Lanier seems to be poorly off." The work Sidney refers to is supervision of the second printing of JFD's autobiography.[38]

By September, Sidney himself was suffering a serious relapse of tuberculosis. On September 27 he wrote to his wife from Washington D.C. that his lungs were bleeding and was invited to stay with the Dunns. "I am admirably tended by Mrs. Dunn and lack for naught."[39]

Both James and Sidney recovered from their illnesses, but James knew he was failing fast. He had one important piece of business to conclude. He planned the provisions of his will for several years, now was the time to put it on paper. Certainly it was an act of love and protection that would extend beyond the grave. He signed the final document on December 31, 1877.[40] The document ran for 16 pages. In contained all of the legal language that protected against challenge.

Many of James Lanier's beliefs stand clear in his will. He believed that men had an obligation to protect the women in their lives. He made sure that Mary and his unwed daughters were provided for. He was ahead of his time in the belief that women needed an education as well as men, and provided for his fatherless granddaughters' schooling.

He named his wife, Charles, William McKee Dunn, and a friend, John W. Ellis as executors. He gave Charles special responsibilities in several sections of the will. After making provision for all of his debts and funeral expenses, he gave Mary the house at Sixteen West Tenth Street, and the stable located on Tenth Street and Sixth Avenue. Included were the furniture, books, plate, horses, carriages, and harness. He ordered that the executors continue paying all expenses of the house and stable, so that Mary could live there without liability. In addition he gave Mary ten thousand dollars per year for the rest of her life. Louisa, who had never married, received the income from $160,000. The principal reverted to JFD's residual estate after her death.

His widowed daughter, Mary Stone received income from $150,000. At her death James directed the principal be divided between her daughters, or their heirs, on a "share and share alike" basis. Mary also received the house on Ninth Street that her father had purchased for her after he husband's death. Each of Mary's daughters, Elisabeth and Mary, received the income from $50,000 for their support and education. Upon reaching 21, the girls received the principal.

James directed the executors to invest $160,000, and give the income to Margaret. The wording of the will was very explicit — Margaret should receive the money "as if she were a feme sole." JFD directed his daughter by her last Will and Testament to leave the $160,000 and any accumulation to the issue of her and her deceased husband James Winslow. If her children by James Winslow preceded her in death, the principal and accumulation was to revert to Lanier's residual estate. It was perfectly clear that her present husband, Josiah C. Pumpelly, was not to get a dime.

Charles' son, JFD Lanier 3, was to receive $10,000 in trust. No later than ten years after his grandfather's death, the boy could claim the gift. He also gave his namesake his watch, watch chain, and seals. James Lanier Cravens, Drusilla's son received $5,000 in trust with similar provisions.

William McKee Dunn became trustee for $5,000 given to his and Elisabeth's son Lanier Dunn. The trust contained the same provisions as those for his other grandsons.

JFD directed that the remainder of his estate be divided into five equal shares. He directed the shares be invested and divided as follows:

One share went to Elisabeth. Another went to Charles. The third share went to Drusilla, and upon her death, to her children with the provision that each daughter would receive $6,000 more than any son. The fourth share was for the benefit of Katherine (Sidney's Kate with hands like lilies). Upon her death, the inheritance was to pass to her children.

Another of JFD's beliefs, that men were to marry and have a family manifested itself concerning Alexander's bequest. James instructed Charles to hold the final share in trust for Alexander. Income, up to $7,000 per year, accrued to Alexander. The trust retained any income over that amount. If Alexander married and had children, he received all of the income from the trust. Upon Alexander's death, the principal held in trust went to his children, share and share alike. Alexander was 56 and unmarried at the time his father executed the will. James was obviously pushing Alex toward marriage and fatherhood with the biggest incentive at his disposal. Alexander needed to act quickly.

In a clause which reinforces his belief that men should be responsible for their actions, he states that he had made considerable cash advances to several of his children. JFD directs the executors to subtract these advances from the inheritance of each child. Their father released Mary, Louisa, and Margaret from their loans. To preclude an argument from any of the others, Lanier stated that only his record book would be the evidence of what had been borrowed.

All through the will, JFD protected his daughters and granddaughters' shares from exploitation. To reinforce that protection, he inserted a specific clause that stated:

> It is my will that all bequests herein made for or which shall inure to, the benefit of any female, shall be received and held by such female in her own sole right, and as and for her separate estate, and shall in no event shall be liable for or to the debts, control or interference of any husband of such female.

Lanier mandated that no inventory of his possessions be taken, and no bond or surety be required of the executors. Still fiscally conservative, he did not allow his executors a commission based on the value of the estate, he dictated that they each be paid a flat fee of $5,000. A banker to the end, JFD stated that if any of the executors were bankers, they be paid the usual banker's commission charges in addition to their fee.

It did not take James long to change his will. On February 6, 1878, he made the first change. In the next three years, James changed his will seven times. Twice to protect his heirs from new business ventures, and five times to reflect changes in family situations.

Although physically debilitated by chronic illness, the will proved JFD retained his mental capacities. He was still willing to join a promising business deal. His signature on a business deal still carried the promise of success.

On April 24, 1878, James joined forces with Charles, John W. Ellis, Edward D. Adams, Edward Winslow, (Mary's son, and JFD's grandson) and Daniel B. Stafford to renew the partnership of Winslow, Lanier and Company. The partnership agreement ran for five years, until 1883. The business relocated to 26 Nassau Street, a short distance off Wall Street. JFD continued as president, and contributed $500,000 additional capital to the venture. Charles was treasurer.

Katherine married Edward A. Farrington, and James apparently liked the young man a great deal. He changed Katherine's bequest to allow a payment of $50,000 to her husband if he survived. Ingersoll records no children from the marriage. but Diana Lanier Smith recalls:

> Kate Lanier Farrington evidentally did have a child. She said to me when I was seventeen; 'Gracoius child, I was a mother at your age' But the son apparently died young and there is no record. She (Katherine) claimed Farrington ran off with her money

James changed his will on June 11, 1879, to protect the new Winslow, Lanier and Company partnership in the event of his death. Charles' 1/5 share now covered JFD's investment in the company. The fact that Charles was willing to back up his beliefs with his inheritance must have pleased JFD.

In January of 1880, the co-partnership of Winslow, Lanier and Company was extended for an additional 5 years, to expire in 1888. They formed the new partnership to take advantage of a great opportunity to cooperate with J.P. Morgan.

J. Pierpont Morgan had become a famous man, and yet it could be argued that he and JFD were very similar. Both were conservative, religious, and traditionalists. Both used money as a tool. Lanier went with the ebb and flow of capital, and forecasting that ebb and flow was his greatest asset. Morgan, on the other hand, actually tried to control the supply of capital, and succeeded to a great extent. Unlike JFD, Morgan was ruthless in his business dealings, and gained many envious enemies. Still, he had the best understanding of the role of money in a developing economy, and used that understanding to catapult the United States into a leader among capitalist nations.

The business opportunity came about because Morgan respected both JFD and Charles. Charles was a long-time friend, and a member of the exclusive Corsair Club. headed by Morgan. The group met on Morgan's yacht and entertained themselves by taking turns trying to devise a meal menu that would surpass the previous effort.[41] Many successful business dealings solidified the friendship. The most important was the agreement to combine forces with one other agent and sell the entire 40 million dollar bond issue of the newly formed Northern Pacific Railroad. The railroad secured the rights to build a line to the Pacific Ocean over the northern route. Until the 1940's this was the largest single railroad transaction in the history of the United States.[42]

In a second transaction Winslow, Lanier & Company, in cooperation with two other banks began selling securities to finance the construction of the Panama Canal.[43] James acted solely as an advisor to his son on these deals, but he was extremely proud of Charles business acumen. The company was in good hands.

President Grant embarked on a world tour after leaving office in 1878. He returned in 1880 with a depleted bank account and with no house to live in. A group of New York business men alerted to the problem became concerned that a national hero was destitute. They organized a subscription campaign that collected $200,000 for the general. Grant used at least $48,000 to purchase a home in New York City.[44] Patriotism still burned brightly in JFD's failing heart. He contributed $1,000 to the fund.

The Louisville Courier Journal, a Democratic paper, could not pass up the opportunity to attack William McKee Dunn, and take a swipe at JFD in the process:

> . . . McKee Dunn does just as suits his family interest best, for you must understand that Dunn uses the power of old J.F.D. Lanier, the head of the famous New York Banking House of Winslow, Lanier and Co., and the old man Lanier has always seen where to put his money where it would do the most good. He gave Grant $10, 000 to buy his home with — that is he was one of the contributors.[45]

In a letter to Robert Cravens, who still lived in Madison, and to the Courier Journal, William McKee Dunn explains that the contribution was $1,000 and refutes the charges of the paper.[46]

On December 30, 1880, James wrote the last codicil to his Last Will and Testament. He made extensive changes. He revoked the original bequests to Mary and her daughters. He also revoked the section that released Mary from repaying any debts she owed him. Instead of dividing his residual property five ways, JFD directed that it be divided 6 ways. He directed the sixth share be subdivided into three shares, with one such share each going to Mary and her two daughters. He must have decided that one-sixth of his residual estate was now worth more than the original $250,000 he gave to Mary and her daughters. He must have felt that the new distribution allowed Mary to repay her debts to him. He also instructed Charles to increase Alexander's yearly allowance to $12,000 if the trust could support it.

The distribution of his assets now satisfied James Lanier. Without the mental stimulation of revising the will to best serve his wishes, his mental capacities failed quickly. The spring heat aggravated his physical infirmities. JFD was never comfortable, and could do little for himself. His mind was still sharp enough to loathe the need for assistance.

James lived with his memories, reliving the many successes. It was a shock when he toted up the number of friends and business acquaintances that had died. He had never compiled such a ledger in the past. As he increasingly looked back, JFD realized there was no future. The heat of the New York summer sapped his ebbing strength. He could escape to the cooling summer of Europe only in memory. As the world followed the life and death struggle of President Garfield, few knew of the final struggles of JFD Lanier.

In the stifling heat of August 29, 1881, James Franklin Doughty Lanier passed to a world without means and liabilities. Three of his children, three grand children and two sons-in-law preceded him in death.

Although he died a very rich man, with many accomplishments that outlasted him, James Lanier's greatest legacy was his descendants. Eight children, 25 grandchildren and two great grandchildren survived him. Whether learned or residing in the blood, his progeny continued the Lanier ethic of work, service, and patriotism. Today several hundred people trace their lineage to JFD Lanier. Most possess his strong moral code.

On Wednesday, August 30, 1881, James' funeral was held in the Presbyterian Church at University Place and Tenth Street. The church was full to overflowing, and the mourners included many and well-known citizens of New York City. The Reverend Dr. Edward Gilman, and the Reverend Dr. Brown officiated, each giving a short eulogy.[47]

His pallbearers included Thomas A. Hendricks, former Democratic governor of Indiana, future vice president, and lifelong political opponent of Oliver Morton; General George W. Cass, partner in the Fort Wayne & Chicago Railroad; and business associates William A. Booth, John W. Ellis, and George E. Storm. The final pall-bearer was an old friend from New Orleans, Joseph H. Oglesby.[48] They placed JFD 's body in the mausoleum in Greenwood Cemetery in Brooklyn that he had purchased from Richard Winslow.

Sidney Lanier could not attend the funeral. He himself lay dying of the malady he contracted in the Union prison-pen. He died 11 days after his relative, friend, and benefactor, on September 7. Sidney was 39 years old.

The attendance at JFD's funeral was a tribute to the man and his ledger of impressive accomplishments. Unfortunately, after closing the crypt, people often forget a man's good works. So it was with JFD Lanier.

Those that take the time to study the man, however, will find a set of principles that will direct them to a successful life just as those same principles guided James Lanier over a century ago.

**". . . to respect scrupulously the rights of others, but always to be firm in the assertion of my own."**

**". . . to be punctual in every duty and appointment."**

**". . . to make the causes of my clients my own."**

**". . . I would never allow my liabilities to exceed my means."**

**"I would make any sacrifice before I would do an unjust act."**

**". . . I felt, however, that on no account should the debt of a great state be discredited. . ."**

# Notes

## Prologue

The genealogical information was supplied by Diana Lanier Smith, great granddaughter of JFD Lanier, and Chairman of the Genealogical Committee of the Lanier Mansion Association. She cited the following sources:

> *The Virginia Magazine of History and Biography* published Quarterly by the Virginia Historical Society for the year ending December 31, 1935 Vol XLIII Richmond ,VA. pp. 160–168.
>
> Atwood Violett, *Tyler's Quarterly Historical and Genealogical Magazine* Vol.III pp. 122–147 July 1921. The author is a Lanier descendant.
>
> Thomas Forsythe Nelson *Washinton-Lanier Ancestry and Descendants: The Ancestry of Mr. Charles Lanier* Washington D.C n.d.
>
> F. Lanier Graham *The Earlier Life and Work of Nicholas Lanier (1588–1666) Collector of Paintings and Drawings* submitted in partial fulfilment of the requirements for the degree Master of Arts . . . Columbia University 1955 unpublished.

[1] Lanier, JFD, Sketch in the Life . . . 389
[2] Lanier, JFD, Sketch in the Life . . . 390
[3] Lanier, JFD, Sketch in the Life . . . 390
[4] Lanier, JFD, Sketch in the Life . . . 390
[5] Lanier, JFD, Sketch in the Life . . . 390

## Chapter 1

[1] Lanier, JFD, Sketch in the Life . . . 389
[2] George Washington to Thomas Jefferson, letter 3/29/1774; Old South Leaflet No. 16, p9; George Washington to Governor Benjamin Harrison of Virginia, letter 10/10/ 1774, Old South Leaflet No. 16, p1 Directors of Old South Works, Boston nd.
[3] Richard B. Morris *Encyclopedia of American History*, Harper Row, 6th Edition, 1982 733
[4] Lanier, JFD, Sketch in the Life . . . 390
[5] Land Records, Pendleton County, Falmouth, Kentucky
[6] Morris, 733

## Chapter 2

[1] Lanier, JFD, Sketch in the Life . . . 390

[2] B.F.Morgan, Directory of Preble County, Ohio, Eaton, Ohio, 1875, 21,33

[3] U. S. Government Land Ordinance 1785

[4] Louise V. Ingersoll, *Lanier* (Genealogy),Goetz Printing Co. Washington D.C., 1975, 348

[5] Logan Esarey, *State Banking in Indiana, 1814–1873*, Indiana University History Department No. 15, Bloomington, Indiana, n.d. 221

[6] Deed Records, Preble County Ohio Historical Society, Eaton, Ohio

[7] H. A. Williams & Bros., History of Preble County, Cleveland, Ohio, 1881, 59

[8] Deed Records, Preble County Ohio Historical Society, Eaton, Ohio

[9] Lanier, JFD, Sketch in the Life . . . 391

[10] H.A. Williams & Bros., 59–60

[11] Deed Records, Preble County Ohio Historical Society, Eaton, Ohio

# Chapter 3

[1] Lanier, JFD, Sketch in the Life . . . 391

[2] War of 1812 Records, Preble County Ohio Historical Society, Eaton

[3] War of 1812 Records

[4] Louise Ingersoll, *Lanier* (Genealogy), 348

[5] Bray Hammond, *Banks and Politics in America From the Revolution to the Civil War*, Princeton University Press, 1957, 228

[6] Henry Adams, *Life of Albert Gallatin*, J.B, Lippencott & Co. Philadelphia & London, 1879

[7] Adams

[8] Vincent P. Carusso, *Investment Banking in America—A History*, Harvard University Press, 1970 1

[9] Morris, 734

[10] Lanier, JFD, Sketch in the Life . . . 391

[11] Lanier, JFD, Sketch in the Life . . . 391

[12] Lanier, JFD, Sketch in the Life . . . 391–392

[13] Lanier, JFD, Sketch in the Life . . . 392

[14] Cottman, George S. *The James F.D. Lanier Home, an Indiana Memorial*, Department of Conservation, Indianapolis, 1926, 6

[15] War of 1812 Records

[16] War of 1812 Records

[17] War of 1812 Records

[18] M.H. Railsback. "Builders of Destiny." D.A.R. Magazine 787 n.d.

[19] Morris,184

[20] Morris, 185

[21] H.A. Williams & Bros, 60

[22] Lanier, JFD, Sketch in the Life . . . 393

[23] *Niles Weekly Register*, 76 volumes, Washington, Baltimore, Philadelphia, February 1815

# Chapter 4

1 Lanier, JFD, Sketch in the Life . . . 393
2 G.W. Hawes *Hawes' Indiana State Gazetteer and Business Directory*, 1858–1863 246
3 Logan Esarey, *State Banking in Indiana 1814–1873*, n.d. 223
4 Lanier, JFD, Sketch in the Life . . . p 386
5 Jefferson County Indiana Court records, Jefferson County Historical Society, Madison, Indiana, cited in George S. Cottman Thesis, 7
6 Logan Esarey *Internal Improvements in Early Indiana*. Indianapolis; Indiana Historical Society, 1912, 80
7 Logan Esarey *Internal Improvements in Early Indiana*. Indianapolis; Indiana Historical Society, 1912, 52
8 Logan Esarey *Internal Improvements in Early Indiana*. Indianapolis; Indiana Historical Society, 1912, 67
9 Carrusso, 3
10 Logan Esarey *State Banking In Indiana 1814–1873*. Indianapolis; Indiana Historical Society. n.d. 224
11 *Madison Courier*, 1/12/1938
12 Logan Esarey *State Banking In Indiana 1814–1873*. Indianapolis; Indiana Historical Society. n.d. 223
13 Logan Esarey *State Banking In Indiana 1814–1873*. Indianapolis; Indiana Historical Society. n.d. 225
14 Logan Esarey *State Banking In Indiana 1814–1873*. Indianapolis; Indiana Historical Society. n.d. 225
15 Madison, Indiana *Republican*, various dates
16 Zimmer, Ph.D. Thesis Indiana University 1974 *Madison Indiana 1811–1860 A Study in the Process of City Building*, 151
17 Madison *Indiana Republican*, 8/24/1819
18 Madison *Indiana Republican* 10/9/1819
19 Lanier, JFD, Sketch in the Life . . . 393
20 Ingersoll, 347
21 Alexander Lanier, *Last Will and Testament* Lanier State Historic Site, Madison, IN.
22 Alexander Lanier, *Last Will and Testament*
23 Alexander Lanier, *Last Will and Testament*

# Chapter 5

1 Ingersoll, 348
2 Logan Esarey, *State Banking in Indiana 1814–1873*, Indiana Historical Society, Indianapolis, n.d. 232,
3 Logan Esarey, *State Banking in Indiana 1814–1873*, Indiana Historical Society, Indianapolis, n.d. 236

[4] Logan Esarey, *State Banking in Indiana 1814–1873*, Indiana Historical Society, Indianapolis, n.d. 237

[5] Logan Esarey, *State Banking in Indiana 1814–1873*, Indiana Historical Society, Indianapolis, n.d. 238

[6] Logan Esarey, *Internal Improvements in Early Indiana*, Indiana Historical Society, Indianapolis; 1912, 53

[7] Logan Esarey, *Internal Improvements in Early Indiana*, Indiana Historical Society, Indianapolis, 1912, 53

[8] Lanier, JFD, Sketch in the Life . . . 394

[9] *Indiana Republican Banner*, June 15,1821

[10] Logan Esarey, *State Banking in Indiana 1814–1873*, Indiana Historical Society, Indianapolis, n.d. 255

[11] Logan Esarey, *State Banking in Indiana 1814–1873*, Indiana Historical Society, Indianapolis, n.d. 226

[12] Madison *Republican*, August 31, 1821

[13] Ingersoll, 348

[14] *Indiana Democrat*, (Indianapolis), Editorial March 26, 1831

[15] Fredrick Hill, *William Hendricks, Indiana Politician and Western Advocate 1812-1856* Ph.D. Thesis Indiana State Library,113–114

[16] *Indiana Republican Banner*, January 10, 1822

[17] *Republican Banner*, May 11, 1826

[18] Letter to authors from Carol Denton, Curator of Special Collections, Transylvania University, April 7, 1992

[19] Sanford Cox, *Recollections of the Early Settlement of the Wabash Valley*, Courier Steam Book and Job Printing, Lafayette, 1860, 99

[20] Hugh McCulloch, *Men and Measures of Half a Century*, Scribner, New York, 1888, 92-93

[21] Lanier, JFD, Sketch in the Life . . . 394

[22] Logan Esarey, *State Banking in Indiana 1814–1873*, Indiana Historical Society, Indianapolis, n.d. 226

[23] Jacob P. Dunn, *Indiana and Indianians*, American Historical Society, Chicago and New York, 1919, V 1, 333

[24] Lanier, JFD, Sketch in the Life . . . 394

[25] Lanier, JFD, Sketch in the Life . . . 394–395

[26] Ray Boomhower "Lafayette's Triumphal Return" *Outdoor Indiana*, May/June 1995, 32

[27] Ingersoll, 349

[28] Logan Esarey, *Internal Improvements in Early Indiana*, Indiana Historical Society, Indianapolis, 1912, 51

[29] Lanier, JFD, Sketch in the Life . . . 395

[30] Logan Esarey, *Internal Improvements in Early Indiana*, Indiana Historical Society, Indianapolis, 1912, 74

[31] *Western Sun*, (Vincennes) March 5, 1825

[32] Logan Esarey, *Internal Improvements in Early Indiana*, Indiana Historical Society, Indianapolis, 1912, 97

[33] Lanier, JFD, Sketch in the Life . . . 395

[34] Logan Esarey, *Internal Improvements in Early Indiana*, Indiana Historical Society, Indianapolis, 1912, 97

[35] Logan Esarey, *Internal Improvements in Early Indiana*, Indiana Historical Society, Indianapolis, 1912, 54

[36] Logan Esarey, *Internal Improvements in Early Indiana*, Indiana Historical Society, Indianapolis, 1912, 54

[37] Logan Esarey, *Internal Improvements in Early Indiana*, Indiana Historical Society, Indianapolis, 1912, 55

[38] Logan Esarey, *Internal Improvements in Early Indiana*, Indiana Historical Society, Indianapolis, 1912, 80

[39] Logan Esarey, *Internal Improvements in Early Indiana*, Indiana Historical Society, Indianapolis, 1912, 81

[40] Logan Esarey, *Internal Improvements in Early Indiana*, Indiana Historical Society, Indianapolis, 1912, 81

[41] Jefferson County, Indiana Tax Records, 1825

[42] Logan Esarey, *Internal Improvements in Early Indiana*, Indiana Historical Society, Indianapolis, 1912, 52

[43] Logan Esarey, *Internal Improvements in Early Indiana*, Indiana Historical Society, Indianapolis, 1912, 55

[44] Ingersoll, 349

[45] Logan Esarey, *Internal Improvements in Early Indiana*, Indiana Historical Society, Indianapolis, 1912, 59

[46] Logan Esarey, *Internal Improvements in Early Indiana*, Indiana Historical Society, Indianapolis, 1912, 75

[47] *Messages and Papers of Noah Noble*, Indiana Historical Bureau, Indianapolis, 1958, 43–44

[48] Logan Esarey, *Internal Improvements in Early Indiana*, Indiana Historical Society, Indianapolis, 1912, 83

# Chapter 6

[1] Knapp, *History of the Maumee Valley*, Blade Publishing House, Toledo, Ohio 397

[2] Logan Esarey, Internal Improvements in Early Indiana, Indiana Historical Society, Indianapolis, 1912, 86

[3] Logan Esarey, Internal Improvements in Early Indiana, Indiana Historical Society, Indianapolis, 1912, 90

[4] *Messages and Papers of Noah Noble*, Indiana Historical Bureau, Indianapolis, 1958, 15

[5] *Indiana Republican Banner*, January 14, 1828

[6] *Indiana Republican Banner*, February 25, 1828

[7] *Indiana Republican Banner*, May 28, 1828 and August 12, 1828

[8] *Indiana Republican Banner*, May 28, 1828

[9] *Indiana Republican Banner*, October 8, 1828

[10] *Indiana Republican Banner*, August 27, 1828 and October 8, 1828

[11] *Indiana Republican Banner*, October 15, 1828

[12] *Indiana Republican Banner*, August 27, 1828

[13] Gail Thornbrough, ed. *Diary of Calvin Fletcher*, Vol. I, Indiana Historical Society, Indianapolis, 1972, 153 fn 49

[14] Jacob Dunn, *Indiana and Indianans*, New York, 1919, V 2, 1031–1033

[15] Gail Thornbrough, ed. *Diary of Calvin Fletcher*, Vol. I, Indiana Historical Society, Indianapolis, 1972, 186 fn 38

[16] Letter J. F.D. to Tipton April 20, 1829, *John Tipton Papers*: V2, edited by Robertson & Riker, Indiaia Historical Bureau, Indianapolis, 1942, 136

[17] Ingersoll, 349

[18] *Indiana Republican Banner*, August 13, 1828

[19] *Indiana Republican Banner*, August 29, 1828

[20] *Indiana Republican Banner*, September 30,1829

[21] *Indiana Republican Banner*, September 30, 1829

[22] *Indiana Republican Banner*, February 2, 1830

[23] *Indiana Republican Banner*, February 17, 1830

[24] *Indiana Republican Banner*, July 8, 1830

[25] *Indiana Republican Banner*, August 12, 1830

[26] Logan Esarey, *Internal Improvements in Early Indiana*, Indiana Historical Society, Indianapolis, 1912, 90

[27] Logan Esarey, *Internal Improvements in Early Indiana*, Indiana Historical Society, Indianapolis, 1912, 90

[28] Logan Esarey, *Internal Improvements in Early Indiana*, Indiana Historical Society, Indianapolis, 1912, 116

[29] Logan Esarey, *Internal Improvements in Early Indiana*, Indiana Historical Society, Indianapolis, 1912, 117

[30] Gail Thornbrough, ed. *Diary of Calvin Fletcher*, Vol. I, Indiana Historical Society, Indianapolis, 1972, 190

# Chapter 7

[1] Letter, Palmer to President Andrew Jackson Andrew Jackson Papers, manuscript Division, Library of Congress. Washington D.C. as reported Fredrick Hill, *William Hendricks, Indiana Politician and Western Advocate 1812–1856* Ph.D. Thesis Indiana State Library, 149

[2] Letter, William Hendricks to President Andrew Jackson 3/5/1831, Andrew Jackson Papers, as reported in Hill, 150

[3] Letter Tipton to Calvin Fletcher, November 30,1830, *John Tipton Papers*; V2, 376–377; edited by Robertson & Riker, Indiaia Historical Bureau, Indianapolis, 1942

[4] Letter Lanier to Hendricks December 12,1830, Collection 278, W.H. Smith Library, Indiana Historical Society, Indianapolis,

[5] Indiana House Journal 1830–1831, 137–138.

[6] *Indiana Democrat*, March 26, 1831

[7] *Messages and Papers of Noah Noble*, Indiana Historical Bureau, Indianapolis, 1958, 16

[8] *Messages and Papers of Noah Noble*, Indiana Historical Bureau, Indianapolis, 1958, 19

[9] *Messages and Papers of Noah Noble*, Indiana Historical Bureau, Indianapolis, 1958, 27

[10] Madison *Republican* August 12, 1828

[11] Ingersoll, 350

[12] Hendricks to Tipton, Oct. 27, 1831, Fredrick Hill, *William Hendricks, Indiana Politician and Western Advocate 1812–1856* Ph.D. Thesis Indiana State Library.

[13] Riker & Thornbrough *Indiana Election Results 1816–1851*, 1960, 128.

[14] Logan Esarey, *Internal Improvements in Early Indiana*, Indiana Historical Society, Indianapolis, 1912, 93

[15] *Republican Banner*, February, 1832

[16] Gail Thornbrough, ed. *Diary of Calvin Fletcher*, Vol. I, Indiana Historical Society, Indianapolis, 1972

[17] *Republican Banner* March 4, 1832

[18] JFD Lanier letter to Robert Buchanan, March 31,1832, item #38 from the Robert Buchanan Correspondence and Papers, MSS qb918R.M. Cincinnati Historical Society Library, Cincinnati Museum Center, Cincinnati, Ohio

[19] Zimmer, 120

[20] Logan Esarey, *Internal Improvements in Early Indiana*, Indiana Historical Society, Indianapolis, 1912, 94

[21] Logan Esarey, *Internal Improvements in Early Indiana*, Indiana Historical Society, Indianapolis, 1912, 96

[22] Letter Lanier to Tipton, May 11, 1832, *John Tipton Papers*; Vol 2; edited by Robertson & Riker, Indiaia Historical Bureau, Indianapolis, 1942, 309

[23] *Messages and Papers of Noah Noble*, Indiana Historical Bureau, Indianapolis, 1958, 104–115

[24] *Messages and Papers of Noah Noble*, Indiana Historical Bureau, Indianapolis, 1958, 30

[25] Logan Esarey, *Internal Improvements in Early Indiana*, Indiana Historical Society, Indianapolis, 1912, 92

[26] Ingersoll 348–350
[27] Morris, 147–148
[28] Morris, 147
[29] Morris, 148
[30] Morris, 733
[31] *Republican Banner* September 27,1832
[32] Letter Lanier to Buchanan 11/22/32, item #37 from the Robert Buchanan Correspondence and Papers, MSS qb918R.M. Cincinnati Historical Society Library, Cincinnati Museum Center, Cincinnati, Ohio

## Chapter 8

[1] Riker & Thornbrough *Indiana Election Results 1816–1851*, 1960, 129.
[2] Letter JFD Lanier to John Tipton, January 4, 1834, *John Tipton Papers*: Vol 3, 4
[3] Catterall, Ralph C.H., *The Second Bank of the United States*, University of Chicago Press, 1907, 291
[4] Catterall, 295
[5] Catterall, 295
[6] ___ *JFD Lanier, Banker Patriot*, Jefferson County Historical Society, nd, 15
[7] ___ *JFD Lanier, Banker Patriot*, Jefferson County Historical Society, nd, 15
[8] Zimmer
[9] Letter John Tipton to Lanier, November 3, 1834, *John Tipton Papers*; V3, 79; edited by Robertson & Riker, Indiaia Historical Bureau, Indianapolis, 1942
[10] Logan Esarey, *State Banking in Indiana 1814–1873* Indiana Historical Society, Indianapolis, n.d. 251
[11] Logan Esarey, *State Banking in Indiana 1814–1873* Indiana Historical Society, Indianapolis, n.d. 256
[12] Logan Esarey, *State Banking in Indiana 1814–1873* Indiana Historical Society, Indianapolis, n.d. 253
[13] Logan Esarey, *State Banking in Indiana 1814–1873* Indiana Historical Society, Indianapolis, n.d. 252
[14] Logan Esarey, *State Banking in Indiana 1814–1873* Indiana Historical Society, Indianapolis, n.d. 252–253
[15] Logan Esarey, *State Banking in Indiana 1814–1873* Indiana Historical Society, Indianapolis, n.d. 253
[16] Logan Esarey, *State Banking in Indiana 1814–1873* Indiana Historical Society, Indianapolis, n.d. 253
[17] Logan Esarey, *State Banking in Indiana 1814–1873* Indiana Historical Society, Indianapolis, n.d. 253

[18] Logan Esarey, *State Banking in Indiana 1814–1873* Indiana Historical Society, Indianapolis, n.d. 253

[19] Logan Esarey, *State Banking in Indiana 1814–1873* Indiana Historical Society, Indianapolis, n.d. 253

[20] Logan Esarey, *State Banking in Indiana 1814–1873* Indiana Historical Society, Indianapolis, n.d. 252

[21] Logan Esarey, *State Banking in Indiana 1814–1873* Indiana Historical Society, Indianapolis, n.d. 252

[22] W.W. Woollen, *Biographical and Historical Sketches of Early Indiana*, n.d. 531

[23] Logan Esarey, *State Banking in Indiana 1814–1873* Indiana Historical Society, Indianapolis, n.d. 255

[24] Logan Esarey, *State Banking in Indiana 1814–1873* Indiana Historical Society, Indianapolis, n.d. 255

[25] Second State Bank of Indiana Journal Minutes, 2/13/1834, Indiana State Archives, 2

[26] Second State Bank of Indiana Journal Minutes, 2/13/1834, Indiana State Archives, 2

[27] Second State Bank of Indiana Journal Minutes, 2/13/1834, Indiana State Archives, 3

[28] Second State Bank of Indiana Journal Minutes, 2/13/1834, Indiana State Archives, 4

[29] Second State Bank of Indiana Journal Minutes, 2/13/1834, Indiana State Archives, 4

[30] Second State Bank of Indiana Journal Minutes, 5/21/1834, Indiana State Archives, 8

[31] *Messages and Papers of Noah Noble*, Indiana Historical Bureau, Indianapolis, 1958. 34

[32] Ingersoll, 350

[33] Richard Meldrum, Letter to "friend" in Madison, April 21, 1879, cited in Emory O. Muncie, *A History of Jefferson County* M.A. Thesis, Indiana University , Bloomington, 1932.

[34] Second State Bank of Indiana Journal Minutes, 11/13/1834, Indiana State Archives, 19

[35] Second State Bank of Indiana Journal Minutes, 11/13/1834, Indiana State Archives, 19

[36] Second State Bank of Indiana Journal Minutes, 11/20/1834, Indiana State Archives, 31

[37] Second State Bank of Indiana Journal Minutes, 11/20/1834, Indiana State Archives, 31

[38] Second State Bank of Indiana Journal Minutes, 11/21/1834, Indiana State Archives, 35

[39] Second State Bank of Indiana Journal Minutes, 11/18/1834, 24 & 11/19/1834, 27. Indiana State Archives

[40] Second State Bank of Indiana Journal Minutes, 11/20/1834, Indiana State Archives, 30

[41] Richard Meldrum, Letter to "friend" in Madison, April 21, 1879, cited in Emory O. Muncie, *A History of Jefferson County* M.A. Thesis, Indiana University , Bloomington, 1932.

# Chapter 9

[1] Ingersoll, 349

[2] Second State Bank of Indiana Journal Minutes, 3/9/1835, Indiana State Archives, 44

[3] Second State Bank of Indiana Journal Minutes, 3/11/1835, Indiana State Archives, 54

[4] Second State Bank of Indiana Journal Minutes, 3/11/1835, Indiana State Archives, 56

[5] Second State Bank of Indiana Journal Minutes, 3/10/1835, Indiana State Archives, 41

[6] Second State Bank of Indiana, Madison Branch Correspondence File, Indiana State Archives

[7] Hugh McCulloch, *Men and Measures of Half a Century*, Scribner, New York, 1888, 122

[8] Gail Thornbrough, ed. *Diary of Calvin Fletcher*, Vol. VI, Indiana Historical Society, Indianapolis, 1972, 254

[9] Second State Bank of Indiana Journal Minutes, 5/19/1835, Indiana State Archives, 60

[10] Second State Bank of Indiana Journal Minutes, 5/19/1835, Indiana State Archives, 60

[11] Second State Bank of Indiana Journal Minutes, 5/19/1835, Indiana State Archives, 65

[12] Second State Bank of Indiana Journal Minutes, 5/21/1835, Indiana State Archives, 68

[13] Gail Thornbrough, ed. *Diary of Calvin Fletcher*, Vol. VI, Indiana Historical Society, Indianapolis, 1972, 257

[14] Gail Thornbrough, ed. *Diary of Calvin Fletcher*, Vol. VI, Indiana Historical Society, Indianapolis, 1972, 256

[15] Second State Bank of Indiana, Madison Branch Correspondence File, Indiana State Archives

[16] Letter- JFD Lanier to Samuel Merrill, 6/25/1835, Samuel Merrill Collection, M204, Indiana Historical Society

[17] *Madison Courier*, July, 1835

[18] List of officers, Christ Episcopal Church of Madison, Lanier Mansion State Historic Site, Madison, Indiana.

[19] Second State Bank of Indiana Journal Minutes, 8/19/1835, Indiana State Archives, 74 Also letter Morris to Madison branch 7/21/1835.

[20] Second State Bank of Indiana Journal Minutes, 8/19/1835, Indiana State Archives, 74

[21] Gail Thornbrough, ed. *Diary of Calvin Fletcher*, Vol. VI, Indiana Historical Society, Indianapolis, 1972, 273–276

[22] Letter Lanier to Polke, 10/17/1835, William Polke Letters, Lilly Library, Indiana University Library

[23] Second State Bank of Indiana, Madison Branch Correspondence File, Indiana State Archives

[24] Gail Thornbrough, ed. *Diary of Calvin Fletcher*, Vol. VI, Indiana Historical Society, Indianapolis, 1972, 271

[25] Lanier, JFD, Sketch in the Life . . . 398

[26] Second State Bank of Indiana, Madison Branch Correspondence File, Indiana State Archives

[27] Second State Bank of Indiana, Madison Branch Correspondence File, Indiana State Archives

[28] Gail Thornbrough, ed. *Diary of Calvin Fletcher*, Vol. VI, Indiana Historical Society, Indianapolis, 1972, 273

[29] Gail Thornbrough, ed. *Diary of Calvin Fletcher*, Vol. VI, Indiana Historical Society, Indianapolis, 1972, 292

[30] Gail Thornbrough, ed. *Diary of Calvin Fletcher*, Vol. VI, Indiana Historical Society, Indianapolis, 1972, 293

## Chapter 10

[1] Second State Bank of Indiana, Madison Branch Correspondence File, Indiana State Archives

[2] Second State Bank of Indiana, Madison Branch Correspondence File, Indiana State Archives

[3] Second State Bank of Indiana, Madison Branch Correspondence File, Indiana State Archives

[4] Logan Esarey, *Internal Improvements in Early Indiana*, Indiana Historical Society, Indianapolis; 1912, 101

[5] Logan Esarey, *Internal Improvements in Early Indiana*, Indiana Historical Society, Indianapolis; 1912, 101 Also General Laws of Indiana, 1835, Chapter 2, Indiana State Archives

[6] Logan Esarey, *Internal Improvements in Early Indiana*, Indiana Historical Society, Indianapolis; 1912, 103

[7] Gail Thornbrough, ed. *Diary of Calvin Fletcher*, Vol. VI, Indiana Historical Society, Indianapolis, 1972, 299

[8] Gail Thornbrough, ed. *Diary of Calvin Fletcher*, Vol. VI, Indiana Historical Society, Indianapolis, 1972, 299

[9] Logan Esarey, *Internal Improvements in Early Indiana*, Indiana Historical Society, Indianapolis; 1912, 105

[10] Logan Esarey, *State Banking in Indiana 1814–1873* Indiana Historical Society, Indianapolis, n.d. 253

[11] Second State Bank of Indiana Journal Minutes, 2/18/1836, Indiana State Archives, 95

[12] Second State Bank of Indiana Journal Minutes, 2/18/1836, Indiana State Archives, 93

[13] Second State Bank of Indiana Journal Minutes, 2/18/1836, Indiana State Archives, 93

[14] Second State Bank of Indiana Journal Minutes, 2/18/1836, Indiana State Archives, 94

[15] Second State Bank of Indiana Journal Minutes, 2/18/1836, Indiana State Archives, 95

[16] Second State Bank of Indiana Journal Minutes, 2/18/1836, Indiana State Archives, 97

[17] Second State Bank of Indiana Journal Minutes, 2/18/1836, Indiana State Archives, 97

[18] Second State Bank of Indiana, Madison Branch Correspondence File, Indiana State Archives

[19] Letter Lanier to Polke. 3/2/1836, William Polke Letters, Lilly Library, Indiana University Library

[20] Letter Lanier to Polke. 3/22/1836, William Polke Letters, Lilly Library, Indiana University Library

[21] Letter Lanier to Polke. 4/15/1836, William Polke Letters, Lilly Library, Indiana University Library

[22] Second State Bank of Indiana, Madison Branch Correspondence File, Indiana State Archives

[23] Second State Bank of Indiana, Madison Branch Correspondence File, Indiana State Archives

[24] Meldrum letter

[25] Meldrum letter

[26] Second State Bank of Indiana, Madison Branch Correspondence File, Indiana State Archives

# Chapter 11

[1] Morris, 529

[2] Logan Esarey, Internal Improvements in Early Indiana, Indiana Historical Society, Indianapolis; 1912, 103

[3] Morris, 529

[4] Letter William Henry Harrison to Governor Noble December 31, 1836, *Messages and Papers of Noah Noble*, Indiana Historical Bureau, Indianapolis, 1958

[5] *International Newsweek* 1/23/95, 15

[6] Morris, 127

[7] Gail Thornbrough, ed. *Diary of Calvin Fletcher*, Vol. I, Indiana Historical Society, Indianapolis, 1972, 343.

[8] Second State Bank of Indiana Journal Minutes, 5/18/1836, , Indiana State Archives, 102

[9] Second State Bank of Indiana Journal Minutes, 5/18/1836, Indiana State Archives, 104

[10] Second State Bank of Indiana Journal Minutes, 5/18/1836, Indiana State Archives, 106

[11] Second State Bank of Indiana Journal Minutes, 5/18/1836, Indiana State Archives, 106

[12] Second State Bank of Indiana Journal Minutes, 5/19/1836, Indiana State Archives, 109

[13] Second State Bank of Indiana Journal Minutes, 5/18/1836, Indiana State Archives, 104

[14] Second State Bank of Indiana Journal Minutes, 5/18/1836, Indiana State Archives, 106

[15] Second State Bank of Indiana Journal Minutes, 5/19/1836, Indiana State Archives, 108

[16] Second State Bank of Indiana Journal Minutes, 5/19/1836, , Indiana State Archives, 108–109

[17] Second State Bank of Indiana Journal Minutes, 5/19/1836, Indiana State Archives, 108

[18] Second State Bank of Indiana Journal Minutes, 5/19/1836, Indiana State Archives, 108

[19] Second State Bank of Indiana Journal Minutes, 5/19/1836, Indiana State Archives, 107

[20] Second State Bank of Indiana Journal Minutes, 5/19/1836, Indiana State Archives, 107

[21] Letter Lanier to Polke, 6/25/1836, William Polke Letters, Lilly Library, Indiana University Library

[22] Letter Lanier to Polke, 7/7/1836, William Polke Letters, Lilly Library, Indiana University Library

[23] Morris, 177

[24] Second State Bank of Indiana, Madison Branch Correspondence File, Indiana State Archives

[25] Second State Bank of Indiana Journal Minutes, 7/27/1836, Indiana State Archives, 115–116

[26] Second State Bank of Indiana Journal Minutes, 7/27/1836, Indiana State Archives, 116

[27] Second State Bank of Indiana, Madison Branch Correspondence File, Indiana State Archives

[28] Frank C. Diedrich, *An Introduction to the Madison and Indianapolis Railroad*, October 1986 Quarterly Newsletter of the Jefferson County Historical Society

[29] Diedrich

[30] Minutes, Porter County Commissioners, June 1836

[31] Plat Book, Porter County, Indiana

[32] Second State Bank of Indiana, Madison Branch Correspondence File, Indiana State Archives

[33] Second State Bank of Indiana, Madison Branch Correspondence File, Indiana State Archives

[34] Letter Lanier to Polke, 10/29/1836, William Polke Letters, Lilly Library, Indiana University Library

[35] Gail Thornbrough, ed. *Diary of Calvin Fletcher*, Vol. VI, Indiana Historical Society, Indianapolis, 1972, 384–385.

[36] Second State Bank of Indiana, Madison Branch Correspondence File, Indiana State Archives

[37] Second State Bank of Indiana, Madison Branch Correspondence File, Indiana State Archives

[38] Second State Bank of Indiana, Madison Branch Correspondence File, Indiana State Archives

[39] Letter Lanier to Polke, 11/18/1836, William Polke Letters, Lilly Library, Indiana University Library

[40] Second State Bank of Indiana, Madison Branch Correspondence File, Indiana State Archives

[41] Second State Bank of Indiana Journal Minutes, 11/25/1836, Indiana State Archives, 124

[42] Second State Bank of Indiana Journal Minutes, 11/25/1836, Indiana State Archives, 124

[43] Second State Bank of Indiana Journal Minutes, 11/28/1836, Indiana State Archives, 127

[44] Second State Bank of Indiana Journal Minutes, 11/28/1836, Indiana State Archives, 126

[45] Second State Bank of Indiana Journal Minutes, 11/28/1836, Indiana State Archives, 131–132

[46] Letter Polke to Lanier, 12/20/1836, William Polke Letters, Lilly Library, Indiana University Library

[47] Letter Lanier to Polke, 12/25/1836, William Polke Letters, Lilly Library, Indiana University Library

[48] Letter Fletcher to Tipton, December 21–22, 1836 *John Tipton Papers*; V 3, 329–331; edited by Robertson & Riker, Indiaia Historical Bureau, Indianapolis, 1942

## Chapter 12

[1] Second State Bank of Indiana, Madison Branch Correspondence File, Indiana State Archives

[2] Ingersoll, 350

[3] Second State Bank of Indiana, Madison Branch Correspondence File, Indiana State Archives

[4] Second State Bank of Indiana Journal Minutes, 2/25/1837, Indiana State Archives, 141

[5] Second State Bank of Indiana Journal Minutes, 2/25/1837, Indiana State Archives, 141

[6] Second State Bank of Indiana Journal Minutes, 2/25/1837, Indiana State Archives, 141

[7] Second State Bank of Indiana Journal Minutes, 2/25/1837, Indiana State Archives, 141

[8] Second State Bank of Indiana, Madison Branch Correspondence File, Indiana State Archives

[9] Second State Bank of Indiana Journal Minutes, 5/17/1837, Indiana State Archives, 150

[10] Second State Bank of Indiana Journal Minutes, 5/17/1837, Indiana State Archives, 150

[11] Gail Thornbrough, ed. *Diary of Calvin Fletcher*, Vol. VI, Indiana Historical Society, Indianapolis, 1972, 429

[12] Logan Esarey, *State Banking in Indiana 1814–1873* Indiana Historical Society, Indianapolis, n.d. 258

[13] Gail Thornbrough, ed. *Diary of Calvin Fletcher*, Vol. VI, Indiana Historical Society, Indianapolis, 1972, 429

[14] Second State Bank of Indiana Journal Minutes, 5/18/1837, Indiana State Archives, 152

[15] Second State Bank of Indiana Journal Minutes, 5/18/1837, Indiana State Archives, 152–153

[16] Second State Bank of Indiana Journal Minutes, 5/19/1837, Indiana State Archives, 153

[17] Second State Bank of Indiana Journal Minutes, 5/19/1837, Indiana State Archives, 154

[18] Second State Bank of Indiana Journal Minutes, 5/19/1837, Indiana State Archives, 154

[19] Second State Bank of Indiana Journal Minutes, 5/19/1837, Indiana State Archives, 154–155

[20] Second State Bank of Indiana Journal Minutes, 5/20/1837, Indiana State Archives, 156

[21] Charles Latham Jr. *Miles Apart* a presentation to the Indianapolis Literary Club, February, 1987

[22] Gail Thornbrough, ed. *Diary of Calvin Fletcher*, Vol. VI, Indiana Historical Society, Indianapolis, 1972, 431

[23] *David Wallace Papers*, Indiana Historical Society, Indianapolis, 1963, 14

[24] *David Wallace Papers*, Indiana Historical Society, Indianapolis, 1963, 14–15

[25] *David Wallace Papers*, Indiana Historical Society, Indianapolis, 1963, 14–15

# Chapter 13

[1] Lanier, JFD, Sketch in the Life . . . 396–397
[2] Second State Bank of Indiana Journal Minutes, 8/11/1837, Indiana State Archives, 163
[3] Lanier, JFD, Sketch in the Life . . . 397
[4] Lanier, JFD, Sketch in the Life . . . 397
[5] Second State Bank of Indiana Journal Minutes, 8/10/1837, Indiana State Archives, 158; 162–163
[6] McCullough, 119
[7] Second State Bank of Indiana Journal Minutes, 8/10/1837, Indiana State Archives, 160
[8] Second State Bank of Indiana Journal Minutes, 8/12/1837, Indiana State Archives, 167
[9] Second State Bank of Indiana Journal Minutes, 8/12/1837, Indiana State Archives, 167
[10] Second State Bank of Indiana Journal Minutes, 8/13/1837, Indiana State Archives, 169
[11] Letter, Lanier to Polke, 8/29/1837, William Polke Letters, Lilly Library, Indiana University Library
[12] Letter, Lanier to Governor Noble, September 23, 1837, Noah Noble, Messages and Papers of Noah Noble, ed Dorothy Riker & Gail Thornbrough, Indiana Historical Bureau, 1958, Indianapolis
[13] Letter, Lanier to Governor Noble, September 23, 1837, Noah Noble, Messages and Papers of Noah Noble, ed Dorothy Riker & Gail Thornbrough, Indiana Historical Bureau, 1958, Indianapolis
[14] Letter Lanier to Polke, 11/9/1837, William Polke Letters, Lilly Library, Indiana University Library
[15] Second State Bank of Indiana Journal Minutes, 11/25/1837, Indiana State Archives, 179–180
[16] Second State Bank of Indiana Journal Minutes, 11/25/1837, Indiana State Archives, 181
[17] Second State Bank of Indiana Journal Minutes, 11/23/1837, Indiana State Archives, 174
[18] Second State Bank of Indiana Journal Minutes, 11/23/1837, Indiana State Archives, 173
[19] Second State Bank of Indiana Journal Minutes, 11/27/1837, Indiana State Archives, 184
[20] Second State Bank of Indiana Journal Minutes, 11/27/1837, Indiana State Archives, 184
[21] Logan Esarey, *Internal Improvements in Early Indiana*, Indiana Historical Society, Indianapolis; 1912, 107–108
[22] Gail Thornbrough, ed. *Diary of Calvin Fletcher*, Vol. VI, Indiana Historical Society, Indianapolis, 1972, 465

[23] *Messages and Papers of David Wallace, 1837–1840*, Indiana Historical Bureau, 1963, 3–6

# Chapter 14

[1] Logan Esarey, *Internal Improvements in Early Indiana*, Indiana Historical Society, Indianapolis; 1912, 107;115

[2] Logan Esarey, *Internal Improvements in Early Indiana*, Indiana Historical Society, Indianapolis; 1912, 118

[3] Second State Bank of Indiana Journal Minutes, 2/16/38, Indiana State Archives, 190

[4] Wallace Papers, 21

[5] Second State Bank of Indiana Journal Minutes, 2/16/38, Indiana State Archives, 190

[6] Second State Bank of Indiana Journal Minutes, 2/17/38, Indiana State Archives, 201

[7] Second State Bank of Indiana Journal Minutes, 2/17/38, Indiana State Archives, 201

[8] Second State Bank of Indiana Journal Minutes, 2/16/38, Indiana State Archives, 192

[9] Second State Bank of Indiana Journal Minutes, 2/16/38, Indiana State Archives, 192

[10] Second State Bank of Indiana Journal Minutes, 2//38, Indiana State Archives, 188-203

[11] Second State Bank of Indiana Journal Minutes, 2/17/38, Indiana State Archives, 200

[12] Second State Bank of Indiana Journal Minutes, 2/16/38, Indiana State Archives, 193–195

[13] Second State Bank of Indiana Journal Minutes, 2/16/38, Indiana State Archives, 193–195

[14] Second State Bank of Indiana Journal Minutes, 2/16/38, Indiana State Archives, 193

[15] Second State Bank of Indiana Journal Minutes, 2/16/38, Indiana State Archives, 193

[16] Lanier, JFD, Sketch in the Life . . . 397

[17] Raymond Walker Jr., *Albert Gallatin*, Macmillian & Company, New York, 1957, 367

[18] Second State Bank of Indiana Journal Minutes, 5/11/38, Indiana State Archives, 207–208

[19] Second State Bank of Indiana Journal Minutes, 5/11/38, Indiana State Archives, 208

[20] Second State Bank of Indiana Journal Minutes, 5/11/38, Indiana State Archives, 213

[21] Second State Bank of Indiana Journal Minutes, 5/11/38, Indiana State Archives, 211–212

[22] Second State Bank of Indiana Journal Minutes, 5/12/38, Indiana State Archives, 218–219

[23] Second State Bank of Indiana Journal Minutes, 5/14/38, Indiana State Archives, 224

[24] Second State Bank of Indiana Journal Minutes, 5/14/38, Indiana State Archives, 224

[25] Second State Bank of Indiana Journal Minutes, 5/12/38, Indiana State Archives, 214

[26] Second State Bank of Indiana Journal Minutes, 5/14/38, Indiana State Archives, 220

[27] Second State Bank of Indiana Journal Minutes, 5/14/38, Indiana State Archives, 221

[28] Second State Bank of Indiana Journal Minutes, 5/14/38, Indiana State Archives, 222

[29] Second State Bank of Indiana Journal Minutes, 5/14/38, Indiana State Archives, 223

[30] Letter, Lanier to Polke, 7/27/1838, William Polke Letters, Lilly Library, Indiana University Library

[31] Second State Bank of Indiana, Madison Branch Correspondence File, Indiana State Archives

[32] Second State Bank of Indiana Journal Minutes, 8/15/38, Indiana State Archives, 236

[33] Second State Bank of Indiana Journal Minutes, 8/15/38, Indiana State Archives, 236

[34] Second State Bank of Indiana Journal Minutes, 8/13/38, Indiana State Archives, 230

[35] Second State Bank of Indiana Journal Minutes, 8/14/38, Indiana State Archives, 233

[36] Second State Bank of Indiana Journal Minutes, 8/14/38, Indiana State Archives, 234

[37] Second State Bank of Indiana Journal Minutes, 8/16/38, Indiana State Archives, 241–243

[38] Second State Bank of Indiana Journal Minutes, 8/16/38, Indiana State Archives, 243

[39] Diederich

[40] *Messages and Papers of David Wallace*, 22–23

[41] *Messages and Papers of David Wallace*, 23

[42] Second State Bank of Indiana, Madison Branch Correspondence File, Indiana State Archives

[43] *Messages and Papers of David Wallace*, 23

[44] Second State Bank of Indiana, Madison Branch Correspondence File, Indiana State Archives

# Chapter 15

[1] Second State Bank of Indiana Journal Minutes, 11/14/38, Indiana State Archives, 253–254,

[2] Second State Bank of Indiana Journal Minutes, 11/14/38, Indiana State Archives, 252

[3] Second State Bank of Indiana Journal Minutes, 11/14/38, Indiana State Archives, 252

[4] Second State Bank of Indiana Journal Minutes, 11/14/38, Indiana State Archives, 252

[5] Second State Bank of Indiana Journal Minutes, 11/14/38, Indiana State Archives, 253

[6] Second State Bank of Indiana Journal Minutes, 11/14/38, Indiana State Archives, 252

[7] Second State Bank of Indiana Journal Minutes, 11/14/38, Indiana State Archives, 256

[8] Logan Esarey, *A History of Indiana from Its Exploration to 1850*, Hoosier Heritage Press, Indianapolis, (Reprint) 1970, 339

[9] Undated pamphlet, *The Madison & Indianapolis Railroad*

[10] Logan Esarey, *Internal Improvements in Early Indiana*, Indiana Historical Society, Indianapolis; 1912, 105

[11] *Messages and Papers of David Wallace*, 26

[12] Undated pamphlet, *The Madison & Indianapolis Railroad*

[13] *Messages and Papers of Noah Noble*, Indiana Historical Bureau, Indianapolis, 1958, 49

[14] Second State Bank of Indiana, Madison Branch Correspondence File, Indiana State Archives

[15] *Messages and Papers of Noah Noble*, Indiana Historical Bureau, Indianapolis, 1958, 49

[16] Second State Bank of Indiana Journal Minutes, 2/14/1839, Indiana State Archives, 280

[17] Second State Bank of Indiana Journal Minutes, 2/14/1839, Indiana State Archives, 280

[18] Gail Thornbrough. Ed. *Diary of Calvin Fletcher*, Vol. VI, Indiana Historical Society, Indianapolis, 1972, 226

[19] Second State Bank of Indiana Journal Minutes, 2/14/1839, Indiana State Archives, 298

[20] Second State Bank of Indiana Journal Minutes, 2/14/1839, Indiana State Archives, 298

[21] Second State Bank of Indiana Journal Minutes, 2/14/1839, Indiana State Archives, 298–299

[22] *Messages and Papers of David Wallace*, p29

[23] Fredia Bridenstein *The Madison and Indianapolis Railroad*, Thesis, Butler University, 1930, 26

[24] *Indianapolis Journal* May, 1840

[25] *Messages and Papers of David Wallace*, 386–387

[26] *Messages and Papers of Noah Noble*, Indiana Historical Bureau, Indianapolis, 1958. cited in George S.Cotterman Thesis, 43, Lanier State Historic Site, Madison.

[27] Second State Bank of Indiana, Madison Branch Correspondence File, Indiana State Archives

[28] Letter Lanier to Polke, 4/25/1839, William Polke Letters, Lilly Library, Indiana University Library

[29] Second State Bank of Indiana Journal Minutes, 5/9/1839, Indiana State Archives, 305

[30] Second State Bank of Indiana Journal Minutes, 5/9/1839, Indiana State Archives, 312

[31] Second State Bank of Indiana Journal Minutes, 5/9/1839, Indiana State Archives, 311

[32] *Indianapolis Journal* May, 1840

[33] *Messages and Papers of Noah Noble*, Indiana Historical Bureau, Indianapolis, 1958. cited in George S.Cottman Thesis, 43, Lanier State Historic Site, Madison.

[34] Second State Bank of Indiana Journal Minutes, 8/14/1839, Indiana State Archives, 326

[35] Second State Bank of Indiana Journal Minutes, 8/14/1839, Indiana State Archives, 328

[36] Second State Bank of Indiana Journal Minutes, 8/14/1839, Indiana State Archives, 327

[37] Second State Bank of Indiana Journal Minutes, 8/14/1839, Indiana State Archives, 327

[38] Second State Bank of Indiana Journal Minutes, 8/14/1839, Indiana State Archives, 327

[39] Second State Bank of Indiana Journal Minutes, 8/14/1839, Indiana State Archives, 328

[40] Second State Bank of Indiana Journal Minutes, 8/13/1839, Indiana State Archives, 322

[41] Second State Bank of Indiana Journal Minutes, 8/14/1839, Indiana State Archives, 327–328

[42] Second State Bank of Indiana Journal Minutes, 8/14/1839, Indiana State Archives, 328

[43] Second State Bank of Indiana Journal Minutes, 8/14/1839, Indiana State Archives, 328

[44] Second State Bank of Indiana Journal Minutes, 8/14/1839, Indiana State Archives, 328

[45] Second State Bank of Indiana Journal Minutes, 8/14/1839, Indiana State Archives, 328

[46] Second State Bank of Indiana Journal Minutes, 8/14/1839, Indiana State Archives, 325

47 Second State Bank of Indiana Journal Minutes, 8/14/1839, Indiana State Archives, 325
48 Second State Bank of Indiana Journal Minutes, 8/14/1839, Indiana State Archives, 329
49 Second State Bank of Indiana, Madison Branch Correspondence File, Indiana State Archives
50 Second State Bank of Indiana, Madison Branch Correspondence File, Indiana State Archives
51 Second State Bank of Indiana, Madison Branch Correspondence File, Indiana State Archives
52 Letter JFD Lanier to Governor Noble, reported in Cottman, 95
53 General Records on Commutations and Pardons Filed by Governor, Indiana State Archives
54 Second State Bank of Indiana, Madison Branch Correspondence File, Indiana State Archives
55 Second State Bank of Indiana, Madison Branch Correspondence File, Indiana State Archives
56 Letter Lanier to Polke, 10/18/1839, William Polke Letters, Lilly Library, Indiana University Library
57 Letter Lanier to J.B. Niles, Oct. 18, 1839, John Barron Niles Manuscripts, Lilly Library, Indiana University
58 Second State Bank of Indiana, Madison Branch Correspondence File, Indiana State Archives
59 Logan Esarey, *State Banking in Indiana 1814–1873* Indiana Historical Society, Indianapolis, n.d. 261

# Chapter 16

1 Second State Bank of Indiana Journal Minutes, 11/11/39, Indiana State Archives, 334
2 Second State Bank of Indiana Journal Minutes, 11/12/39, Indiana State Archives, 336–339
3 Second State Bank of Indiana Journal Minutes, 11/12/39, Indiana State Archives, 339
4 Second State Bank of Indiana Journal Minutes, 11/12/39, Indiana State Archives, 340
5 Second State Bank of Indiana Journal Minutes, 11/12/39, Indiana State Archives, 341
6 *Messages and Papers of David Wallace*, 32
7 Second State Bank of Indiana Journal Minutes, 11/13/39, Indiana State Archives, 345
8 Second State Bank of Indiana Journal Minutes, 11/12/39, Indiana State Archives, 343

9  Second State Bank of Indiana Journal Minutes, 11/12/39, Indiana State Archives, 343
10  McCullough, 117
11  Second State Bank of Indiana Journal Minutes, 11/12/39, Indiana State Archives, 337
12  Letter, Lanier to J.B. Niles, 11/26/1839, John Barron Niles Manuscripts, Lilly Library, Indiana University
13  Logan Esarey, *Internal Improvements in Early Indiana*, Indiana Historical Society, Indianapolis, 1912, 121
14  *Messages and Papers of David Wallace*, 32
15  Logan Esarey, *Internal Improvements in Early Indiana*, Indiana Historical Society, Indianapolis, 1912, 119
16  *Messages and Papers of David Wallace*, 41
17  Second State Bank of Indiana Journal Minutes, 2/11/1840, Indiana State Archives, 359
18  Second State Bank of Indiana Journal Minutes, 2/11/1840, Indiana State Archives, 360–361
19  Second State Bank of Indiana Journal Minutes, 2/11/1840, Indiana State Archives, 356–357
20  Letter, Lanier to J.B. Niles, 4/2/1840, John Barron Niles Manuscripts, Lilly Library, Indiana University
21  Second State Bank of Indiana Journal Minutes, 5/1840, Indiana State Archives, 371
22  Second State Bank of Indiana Journal Minutes, 5/1840, Indiana State Archives, 373–374
23  Second State Bank of Indiana Journal Minutes, 5/1840, Indiana State Archives, 374–375
24  Second State Bank of Indiana Journal Minutes, 5/1840, Indiana State Archives, 376
25  Second State Bank of Indiana Journal Minutes, 5/1840, Indiana State Archives, 376–377
26  Second State Bank of Indiana Journal Minutes, 5/1840, Indiana State Archives, 377
27  Second State Bank of Indiana Journal Minutes, 5/1840, Indiana State Archives, 367
28  Second State Bank of Indiana Journal Minutes, 5/1840, Indiana State Archives, 367
29  Second State Bank of Indiana Journal Minutes, 5/1840, Indiana State Archives, 368
30  Second State Bank of Indiana Journal Minutes, 5/1840, Indiana State Archives, 368
31  Second State Bank of Indiana Journal Minutes, 5/1840, Indiana State Archives, 369

[32] Second State Bank of Indiana Journal Minutes, 5/1840, Indiana State Archives, 382
[33] Second State Bank of Indiana Journal Minutes, 5/1840, Indiana State Archives, 379

# Chapter 17

[1] Bridenstein, 26
[2] Bridenstein, 27, Quoting *Madison Courier*, August 22, 1840
[3] Bridenstein, 27, Quoting *Madison Courier*, August 22, 1840
[4] Letter Merrill to Stapp, 8/10/1840, Indiana Historical Society, Indianapolis, Samuel Merrill Collection, M 204
[5] Second State Bank of Indiana Journal Minutes, 8/1840, Indiana State Archives, 385
[6] Second State Bank of Indiana Journal Minutes, 8/1840, Indiana State Archives, 385
[7] Second State Bank of Indiana Journal Minutes, 8/1840, Indiana State Archives, 385
[8] Second State Bank of Indiana Journal Minutes, 8/1840, Indiana State Archives, 385
[9] Second State Bank of Indiana Journal Minutes, 11/11/1840, Indiana State Archives, 397
[10] Second State Bank of Indiana Journal Minutes, 11/11/1840, Indiana State Archives, 398
[11] Second State Bank of Indiana Journal Minutes, 11/11/1840, Indiana State Archives, 401
[12] Second State Bank of Indiana Journal Minutes, 11/11/1840, Indiana State Archives, 399
[13] Second State Bank of Indiana Journal Minutes, 11/11/1840, Indiana State Archives, 401
[14] T.B. Anderson & R. G. Moore M*eaning and the Built Environment* Published in *The Recovery of Meaning* Edited by Leone & Potter, Smithsonian Institution Press Washington & London, 1988, 389–390.
[15] *Madison Banner*, October 7, 1840
[16] *Madison Banner*, October 7, 1840
[17] Gail Thornbrough, ed. *Diary of Calvin Fletcher*, Vol. III, Indiana Historical Society, Indianapolis, 1972, 226
[18] Gail Thornbrough, ed. *Diary of Calvin Fletcher*, December 25, 1840, Vol. II, Indiana Historical Society, Indianapolis, 1972, 261
[19] Gail Thornbrough, ed. *Diary of Calvin Fletcher*, December 25, 1840, Vol. VI, Indiana Historical Society, Indianapolis, 1972, 261

# Chapter 18

[1] Gail Thornbrough, ed. *Diary of Calvin Fletcher*, January 23, 1841, Vol. II, Indiana Historical Society, Indianapolis, 1972, 273

[2] Logan Esarey, *Internal Improvements in Early Indiana*, Indiana Historical Society, Indianapolis; 1912, 118, cites legislative report, 1841

[3] Logan Esarey, *State Banking in Indiana 1814–1873* Indiana Historical Society, Indianapolis, n.d. 262

[4] Letter, Lanier to J.B. Niles, 1/29/1841, John Barron Niles Manuscripts, Lilly Library, Indiana University

[5] Second State Bank of Indiana Journal Minutes, 2/8/41, Indiana State Archives, 415

[6] Second State Bank of Indiana Journal Minutes, 2/8/41, Indiana State Archives, 420

[7] Second State Bank of Indiana Journal Minutes, 2/9/41, Indiana State Archives, 428

[8] Second State Bank of Indiana Journal Minutes, 2/9/41, Indiana State Archives, 411–413

[9] Letter, Lanier to J.B. Niles, 3/8/1841, John Barron Niles Manuscripts, Lilly Library, Indiana University

[10] *Biographical Directory of the American Congress 1774–1971*, U.S. Government Printing Office, 1971

[11] Letter, Merrill to Noble, 3/24/1841, Merrill Collection, M 204, Smith Library, Indiana Historical Society

[12] *Madison Banner*, April 17, 1841

[13] Second State Bank of Indiana Journal Minutes, 5/10/41, Indiana State Archives, 433

[14] Second State Bank of Indiana Journal Minutes, 5/10/41, Indiana State Archives, 431

[15] Second State Bank of Indiana Journal Minutes, 5/10/41, Indiana State Archives, 432

[16] Second State Bank of Indiana Journal Minutes, 5/10/41, Indiana State Archives, 434

[17] Third Annual Report to the Stockholders, M&I Railroad, Indiana State Library

[18] Bridenstein, 28

[19] Second State Bank of Indiana Journal Minutes, 8/9/41, Indiana State Archives, 446

[20] Second State Bank of Indiana Journal Minutes, 8/9/41, Indiana State Archives, 447

[21] Second State Bank of Indiana Journal Minutes, 8/9/41, Indiana State Archives, 449

[22] Letter, Lanier to J.B. Niles, 10/5/1841, John Barron Niles Manuscripts, Lilly Library, Indiana University

[23] Second State Bank of Indiana, Madison Branch Correspondence File, Indiana State Archives

[24] Second State Bank of Indiana Journal Minutes, 11/8/41, Indiana State Archives, 460

[25] Second State Bank of Indiana Journal Minutes, 11/8/41, Indiana State Archives, 460

[26] Second State Bank of Indiana Journal Minutes, 11/8/41, Indiana State Archives, 461

[27] Second State Bank of Indiana Journal Minutes, 11/9/41, Indiana State Archives, 477–480

[28] Second State Bank of Indiana Journal Minutes, 11/9/41, Indiana State Archives, 479

[29] Second State Bank of Indiana Journal Minutes, 11/9/41, Indiana State Archives, 483

[30] Letter, Lanier to J.B. Niles, 12/11/1841, John Barron Niles Manuscripts, Lilly Library, Indiana University

[31] Second State Bank of Indiana, Madison Branch Correspondence File, Indiana State Archives

[32] Second State Bank of Indiana, Madison Branch Correspondence File, Indiana State Archives

[33] Letter, Lanier Correspondence, Indiana State Museums & Historic Sites

[34] Second State Bank of Indiana, Madison Branch Correspondence File, Indiana State Archives

[35] Letter, Lanier to J.B. Niles, 3/26/1842, John Barron Niles Manuscripts, Lilly Library, Indiana University

[36] Nathan B. Palmer, *Report of Agent to Examine the State Bank*, December, 1842, Indiana State Archives

[37] Nathan B. Palmer, *Report of Agent to Examine the State Bank*, December, 1842, Indiana State Archives

[38] Second Annual Report, Madison and Indianapolis Railroad, 1842

[39] Logan Esarey, *Internal Improvements in Early Indiana*, Indiana Historical Society, Indianapolis; 1912, 124

[40] Logan Esarey, *Internal Improvements in Early Indiana*, Indiana Historical Society, Indianapolis; 1912, 124

[41] Second State Bank of Indiana Journal Minutes, 2/14/1842, Indiana State Archives, 484

[42] Second State Bank of Indiana Journal Minutes, 2/14/1842, Indiana State Archives, 488

[43] Second State Bank of Indiana Journal Minutes, 2/14/1842, Indiana State Archives, 499

44 Second State Bank of Indiana Journal Minutes, 2/14/1842, Indiana State Archives, 491

45 Second State Bank of Indiana Journal Minutes, 2/14/1842, Indiana State Archives, 491

46 Second State Bank of Indiana Journal Minutes, 2/17/1842, Indiana State Archives, 504

47 Second State Bank of Indiana Journal Minutes, 2/16/1842, Indiana State Archives, 492

48 Second State Bank of Indiana Journal Minutes, 5/10/1842, Indiana State Archives, 511

49 Second State Bank of Indiana Journal Minutes, 5/10/1842, Indiana State Archives, 513

50 Second State Bank of Indiana Journal Minutes, 5/10/1842, Indiana State Archives, 515

51 Second State Bank of Indiana Journal Minutes, 5/10/1842, Indiana State Archives, 506

52 Second State Bank of Indiana Journal Minutes, 5/10/1842, Indiana State Archives, 512

53 Second State Bank of Indiana, Madison Branch Correspondence File, Indiana State Archives

54 Ingersoll, 348

55 General Records on Commutations and Pardons, filed by governor, Indiana State Archives

56 Letter Lanier to Polke, August 26, 1842, William Polke letters, Lilly Library, Indiana University Library

57 Letter, Lanier to J.B. Niles, August 27, 1842, John Barron Niles Manuscripts, Lilly Library, Indiana University

58 Letter, Lanier to J.B. Niles, August 27, 1842, John Barron Niles Manuscripts, Lilly Library, Indiana University

59 Second State Bank of Indiana, Madison Branch Correspondence File, Indiana State Archives

60 Ingersoll, 348

61 Second State Bank of Indiana, Madison Branch Correspondence File, Indiana State Archives

## Chapter 19

1 Logan Esarey, *Internal Improvements in Early Indiana*, Indiana Historical Society, Indianapolis, 1912, 124

2 Logan Esarey, *Internal Improvements in Early Indiana*, Indiana Historical Society, Indianapolis, 1912, 124

3 Logan Esarey, *Internal Improvements in Early Indiana*, Indiana Historical Society, Indianapolis, 1912, 123

[4] Bridenstein, 35

[5] Bridenstein, 36

[6] Bridenstein, 35 quoting General Laws of Indiana, 1841–1842 Chapt.1

[7] Diederich

[8] General Laws of Indiana, 1841–1842, Chapter 1 cited in Bridenstein, P 35

[9] Logan Esarey, *Internal Improvements in Early Indiana*, Indiana Historical Society, Indianapolis, 1912, 123

[10] Bridenstein, 37

[11] Bridenstein, 38

[12] Daniels, 19

[13] Second Annual Report, Madison and Indianapolis Railroad, 1842

[14] Letter, Lanier to J.B. Niles, May 14, 1843, John Barron Niles Manuscripts, Lilly Library, Indiana University

[15] Ingersoll, 348

[16] Bridenstein, 38

[17] Gail Thornbrough, ed. *Diary of Calvin Fletcher*, Vol. II, Indiana Historical Society, Indianapolis, 1972, 523

[18] Gail Thornbrough, ed. *Diary of Calvin Fletcher*, Vol. II, Indiana Historical Society, Indianapolis, 1972, 523

[19] Gail Thornbrough, ed. *Diary of Calvin Fletcher*, Vol. III, Indiana Historical Society, Indianapolis, 1972, 5

[20] Letter, Merrill to brother, 1/17/1844, Merrill Collection, M 204, Smith Library, Indiana Historical Society

[21] Gail Thornbrough, ed. *Diary of Calvin Fletcher*, Vol. III, Indiana Historical Society, Indianapolis, 1972, 5

[22] Gail Thornbrough, ed. *Diary of Calvin Fletcher*, Vol. III, Indiana Historical Society, Indianapolis, 1972, 6

[23] Gail Thornbrough, ed. *Diary of Calvin Fletcher*, Vol. III, Indiana Historical Society, Indianapolis, 1972, 24

[24] Second State Bank of Indiana, Madison Branch Correspondence File, Indiana State Archives

[25] Letter, Lanier to Merrill, June 14, 1844 Merrill Collection, M 204, Indiana Historical Society

[26] Second State Bank of Indiana, Madison Branch Correspondence File, Indiana State Archives

[27] Second State Bank of Indiana, Madison Branch Correspondence File, Indiana State Archives

## Chapter 20

[1] All information about the trial is from the *Madison Republican Banner* September 1844 issues.

# Chapter 21

1 Letter JFD to John Tipton, 9/19/1835, *John Tipton Papers*; V3, 177; edited by Robertson & Riker, Indiaia Historical Bureau, Indianapolis, 1942
2 C.S. Cottman, 25
3 Elizabeth D. Garrett, *At Home: The American Family 1750–1870*, Harry N. Abrams Inc. New York, 1990, 21
4 Garrett, 21
5 Garrett, 22
6 Garrett, 20
7 Garrett, 27
8 Garrett, 26
9 Letter Merrill to his wfe March 8, 1846, Indiana Historical Society.
10 Jefferson County Court records, Jefferson County Historical Society records, Madison, Indiana
11 Burley, *The Old Northwest*, V1, 258

# Chapter 22

1 Logan Esarey, *Internal Improvements in Early Indiana*, Indiana Historical Society, Indianapolis, 1912, 130
2 Logan Esarey, *Internal Improvements in Early Indiana*, Indiana Historical Society, Indianapolis, 1912, 121
3 Logan Esarey, *Internal Improvements in Early Indiana*, Indiana Historical Society, Indianapolis, 1912, 124
4 *Indianapolis Sentinal*, March 13, 1845, cited in Wylie Daniels, *Village at the End of the Road*, Indiana Historical Society, Indianapolis, 1938, 5
5 Presentation by A.J. Grayson to Madison Historical Society, 12/13/1898, Madison Indiana
6 A.J. Grayson
7 Letter, Lanier to J.B. Niles, April 7, 1845, John Barron Niles Manuscripts, Lilly Library, Indiana University
8 Daniels, 24
9 Daniels, 22
10 Daniels, 28
11 Daniels, 28
12 Daniels, 28
13 Daniels, 28
14 *Madison Courier*, 10/20/1845
15 *Madison Banner*, 11/15/1845
16 *Madison Banner*, 11/15/1845

[17] Ingersoll, P 348
[18] Gail Thornbrough, ed. *Diary of Calvin Fletcher*, 1/29/1846–2/4/1826, Vol. III, Indiana Historical Society, Indianapolis, 1972, 224–225
[19] Logan Esarey, *Internal Improvements in Early Indiana*, Indiana Historical Society, Indianapolis, 1912, 131
[20] Logan Esarey, *Internal Improvements in Early Indiana*, Indiana Historical Society, Indianapolis, 1912, 131
[21] Logan Esarey, *Internal Improvements in Early Indiana*, Indiana Historical Society, Indianapolis, 1912, 133
[22] Logan Esarey, *Internal Improvements in Early Indiana*, Indiana Historical Society, Indianapolis, 1912, 133
[23] Logan Esarey, *Internal Improvements in Early Indiana*, Indiana Historical Society, Indianapolis, 1912, 133
[24] Logan Esarey, *Internal Improvements in Early Indiana*, Indiana Historical Society, Indianapolis, 1912, 133
[25] Logan Esarey, *Internal Improvements in Early Indiana*, Indiana Historical Society, Indianapolis, 1912, 134
[26] Ingersoll, 348
[27] Letter, Samuel Merrill to David Merrill, April 26, 1846, Merrill Collection M207, Indiana Historical Society.
[28] Letter, Lanier to J.B. Niles, May 30, 1846, John Barron Niles Manuscripts, Lilly Library, Indiana University
[29] *Madison Banner*, August 12, 1846
[30] *Indianapolis Sentinal*, August 5, 1846, citiing *Boston Globe*
[31] *Madison Banner*, August 12, 1846
[32] Letter, Lanier to J.B. Niles, July 18, 1846, John Barron Niles Manuscripts, Lilly Library, Indiana University
[33] *Madison Banner*, November, 1846
[34] *Madison Banner*, November, 1846
[35] Gail Thornbrough, ed. *Diary of Calvin Fletcher*, 11/16/1846, Vol. III, Indiana Historical Society, Indianapolis, 1972, 322

## Chapter 23

[1] Lanier, JFD, Sketch in the Life . . . 415
[2] Lanier, JFD, Sketch in the Life . . . 415
[3] Indiana Department of Conservation *The James F.D. Lanier Home* 1928
[4] Ingersoll, 348
[5] Gail Thornbrough, ed. *Diary of Calvin Fletcher*, April 10, 1847, Vol. III, Indiana Historical Society, Indianapolis, 1972, 365
[6] Daniels, 30
[7] Lanier, JFD, Sketch in the Life . . . 415

[8] Lanier, JFD, Sketch in the Life . . . 415–416
[9] Lanier, JFD, Sketch in the Life . . . 416
[10] Lanier, JFD, Sketch in the Life . . . 416
[11] Lanier, JFD, Sketch in the Life . . . 416
[12] Bridenstein, 44a, cites Dunn, J.C., *Greater Indianapolis*, 149
[13] *Indianapolis Sentinal*, October 6, 1847
[14] *Indianapolis Journal*, October 11, 1847
[15] Letter, Lanier to Samuel Merrill, n.d. Samuel Merrill Collection M207, Indiana Historical Society.
[16] Ingersoll, 348
[17] *Madison Banner*, December 17, 1847

## Chapter 24

[1] Daniels, 51–52
[2] *Madison Banner*, February 2, 1848
[3] Gail Thornbrough, ed. *Diary of Calvin Fletcher*, March 8, 1848 Vol. IV, Indiana Historical Society, Indianapolis, 1972, 21
[4] Charles Latham Jr.
[5] Charles Latham Jr.
[6] Letter, Lanier to Merrill, August, 1848, Merrill Collection, M 204, Indiana Historical Society
[7] Bridenstein, 46
[8] *Biographical Directory of the American Congress, 1774–1971*, U.S. Government Printing Office, 1971
[9] Gail Thornbrough, ed. *Diary of Calvin Fletcher*, Vol. IV, Indiana Historical Society, Indianapolis, 1972, 147
[10] Diederich
[11] Ingersoll, P 349
[12] Ingersoll, P 348
[13] Ingersoll, P 349
[14] Springdale Cemetery records, Madison, In.
[15] Ingersoll, 350
[16] Daniels, 52
[17] Gail Thornbrough, ed. *Diary of Calvin Fletcher*, August 13, 1850, Vol. IV, Indiana Historical Society, Indianapolis, 1972, 207
[18] Gail Thornbrough, ed. *Diary of Calvin Fletcher*, November 11, 1850, Vol. IV, Indiana Historical Society, Indianapolis, 1972, 241
[19] Presentation by A.J. Grayson to Madison Historical Society, 12/23/1898, Madison Indiana
[20] A.J. Grayson
[21] A.J. Grayson
[22] A.J. Grayson

[23] Letter, Judge Jeremiah Sullivan to son Algernon, April 17, 1851, Jeremiah Sullivan Collection M270, W. H. Smith Library, Indiana State Historical Society, Indianapolis
[24] Ingersoll, 350
[25] Ingersoll, 349
[26] Ingersoll, 348
[27] Gail Thornbrough, ed. *Diary of Calvin Fletcher*, May 13 & 14, 1851, Vol. IV, Indiana Historical Society, Indianapolis, 1972, 288

## Chapter 25

[1] New York City Directory 1851–1852
[2] Pamphlet: Jefferson Market Regional Library
[3] Exhibit New York State Museum-Albany
[4] Exhibit New York State Museum-Albany
[5] New York City Directory 1853–1854
[6] Charles Latham Jr.
[7] Ingersoll, 348–349
[8] Arthur Tayler, *Illustrated History of North American Railroads*, 25
[9] Lanier, JFD, Sketch in the Life . . . 398
[10] Lanier, JFD, Sketch in the Life . . . 400
[11] Letter Lanier to Merrill July 4, 1851, Merrill Collection M204, Indiana Historical Society, Indianapolis.
[12] Vincent P. Carosso, 12
[13] Lanier, JFD, Sketch in the Life . . . 400
[14] Vincent P. Carosso, 12
[15] Lanier, JFD, Sketch in the Life . . . 400
[16] Lanier, JFD, Sketch in the Life . . . 400
[17] Vincent P. Carosso, 12
[18] Lanier, JFD, Sketch in the Life . . . 400–401

## Chapter 26

[1] Lanier, JFD, Sketch in the Life . . . 402
[2] Letter- Steven Miller, Curator Museum of the City of New York to Diana Lanier Smith, 6/29/1981
[3] Logan Esarey, *State Banking in Indiana 1814–1873* Indiana State Historical Society, Indianapolis, n.d. 289
[4] Logan Esarey, *State Banking in Indiana 1814–1873* Indiana State Historical Society, Indianapolis, n.d. 289
[5] Logan Esarey, *State Banking in Indiana 1814–1873* Indiana State Historical Society, Indianapolis, n.d. 288
[6] Logan Esarey, *State Banking in Indiana 1814–1873* Indiana State Historical Society, Indianapolis, n.d. 291

[7] Logan Esarey, *State Banking in Indiana 1814–1873* Indiana State Historical Society, Indianapolis, n.d. 291

[8] Logan Esarey, *State Banking in Indiana 1814–1873* Indiana State Historical Society, Indianapolis, n.d. 293–294

[9] Logan Esarey, *State Banking in Indiana 1814–1873* Indiana State Historical Society, Indianapolis, n.d. 294

[10] Logan Esarey, *State Banking in Indiana 1814–1873* Indiana State Historical Society, Indianapolis, n.d. 293–294

[11] Logan Esarey, *State Banking in Indiana 1814–1873* Indiana State Historical Society, Indianapolis, n.d. 295

[12] Sandburg, *Abraham Lincoln, The Prairie Years and the War Years*, Harcourt Brace, Jovanovich, New York, 1954, 111

[13] Ingersoll, 350

[14] Greenwood Cemetery records, lot 7131-7134 Brooklyn N.Y.

[15] Ingersoll, 349

[16] Ingersoll, 349

[17] Ingersoll, 349

[18] Greenwood Cemetery records, lot 7131-7134 Brooklyn N.Y.

[19] Lanier, JFD, Sketch in the Life . . . 403

[20] Esarey, *Internal Improvements in Early Indiana*, Indiana State Historical Society, Indianapolis, 1912, 150

[21] *New York Times*, March 8, 1926.

[22] Ingersoll 350

[23] Letter to all Wabash and Erie Canal bondholders from JFD Lanier, November 26, 1858, Canals: Wabash & Erie Canal Collection #1758 Indiana State Historical Society, Indianapolis.

[24] Esarey, *Internal Improvements in Early Indiana*, Indiana State Historical Society, Indianapolis, 1912, 151–152

[25] Letter to all Wabash and Erie Canal bondholders from JFD Lanier, November 26, 1858, Canals: Wabash & Erie Canal Collection #1758 Indiana State Historical Society, Indianapolis.

[26] Letter, Jerimiah Sullivan to son Algernon, November 1859, Jerimiah Sullivan Papers, Collection #270 Indiana State Historical Society

[27] Ingersoll 350

[28] Ingersoll, 349

[29] *Biographical Directory of the American Congress 1771–1971*, U.S. Government Printing Office 1971.

[30] Lanier, JFD, Sketch in the Life . . . 403

[31] *New York Times* 7/21/69

[32] *Madison Courier* 8/7/58

[33] *New York Times* 7/21/69

[34] *New York Times* 7/21/69

[35] *New York Times* 7/21/69

[36] Sandburg, 148

37 Sandburg, 146
38 Sandburg, 148
39 *Madison Daily Evening Courier*, May 22, 1860
40 Jefferson County Deed Records, 1861
41 The James F.D. Lanier Home, Indiana Department of Conservation, 23
42 The James F.D. Lanier Home, Indiana Department of Conservation, 23
43 *New York Times* 7/21/69 quoted in Lanier, 404
44 *New York Times* 3/8/26
45 Sandburg, 195
46 Lanier, JFD, Sketch in the Life . . . 408
47 Sandburg, 160

## Chapter 27

1 Sandburg, 162
2 Sandburg, 162
3 Sandburg, 162
4 Sandburg, 163
5 Sandburg, 164–165
6 Sandburg, 165
7 Lanier, JFD, Sketch in the Life . . . 408
8 Ingersoll, 349
9 William D. Foulke, *The Life of Oliver P. Morton*, V1, 112
10 Lanier, JFD, Sketch in the Life . . . 409
11 Morton Telegraph Books, bk. 1, 120
12 Morton telegraph Books bk. 2, 186
13 Morton Telegraph Books bk 2, 192
14 Morton Letter Book
15 William Wesley Woolen, Biographical Sketches of early Indiana, P 404.
16 Ingersoll, 350
17 *New York Times* 7/21/69 quoted in Lanier, 400
18 *New York Times* 7/21/69 quoted in Lanier, 399
19 *New York Times* 7/21/69 quoted in Lanier, 400
20 Lanier, JFD, Sketch in the Life . . . 409
21 Madison *Courier*, 11/27/1861
22 William D. Foulke, *The Life of Oliver P. Morton*, V1, 180–181
23 *Indianapolis Daily Journal* June 24, 1862
24 *Indianapolis Daily Journal* June 24, 1862
25 *Indianapolis Daily Journal* June 24, 1862
26 *Indianapolis Daily Journal* June 24, 1862

[27] *Indianapolis Daily Journal* June 24, 1862
[28] Sandburg, 352
[29] Morton Telegraphic Messages 5/21/62
[30] Morton Telegraphic Messages 5/23/62
[31] Morton Telegraphic Messages 5/23/62
[32] Morton Telegraphic Messages 5/26/62
[33] Morton Telegraphic Messages 5/27/62
[34] Morton Telegraphic Messages 5/29/62
[35] Oakey letter of June 3, 1862, published in the *Indianapolis Daily Journal*
[36] Morton Telegraphic Messages 6/2/62
[37] Morton Telegraphic Messages 6/21/62
[38] James Madison, *The Indiana Way* p 201
[39] William D. Foulke, *The Life of Oliver P. Morton*, V1, 214
[40] William D. Foulke, *The Life of Oliver P. Morton*, V1, 214
[41] William D. Foulke, *The Life of Oliver P. Morton*, V1, p 229–230
[42] William D. Foulke, *The Life of Oliver P. Morton*, V1, p 234
[43] William D. Foulke, *The Life of Oliver P. Morton*, V1, p 232
[44] William D. Foulke, *The Life of Oliver P. Morton*, V1, p 233
[45] William D. Foulke, *The Life of Oliver P. Morton*, V1, p 234
[46] William D. Foulke, *The Life of Oliver P. Morton*, V1, p 235
[47] William D. Foulke, *The Life of Oliver P. Morton*, V1, p 236
[48] William D. Foulke, *The Life of Oliver P. Morton*, V1, p 255
[49] Lanier, JFD, Sketch in the Life . . . 410
[50] Lanier, JFD, Sketch in the Life . . . 431
[51] Lanier, JFD, Sketch in the Life . . . 431
[52] Lanier, JFD, Sketch in the Life . . . 431
[53] Lanier, JFD, Sketch in the Life . . . 431
[54] Lanier, JFD, Sketch in the Life . . . 432

## Chapter 28

[1] Indiana State Archives A2942 094321 folder 16
[2] William D. Foulke, V1, 263–266
[3] U.S. Grant Personal Memoirs of U.S. Grant.Greenwich Conn.: Fawcet Publications, 1962, Edited by Phillip Van Doren Stern. 221
[4] Julia Dent Grant Personal Memories of Julia Dent Grant. New York, G.P. Putnam's Sons. Edited by John Y Simon. 114, 119
[5] Julia Dent Grant, 126.
[6] Sandburg, 351
[7] Sandburg, 350
[8] Sandburg, 350
[9] Sandburg, 350

[10] Sandburg, 350
[11] Sandburg, 350
[12] Sandburg, 350
[13] Sandburg, 351
[14] Sandburg, 352
[15] Transcribed from National Archives by Wm. Marshall Shaw Jr. 323 Forest Ave. Shreveport La. 71104
[16] William D. Foulke, *The Life of Oliver P. Morton*, V1, 270
[17] Lanier, JFD, Sketch in the Life . . . 411
[18] William English Papers, Biographical Notes p5, Collection M98, Indiana State Historical Society, Indianapolis, Indiana.
[19] William English Papers
[20] Lanier, JFD, Sketch in the Life . . . 407
[21] Greenwood Cemetery records, lot 7131-7134 Brooklyn NY
[22] Ingersoll, 349
[23] Ingersoll, 350
[24] Burke Davis, *The Civil War: Strange and Fascinating Facts*, The Fairfax Press, Crown Publishers Inc. New York, NY, 1982, 77–78
[25] Lanier correspondence National Archives.
[26] Examiner's Report, Third National Bank of the City of New York, June 8, 1866.
[27] Examiner's Report Third National Bank of the City of New York, June 8, 1866.
[28] Burke Davis, 78
[29] Sidney Lanier, *Letters*, Edited by Charles Anderson and Audrey Starke, Johns Hopkins University Press, 1945, Vol 7, fn 3, 213

## Chapter 29

[1] Ingersoll, 349
[2] Lanier, JFD, Sketch in the Life . . . 433
[3] Lanier, JFD, Sketch in the Life . . . 433
[4] Lanier, JFD, Sketch in the Life . . . 418
[5] Lanier, JFD, Sketch in the Life . . . 418
[6] Lanier, JFD, Sketch in the Life . . . 419
[7] Lanier, JFD, Sketch in the Life . . . 418
[8] Lanier, JFD, Sketch in the Life . . . 419
[9] Lanier, JFD, Sketch in the Life . . . 419
[10] Lanier, JFD, Sketch in the Life . . . 420
[11] Lanier, JFD, Sketch in the Life . . . 420
[12] Lanier, JFD, Sketch in the Life . . . 420
[13] Lanier, JFD, Sketch in the Life . . . 421
[14] Lanier, JFD, Sketch in the Life . . . 421

[15] Lanier, JFD, Sketch in the Life . . . 421–422
[16] Lanier, JFD, Sketch in the Life . . . 423
[17] Examiner's Report Third National Bank of the City of New York, June 8, 1866.
[18] Ingersoll, 349
[19] Sidney Lanier, *Letters*, V8, 279–280
[20] Sidney Lanier, *Letters*, Introduction fn #40
[21] Ingersoll, 349
[22] Lanier, JFD, Sketch in the Life . . . 425
[23] Sidney Lanier, *Letters*, V8, 20
[24] Sidney Lanier, *Letters*, V8, 20
[25] Sidney Lanier, *Letters*, V8, 22–23
[26] Sidney Lanier, *Letters*, V8, 25–26
[27] Sidney Lanier, *Letters*, V8, 100
[28] Ingersoll, 348
[29] Ingersoll, 350
[30] Sidney Lanier, *Letters*, V8, 213
[31] Sidney Lanier, *Letters*, V8, 390
[32] Sidney Lanier, *Letters*, V8, 412
[33] Sidney Lanier, *Letters*, V9, 91
[34] Sidney Lanier, *Letters*, V9, 389-90
[35] Sidney Lanier, *Letters*, V9, 432
[36] Sidney Lanier, *Letters*, V9, 453 & V9, 464
[37] Sidney Lanier, *Letters*, V9, 433
[38] Sidney Lanier, *Letters*, V9, 467
[39] Sidney Lanier, *Letters*, V9, 477
[40] A copy of JFD Lanier's will is on file at the Lanier State Historic Site in Madison Indiana.
[41] *New York Times*, March 8, 1926.
[42] Records on file at the Lanier State Historic Site, Madison, Indiana
[43] Records on file at the Lanier State Historic Site, Madison, Indiana
[44] Cottman Thesis, 76 citing William O. Stoddard *Ulysses S. Grant*, New York, 1888, 343
[45] Cottman Thesis, 76
[46] Cottman Thesis, 76
[47] *New York Times*, August 31, 1881
[48] *New York Times*, August 31, 1881

# Bibliography

Adams, Henry, *Life of Albert Gallatin*, J.B. Lippencott & Co., Philadelphia and London, 1879

Anderson, T.B & R. G. Moore, *Meaning and the Built Environment* Published in *T'he Recovery of Meaning*. Edited by Leone & Potter, Smithsonian Institution Press, 1988.

Baird, C. W. D.D. *History of the Huguenot Emigration to America*, Genealogical Publishing Co. Inc., Baltimore, 1973,

_____ *Biographical Directory of the American Congress 1774–1971*, U.S. Government Printing Office, 1971

Boomhower, Ray, "Lafayette's Triumphal Return" *Outdoor Indiana*, May/June 1995

Bridenstein, Freda, *The Madison and Indianapolis Railroad*, Thesis Butler University, 1930

Burley, *The Old Northwest, Pioneer period 1815–1868* Indiana Historical Society, Indianapolis, 1950, V 1.

Canals: Wabash & Erie Canal Collection #1758 Indiana State Historical Society, Smith Library, Indianapolis.

Carusso, Vincent P., *Investment Banking in America—A History*, Harvard University Press, 1970

Catterall, Ralph C. H., *The Second Bank of the United States*, University of Chicago Press, 1903

Cottman, George S., Thesis, n.d., Lanier State Historic Site, Madison,

Cottman, George S., *The James F.D. Lanier Home, An Indiana Memorial*, Indiana Department of Conservation, Indianapolis, 1926

Cox, Sanford *Recollections of the Early Settlement of the Wabash Valley*, Courier Steam Book and Job Printing, Lafayette, Indiana, 1860

Daniels, Wiley, *Village at the End of the Road*, Indiana Historical Society, Indianapolis,1938

Davis, Burke, *The Civil War: Strange and fascinating Facts*, The Fairfax Press, Crown Publisher's Inc., New York, NY, 1982

Diederich, Frank C., *An Introduction to the Madison & Indianapolis Railroad*, October 1986 Quarterly Newletter of the Jefferson County Historical Society

Dunn, Jacob B., *Indiana and Indianians*, American Historical Society, Chicago and New York, 1919, V 1 & 2

English, William, Papers, Indiana State Historical Society, Collection M98, Smith Library, Indiana Historical Society, Indianapolis

Esarey, Logan, *State Banking in Indiana 1814–1873*, Indiana University History Department No. 15, Bloomington Indiana, nd

Esarey, Logan, *Internal Improvements in Early Indiana*. Indianapolis; Indiana Historical Society, 1912.

Esarey, Logan, *A History of Indiana from Its Exploration to 1850*, Hoosier Heritage Press, Indianapolis, (Reprint) 1970.

Fletcher, Calvin, *Diary of Calvin Fletcher*, Vol. I-IX, Gail Thornbrough, ed., Indiana Historical Society, Indianapolis, 1972

Foulke, William D., *The Life of Oliver P. Morton*, Bowen Merrill Co. Indianapolis, 1899, V 1

Garrett, Elizabeth D., *At Home: The American Family 1750–1870*, Harry N. Abrams Inc., New York, 1990

Grant, Julia Dent, *Personal Memories of Julia Dent Grant*, New York, G.P. Putnam's Sons. Edited by John Y Simon.

Grant, U.S., *Personal Memoirs of U.S. Grant*. Greenwich Conn.: Fawcet Publications, 1962, Edited by Phillip Van Doren Stern.

Grayson, A.J. Presentation to Madison Historical Society December 23, 1898, Madison Indiana.

Hammond, Bray, *Banks and Politics in America From the Revolution to the Civil War*, Princeton University Press, 1957

Hawes, G. W. *Hawes' Indiana State Gazetteer and Business Directory*, 1858–1863

Hill, Fredrick, *William Hendricks, Indiana Politician and Western Advocate 1812–1856* Ph.D. Thesis Indiana State Library, Indianapolis 1972

Indiana Department of Conservation *The James F.D. Lanier Home*, n.p. 1928, Indianapolis.

Ingersoll, Louise V., *Lanier* (Genealogy), Goetz Printing Co. Washington D.C., 1975

Knapp, H.S., *History of the Maumee Valley*, Blade Publishing House, Toledo, Ohio, 1872

Lanier, JFD, *Sketch in the Life of JFD Lanier*, privately published, New York, 1871, Second edition 1877

Lanier, JFD collection, Lanier Mansion S.H. S., Madison, Indiana

Lanier, Sidney, Letters, Edited by Charles Anderson and Audrey Starke, John Hopkins University Press, 1945, Vols 7–9

Latham, Charles Jr. *Miles Apart* a presentation to the Indianapolis Literary Club, February 1987

Madison, James, *The Indiana Way*, Indiana University Press, Bloomington; Indiana Historical Bureau, Indianapolis, 1986

McCulloch, Hugh, *Men and Measures of Half a Century*, Scribner, 1888

Merrill, Samuel, Collection M204 W.H. Smith Memorial Library, Indiana Historical Society, Indianapolis,

Morgan, B.F., Directory of Preble County Ohio, Eaton Ohio, 1875

Morris, Richard B., *Encyclopedia of American History*, Harper Row, 6th Edition, 1982

Morton, Oliver P., Governor, Letter Book Indiana State Archives, Indianapolis

Morton, Oliver P., Governor, Telegraph Books, bk. 1 & 2 Indiana State Archives, Indianapolis, IN,

Muncie, Emery, *A History of Jefferson County, Indiana*, submitted as a pairtial requirement for MA degree, Indiana University, Bloomington, Indiana, 1932.

Niles, John Barron, Manuscripts, Lilly Library, Indiana University, Bloomington, Indiana

*Niles Weekly Register*, 76 volumes, Washington, Baltimore, Philadelphia, February 1815

Noble, Noah, *Messages and Papers of Noah Noble*, Dorothy Riker & Gail Thornbrough ed. Indiana Historical Bureau, Indianapolis, 1958,

Palmer, Nathan B., *Report of Agent to Examine the State Bank*, December 1842, Indiana State Archives, Indianapolis.

Polke, William Letters, Lilly Library, Indiana University Library, Bloomington Indiana

Railsback., M.H. "Builders of Destiny." D.A.R. Magazine

Riker & Thornbrough Indiana Election Results 1816–1851, Indiana Historical Society, 1960

Sandburg, Carl, *Abraham Lincoln, The Prairie Years and the War Years*, Harcourt Brace, Jovanovich, New York, 1954

Second State Bank of Indiana Board of Directors Minutes Indiana State Archives, Indianapolis.

Second State Bank of Indiana, Madison Branch Correspondence File, Indiana State Archives, Indianapolis.

Smith, Diana Lanier, personal correspondence

Sullivan, Jerimiah Collection, Jefferson County, Indiana Historical Society

Sullivan, Jerimiah Papers, Collection M270, Indiana State Historical Society, Smith Library, Indianapolis

Tayler, Arthur, *Illustrated History of North American Railroads*, Chartwell Books, Inc., Edison, New Jersey, 1996

Third Annual Report to the Stockholders, M&I Railroad, Indiana State Library, Indianapolis.

Tipton, John, *John Tipton Papers*; Vol. 1–3, edited by Robertson & Riker, ed., Indiana Historical Bureau, Indianapolis, 1942

Tipton, John, Papers, W. H. Smith Library, Indiana Historical Society, Indianapolis.

Washington, George, letter to Thomas Jefferson, 13/29/1774, Old South leaflet No. 16, p9; George Washington to Governor Benjamin Harrison of Virginia, letter 10/10/ 1774, Old South Leaflet No. 16, p1 Directors of old South Works, Boston nd

Walker, Raymond Jr., *Albert Gallatin*, Macmillian & Company, New York, 1957

Wallace, David, *Messages and Papers of David Wallace, 1837–1840*, Indiana Historical Bureau, Indianapolis., 1963

Williams, H.A & Bros, History of Preble County, Cleveland, Ohio, 1881

Woollen, W.W., *Biographical and Historical Sketches of Early Indiana*, nd, np

Zimmer, Ph.D. Thesis Indiana University 1974 *Madison Indiana 1811–1860 A Study in the Process of City Building*

# SKETCH OF THE LIFE

OF

# J. F. D. LANIER.

(Printed for the use of his Family only.)

NEW YORK.
1877

# TO MY CHILDREN.

*In the following pages I have prepared for you a brief sketch of some of the leading events of my Life, believing that I can leave to you no legacy more acceptable.*

I was born in Washington, in the County of Beaufort, in the State of North Carolina, on the 22d day of November, 1800. My father was Alexander Chalmers Lanier. His mother's maiden name was Sarah Chalmers. She was nearly allied to the family of Chalmers in Scotland, of which Dr. Chalmers, the celebrated divine, was afterward a member. It was this connection that gave my father his middle name. My mother was a native of Virginia. Her maiden name was Drusilla Doughty.

My first paternal ancestor in this country was Thomas Lanier, a Huguenot of Bordeaux, France, who was driven out of that country by religious persecution, near the middle of the seventeenth century. He went first to England, and came from that country to this, either in company with, or about the time that John Washington, the ancestor of George Washington, emigrated to it. He subsequently married Elizabeth, a daughter of John Washington, and ultimately settled in North Carolina. In his native country he was a man of high social position, and possessed a large estate, a considerable portion of which he contrived to bring away with him, although confiscated by law. He also brought with him a portion of the family furniture which was long retained by his descendants as interesting and valued heirlooms. His children were Richard, Thomas, James, Elizabeth and Sarnpson Lanier. It was from the first-named that our branch of the family descended. His children were Lewis, Buckner, Burrill and Winifred. Lewis, our ancestor, married a Miss Ball, a sister of the mother of General Washington. He was my great-grandfather. His son, James Lanier, was my grandfather. My account of the emigration of our ancestor to this country, and of his marriage into the Washington family, is derived from a statement of the late George Washington Parke Custis, the grandson of Mrs. General Washington, taken from the records of the Washington family in his possession. The marriage of my great-grandfather with a sister of the mother of General Washington is a well established tradition in our family, but I possess no authentic record of the fact.

My grandfather, James Lanier, was a planter. He was well educated, a cultivated gentlemen, energetic and public spirited, and took an active part in the war of the Independence, serving through the whole of it as captain in Col. William Washington's regiment of light cavalry which was particularly distinguished for its efficient service. He was in the battles of Eutaw Springs, Guilford Court House, the Cowpens and, I believe, of King's Mountain. These were among the most brilliant achievements of the war. He also served as captain in General Wayne's expedition against the Northwestern Indians, in 1794, which not only avenged the defeat of General St. Clair, but completely destroyed their power, and for the first time gave peace to, and prepared the way for the future settlement of, the great Mississippi Valley.

In 1789, I think, my grandfather moved to Nashville, Tennessee. The South-west was then just coming into notice. Among the immigrants into that section was General Andrew Jackson, afterward so famous in the history of the country. For some time after his arrival at Nashville he was an inmate of my grandfather's family. My grandfather subsequently, about 1791, removed to Bourbon County, Kentucky, of which he was soon appointed Prothonotary, or County Clerk. From thence he moved to Pendleton County, Kentucky, where he passed the remainder of his days.

Soon after my birth, my father moved to Bourbon County, Kentucky. He invested his property in lands, and lost it by defect of title, with which much of the real estate of that State was tainted, and which produced wide-spread disaster and ruin. In consequence of these losses, he moved, in 1807, to the town of Eaton in Preble County, Ohio. Upon reaching this State, he manumitted two valuable family slaves, the only ones he held, being prohibited from doing so in Kentucky by the laws of the latter. He had the satisfaction of seeing them both useful and respected in their new condition of freedom. I have always greatly valued this act of my father, as these slaves constituted quite a portion of his property. The act was, however, only in harmony with his whole character.

390

For a considerable portion of the time that my father resided at Eaton, he was clerk of the courts of the county. Upon the breaking out of the war of 1812, he entered the army and served during the whole of it. He served under General Harrison, with the rank of Major, in his north-western campaigns, and had in charge a long line of defences, extending westerly from Lake Erie, and following up the valley of the Maumee, the most important of which was *Fort Wayne*, situated on a narrow neck of land separating the waters flowing into Lake Erie from those flowing into the Gulf of Mexico, and named in honor of General Wayne and in commemoration of his celebrated north-western campaign, in which my grandfather served. Upon the site of the fort, erected in the last century for the purpose of preventing the incursions of hostile savages, has grown up one of the most flourishing towns of the West, which has now become the centre of a vast system of railroads, the most important of which is the Pittsburg, Fort Wayne and Chicago. By a singular coincidence, the very ground which my father and grandfather periled their lives to wrest from savage tribes, I have labored long and earnestly, though in a different way, to improve and enrich by the arts of peace, and thus to complete their work. The territory, once so remote and inaccessible, and whose forests were the covert for the treacherous Indian, has, through the instrumentality of the railway, been brought within easy distance of Eastern markets, and is now one of the most populous, flourishing and prosperous portions of the West.

While at Eaton I attended the village school for about eighteen months. It was kept by a Mr. Stevens, who taught only the rudiments of an English education. While there I served as a clerk in the store of a Mr. Cornelius Van Ausdall, an immigrant of Dutch descent from Hagerstown, Maryland, and a very worthy man. I believe he is still living. I have always looked upon my service with him as one of the most valuable periods of my early life. It taught me to be industrious, active, and methodical, and the value, if I may use the word, of small things. I was brought into contact with all varieties of people, had to turn my hand to every kind of work, and learned how to be respectful and obliging to all. The stock in the store consisted chiefly of light cotton goods, twists, buttons, and the smaller articles of hard and tin ware, and other articles suited to the primitive condition of the people with whom we dealt. The greater part of the trade consisted of *barter*. The most valuable articles received in exchange for goods were peltries of one kind or another. The route to the Eastern markets was up the Ohio River to Pittsburg and Wheeling in keel-boats; thence by wagons to Philadelphia or Baltimore. There were in those days neither roads nor steamboats in the West. The cost was too great to allow the transportation of the produce of the Western county to market, except a small amount of flour, corn and provisions sent down the river in arks, or flatboats, to New Orleans. Nearly everything was produced in the family that was consumed in it. The only money then in circulation was silver — Spanish coins chiefly, received by way of New Orleans. This was packed on horses when the merchant went East to make his purchases, and the lighter kinds of goods brought back in the same manner. The trip to and from the Eastern States was then an affair of greater magnitude and peril, and required a greater length of time than that at present between New York and San Francisco, or between New York and Europe. The country was wholly without good roads and almost the only mode of travel, as well as of transporting merchandise was upon the backs of horses and mules.*

---

* Only six years before my grandfather moved to Tennessee, General Washington crossed the Allegheny mountains for the purpose of ascertaining the practicability of constructing a navigable water line from the Potomac to the Ohio. The report of his journey and observations describes so accurately the condition of the Western country at the time and the necessity of improved highways to unite it firmly with the Eastern States., that I cannot refrain from copying a portion of his communication addressed to the Governor of Virginia:

"I need not remark; to you," said Washington in the communication referred to, "that the flanks and rear of the United States are possessed by other powers, and formidable ones too, and how necessary it is to apply the cement of interest to bind all parts of the Union together by indissoluble bonds — especially that part of it which lies immediately west of us — with the Middle States. For what ties, let me ask, should we have upon those people (in the Mississippi Valley)? How entirely unconnected with them shall we be, and what troubles may we not apprehend, if the Spaniards on their right and Great Britain on their left, instead of throwing stumbling blocks in their way, as they now do, should hold out lures for their trade and alliance? What, when they gain strength, which will be sooner than most people conceive (from the immigration of foreigners who will have no predilection for us, as well as the removal of our own citizens), will be the consequence of having formed close connections with both or either of these powers, in a commercial way? It needs not, in my opinion, the gift of prophecy to foretell.

"The Western States (I speak now from my own observation) hang upon a pivot. The touch of a feather would turn them any way. They have looked down the Mississippi till the Spaniards very impoliticly, I think, for themselves, threw difficulties in the way and they looked that way for no other reason than because they could glide gently down

In 1815 I attended; for about a year and a half, an academy taught by Messrs. Morse and Jones, at Newport, Kentucky. They were excellent teachers and I derived great benefit from their instruction. In 1817 my father moved to Madison, Indiana. This State was admitted into the Union the year previous, and contained about 60,000 inhabitants, scattered very sparsely over the southern portion of it. At that time the Indian titles were extinguished only twenty miles north of Madison. At this place my father opened a dry-goods store. The town at that time contained about one hundred and fifty people. It had been so recently settled that it was still a forest — the trees that were not standing almost covered the ground where they fell. It was wholly without streets or any improvements fitted to make it an attractive or agreeable place. After our removal to Madison I had, for a year and a half, the almost inestimable advantage of a private school taught by a very superior person from the Eastern States. When not at school I assisted my father in his store. At this period General Harrison, afterward President of the United States, and who was a warm and life-long friend of our family, procured for me a cadetship at West Point. I was very eager to accept the appointment, but relinquished it, seeing that my mother was greatly distressed at the thought of my leaving home, I being her only child.

In March, 1820, my father, who had long been ill from diseases contracted while in military service under General Harrison, died. My father, from his infirm health, was not successful in his business in Madison, and died insolvent. I settled up the estate, and ultimately, as I acquired property of my own, paid all his debts in full.

---

the stream, without considering, perhaps, the difficulties of the voyage back again and the time necessary to perform it; and because they had no other means of coming to us but by land transportation and unimproved roads. These causes have hitherto checked the industry of the present settlers; for except the demand for provisions occasioned by the increase of population, and the little flour which the necessities of the Spaniards compel them to buy, they have no incitements to labor. But smooth the road, and make easy the way for them,, and then see what an influx of articles will be poured upon us, how amazingly our exports will increase, and how amply we shall be compensated for any trouble and expense we may encounter to effect it."

It has been reserved to the present generation, by the construction of railways, to "smooth the road and make easy the way" for the West. The results have vastly more than fulfilled the anticipation of the Father of his Country. These works have not only rendered the country indissoluble, but have created a commerce the magnitude of which really exceeds belief.

In 1819 I commenced the study of law in the office of Gen. Alexander A. Meek, of Madison. I finished my legal course by graduating at the Transylvania law school in Kentucky in 1823. I immediately commenced the practice of law in Madison, which at that time had a population of about 300. I was diligent, strove to be respected, and made it a point to be punctual in every duty and appointment. It was early my purpose of life to respect scrupulously the rights of others, but always to be firm in the assertion of my own. It was the rigid adherence to this plan of life, if it can be so called, that I owed my success. My diligence and fidelity in every engagement gave me the command of whatever money I wanted, as it was well known that I would never allow my liabilities to exceed my means. While in the practice of the law I made the cause of my clients my own. Success or defeat, consequently, gave me more pleasure, or pain, than it did them. I was for this reason very successful; but I found the labor and anxiety, of my profession too much for my strength, which led me to give it up as soon as other satisfactory openings for business presented themselves. While in the practice of the law I traveled what was called the South-eastern District of Indiana, practicing in a large number of counties. The only mode of traveling in those days was by horseback. On most of the routes traveled we were guided by trails or *blazed* lines, which were often preferable to what were called roads which, from the friable nature of the soil, were speedily so cut up as to be almost impassable, particularly in the wet seasons of the years. The rivers were crossed in log canoes, and by swimming our horses, when they could not be forded.

In 1824 I was appointed assistant clerk of the House of Representatives of the State, at the last Sitting of the Legislature at Corydon. The next meeting was at Indianapolis, the present capital. I continued assistant clerk until 1827, when I was elected chief clerk. My compensation was $3.50 per day. I kept the journal in which was entered all the proceedings of the House, and did the reading. My duties required the greatest diligence and the closest attention. I soon became master of the rules and modes of conducting business, and was in this way enabled to be of service to members, many of whom, although men of sense and ability, often found themselves in positions of embarrassment from want of familiarity with legislative proceedings. My good offices were often availed of in the drawing up of motions and bills, and in guiding the conduct of members on the floor. I regard my office of clerk of the House as one of the chief causes of my future success. It enabled me to form an intimate acquaintance with all the leading men of the State, many of whom, in after life, were not slow to reciprocate the good offices I had done them.

With my practice and my salary as clerk of the House, I was in receipt of quite an income, for those days, in the West. My habits were simple and economical, at the same time I studied to make every one dependent upon me, among whom was my mother, comfortable and happy. My surplus means were, as fast as acquired, invested in real estate which, as in all new States, rose rapidly in value.

When clerk of the House, the trip from Madison to Indianapolis required three days of fatiguing travel on horse-back. It is now performed, by railroad in about four hours.

In 1833, upon the chartering of the State Bank of Indiana, I retired from the practice of the law, and took a prominent share in the management of that institution. I held a larger amount of the stock first subscribed than any other individual. This bank consisted of a Central Bank, located at Indianapolis, with ten branches in as many leading towns of the State. I was the first President of the Madison branch. The Central Bank was not one of discount or issue. Its functions were a general supervision of the branches, being a Board of Control, of which Mr. McCulloch, afterward Secretary of the Treasury of the United States, and myself, were among the leading members. Notwithstanding the managers of the Bank, at the time it went into operation, were wholly without training or experience in such matters, many of them never having been inside of such an institution, it proved a model of success, and consequently most beneficial to all the interests of the State. The capital was almost wholly borrowed from abroad, and through the credit of the State, which took $1,000,000 of the stock, and loaned its credit to individual stockholders to the extent of one-half the stock subscribed by them, taking as security therefor, real estate at one-half of its unimproved value. The credit of the State was high, its five per cent. bonds selling at a premium averaging from twelve to fifteen per cent. It may seem incredible that a bank, based almost wholly upon capital borrowed, and that, too, through the instrumentality of the State, should have proved such a success. It would appear to have been almost inevitable that in a country lacking in commercial training, where the demand for capital is always excessive, where the managers of trust funds have every inducement to make a reckless use of them, and where, among the great mass, there is very little idea of the importance and value of promptness in the payment of obligations, that the bank, if it did not lose its capital, would soon find it converted into various kinds of property taken in payment of loans, or in the overdue notes of its borrowers. The bank commenced business at one of the most critical periods of the history of the country — at the very beginning of that great era of speculation which nearly bankrupted the whole nation, and which culminated in the terrible catastrophe of 1837. At this disastrous crisis nearly every bank in the Western and South–western States failed, with the exception of that of Indiana. A very large number of those of the Eastern States were totally ruined. It would seem to have been almost impossible that the Bank of Indiana, then one of the newest of the Western States, should not have become involved in the general catastrophe. So far from this being the case, the bank not only paid dividends averaging from twelve to fourteen per cent. annually, but returned to its stockholders nearly double the original investment when it was wound up at the expiration of its charter in 1854. For the $1,000,000 invested by it in this institution, the State received, in profits alone, fully. $3,500,000. These profits now constitute the school fund of the State, the increase of which, being invested in the State indebtedness, is rapidly converting the whole of it into an irredeemable fund to be devoted to educational purposes. The bank was the only one of the numerous enterprises in which the State embarked that did not prove an almost total failure.

As we had always intended to keep our banks in position to meet any emergency that might arise, we had not in the least anticipated the general suspension, in 1837, in the Eastern States till that event happened. Our Board of Control were then in session at Indianapolis. We were at the time the depository of $1,500,000 of Government funds. I was instructed by the Board to proceed immediately to Washington to represent our condition, and to confer with the Secretary of tile Treasury as to what we, in the emergency, should do. I took with me $80,000 in gold. I went up the Ohio River in a steamboat to Wheeling, and thence by stage, chartered for the purpose, alone across the mountains to Frederick, at that time the Western terminus of the Baltimore and Ohio Railroad, and 61 miles west from Baltimore. I suffered not a little anxiety on account of the treasure I carried more than 300 miles, through a wild and comparatively uninhabited region, and was not a little relieved on reaching the safe conduct of a railroad. On arriving at Washington I obtained an interview with the Secretary of the Treasury, the Hon. Levi Woodbury, explained to him the position and the entire solvency of our bank, and delivered to him the gold I had brought with me, in part payment of our balances. He received me with great cordiality, and said that our bank was the only one that had offered to pay any portion of its indebtedness in specie. We were allowed to retain the Government deposits till they were drawn in its regular disbursements. At his solicitation I consented to act as Pension Agent for a portion of the Western States. For the pensions I paid, drafts were made upon the Government deposits in our bank. Drafts were also made upon us in payment of troops, transportation of the mails, and other services. In all these payments our bank-notes, from our well-known credit. were received equally with specie. In such payments all the balances against us were liquidated in a manner entirely satisfactory to the Government, and greatly to our convenience and advantage.

In April, 1838, a convention of the officers of the banks of the United States was held in New York, for the purpose of considering the subject of resuming specie payments. I attended the convention as the representative of our bank. In the debates that took place I earnestly favored the proposition for immediate resumption. The position I took greatly pleased the venerable Albert Gallatin who, aged as he was, was the leading spirit of the convention, and who was much gratified in finding himself earnestly supported from a quarter from which he had not expected aid. He took occasion to thank me personally and warmly for the grounds I took. I recollect my interviews with him on this occasion with great pleasure.

At the period of which I have been last speaking nearly all the Western States, Indiana among them, embarked in elaborate systems of internal improvements. These were entered upon without proper reference to the wants or conditions of the country, and embraced extensive water lines, which were either impracticable or of little value when completed. The different States assumed to provide, by an issue of their bonds, the means for their construction. These proving wholly inadequate, failure on a gigantic scale was inevitable. For such works the State of Indiana incurred a debt of about $10,000,000, without realizing any substantial benefit therefor. It was still without the works necessary to give value to its products, by opening to them the markets of the East. Wheat raised in the interior of the State, at the period referred to, would not bring more than 20 cents the bushel. Indian Corn would not bring more than one-half this amount. The chief value of the latter was to feed it to live stock. There could be no substantial recovery till the works were constructed, which have since quadrupled the value of these as well as of all other products of the States. But years had to elapse before their construction could be undertaken with any hope of success. The people were too poor to construct them. The credit of the States was destroyed: and if it had not been, constitutional provisions were enacted by most of them forbidding them to create a debt for any work of internal improvement. A paralysis for a long time seemed to rest upon the whole country. After the resumption of specie payments in 1838-9, most of the banks of the country again suspended in 1841. In fact, no decided recovery took place till the acquisition of and discovery of gold in, California, in 1848, from which event may be said to date the physical development of the country, which is now the marvel of the world.

One of the most important branches of our banking business was the purchase and sale of exchange made by the internal commerce of the country. At that time the only outlets of the interior, as far west as Indiana, were the Ohio and the Mississippi Rivers. New Orleans was the sole port of export. We purchased largely bills drawn against shipments of produce to this port. As these bills were about to mature it was my custom to go to New Orleans to invest their proceeds, and such other means as our bank could spare, in the purchase of bills drawn in New Orleans upon shipments of produce from thence to the Eastern States. The proceeds of the latter bills, at their maturity, supplied us amply with exchange for our Western merchants, in payment of their purchases of merchandise. In this way we were enabled to turn our capital several times each year, and at a good profit, without the loss, I believe, of a single dollar in any transaction.

I continued in the management of the Madison Branch Bank and a member of the Board of Control till 1849, when the subject of railroad construction again began to excite general attention and interest. During the twelve years that had elapsed since the great calamity of 1837, the West had increased rapidly in population and wealth, and the necessity for improved highways was felt to be more imperative than ever. The acquisition of California, and the discovery of immense deposits of gold within it, gave to the whole nation an impulse never before felt. Numerous railway enterprises were again proposed in the West, and I felt that the time had at last come when they could be safely undertaken as remunerative investments for capital. Residing at Madison, Indiana, I had been instrumental in the resuscitation of the Madison and Indianapolis Railroad, originally a part of the system of public work which the State had attempted to construct, and had learned from the early success of that road what might be expected of other lines more favorably situated. For the purpose, therefore, of embarking in the construction of railroads on a wider scale, I went to New York in the latter part of 1848, and on the first day of January, 1849, I formed a copartnership with Mr. Richard H. Winslow, the chief object of which was the negotiation of railway securities, although we contemplated, in connection therewith, a general banking business. At that time there were in operation in the West only about 600 miles of line.*

These roads were chiefly the remains of the old State systems which had been sold out to private companies, and were almost without exception badly located and imperfectly built. They were in all cases laid with the light flat bar, upon longitudinal sills, and were utterly incapable of sustaining heavy trains, high speed, or a large traffic. They had, consequently, involved in heavy loss all who had been engaged in their construction. I felt, however, their want of success to be no argument against

---

* On the first day of January, 1849, the following lines of railroad were in operation in the States north and west of the Ohio River.

|  |  | Length of Line |  |
|---|---|---|---|
| Ohio. | Little Miami | 84 | miles |
|  | Mansfield and Sandusky | 56 | " |
|  | Mad River | 102 | " |
| Indiana | Madison and Indianapolis | 86 | " |
| Michigan | Michigan Central | 146 | " |
|  | Michigan Southern | 70 | " |
|  | Erie and Kalamazoo | 33 | " |
|  | Detroit and Pontiac | 25 | " |
| Illinois. | Sangamon and Morgan | 53 | " |
|  | Total | 655 | miles |

399

lines properly constructed upon good routes. I undertook to demonstrate this in every way in my power, particularly in newspaper articles and pamphlets, of which I published great numbers in connection with the negotiation of the securities of various companies which we undertook. The result of our efforts soon far exceeded our expectations. Although we began in a very small way, every step we took gave us increased business and strength, and we soon had all the business we could attend to. Commencing with the bonds of the Madison and Indianapolis Railroad, which were the first securities of the kind ever brought out in the New York market, we followed them with the bonds of the Little Miami; Columbus and Xenia; Cleveland, Columbus and Cincinnati; Cleveland, Painesville and Ashtabula; Ohio and Pennsylvania (now a part of the Pittsburg, Fort Wayne and Chicago); Michigan Southern, and other important lines. We not unfrequently negotiated a million of bonds daily. The aggregate for the year was enormous. We were without competitors for a business we had created, and consequently made money very rapidly. The commissions for the negotiation of bonds averaged at first five per cent. With their negotiation we often coupled contracts for the purchase, at a large commission, of rails. Our business soon became so great that it was a question with us, not so much what we would undertake, as what we would reject. We not unfrequently took, on our own account, an entire issue of bonds of important lines.

The negotiation of the securities of companies was followed by arrangements that made our house the agent for the payment of interest accruing them, as well as transfer agents. Such arrangements naturally led the way to the banking business to which we afterward chiefly confined ourselves. The extent of our business as well as of our success exceeded all expectation. During the period of six years, from 1849 to 1854 inclusive, in which we were actually engaged in the negotiation of railway securities, 10,724 miles of line were constructed, nearly one-half of which were in the Western States. With all the more important lines we were, in one way or another, connected. At one period we paid the interest on fifty different classes of securities. These facts will convey some idea of the magnitude of our business and the vigor and energy with which it was conducted.

The uniform success of the enterprises in behalf of which we acted was something remarkable, and has since been a source of great satisfaction. I feel that investors, as well as the country at large, have been greatly benefited by my labors. The interest on almost all the securities brought out by us has been regularly paid, while in not a few instances there has been an enormous profit upon the prices paid. Our house was the first to bring out county and city securities, issued for the construction of railroads. These securities were instrumental in the construction of an immense extent of line, which, but for them, could not have been built, while they have proved a most excellent investment. In no instance, I believe, have the counties and cities, the bonds of which we negotiated, made default, either in principal or interest.

Rapid as has been the progress of railroads since we first engaged in their construction, that of their commerce is a matter of still greater surprise and wonder. Considered in reference to its magnitude, they have created the present immense wealth of the nation. Previous to their construction, the products of the interior, only a short distance removed from navigable watercourses, had no commercial value. The greatest abundance of the peculiar products of a section might give only an inconsiderable amount of comfort, and no wealth. With such works, the whole natural wealth of the country became at once available to the uses of man. When we consider that the commerce of the country, borne upon railroads, dates from a period considerably subsequent to the time I left the West for New York to embark in these enterprises, and that this commerce to-day measures, in bulk, 100,000,000 tons, having a value of $10,000,000,000, and that the earnings of our railroads equaled $400,000,000 in 1868, against $40,000,000 in 1851, and that the investment in them, now amounting to $1,800,000,000, has increased in like ratio, the vastness and rapidity of this development will be in some degree appreciated. I have not only been contemporaneous with all this growth, and, to some extent, instrumental in promoting it, but I reach far beyond its first inception. In one respect, therefore, my life, as does, in fact, that of every middle-aged man, covers a wider experience than that of all the generations of men from earliest history to the present time.

In the West, twenty years ago, precisely the same means were used for the transportation of persons and property that were used in the very infancy of the race. So, too, nearly all the other methods of domestic economy were entirely similar for the two widely separated periods. When a child, and till I reached manhood, the clothing, I wore was made up at home, and by the members of the family. The present generation consequently have, in all that relates to the economy of life, what might be termed an universal experience. The coming one will have only that which belongs to itself.*

At the close of 1854 we withdrew from the negotiation of railway securities, and confined ourselves chiefly to Banking, for which our previous success had opened a wide field. We however continued to be the financial and transfer agents of a large number of railway companies whose securities we had negotiated.

In 1857 the health of Mr. Winslow began to fail. In consequence of this he retired from our firm in 1859. He died on the 14th of February, 1861. He was a man of rare force and energy of character, and by thoroughly comprehending the value of railways, admirably adapted to the business in which we embarked. He had, above all men I ever knew, the faculty of inspiring others with the zeal and confidence which he himself felt. Whatever he undertook was certain to be accomplished. When we con-

---

* As already stated, the number of miles of railway in operation in the Western States in 1849, the year I removed to New York, was 653. On the first day of January, 1869, twenty years thereafter, there were 16,889 miles in operation. The number in each State, at the dates named, is shown in the following table:

| | | |
|---|---|---|
| Ohio | 242 | 3 398 |
| Michigan | 274 | 1,199 |
| Indiana | 86 | 2,600 |
| Illinois | 53 | 3,440 |
| Wisconsin | — | 1,235 |
| Minnesota | — | 572 |
| Iowa | — | 1,523 |
| Kansas | — | 648 |
| Nebraska | — | 920 |
| Missouri | = | 1,354 |
| Total miles | 655 | 16,889 |

The increased railroad mileage in these States, in twenty years, was 16,234 miles, or an average of 812 miles annually. The capital invested in them on the first day of January 1869, at the rate of $40,000 per mile, equaled $675,556,000 — the increase in the twenty years being fully $665,000,000. The aggregate tonnage of the roads, for 1869, equaled 1,500 tons to the mile, or an aggregate of 25,333,000 tons, of which the increase exceeded 25,000,000 tons. The value of this tonnage, at $150 per ton, equaled $3,750,000,000 nearly the whole of which was a creation of the period named. These illustrations will show how rapid has been the growth of the West for the past twenty years. When I compare its present condition with what it was forty years ago, I am at a loss for language to express adequately the change.

sider the results that railroads secure — that every mile of line built adds, immediately, four-fold its cost to the aggregate value of the property of the country, and that the traffic which it creates and which passes over it exceeds annually six times such cost, we can form some idea of the services rendered to society by a man whose energy and influence was instrumental in the construction of an immense extent of line. He was one of the leading spirits that inaugurated and sustained the great movement that led to the construction of the vast system of works that are now spread, like a network, over the whole country, and which now embraces nearly 50,000 miles of line. He never ceased from his labors till compelled to do so by his declining health. All my relations with him were of a most harmonious character, and it gives me great pleasure to pay this tribute to his memory.

Although our firm did not, after 1854 negotiate railway securities to any considerable extent, we continued to cherish a lively interest in those enterprises in behalf of which we had acted, and frequently rendered them pecuniary assistance in emergencies in which they not unfrequently found themselves placed. The great movement which commenced in 1848 culminated in 1857, in a suspension of specie payments by the banks, and in an excessive prostration of business throughout the country. No interest suffered so severely as the railroads. Nearly all of them had been constructed upon borrowed capital, and most of the companies owed large floating debts. All wanted large additional means, either to complete their works or to discharge pressing liabilities. Even so late as 1858 the earnings of roads were not one quarter their present amount. These earnings, owing to the embarrassments into which every kind of industry and business had fallen, decreased largely for several years, and in many cases proved wholly inadequate to meet even the calls for interest. Many of our most valuable enterprises were forced into bankruptcy, and had to be reorganized by new adjustments of interests, and, in most cases, by large sacrifices on the part of the stock and bondholders. A period of great general depression and discouragement followed one of previous confidence and hope. In this crisis it devolved naturally upon parties who had been instrumental in providing the means for the construction of roads to raise them from their depressed condition, and place them, if possible, in a position in which they could be successfully worked and realize the expectations formed of them. Among the companies that yielded to the financial storm was the Pittsburg, Fort Wayne and Chicago — a company with which I had been early identified, whose securities we had negotiated, and for whose good name and success I was most solicitous. To its restoration I consequently devoted no small portion of my time, till all its embarrassments were happily surmounted, and the road placed in a position of perfect independence, in which it proved itself to be one of the most valuable enterprises of the kind in the United States. Perhaps I cannot better show the difficulties into which this work, in common with many others, had fallen, and of its subsequent recovery, than by copying the following article in reference thereto, from the New York Times newspaper, under date of July 21, 1869:

"In 1859 the Pittsburg, Fort Wayne and Chicago Railroad, in common with most other lines, was overwhelmed in the financial revulsion which had swept with resistless force over the whole country. The road had been just opened to Chicago. The line was originally undertaken by three companies, none of which possessed means at all adequate to the construction of their several links. The road when opened was hardly more than half completed. Its earnings, not equaling one quarter their present amount, were wholly insufficient to meet current expenses and the interest on its funded debt. Default, by necessary consequence, was made on all classes of its securities. Bankruptcy stared the concern full in the face, threatening the loss of nearly the whole amount invested.

In this crisis a meeting of its creditors, chiefly first mortgage bondholders, was called at the office of Winslow, Lanier & Co., to consider what was to be done. This class of creditors, of course, had the precedence. If they insisted upon the letter of the law, they would inevitably cut off all subsequent parties in interest, who represented an amount of capital invested in the road twice greater. After much deliberation it was decided to raise a committee to be invested with full power, and if possible, save the interests of all. This committee consisted of Mr. J. F. D. Lanier, who was appointed by the creditors its chairman; Mr. Samuel J. Tilden, Mr. Louis H. Meyer, Mr. J. Edgar Thomson, President of the Pennsylvania Railroad, and Mr. Samuel Hanna of Fort Wayne. To give some idea of the chaos existing in the affairs of the Company, we may state that there were outstanding, at the time, nine different classes of bonds, secured, in one way or another, upon the different portions of the road; two classes secured by real estate belonging to the Company, and several issued in the funding of coupons. Upon all these, interest for several years, amounting to many millions of dollars, was overdue. The principal sums of several of the first mortgages were speedily to mature. The Company also owed more than $2,000,000 of floating debt, portions of it in the form of judgments recovered in the State courts. The road was in extremely bad condition, and required the expenditure of a large sum to enable it to conduct its business with any degree of economy or dispatch.

Such was the condition of affairs when the Committee commenced work. The value of the securities of the Company was merely nominal. Its stock would not sell for five cents on the dollar. Each class of creditors was striving to gain some advantage at the expense of the others. The first step of the Committee, consequently, was to put the property beyond the reach of individuals and in the custody of the courts. An order for this purpose was obtained in the United States District Court for the Northern District of Ohio, on the 17th of January, 1860, and Mr. Wm. B. Ogden was appointed receiver.

The Committee set out with the determination of preserving, if possible, the rights of all the parties in interest — not alone those of the first mortgage bondholders. It was hoped that when the property was put beyond the reach of individual creditors, an arrangement might be effected and the rights of the various parties preserved in the relations they had previously maintained. But such an adjustment required the assent of each creditor and stockholder. This, in the multiplicity and conflict of interests, it was found impossible to obtain. The next, and only remaining course, was to sell the road and property of the Company by an order of Court in behalf of the first mortgagees. Such sale would vest absolutely the title to the road in the hands of the purchasers, who would thus be in position to make such disposition of it as in their view equity and justice might demand. It would also enable them to apply the net earnings to the construction of a good road, without which the investment itself would be of no value.

With this purpose a full plan of reorganization, such as was finally adopted, was prepared and published, and brought, as far as possible, to the attention of every party in interest. Decrees for sale had to be obtained in the Courts of the United States for four different States. The time required for this purpose was occupied by the Committee in incessant efforts in removing one impediment after another thrown in their way by importunate and dissatisfied creditors, who were indifferent to the fate of the concern, provided they could get their pay. All difficulties were at last overcome, and on the 24th of October, 1861, the road and property was sold at auction, and purchased by Mr. Lanier, in behalf of himself and his associates, for the sum of $2,000,000. The Courts, we are happy to say, facilitated legal proceedings as far as this could be properly done. They had full confidence in the Committee, and sympathized with the unfortunate creditors of the concern, and not, as at the present day, in our State, with bands of conspirators against the public welfare, who seek the control of great lines with no other purpose but to plunder them. Eight years ago, measured by what has since transpired, was a golden age of judicial purity.

By the sale of the road a most important step was gained. The title to it vested, absolutely, in the purchasers. They could convey it to whom, at what price and upon what terms they pleased. What followed was more a matter of detail, though involving great patience and labor. For the creation of a new Company, according to the origi-

405

nal plan of reorganization, legislation had to be obtained in the States of Pennsylvania, Ohio, Indiana and Illinois. Such legislation was at last secured, a new Company formed, to which was conveyed the railroad and everything appertaining thereto, the Committee receiving therefor, first, second and third mortgage bonds, in amounts sufficient to meet the sums due the different classes of creditors in the old Company; and also certificates of stock corresponding in amount to that outstanding in the old. First mortgage bonds, to the amount of $5,200,000, were issued to the first mortgage bondholders of the old Company, and of the several links of which its road was composed, and for accrued interest. The bondholders were also required to fund, for two years, the interest accruing on the new bonds, so as to allow, for such a period, the application of the net earnings to construction. The second mortgage bondholders received, in the same manner, and subject to similar conditions, second mortgage bonds to the amount of $5,250,000. The unsecured creditors were paid off in third mortgage bonds to the amount of $2,000,000. The shareholders received new certificates in exchange for the old. By such means each class of creditors, without the abatement of a dollar, were fully and completely reinstated in the new Company in the order they stood in the old. The proper transfers and exchanges were made, and on the 1st day of May, 1862, two years and six months after the road was placed in the hands of a receiver, and six months after the sale, the trust, so long held and faithfully executed, was brought to a virtual close, to the entire satisfaction of every party in interest in the road.

During the period of reorganization the road was operated, under the general direction of the Committee, by Geo. W. Cass, its former and subsequent President. His well-known abilities as a railroad manager were never more conspicuously displayed than in this service. He had every difficulty to contend with — an impoverished and half completed road, with clamorous creditors at every turn. The Chairman of the Committee was not unfrequently called upon to advance, from his private funds, considerable sums in aid of the operations of the road. Such advances were, of course, repaid, but only with simple interest. The good name and financial strength of Mr. Lanier, joined to his well-known prudence and caution, tended to inspire great confidence in the action of the Committee in which he justly exerted great influence. Mr. Thomson's position as chief of a great and successful enterprise, enabled him to render very great aid to the Committee in the operations of the road. Indeed, it was through his instrumentality that the old Company was enabled to push its line through to Chicago. Mr. Tilden was the chief legal adviser of the Committee and Company throughout. He had charge of the proceedings, not only for the winding up of the old; but for the formation of the new Company, and for the recent transfer of the road to the Pennsylvania Company, and drew up all the documents and guarantees relating to the same. The proper discharge of his duties involved the fate and security of the whole investment. Not a suggestion has been ever raised that they were not ably and faithfully performed. The directors of the Company, pending its reorganization, rendered valuable assistance. Many of them resided upon the line of the road, and were enabled to exert a salutary influence, not only

406

among the creditors of the Company, but in securing the legislation required. But it is, perhaps, invidious to particularize when all worked faithfully and well. Not a dollar was ever paid to secure the legislation required for the formation of the new Company; not a dollar to buy off importunate or unreasonable creditors. The Committee never had a secret which they turned to account at the expense of the stock and bondholders. Their plans were prepared and published in the outset, and scrupulously adhered to.

Soon after the new Company commenced operations it was seen the enterprise had passed its darkest days. For the year ending December 31, 1862, the net earnings of the road equaled nearly $2,000,000, all of which were applied to construction. The Committee was enabled to add largely to its available means by the sale of property purchased with the road, but not needed in its future operations, and which, in fact, they were not, by the terms of the trust, to account for to the new Company. The sums realized from these sources, and paid over to the Company, equaled about $600,000, of which some $400,000 was saved by a compromise which the Committee were enabled to make with European holders of bonds secured by real estate. All the advantages gained by such settlements were given to the new Company.

In 1863 the net earnings equaled nearly $3,000,000. These sums enabled the Company to place its road in first-rate condition; and on the 1st day of April, 1864, it commenced the payment of dividends at the rate of 10 per cent. per annum, free of Government tax, in quarterly payments of 2 1/2 per cent. each. These were continued regularly to the 1st day of July, 1869, when the road was leased to the Pennsylvania Railroad Company for 999 years; at an annual rental of 12 per cent. on its share capital.

In this lease the Pennsylvania Company assumes every obligation or charge for which the Fort Wayne Company are, or may be, liable. It pays the sum of $19,000 annually for the maintenance of the organization of the former. It keeps up the annual contributions to the sinking fund. These contributions will, in twenty-six years, wholly pay off the bonded debt of the Fort Wayne Company, leaving the stockholders the sole owners of the road; and, in conclusion, it agrees to pay an annual rental of $1,380,000, a sum which equals 12 per cent. annually upon the stock, *free of Government tax*, or of any other charge. The terms of the lease also allow the Fort Wayne Company to increase its share capital *seventy-one and three-sevenths per cent.*, and to issue certificates for the whole capital, upon which, for the entire period of the lease, *seven per cent. a year, in quarterly payments of one and three-quarters per cent.*, free of Government tax, is to be paid. All these payments, as well as the accruing interest, are to be made directly to the agency of the Fort Wayne Company, in New York. When we consider that the net earnings of the road largely exceed the rental paid, and that this rental is guaranteed by the most powerful and successful railroad corporation on this Continent, and that the lease will inure even more to its advantage than to that of the lessors, in placing a common line under a common head and management, certainly it is not within the power of man to make a better security, or one in which trust funds can be more securely placed.

We have thus put on record a detailed statement of the resuscitation and success of a great enterprise, as an example of what has been and may be accomplished by upright, able and public-spirited men. In no country do railways bear a relation to the internal economy of a people so intimate as in ours. No investments, consequently, can be so productive as those made in good and well-managed lines. There is no doubt that the gross earnings of the railroads of the Northern States equal fully 30 per cent. annually of their actual cost. One-third of this, at least, should be net, and we take pleasure in placing an illustration before our readers, where the best possible net result has not only been secured, but secured as it should be, to those who are and have been the owners of the property."

I have given this statement as an example of what patient labor and watchfulness may accomplish under similar circumstances. We not only saved a vast property, at one time, to all appearances, wholly wrecked, but made it one of the most productive railroads in the country, and finally leased it in perpetuity to one of the richest and most prosperous corporations in the United States — the Pennsylvania Railroad Company — at an annual rental of 12 per centum per annum, after making full provision for the principal and interest of its debts. An immense investment was not only saved, but rendered productive almost beyond precedent; and with it, great numbers of persons whose means were invested in the road, saved from poverty and want. In their comfort and happiness I am well repaid for the toil and anxiety which I underwent on account of this work.

In 1860, the election of Mr. Lincoln to the Presidency of the United States, an event which I earnestly desired, was followed by mutterings of the coming storm, which soon burst upon the country with resistless violence. I was too old to take the field, but I gave whatever aid and encouragement I could to the cause of the Union. It was not long, however, before I was called upon to assume more responsible duties, on account of the relations which I had sustained to the State of Indiana. That State voted for Mr. Lincoln, and at the same time elected State officers in political sympathy with him. The Hon. Henry S. Lane, who had been elected Governor of the State, was chosen by the Legislature, upon its assembling, as Senator in the Congress of the United States. By this event, the Hon. O. P. Morton, Lieutenant Governor, became the Chief Magistrate. The war found the State almost wholly without means for arming, equiping or sending into the field the quota of troops required of it. It had no money in its treasury, and in the general distrust which prevailed, and in the universal scramble for money, for all the loyal States, as well as the Federal Government, were in the market for it, it was found impossible to sell its bonds, or to provide in season, from its own resources, the means required. In this dilemma Governor Morton applied to me for a loan of money to arm and equip the quota of troops required of his State. I complied with his request, and continued such advances as they were required, till the whole amount reached $400,000. With this sum he was enabled to arm and equip his quota in a most satisfactory manner, and despatch it to the field more promptly than that of any other Western State. Indiana at all times was nearly equally divided upon the subject of the war. Whatever, consequently, tended to inspire the confidence and raise the spirits of tile Union party within it, greatly strengthened the hand of the Executive, and had a most important and favorable influence upon the great contest.

In 1862, owing to the reverses that had befallen the Union arms, the elections in many of the States went adversely to the National cause. In Indiana a majority of the members returned to the Legislature for that year were bitterly opposed to the war, and to all measures necessary for its vigorous prosecution. They were determined, if possible, to take the State out of the Union ranks, and place it in direct antagonism to the Government at Washington. The success of their disloyal schemes might have proved fatal to the great cause. None understood this better than themselves. Indiana was not only one of the leading States of the West, but in many respects it occupied a position of first-rate importance. It was centrally situated, and, extending from Lake Michigan to the Ohio, it would, in disloyal hands, have been in a position to cut off all communication between the West and the East. Its southern border rested upon territory where the great mass of the people were strongly infected with the spirit of rebellion. This State, consequently, became emphatically the battle-ground of the contest in the North. If its influence had been arrayed against the Union, the infection might have spread to other States, as there were in all abundant material eager to take advantage of any event that might embarrass or defeat the action of the Government. A united front on the part of all the Northern States was absolutely essential to success. Such a front, happily, was preserved throughout the whole war.

The plan adopted by the disloyal members of the Legislature of Indiana was to divest the Governor of all power over the militia, and to vest the control of the same in a committee of their own creatures. They refused to pass the necessary appropriation bills till their schemes should become a law. To defeat their plans the only course left to the loyal members was to retire from the Legislature, which they did. That body, consequently, was left without a quorum. Their retirement put an end to the iniquitous projects, but it left the Governor without the means of preserving the credit of the State. It was held by the Supreme Court of the State that without a special act he could not pay the interest accruing on the State debt, although it had been previously supposed that the Constitution of the State had provided for such a payment without any special law.

In this emergency Governor Morton, most anxious to preserve the honor and credit of the State, applied to me to advance the sums necessary for the purpose. Unless this could be done he felt that he could not justify, before his own State and the country, the position which his friends in the Legislature had taken through his council and advice. The application was made at the darkest period of the whole war. I could have no security whatever, and could rely for reimbursement only on the good faith of a Legislature to be chosen at a future and distant day, and upon the chances of its being made up of more upright and patriotic members than those composing the one then in existence. If the great contest should turn out disastrously to the cause of the Union and of freedom, I could never expect to be repaid a dollar. I felt, however, that on no account must the debt of a great State be discredited, nor the position of its Chief Magistrate, the ablest and most efficient of all the loyal Governors, and who of all contributed most to our success, be compromised or weakened. No alternative was left to me but to advance the sums required. I would not allow myself to be responsible for the consequences of a refusal of his request. If the credit of the State in such a critical period should be destroyed, that of the other States, and even the Federal Government, might be so impaired as to render it impossible for them to sustain the immense burdens of the war. Another influence of very great weight with me was an ambition to maintain the credit of a State with which I had so long been identified, to which I was indebted for my start in life, and for whose credit in former times

410

I had earnestly labored. The last, perhaps, was the ruling motive. I accordingly addressed a note to the agent of the State for the payment of the interest, offering to pay that falling due July 1st, 1863, and requesting him to supply me with a list of the holders of the State stocks. He peremptorily refused to furnish such list, being himself one of the conspirators in destroying the State credit. A list had to be procured from other sources of information. As soon as this was obtained, I commenced the payment of interest, which was thereafter promptly paid by me on the days it fell due. These payments were continued two years. The whole amount advanced by me on this account was $640,000. In the meantime the State was practically without a Legislature. The disloyal members were constantly in the expectation that the Governor would be compelled to call them together, as the only means of enabling him to carry on the government. The Governor well knew that if they were called together, they would take from him the power to control the militia of the State, and he determined to hold out, which he did, till a new Legislature should be chosen.

The following extracts taken from the message of Gov. Morton, made to the General Assembly of Indiana, Jan. 6, 1865 gives a brief and succinct history of the efforts made to destroy the credit of the State, and to embarrass its action in the war, and of the aid rendered by our house in defeating them:

"Shortly after the Legislature adjourned, the question was sprung as to the existence of legal appropriations for the payment of the interest upon the public debt, and the opinion of the Attorney General was published, denying their existence and any power to withdraw the money from the Treasury to pay the interest, which opinion was indorsed and acted upon by Mr. Ristine, the Auditor of State. Believing that the question had its origin in political considerations, and that there was little room to doubt as to the legal right and duty of the Treasurer to remit the money to New York to pay the interest, I at once took issue with these gentlemen. The State had failed to pay the interest upon her bonds from 1841 to 1847, during which time she acquired a reputation for repudiation and bankruptcy, from which she only recovered after many years of faithful discharge of her obligations. The dark cloud which had thus been placed upon her financial character had seriously retarded her growth in wealth and population, deterring emigration from other States. In 1846, she effected a compromise with most of her creditors, by the transfer of the Wabash and Erie Canal for one-half of her debt, and issuing new stock for the other half, upon which she solemnly pledged herself to pay the interest semi-annually.

411

This pledge, and the legislation had in pursuance of the compromise, was treated by Governor Whitcomb, and the various officers of State, as a valid appropriation of the money necessary to pay the interest under the old Constitution, which, upon this subject, is like the present. In 1850 the framers of the new Constitution, by the twentieth section of the tenth article, solemnly ratified this contract with the bondholders, by appropriating all the revenue of the State, derived from taxation for general State purposes, after defraying the ordinary expenses of the State government, to the payment of the interest and the liquidation of the principal of the public debt. It was clearly the purpose of the new Constitution to place the credit of the State beyond the contingency of dishonor by acts of omission or prohibition on the part of the Legislature. Under the new Constitution, further legislation to pay the interest was not deemed necessary, and this construction was acted upon by all administrations down to 1863; although, perhaps, in one case, a formal appropriation was made with out any definite purpose. An action for a mandamus against the Auditor was commenced by Mr. W. H. Talbott, President of the Sinking Fund Board, for the avowed purpose of having the question settled, which was carried through the Circuit and Supreme Courts, and resulted in a decision, by the latter, against the existence of an appropriation. Without intending any disrespect to the eminent tribunal by which this case was decided, I must be permitted to observe that the history of its origin, progress and conclusion was such as to deprive it of any moral influence, and that the principles upon which the decision was made have been since openly disregarded by the Auditor and Treasurer of State in the payment of large sums of money to the Public Printer. But leaving out of view wholly who was right or wrong upon the legal question, it was a matter of the first importance that the obligations of the State should be promptly met, and her credit rescued from the disaster of a new dishonor. It had received a shock in the discovery and exposure of the Stover forgery of our State stocks amounting to nearly three millions of dollars, from the evil consequences of which it was relieved only by a determined effort on the part of the State authorities to bring the criminals to justice. No argument was required to prove that, should it again become impaired by a serious failure upon the part of the State to meet her engagements, it could not be restored during this generation, and the progress of the State in wealth and population would receive a serious check. Determined, if possible, to avert the threatened calamity, I went to New York and laid the whole matter before the house of Messrs. Winslow, Lanier & Co., with the request that they should advance the amount necessary to pay the interest, until such time as the Treasury might be unlocked, and the money obtained therefrom. My request was generously met, and, after full consideration, acceded to, provided a correct list of the stockholders could be obtained. It is proper to state that, in making this arrangement, no stipulation was asked for or given, in regard to the compensation they should receive for the use of their money, and the risk and trouble they should incur; but the whole matter was referred to the future action and good faith of the State. They at once notified John C. Walker, Agent of State, of their readiness to pay the interest, and asked him to furnish, from his books, a list of the stockholders, for the making out of which they offered to pay. This he peremptorily refused, and denied access to his

412

books, from which they desired to copy the list. They then proposed to him that he should pay the interest in the usual way upon his own books, agreeing to honor his checks issued therefor, at the same time exonerating him from all personal liability for any moneys so paid. This offer was likewise refused. The correspondence between Winslow, Lanier & Co. and Walker upon this subject, is herewith submitted for your consideration.

As Messrs. Winslow, Lanier & Co. would not take the responsibility of paying, in the absence of a correct list, owing to the existence of a large amount of spurious stock, which otherwise they had no means of detecting, the interest which fell due on the first day of July, 1863, went unpaid. Determined not to be defeated, if possible, in the effort to preserve the credit of the State, I attempted to secure from other sources a correct list of the stockholders, and in this attempt succeeded, in November. In the meantime the necessity for action had become more manifest and imperative than before. While the American stockholders had a correct knowledge of the state of affairs, and but few stocks were changing hands or being offered in the market, the case was quite different with our stockholders in Europe. In Europe, American politics are always badly understood, and the principal fact, which they clearly comprehended was, that they did not receive their interest. They associated this failure with that of 1841, and began to say that there was some strange fatality attending Indiana securities, and declared their intention of sending them back to America and getting clear of them at once and forever. Such a measure would have given the State a bad name abroad, seriously affecting emigration to her borders, and would have been followed by great depreciation and loss of credit throughout the United States.

Having presented the list to Messrs. Winslow, Lanier & Co., they promptly renewed their offer, and gave public notice that they would pay the back interest which fell due in July, and afterward gave further notice that they would pay the interest accruing on the 1st day of January, 1864; the 1st day of July, 1864, and the 1st day of January, 1865; and up to the 31st of November last, as I am advised, had paid out four hundred and sixteen thousand six hundred and seventy-seven dollars and eight cents.

How much they have paid since the 1st of January, 1865, I am not advised, but presume it will make the aggregate as much as five hundred and seventy-five thousand dollars. The noble and generous conduct of this house should and will be appreciated by the people of Indiana; and Mr. Lanier, in his clear comprehension and able management of the affair, has displayed not only financial ability, but a broad statesmanship not often exhibited in financial affairs.

I trust that the generous confidence which he has reposed in the good faith of the people of Indiana will not be disappointed, and that the Legislature will hasten to reimburse him for the money he has expended, and indemnify him for the use of it, and for the trouble he has incurred.

In conclusion, upon this subject, I am glad to be able to say, that the credit of the State has been fully preserved; and that her stocks now command a higher price, relatively, in the market, when compared with stocks of other States, bearing like interest, than at any former period in her history."

In 1864, the Presidential election again took place. Mr. Lincoln was a candidate for re-election to the Presidency of the United States, as was Mr. Morton for the governorship of Indiana This State was one of the first to vote in the fall elections of that year. Its action, in view of the events that had occurred in it, could not fail to be regarded as the key-note of the campaign, if not conclusive of the great contest that was speedily to follow. In that State the canvass necessarily turned upon the extraordinary condition of things that had existed in it for two years; upon the policy of the Union party in breaking up the Legislature; the refusal of the Governor to reassemble it, and upon the responsibility he assumed of paying the interest on the State debt without provision of law. One of the ablest men in the State was nominated as his opponent. The two canvassed the State, Governor Morton in vindication, and his competitor in condemnation, of the policy and course that had been pursued. It was a contest in which Mr. Lincoln took a very deep interest, not only from its significance in reference to his own election, but from the interest he took in that of Mr. Morton, who, of all the civilians in the United States, probably rendered the most efficient and valuable service in putting down the great rebellion.

In the canvass before the people, Mr. Morton acquitted himself with transcendent ability. Mr. Lincoln, in reading a report of the speech of Mr. Morton, by which it was opened, said, "That settles the Presidential election." The result fully justified his expectation. Mr. Morton everywhere carried the people with him, and upon no issues more heartily than in their approval of the policy of the Union party, which, to avert a greater evil, had left the State without a Legislature for two years, and of the steps by which its faith and good name had been maintained. He was elected by more than 20,000 majority, in the most heated canvass ever known in the State. The result there turned public sentiment everywhere in favor of the Administration; and in the following month, Mr. Lincoln was elected to the Presidency by the almost unanimous voice of the North.

At the State election for 1864 a majority of Union members were returned to the Legislature, by whom provision was made for the repayment of the sums I had advanced, with no other compensation than interest on the amount, which was all I desired or would have received. I had, however, the most gratifying proofs of the esteem which my action had secured for me throughout the State. Every loyal man felt that I had averted a disgrace in which he must have shared. The effect upon the politics of the State was decisive. It has ever since been a steady supporter of the Union cause. At the next vacancy occurring in the Senate of the United States, Mr. Morton was chosen to fill the place, which he now holds in a manner both honorable to himself and the State.

I omitted to mention, in its proper order, my connection with the adjustment of the debt of the State of Indiana in 1847. As already remarked, that State had previously embarked in elaborate systems of public works, the means for the prosecution of which were wholly raised by sales of bonds. In the embarrassments which followed, the State made default in the payment of interest on these bonds, and remained in default till the amount due reached the sum of about $12,000,000, of which some $4,000,000 were for interest. At the session of the Legislature of the State for 1846–7, an act was passed for an adjustment of the debt, commonly called the "Butler Act," authorizing an issue to the holders of the old bonds, of a five per cent. inscribed State Stock, to an amount equaling one half that of said bonds; and a transfer, to Trustees, for the benefit of the bondholders, of the Wabash and Erie Canal, with the lands belonging to the same, upon the condition of the surrender of the old bonds — the payment of the other half of these bonds being chargeable upon the canal and its revenues.

It became necessary, therefore, that some person should visit Europe for the purpose of explaining the financial condition of the State, to secure the assent of such bondholders as had not acceded to the proposition made them, and to make the exchanges of securities. I was appointed to this mission, and proceeded to Europe early in the summer of 1847. The new securities to be issued, viz.: the certificates of State stock, and of ownership in the canal, were placed in my hands fully executed, with the exception of dates, amounts, and names of parties to whom they were to be issued. These I was authorized to insert on making the exchanges. I was accredited to Sir J. Horsley Palmer, then Governor of the Bank of England — a staunch friend of the United States, and whose place of business in London I made my headquarters; to Baron N. M. Rothschild, of London; to Baron James Rothschild, of Paris; to the house of Hope

& Company, of Amsterdam — these parties, or the houses with which they were connected, holding or controlling large amounts of the bonds. Immediately upon my arrival in London, I prepared and published a statement embodying the plan of settlement proposed, and urging, with what arguments I could adduce, its acceptance. My duties brought me into intimate contact with the gentlemen named, and also with Mr. Labouchere, then manager of the house of Hope & Co., of Amsterdam. I had occasion, in the execution of my mission, to visit, several times, the cities named, and also Geneva, Switzerland, where some of the State bonds were held. The result was, that I was enabled to get up nearly all the outstanding bonds, and was in this way instrumental in placing the credit of the State on the firm basis upon which it has ever since rested. The State immediately entered upon a career of prosperity which has never flagged to the present moment. A virtual repudiation had destroyed its public spirit, and had been a bar to capital and immigration coming into it. Since the funding of the debt, no state in the Union has made more rapid progress than Indiana. It has constructed 3,000 miles of railroad. These works now penetrate every portion of its territory. Its debt has been almost wholly paid to the holders, by taxation, or from the proceeds of the school fund arising from the profits accruing from the interest of the State in the State Bank. The benefits resulting from the adjustment of this debt have been almost incalculable.

I was not only successful in my mission, but I had a most agreeable visit — my first to Europe. I was most kindly received by all the parties to whom I was accredited, and by others. Mr. Labouchere's ancestors, like my own, were Huguenots, and were driven out of France about the same time that mine were, and for a similar cause — adherence to the principles of the Reformation. His ancestors fled to Holland; mine to America. A kindred ancestry, as it were, and a kindred experience brought us into close sympathy. Sir Horsley Palmer also treated me with gratifying attention, and invited me to his princely country seat at Fulham, on the Thames, a few miles from London. The acquaintances I then made were of immense service to me in the business in which I subsequently engaged, and have added greatly to the pleasure of subsequent visits to England and to the Continent.

On my return home I delivered up the bonds I had taken up,

together with the unused certificates of State and Canal Stock. My accounts were settled most satisfactorily, and I received the thanks of the State authorities for the manner I had executed the trust confided to me.

In 1865, as I was about to visit Europe, I received communications, copies of which I gave elsewhere, from the Secretary of the Treasury and the Secretary of State of the United States, requesting me to act, in its behalf, in explaining to capitalists abroad the character of our public debt and the means and disposition of our people for its payment. This mission I undertook with earnestness, being fully persuaded that no better securities could be made than these of the United States. This conviction I sought, with whatever power I possessed, to impress upon others. At Frankfort-on-the-Maine, I was formally invited to address a public meeting of Bankers and Capitalists upon the subject of my mission. It was largely attended, and I had an opportunity not only to submit some detailed remarks, but for a free and full conference with gentlemen composing the meeting, nearly all of whom could speak my native tongue. My remarks were published in German and English, and freely distributed, through the Consulates, throughout the Continent and England. I believe they were instrumental of much good as they embodied the arguments in favor of our securities in a concise form, and in one that had not been previously presented, and one that could be used by others, particularly my own countrymen, equally with myself. Of these I annex a copy:

" REMARKS OF MR. J. F. D. LANIER, MADE AT A MEETING OF BANKERS AND CAPITALISTS, AT FRANKFORT-ON-THE-MAINE ON THE 14TH DAY OF SEPTEMBER, 1865.

The national debt of the United States, on the first of August of the present year, was, in round numbers, $2,720,000,000, to wit:

| Debt bearing interest payable in gold | $1,108,000,000 |
| " " " " in currency | 1,063,000,000 |
| " " " " no interest | 659,000,000 |

It is estimated, upon the most competent authority, that the national debt, after all the expenses of the war are finally liquidated, will not exceed $3,000,000,000.

The revenues of the Government for the fiscal year ending June 30, 1865, were $318,251,589, of which $82,000,000 were in gold, from Customs.

The revenues for the fiscal year ending June 30, 1866, were estimated at $396,000,000, of which $80,000,000 will be in gold from Customs, $300,000,000 from internal taxes, and $16,000,000 from lands and miscellaneous sources.

The interest on the entire national debt of $3,000,000,000 is estimated at $165,000,000, leaving $231,000,000 for the expenses of the Federal Government and other purposes.

These estimates were made in June last, at the commencement of the fiscal year. Since that time the receipts from Customs have increased so rapidly, that instead of $80,000,000, as estimated, the revenue from this source, in gold, may reach $130,000,000.

This increase is largely owing to the trade which has been opened up at the South since the suppression of the rebellion. Although the war destroyed for a time the commerce and industry of this section, and deprived the people of the ability to maintain their railroads and to navigate their rivers, and left them little but the cotton which had been accumulated, this is found to be sufficient to furnish a very large amount of means with which to supply their wants, and lay, anew, the foundations of their prosperity. The receipts of cotton from the South, at New York, equal 20,000 bales weekly, and have been followed by corresponding exports to that section of supplies, and whatever is necessary to the restoration and development of its resources.

The national debt of England at the end of the war with France, in 1816, amounted to S4,205,000,000. It has since been reduced only $250,000,000. It equaled $218 20 to each individual, and 40 4/10 per cent. of the aggregate value of the whole property of the Kingdom. Since the battle of Waterloo her wealth has grown at a slow but steadily increasing rate – from 20 per cent. in the first, to 41 per cent. in the last ten years, thereby reducing the burden of the debt from 40 4/10 per cent. on the national wealth, to 12 per cent.

The census of 1860 showed the wealth of the loyal States to be $10,716,000,000, and a yearly product $2,870,000,000 in value, or 26 1/2 per cent. of their aggregate capital.

The wealth of the loyal States increased, in the ten years between 1850 and 1860, at the rate of 126 per cent., or 8 1/2 per cent. per annum. Assuming these amounts and rates as a basis, we have for June, 1865, a wealth of $16,112,000,000, and an annual product of $4,318,000,000, without making any estimates on exports.

In 1833 the national wealth of England was estimated at $17,200,000,000. For the United States the figures given are by no means estimates, but are results accurately obtained through the Census Bureau. These results enable us to estimate the amount of the national wealth at the close of future periods, to wit:

In 1870 the national wealth will equal     $24,218,000,000
In 1880  "   "     "     "     "     48,436,000,000
In 1881  "   "     "     "     "     51,516,000,000

In the last-named year, consequently, the interest on the national debt of $3,000,000,000, will equal only 3 3/100 per cent. of the national wealth.

This estimate of the reduced percentage of the interest of the national debt in ratio to the national wealth, is made upon the rate of increase of national wealth prior to the rebellion.

On this calculation, what will be the increase for the next sixteen years ? Let us look a little more carefully into this question. During the last ten years the increase of wealth in nine of the North-western States and Territories of the United States was not less than 411 1/2 per cent. — the aggregate increase being from $452,500,000 to

$1,862,000,000. Four new Territories, which did not appear in the census of 1850, had a valuation in 1860 of $98,000,000. Those since organized — Dacotah, Nevada, Colorado, Arizona and Idaho — are not embraced in this estimate. These last-named States and Territories are as rich in precious metals of all kinds as was California.

As another important source of wealth and revenue, the United States still holds 950,000,000 of acres of unsold lands which, now that the war is closed, will soon come into market, and which should bring $1,000,000,000 into the public Treasury.

But what is of vastly greater importance is the rapidly increased value of these lands, consequent upon their occupation and settlement. The taxable value of property in the Northwestern States, as has been shown, increased at the rate of 411 1/2 per cent. from 1850 to 1860. In 1880 this value will be thirty times greater than it was in 1860, and form the basis of a revenue infinitely greater than what could be derived from the sale of their lands; so that if every dollar derived from this source should be bestowed upon the new States by the Federal Government, in aid of internal improvements and for educational purposes, their taxable wealth and the revenue derived from them would soon exceed many times the sums so bestowed. It is not only in what we now possess, but what we are capable of accomplishing, that our strength lies.

Our minerals are another vast source of yet undeveloped wealth. At least 1,000,000 square miles of our territory are surpassingly rich in gold, silver, copper, lead, quicksilver, coal, gypsum, salt, etc., etc. From their recent discovery our gold and silver deposits, except in California, have hardly begun to be worked. Were they worked even to the extent that they are in that State, they would produce, it is estimated, at least $200,000,000 annually, while the other minerals named would yield at least one-half this sum, were proper means of transportation and communication provided. Such results are not probabilities of a far distant future; their accomplishment is sufficiently near to be an all-important element in enabling the country to bear the burdens imposed upon it. They are, in fact, the necessary and inevitable consequence of the progress of a people who already number 34,000,000 souls – who double their population every twenty-three and a half years – who possess every implement and contrivance that science and art have contributed in aid of labor – who are urged forward by a resistless spirit of enterprise, confident of their future, and of their ability to surmount all obstacles that may oppose their way. Such a people may be safely entrusted with the greatest responsibilities, and are equal to any emergency in which they may be placed.

But upon the future growth of these undeveloped territories we by no means place our confidence of the ability of our people to bear the burdens imposed upon them. The aggregate increase of the wealth of the older States has been vastly greater, though the ratio of the increase may not have been so great. That of Ohio has increased within ten years at the rate of 126 per cent., although the State was founded 77 years ago; that of the States of New Jersey and Connecticut, though founded more than two centuries ago, increased in a like rate; that of Pennsylvania increased, within the same period, at the rate of 96 per cent., upon the already large aggregate of $722,000,000.

For the last four years the Northern States supplied all the means for carrying on the war, and for defraying the expenditures of Government. We are fast being relieved of the former, at the same time that the States recently in rebellion are now contributing their proportion to our already diminished burdens. These are soon to be reduced more than one half, while our increased means from an united country must exceed by at least one-third what they have been. By the census of 1860 the wealth of the Southern States equaled $3,467,000,000. In the period of five years, from 1855 to 1860, they doubled the value of their products. They will, in a very short time, be restored to a condition of prosperity far exceeding anything in their former experience. The great drawbacks to the proper development of their resources have been removed. They possess all the blessings and advantages – which cannot be overestimated – of a temperate zone and of a semitropical climate. What they have lacked have been population, skilled labor, a spirit of enterprise, and the manifold industries of free institutions; all these essentials to prosperity have been secured to them by the war.

A short period, therefore, only is required for the realization of the promise which our natural wealth and resources afford. Taking the past as a basis of calculation for the future, the United States, in 1880, will have a population of 60,000,000, and a national wealth of $60,000,000,000. It will then not only be able to meet the interest on the public debt, but will be able to discharge it with entire ease – and, true to our historic policy, will undoubtedly do so. The national wealth of Great Britain, in 1816, was only half as great as is that of the United States at the present time, yet its debt has already been reduced from 40 to 12 per cent. of its wealth. That of the United States in 1880, will be only 5 per cent. of its wealth, should the amount of the debt, in the meantime, remain unreduced.

Should revenues additional to these already provided be required, they may be easily raised by taxes levied upon cotton and tobacco and other articles of the re-established Union, of which we monopolize the production of the world. It is estimated that our revenue may be increased from these sources from $60,000,000 to $100,000,000, without any diminution in the consumption of the articles taxed, and without injury to our commerce or to any domestic interest.

The manner in which the obligations of the United States are held should add greatly to the confidence of foreigners in them. Of the whole amount outstanding, not more than $300,000,000, or one-tenth of the whole, are held abroad. All classes at home, poor as well as rich, have invested their savings in them. Very large amounts are held in sums not exceeding $50. Preference is universally given to them over all other kinds of investment. No national loan was ever so universally distributed. Each citizen felt himself a party to the contest, and contributed to it according to his ability. All, consequently, are directly interested in maintaining inviolate the public faith.

It is a great error to suppose that the Northern States have been exhausted in consequence of the war. There is most convincing proof to the contrary in the ease and readiness with which they have supplied the Government with money, and whatever was necessary for its prosecution, and have absorbed the vast debt that has been created. The Government has neither directly nor indirectly borrowed a dollar in Europe. The bonds that have found their way there have gone in the regular course of trade.

The vast demand created by the war for munitions, materials and supplies of all kinds, gave to the agriculture of the West and the manufactures of the North a wonderful impulse, which still continues. The resources of those sections remain not only unimpaired, but have been greatly augmented. Great as are their burdens, the people feel themselves perfectly able to bear them, and that they have an ample equivalent for them of a nature far transcending mere material advantages. They have for the first time established their nationality upon an immutable basis. They have removed the great source of discord and alienation – slavery – and they are infinitely stronger and more united than ever before. Under the able and judicious administration of our affairs, the nation has started anew on a career of growth and prosperity unexampled in its own history, or in that of any other people.

The nation has pledged its honor for the fulfilling of all its obligations. Success has given a full equivalent for them. Its wonderful experience has served to give confidence in and ability for the future, and no one who considers our means, our present position, or the guarantees of the past, can doubt the payment of our national debt."

On my return home I received not only the thanks of the Government for the services I had rendered, but gratifying evidences of appreciation of them from private individuals. I annex the following Associated Press Report of my interview with the President and Secretary of the Treasury, on presenting my report:

" WASHINGTON, Friday, Nov. 3, 1865.
Mr. J. F. D. Lanier, the well-known banker of New York, who recently returned from Europe, whither he went some time ago on a confidential mission for the Government in connection with the national finances, yesterday had an interview with the President and the Secretary of the Treasury, to whom he submitted a report of the results of his mission. Mr. Lanier everywhere found the best of feeling prevailing, in financial circles, with relation to the United States, particularly on the Continent, and great confidence in our public securities. At Frankfort-on-the-Maine he addressed, at length, a large meeting of capitalists, embracing representatives from nearly every leading house in Germany. The complete and utter overthrow of the rebellion was a matter of equal surprise and congratulation, and the demonstration made of the power and wealth of the North was a subject of unusual admiration. But the war being ended, the expectation was confidently expressed by the European holders of our securities, that we would immediately commence a return toward specie payments, however gradual the progress in such direction might be. Such a step, it was represented, was absolutely necessary to the maintenance of confidence in our securities and in the policy of the Government. The ability of the country to bear all the burdens of the

421

war was not questioned, especially with the rapid progress of the work of Reconstruction, which bids fair to restore political and social amity to every portion of the country. With a wise and correct policy, there will be no limit to the demand for our securities, not only on the Continent, but in England, where our military successes were fast opening the eyes of their people as to the value of our bonds. But the feeling against any further increase, and in favor of a steady contraction of the currency, was universally expressed as the sole condition on which our credit abroad could be maintained. It is understood that the views of Mr. Lanier were heartily responded to, both by the President and the Secretary of the Treasury."

I also annex a copy of a letter received from Hon. Samuel Hooper, M. C.:

THIRTY-EIGHTH CONGRESS
HOUSE OF REPRESENTATIVES,
WASHINGTON CITY, DEC. 24, 1865.

MY DEAR SIR — I have to thank you for your kindness. in sending me a printed copy of your remarks recently made at a meeting of European capitalists at Frankfort-on-the-Maine, which I have read with much interest and with most hearty approval of them.
I consider you entitled to the thanks of all loyal men for them; and I congratulate you on the results which so soon after added confirmations to your statements.

With great respect, I am,
Your ob'd't servant,

J. F. D. LANIER, Esq.                    (Signed) S. HOOPER.

Since the date of the above remarks, I have had, in common with every American citizen, the gratification of witnessing an uninterrupted improvement of our national credit. All that I, or others, could do was to present the evidence upon which this appreciation has been based, and show what we were and what the future must do for us. But even my anticipations have been far exceeded by the result.

In this connection I also copy the following article from the New York Times newspaper, of January 19, 1866:

"OUR FINANCIAL POSITION ABROAD.
The effects of our great struggle are beginning to be felt in Europe at the moment we are emerging from them here. The wave set in motion is moving round the world, uniform in its course and resistless in its power. We have demonstrated that the nationality of a Republic, based solely upon the conviction of its value, is far more firmly grounded in the hearts of the people than institutions based upon tradition, and fortified by pride of ancestry and the recollection of great deeds; or by that uniformity of life and character which ages alone can produce. Foreigners, for the first time, realize that we are a

422

Nation, with an ideal palpable to the meanest citizen — that chaos has no place in our system, and that we have the will and the power to reduce to obedience every refractory element; and that the strongest of all governments is that in which each citizen has an equal share, and is an equal partaker in the advantages which it secures.

The first sentiment developed toward us is that of respect. Close upon that follows confidence in our material and financial condition. We have provoked a spirit of inquiry which cannot be set at rest. We no longer lack friends to sympathize with us, but hosts are coming forward to share our burdens and our prosperity. Our securities are eagerly sought for investment, particularly on the Continent, at the same time that a new impulse is given to emigration to our shores. The interest felt in us in Germany cannot be better described than by giving an extract from a letter received from Frankfort-on-the-Maine, where a large number of capitalists was recently addressed by our citizen, Mr. Lanier, whose remarks have been circulated, by our Consuls, throughout Europe. It says:

'Gold or paper dollar is the question which agitates the German press and financiers. The more they discuss your financial prospects, the more they invest in your securities. On all 'Changes, the transactions in them are enormous. Since the receipt of the President's Message and the Report of the Secretary of the Treasury, the United States securities rule the market, almost to the exclusion of every other loan. The Wirtemberg official paper has brought out a long article warning the excessive investment in your bonds; over 100,000,000 of guilders having been invested in them, to the detriment of other interests. But to the disappointment of the Government, your bonds next day rose two per cent. – the Liberal press taking the ground that the people could do nothing better than invest in American securities, as the safest loan offered in an age. These bonds are the most powerful and influential emissaries you could have sent over to the Old Continent, to convert the masses to republican principles. They never before heard so much talk about America; your means and resources, your future and your prospects, are discussed everywhere, and in such favorable terms that emigration is the leading topic among the sturdy masses; and the next year will bring you, for every $1,000 of your bonds taken in Germany, at least one of her industrious sons.'

A similar feeling is rapidly developing itself towards us in England, as shown by the operations of the London Stock Exchange. Our securities are constantly forcing their way there, in spite of the efforts of the Bank of England and of the public press to decry their value, and to point out the danger to that country from a large investment in them.

Such a result is not only most gratifying to our national pride, but is the proper reward of our efforts and successes, and proper homage to our national character. It is due very largely to a public spirited gentleman who has visited Europe for the purpose of placing before the people, there, the ground and method of our strength and prosperity, and who supplied the data by which foreigners themselves could arrive at satisfactory conclusions in reference to them. His success was complete. The sentiment everywhere felt toward us is all we could wish. It has increased enormously, not only our politi-

cal influence and power, but it goes far to solve any financial embarrassments that might threaten. The way being prepared, should it be
thought advisable, we could have, any day, a draft upon Europe honored for almost any amount. The object of the bill now in the hands
of the Committee of Ways and Means is to place such power in the
hands of the Secretary of the Treasury, should its exercise ever be
deemed to be expedient. It is not probable, however, that any such
necessity will occur. Our own people are abundantly able to absorb
all our securities, while the amounts going abroad, daily, will fully
equal all we should wish to see placed in foreign hands. Our military
successes, together with the material strength we have displayed,
have settled our financial difficulties; and though these have in times
past been great, every day lessens the burdens they impose."

In 1868, being again about to leave for Europe, I received
from the Treasury Department the following communication:

TREASURY DEPARTMENT,<br>
April 20, 1868.

DEAR SIR — Understanding that you are about visiting Europe, I
take the liberty of requesting that you will, as a friend of the Department and as a representative of it without compensation, avail yourself of such opportunities as may be presented to you to ascertain
what is the sentiment of capitalists in regard to United States securities; what would be the prospect of negotiating a five per cent. loan –
principal and interest, by express provision of law, payable in coin;
and whether or not such bonds could be exchanged, at par, for the
Five-Twenty six per cents now held in Europe ?

I will thank you also to make, from time to time, such suggestions as you may think proper in regard to the finances of the United
States, and the best steps to be taken to place the credit of our securities on the most satisfactory basis.

With many thanks for the very valuable service rendered by you
to the Government when you were last in Europe,

I remain, very truly,<br>
Your ob'd't servant,<br>
(Signed) H. McCULLOCH,

J. F. D. LANIER, Esq.,                    *Secretary of the Treasury.*
New York.

My health during this visit to Europe was such that I could
not give the attention to the requests in the foregoing letter that
I desired. I, however, caused the remarks I had made at Frank-
fort on a previous visit, to be re-printed, with some additional
matter, and circulated, widely, through the Consulates and other
channels. I also conferred, sufficiently, with leading bankers
abroad to satisfy myself that, in a comparatively short period, a
*five* per cent. long bond, payable, principal and interest, in gold,
in New York, could be made to take the place of the six per

424

cents. outstanding, and without loss to the Government which conviction I communicated to the Secretary of the Treasury. Everything that has since transpired has tended to confirm such conviction.

At the close of the war it was estimated that the funded debt of the Government, when all the outstanding claims should be included, would reach $3000,000.000. It would have reached this amount, but for the vast sums which our immense revenues enabled us to pay. At the close of the fiscal year of 1866, the ascertained debt amounted to $2,784,073,379. By the statement made March 1, 1870 and the last made previous to the preparation of this sketch, it amounted to $2,464,390,348, as follows:

| | |
|---|---:|
| Debt bearing coin interest | $2,107,939,650 |
| Debt bearing currency interest | 124,012,320 |
| Debt bearing no interest | 440,442,857 |
| Debt matured and not presented for payment | 3,973,346 |
| Total debt | $2,676,368,173 |
| Less in the Treasury: | |
| Coin | $102,400,739 |
| Currency | 10,280,746 |
| Bonds purchased | 99,287,800 |
| | $211,968,285 |
| Debt less cash and bonds | $2,464,399,888 |

Of the debt bearing *currency* interest, $64,457,320 is for bonds issued on account of the Pacific Railroads, and which were issued subsequently to July 1, 1866. Deducting these from the above statement the total will be $2,399,420,028, or $384,653,351 *less* than it was three years and eight months previous. The rate of payment has exceeded $100,000,000 annually.

The average market value of the 6 per cent. 1881 bonds of the Government, in 1864, was 110; that of gold, for the same year, 220. The value of the bonds in 1865 equaled 106 per cent.; that of gold 138. The market value of the 1881 bonds on the 10th of March, 1870, equaled 114; that of gold, 111. These figures express, better than any language, the rapidity with which the credit of the Government has appreciated.

Since the close of the war I have not taken any active part in public affairs, but have devoted myself to banking – a business which our house has followed for the past fifteen years. We have

425

retained a connection with several of the enterprises which we helped into existence, and have frequently extended to them aid in their financial affairs. I am a business man, from taste as well as from long habit. The period of my business life has probably been the most remarkable one in all history. Steam was first successfully applied to locomotion in the latter part of 1829 – only forty years ago! Since then the progress made in the physical sciences and in the material prosperity of the world has been beyond all precedent. The most sanguine imagination could not have pictured one-half the results that have been realized. The Electric Telegraph followed speedily upon the invention of the railroad, as the necessary condition to the highest value of this wonderful contrivance. In this short period 50,000 miles of railroad have been opened in the United States. A great and unbroken line extends across the Continent from ocean to ocean, traversing, without inconvenience or interruption, the most formidable mountain barriers. The terminus of this line upon the western slope of the Continent, the City of San Francisco, now containing 200,000 people, existed only in name when I removed from Indiana to New York. The railroad, everywhere, has become the common highway of the people. Nor have other countries, though far distanced by our own, been idle in the great race of social and material progress. The same year that witnessed the completion of the Pacific Railroad has also been distinguished by the opening of a ship canal from the Mediterranean to the Red Sea, thus realizing the dreams and hopes of the merchant, as well as the great rulers, for thousands of years. At the moment that this is being written, the great pageant of the opening of this new highway, which shortens by thousands of miles the routes to the Indias, is reported to us, word by word, as it proceeds, by lines of telegraph wholly submerged beneath the seas! The period which embraces my business life has been one of intense activity, and of wonderful and beneficent achievements; and it is a source of the highest gratitude and satisfaction to me to have witnessed the great movements that have taken place, and to have been identified with their progress. I hope my children will be equally fortunate and happy by being equally favored with opportunities for useful and valuable labor, and to see, as I have seen, the fruit of it spring up on every hand.

I now conclude this brief sketch of some of the leading events of my life. Although I have, throughout, been an active business man, I have been subject to but few vicissitudes of fortune. I have been almost uniformly successful. I have, as a rule, enjoyed excellent health. For all these blessings, bestowed by a kind Providence, I am, I trust, truly grateful. It has been my good fortune not only to have had a wide acquaintance with the leading men, and with various portions of this country, but to visit other lands, to return from them only to value more highly our people and our own institutions. As I grow in years the more am I drawn to my family and children. I trust that my example will not be without its uses in teaching my children the worth of industry and prudence in whatever walk of life they may find themselves cast. They may be assured that with these qualities, joined to integrity of character, they can never be unhappy, and never be without a reasonable share of this world's goods, nor without the confidence and respect of their fellow-men.

# THE LATE RICHARD H. WINSLOW.

[From the American Railroad Journal, March 2,1861.]

This gentleman, so well known in the business circles of this city, and for many years a leading mind in the great movement that covered our country with railways, died at his residence at Westport, Connecticut, on the 14th ult. He was born at Albany about fifty-five years ago, and was a direct descendant of Governor Winslow, of Plymouth Colony. He came to New York about thirty years since, and immediately went into business in Wall street. His prominence, however, as a public man, commenced with the great railway era of the country, which almost immediately followed the discovery of California. On the 1st of January, 1849, he formed a copartnership with J. F. D. Lanier, Esq., many years a resident of the West, and who brought to the firm not only all the qualities that can command affection and respect, but a very wide and intimate knowledge of the public men, and the wants and resources of the West. Mr. Lanier brought with him the first Western Railroad bond ever offered in this market, and the firm soon turned its attention to the negotiation of this kind of securities. At that time, Western railroads hardly existed, even in idea. There were no precedents to inspire confidence or to guide in framing a system or plan for presenting these enterprises to the public. Before anything could be accomplished a favorable opinion had to be created — a formidable undertaking where monetary co-operation was to be secured. For this office Mr. Winslow was peculiarly fitted. He was a man whose earnest convictions and great energy seldom failed to impress his own views upon all with whom he came in contact. The commencement made by the firm, however, was in a very small way. It was compelled to take a portion of loans offered, and divide the balance among a very limited circle; the firm, even in such cases, being frequently called upon to guarantee prompt payment of interest on the loans. The bonds of the Madison and Indianapolis Railroad were first brought out, followed by those of the Little Miami, Columbus and Xenia, Cleveland, Columbus and Cincinnati, Lake Shore, and other Western railroads. The immediate success of these works fully vindicated the representations made in reference to them, and realized large profits to the purchasers of their securities. Thenceforward the operations of this firm were distinguished rather for their magnitude than for the difficulties to be surmounted. For several years nearly every loan brought upon the market was proffered it, securing to it a selection of the best offered. In a short time its operations extended to almost every State in the Union where railroads were in progress, and a very long list of our best paying projects might be named, for the construction of which this firm was instrumental in securing the means. So thoroughly had this firm become established in public confidence, that, in the years of 1852, 1853 and 1854, it was no unusual affair for it to make negotiations equaling $1,000,000 in a single day; while sales varying from $100,000 to $500,000 a day were of common occurrence. In 1852, the firm was enlarged by the addition to it of Mr. James Winslow, brother of the deceased.

Considering the immense number of securities negotiated, the firm was very fortunate in the enterprises selected. This was in a great measure due to Mr. Lanier, whose thorough and intimate acquaintance with the West enabled him to foresee with great accuracy the works likely to be successful. Nearly all the securities negotiated have had their interest promptly paid, while many of them rank among the very first class. This firm were also the first to introduce County bonds of the State of Ohio upon this market, and negotiated the greater portion of these, which are still regarded as one among the most reliable Western securities.

After 1854 the firm gradually withdrew from railway negotiations and confined itself almost entirely to banking, in which it transacted a large business. About eighteen months since Mr. Winslow retired from it on account of his health which continued steadily to decline till his decease.

What these gentlemen actually accomplished, however, is to be looked for in the results rather than in the magnitude of their operations. The credit they early established for Western securities, spread till it extended over the whole of Europe as well as of this country. The capital of both was freely proffered to our enterprises. A similar spectacle was never seen. Railroads were commenced simultaneously in every part of the Union, and in the decade just closed 25,000 miles were constructed. In one or two years 4,000 miles were opened each year. The whole system sprang as if by magic into existence, stretching from Quebec, in Canada, to New Orleans, 2,500 miles apart, and from the eastern part of Maine to the western part of Kansas, penetrating every portion of our wide domain. The whole of Europe has yet hardly constructed the extent of mileage opened in the United States within the past ten years.

The commerce of a country like the United States is mainly a creation of its public works, as these are essential to give a commercial value to the products of the interior. A person who provides the means for the construction of a railroad is a public benefactor. Its results are the measure of good he has accomplished. But such persons are often the unseen spring in the mechanism, while the one who superintends the execution of a single piece of the work becomes the conspicuous object. But for the former, the latter could have had no function or name. Now it we take the results that followed the efforts of the pioneers in the great railway movement, we shall have nothing in history to compare with them. In the Western States, where these have been the most conspicuous, there are now 10,500 miles of railroad, constructed at a cost of $400,000,000, carrying freight to the amount of 7,500,000 tons annually, and having a value of at least $500,000,000. The population of these States increased from 4,721,554 in 1850, to 7,797,528 in 1860, or at the rate of about seventy per cent. Their wealth is increased in three-fold ratio. First-class cities have sprung into existence, and the whole face of the country presents the scene of a numerous, active and thriving population, with a vast commerce; nearly all the creation of its public works.

In the Eastern States, the most striking effect of these works is seen in the progress in population and commerce of the city of New York. The population of this city and its environs has increased from 645,000 in 1850, to 1,155,000 in 1859. Its exports, in 1850, were $47,580,357, in 1859, $146,683,450. Its imports, in 1850, were $116,667,558; in 1859, $229,408,130. Its wealth in the same time has more than trebled. This advance is the real measure of the results of the construction of Western railroads, as New York has reaped the same advantage as if each had been constructed for its particular benefit.

Such results, the firm of which Mr. Winslow was an active member was greatly instrumental in achieving, and it is proper that the occasion of his decease should not be passed by without a reference to them, as they are certainly the proudest monument ever erected to the memory of man.

# SNOW-STORM IN THE ALPS.

The following account, written soon after the events described, will interest my children in showing them how narrowly I escaped with my life, in a great storm which I encountered in crossing the Alps in the winter season:

GENOA, Friday, Jan. 23, 1863.

I left Paris on Saturday. I had an agreeable journey by rail to San Meichel, at the foot of Mount Cenis. At San Meichel we were transferred to sleighs, or rather to diligences placed on runners. At 3 P. M., Sunday, we began the ascent of the mountain. The day was a pleasant one — calm, with sunshine. We reached the summit about 12 1/2 o'clock at night — the weather still continuing calm and pleasant, the stars shining brightly — and we congratulated ourselves on the prospect of so pleasant a passage over this Alpine region. We had descended on the Italian side about half an hour, when the wind began to blow, drifting the snow across our route, which impeded our progress. As we continued to descend, the wind increased in violence, making it more and more difficult for us to proceed.

At 3 o'clock in the morning, having reached a point more than half-way down, the gale became terrific, roaring like a thousand Niagaras, dashing and whirling the fine dry snow so as to darken the atmosphere.

By this time the drifts had become deep, and it being dark our progress was stopped. On our left was a precipice of a thousand feet or more deep. The sleigh next in front of ours had upset with the passengers, and was only prevented going over the precipice by its lodging in the soft snow within a few feet of the edge. The conductor now came and told us we would have to sit in the sleigh where we were, until daylight; that he must seek the protection of the lee of some rock with his horses to save himself and them from perishing from cold. This announcement, you may imagine, was anything but agreeable to us. Here we sat until about 9 o'clock Monday morning.

About 5 o'clock we heard the fall of an avalanche across the road before us, and soon after the fall of another in our rear; this greatly increased our alarm, as we did not know what moment another would sweep us over the precipice in its course. It was truly a night of horror. After daylight we anxiously awaited the

431

return of the conductor to know our fate; he came after 9 o'clock and informed that he would endeavor to draw the sleigh a little nearer the avalanche, to shorten the distance we should have to walk to reach it.

We had advanced but a few rods when we came to a stand, the drifts preventing our progress. Our only chance of safety was to walk to the "Cantano," or house of refuge, about four hundred yards off; the avalanches fifteen to twenty feet deep and more than one hundred wide, lying in the way. Each one had to take care of himself.

I was the last to leave the sleigh. With difficulty I reached the avalanche, and in attempting to walk over it I sank, half my length, in the soft snow. I became completely exhausted; the terrible wind took my breath away. I fell on the snow, unable to speak or rise. One of the passengers happened to see me fall, and after reaching the "Cantano" sent up two of the Cantoniers, who carried me to the house nearly in an insensible state. By dint of rubbing with spirits I revived in about half an hour.

The storm continued with unabated fury until about 10 o'clock Tuesday morning, when it began to subside a little. In the afternoon of Tuesday, the chief of the Cantoniers, an active, energetic fellow, came from below with twenty-five of his men; these, added to about ten at the "Cantano," made thirty-five men. The sleighs having been brought down, the joyful order was given to mount, which was readily complied with.

At this place I made the acquaintance of the Marquis D'Azeglio, the Italian Minister at the British Court, then on his way to London. At his request, I gave him a copy of this letter, which he said he would lay before his Government of Turin, that they might consider the subject of providing better accommodation for travelers at these "Cantanos."

I had read in my early years of the fury and power of these Alpine storms; how unfortunate travelers were suddenly overtaken and lost in the drifts and avalanches of snow, but never before did I realize them. The tunneling of' Mount Cenis is progressing as fast as the nature of the case admits of; they have penetrated about one mile at each end; the blasting is through a rock of the hardest kind; the progress is about five feet a day at each end, and when completed will be over eight miles long. The completion of the tunnel is greatly to be desired; it will make the shortest, most direct, and far the most agreeable route from Paris to Italy. This work is being done by the Italian Government.

Copies of letters addressed to me by the Hon. Hugh McCulloch, Secretary of the Treasury, and Hon. William H. Seward, Secretary of State of the United States, as I was about leaving for Europe in 1865.

TREASURY DEPARTMENT,

WASHINGTON, May 29, 1865.

DEAR SIR — Although you are about to visit Europe for the benefit of your health, and desire to be relieved from all cares and responsibilities, I cannot permit a gentleman of your distinguished and well-merited reputation as a financier to visit Europe, without asking of him the benefit of his services in explaining to Capitalists in that country the condition of our financial affairs, and in giving to me the benefit of such suggestions as he may be able to make in regard to the condition of American credit in the countries he may visit, and in the transaction of any business which the Treasury Department may wish to commit to his care.

I inclose herewith a statement of our national debt. You are well advised of our national resources.

I will thank you, while in Europe, on behalf of the Treasury Department, to explain the character of this debt and the extent of the resources of the United States, to gentlemen with whom you may come in contact; and who may be interested in these subjects.

I will from time to time communicate with you upon these subjects, and ask of you to perform specific duties, if I should be under the necessity of requiring your particular services.

Trusting that your journey will be a pleasant one, and that you will return to the United States re-invigorated by relaxation and travel,

I am, very truly, your ob'd't servant,

(Signed) H. McCULLOCH,

J. F. D. LANIER, Esq.,                                     *Secretary of the Treasury.*
New York.


DEPARTMENT OF STATE,

WASHINGTON, 2d June, 1865.

*To the Diplomatic and Consular Agents of the United States in Europe:*

GENTLEMEN — It is my pleasing duty to introduce to you J. F. D. Lanier, Esquire, a distinguished banker of the City of New York, and a most estimable gentleman.

Mr. Lanier has been requested by the Secretary of the Treasury to look after the financial interests of this Government while in Europe, and he has kindly consented to do so.

I commend him to your friendly attention and consideration, and bespeak for him such facilities as may contribute to the effective discharge of the duties confided to him.

I am, gentlemen,

Your very obedient servant,

(Signed) William H. SEWARD,

*Secretary of State.*

# APPENDIX

July 6, 1877.

My Dear Sir:

It has long been matter of common knowledge that ancestors transmit to their progeny those ingrained and radical peculiarities which constitute what might be called Family Individuality. The modern habit of scientific observation would seem to have established a much more extensive range of this process than had hitherto been suspected; and it may probably be considered fairly settled that not only the broader family traits are hereditarily transmissible, but that even the mental acquisitions of any individual parent do, to a certain extent, pass on to his children; so that if a man shall have made himself an expert in any particular branch of human activity, there will result the strong tendency that a peculiar aptitude towards the same branch will be found among some of his descendants.

The slight esteem, therefore, in which genealogical investigations are sometimes held can legitimately attach only to such as are pursued from unseemly motives of display. For, indeed, to the earnest man, the study of his ancestry must be regarded as the study of himself. Christian insight, no less than heathen wisdom, has sanctioned the ancient admonition, Know thyself; and if it be true that in order to know oneself one must know one's ancestors, then the practice of genealogic research must be regarded as a duty, and with a peculiar propriety the Family Tree is inscribed in the Family Bible.

It is therefore with pleasure that I communicate to you such items of family history as have come to my notice, regretting only that a laborious life has never allowed me the opportunity which I desired of making some special research into these matters. Perhaps it will not be amiss to add here, for the behoof of any member of the family who may hereafter have leisure and means to pursue this subject, that without doubt many interesting reminiscences of the Laniers might be obtained by intelligent inquiry prosecuted in the South of France, and in England and Wales, according to the migrations of the family hereinafter set forth. I was once disposed to think that our forefathers had been singularly careless in failing to preserve more ample written records of our descent and history; but a somewhat closer

434

acquaintance with the nomadic habits of the Laniers inclines me to attribute the paucity of our genealogical remains to other causes. The main secret of it appears to have been their continual movements from place to place during the last two hundred years. The original breaking up of the Huguenot Laniers in France, and their flight into England; then their removal to Virginia in the sturdy days of the old colonists, when it must have been of great importance to be encumbered with as little luggage as possible; and, finally, the dispersion of the family throughout the East, West, and South of the United States; have all been circumstances unfavorable to the preservation of family archives. Indeed, I think a certain intolerance of restraint, and a powerful tendency among younger members to break off from the parental stem as soon as possible, may be very distinctly traced as a prominent family characteristic among us. I know of Laniers now existing in New York, Maryland, Virginia, North Carolina, South Carolina, Georgia, Florida, Alabama, Mississippi, Louisiana, Texas, Tennessee, and Indiana; and I do not recall a single instance where any considerable family have remained together continuously for a great while, but all appear to have early felt the hereditary tendency to leave the parental county or State and set up separate existences,

## SIR JOHN LANIER.

Perhaps the first authentic mention of our name in history is that which records the part borne by Sir John Lanier at the battle of the Boyne, July I (12), 1690, where he commanded the Queen's regiment of horse. In Macaulay's "History of England" (page 494, Vol. III., Harper & Bros'. edition, New York, 1856) occurs the following paragraph, among others detailing the array of King William's army on that eventful morning: "Sir John Lanier, an officer who had acquired military experience on the Continent, and whose prudence was held in high esteem, was at the head of the Queen's regiment of horse, now the First Dragoon Guards."

It is not an improbable conjecture that this Sir John, instead of flying with our other Huguenot ancestors to England, may have chosen to seek his asylum in Holland, and may have there made the acquaintance of the great Dutch Prince who so

435

valiantly defended the Protestant cause. However this may be, he appears to have been a brave and faithful officer; for within the next two years we find him rising to the rank of General, and perishing along with the gallant Mackay and Douglas at the battle of Steinkirk. This fact is recorded on page 226, Vol. IV., of Macaulay's " History of England" (edition above cited), where Lanier is mentioned as a General "distinguished among the conquerors of Ireland."

Macaulay does not cite the documents from which he obtained these particular items, further than to give the authorities for his general history of the period. I have an impression, however, that somewhat minute regimental records have long been kept in the British Army and it is very likely that many interesting details of the career of Sir John Lanier might be therein found.

It is a family tradition that he was one of our lineal ancestors. Indeed, putting together all the accounts which have ever come to me from many widely-scattered branches, I find that they all point in one direction, namely, to the existence of a single family of Laniers in the South of France, from whom all persons now bearing that name have descended: so that, in any given instance, I think the fact of the name alone may with perfect security be taken as evidence of kinship.

### THOMAS LANIER

(The materials from which the facts in the following statement have been gathered are: (1) a MS. work entitled "History of the Harris Family," which was kindly sent to me by my friend Iverson Lanier Harris, at that time one of the Justices of the Supreme Court of Georgia, having been compiled by him from documents furnished to his kinsman Henry Clay Harris, of Kentucky, by: Benjamin Watkins Leigh, of Virginia: (2) a work called "The Old Churches and Families of Virginia," by Bishop William Meade, of that State, a copy of which is, I believe, now in your possession: (3) The Family Tree, hereinafter set forth, which, in its present form, first came (I think) to my grandfather, Sterling Lanier, from the papers of the late George Washington Parke Custis, of Virginia: (4) traditions of the Harris and Lanier families.)

Some time between. the years 1691 and 1716 a party of

colonists, consisting of the Laniers, the Maxwells, the Mayhews, the Bondurants, the Howells, the Harrises, and others whose names are frequently met with among the early families of Virginia, came to that colony from Great Britain, and settled upon a grant of land ten miles square which embraced the present site of the city of :Richmond. :

One of these Laniers appears to have been the Thomas Lanier hereinafter mentioned. The grant of land was made by William and Mary in 1691 to Henry Harris and John Jourdan, conveying to them a certain tract of Crown-lands lying along the James river, in the county of Powhatan, Virginia. The original of this grant was in the possession of Benjamin Watkins Leigh, of Virginia, in the year 1844. This Henry Harris (with whose family ours afterwards became intimately connected by intermarriage) belonged to an ancient house of Harrises whose seat was in Glamorgan, Wales. They were enthusiastic members of the "Welsh Baptist" Society; and during the fluctuating religious troubles of that period had been compelled to fly into France. Here they united with the Huguenots: and it is strongly probable that some acquaintance may have been formed at this time between the French Laniers and the Welsh Harrises, which afterwards led to their joint emigration to America.

For, on the promulgation of the Edict of Nantes, the Welsh refugees in France had returned to Wales, where they lived until the Revocation of the Edict. After this event the Huguenot Laniers left their home in the South of France, and appear to have gone first to England or Wales. We find them emigrating thence soon afterward in company with the Harrises and others, as already mentioned, to America; Here they settled a town near the Falls of the James river, which was called Manakin town; or Monacan town. This name (says Bishop Meade, page 466, Vol. I., of "Old Churches and Families of Virginia") "was derived from the Indian Monacan — the name of a warlike tribe of Indians whom the great King Powhatan in vain attempted to subdue," and who "resided on James river from the Falls" (the present site of Richmond) "to Manakin."

Bishop Meade mentions the Laniers as early settlers in Manakin town, and refers to the mixture of French and Welsh elements in that colony.

It is therefore from Manakin town that our family derives its origin in the United States.

Both the Harrises and the Laniers now began to spread about the land. We find Thomas Lanier (according to the Family Tree hereinbefore mentioned) marrying Elizabeth Washington, the paternal aunt of George Washington. In this connection it will be of interest to remark that in the year 1747 Thomas Lanier obtained a grant of Crown-lands in Brunswick County, Virginia, as more fully appears by the following copy of the original instrument conveying the estate to him:

"George the Second, by the Grace of God of Great Britain, France and Ireland King, Defender of the Faith, etc.: To all to whom these presents shall come Greeting: Know ye that for divers good causes and considerations but more especially for and in consideration of the sum of forty shillings of good and lawful money for our use paid to our Receiver General of our revenues in this our Colony and Dominion of Virginia, we have given, granted and confirmed, and by these presents for us, our heirs and successors do give, grant and confirm unto Thomas Lanier, one certain tract or parcel of land containing three hundred and eighty acres lying and being in the County of Brunswick on both sides of Mitchell's Creek, joining Shepard Lanier's line and his own, and bounded as followeth to wit: Beginning at Shepard Lanier's lower corner white oak on the creek, thence along his line south seventeen degrees west one hundred poles to a red oak on his line, thence along his line south seventy-one degrees east sixty poles to a red oak on the creek, thence down the said creek as it meanders to a white oak on the said creek, thence of (sic) north forty-three degrees east one hundred and eighteen poles to a white oak, thence north twenty-three degrees east one hundred and eighty-eight poles to his own corner sweet gum on a branch, thence north fourteen degrees west one hundred and sixty-six poles to a pine on William Hill's line, thence south seventy degrees west one hundred and sixty-six poles to Hill's corner dogwood on a branch, thence down the said branch as it meanders to the mouth of the same, thence down Mitchell's Creek aforesaid as it meanders to the Beginning, With all wood, underwoods, swamps, marshes, low grounds, meadows, feedings, and his due share of all veins, mines and quarries as well discovered as undiscovered within the bounds aforesaid and being part of the said quantity of three hundred and eighty acres of land, and the rivers, waters and watercourses therein contained, together with the privileges of Hunting, Hawking, Fishing, Fowling, and all other profits, commodities and hereditaments whatsoever to the same or any part thereof belonging or in any wise appertaining: To Have, Hold, possess and enjoy the said tract or parcel of land and all other the before-granted premises and every part thereof with their and every of their appurtenances unto the said Thomas Lanier and to his heirs and assigns forever: to the only use and behoof of him said Thomas Lanier his heirs and assigns forever: To be held of us, our heirs and successors, as of our manor of East Greenwich in the County Kent in free and common socage and not in capite or by knight service, Yielding and paying unto us our heirs and successors for every fifty acres of land and so proportionately for a lesser or

438

greater quantity than fifty acres the fee rent of one shilling yearly to be paid upon the feast of Saint Michael the Archangel, and also cultivating and improving three acres part of every fifty of the tract above-mentioned within three years after the date of these presents. Provided always that if three years of the said fee rent shall at any time be in arrear and unpaid, or if the said Thomas Lanier his heirs or assigns do not within the space of three years next coming after the date of these presents cultivate and improve three acres part of every fifty of the tract above-mentioned, then the estate hereby granted shall cease and be utterly determined, and thereafter it shall and may be lawful to and for us, our heirs and successors to grant the same lands and premises with the appurtenances unto such other person or persons as we, our heirs and successors shall think fit: In Witness Whereof we have caused these our Letters Patent to be made. Witness our trusty and well-beloved Sir William Gooch Bar., our Lieutenant Governor and Commander in Chief of our said Colony and Dominion at Williamsburg under the seal of our said Colony the twelfth day of January one thousand seven hundred and forty-seven in the twenty-first year of our reign.

(Signed)     WILLIAM GOOCH."

Information obtained from the Register Of the Virginia Land Office reveals that Thomas Lanier obtained other grants in addition to this: namely, a grant dated August 5, 1751, conveying to him 318 acres of land lying in Lunenburg County, Virginia; one dated March 3, 1760, conveying 400 acres in the same county; and one dated September 20, 1768, conveying 838 acres in the same county.

Besides these conveyances to Thomas Lanier, I find that two grants were issued to "Thomas Bird Lanier," one dated January 2, 1737, for 312 acres of land in Brunswick County, Virginia, and one dated January 12, 1747, for 374 acres in the same county. It seems probable that this Thomas Bird Lanier was a different person from Thomas Lanier: for I observe that two of the grants mentioned above were issued on the same day — January 12, 1747 — and that one of them conveyed land to "Thomas Lanier," while the other conveyed to "Thomas Bird Lanier": which renders it extremely unlikely that these were names of the same individual, particularly as the instruments date from a time when legal technicalities were much more rigorously observed than at present.

It is clear, however, from the deeds cited, that Thomas Lanier was a considerable land-owner in the counties of Brunswick and Lunenburg; and it is to these counties, together with the adjoining county of Rockingham in North Carolina

439

(where my grandfather Sterling Lanier was born), that we may trace the original seat of our family after the initial settlement at Monacan town.

It is proper to subjoin also, at this point, the Family Tree, to which I have already referred. The following is a copy from the Tree furnished by G. W. P. Custis, Esq., with the single addition of the names of the three grandchildren of Winifred Lanier, two of which are taken from the Tree furnished by Mrs. Hallowes, of Florida, and one — that of Mrs. Bryson — added upon information furnished by herself:

John Washington

ELIZABETH WASHINGTON married THOMAS LANIER.     Augustine Washington.

| | | |
|---|---|---|
| Richard, | Thomas, | George Washington. |
| James, | Elizabeth (married Craft), | |
| and | | |

SAMPSON (who married ELIZABETH CHAMBERLIN).

Children of Sampson Lanier and Elizabeth Chamberlin:

LEWIS Lanier, of Screven County,Georgia;

Buckner       "   ;

Burwell       "   ;

WINIFRED     (who married Col. Drury Ledbetter, of Virginia, and was grandmother of Judge John C. Nicoll, of Savannah, Georgia, and of Mrs. Caroline M. S. Hallowes, of Florida, and of Mrs. A. K. S. Bryson, of Kentucky);

Nancy       (who married Major Vaughn, of Roanoke, North Carolina);

Rebecca     (who married Walton Harris, of Virginia; she was grandmother of Judge Iverson L. Harris, of Georgia).

Rebecca Lanier — a granddaughter of Thomas Lanier — was united in marriage to Walton Harris, of Brunswick County, Virginia, a member of the original Harris family of Monacan town. This couple afterwards removed to North Carolina, where, according to the Harris History hereinbefore quoted, "they owned the great fishery at the narrows of the Yadkin River."

Rebecca was the daughter of "Sampson" Lanier. This has long been a family name, both in my own branch of the Lanier family and among the Harrises. My great-uncle Sampson Lanier recently died in Florida, and my father's given name is Robert Sampson.

440

It is in this same Rebecca Lanier's father, Sampson, that your lineage and mine come together. His two sons, Lewis and Buckner, were the heads of our respective families: Lewis of yours, and Buckner of mine. Lewis Lanier was your greatgrandfather through your father Alexander Chalmers Lanier, and your grandfather James Lanier.

Winifred Lanier — a sister of your great-grandfather, Lewis — married Col. Drury Ledbetter, of Virginia. In a letter from their granddaughter, Mrs. A. K. S. Bryson (your "Aunt Bryson"), which I have had the pleasure of perusing, I find the following paragraph: "He" (meaning Lewis Lanier) "married an interesting woman in N. C.: if I mistake not she was a Miss Ball. I think she was a sister of Gen. Geo. Washington's mother, as my grandmother called Mrs. W. aunt." I understand this to be in accordance with the traditions of your own immediate family upon the same subject.

From Lewis Lanier's sister, Winifred, have descended many interesting persons. She was born in North Carolina, where she and her husband appear to have lived until the close of the Revolutionary war, when they moved to Georgia, and thenceforth resided in that State. One of their daughters, Susan W. Ledbetter (the mother of Mrs. Bryson, to whom reference has been made), was born in North Carolina, in the year 1773. After she moved with her father to Georgia, she married Major Thomas Martin, of the United States Army, who was then in command of a fort called Point Peter, a few miles from St. Mary's, Georgia. The marriage, however, occurred in Wilkes County, Georgia. Major Martin was born in Albemarle County, Virginia, in the year 1751. In 1801 he left Georgia and took command of a fort near Norfolk, Virginia: but did not remain there long, for I find that after having been successively ordered to Pittsburg and to Detroit, he finally came, in the year 1804, to Newport Barracks, Kentucky, and assumed command at that place. Major Martin's manners were genial; his wife, Mrs. Susan W. Martin, is described as an accomplished lady, of fine presence, and endowed with many virtues; while their daughters were also estimable and charming women; so that their house soon became a rendezvous for the best society of that region, and appears to have been a point of great social attraction for a long time.

The following are the names of Major Martin's children: Ann K. S. Bryson;

Eliza W. Oldham;

Susan L. Sandford;

Mary F. Winston (whose daughter, Sabella Winston, married Gov. Stevenson, of Kentucky);

Louisa W. Prather;

Harriet Joyce;

Thomas Martin;

James Martin.

It is to the remarkable memory of Mrs. Bryson — the last survivor of Major Martin's children, now residing at Covington, Kentucky — that most of the foregoing recitals concerning the Ledbetter family are due. Mrs. Bryson, now at the age of eighty-seven, retains all her faculties, writing long and intelligent letters, and giving names and dates with great precision.

Col. Ledbetter's daughter, Caroline Agnes, married Col. A. Y. Nicoll, of the United States Army. Their only daughter, Mrs. Caroline M. S. Hallowes, is now residing near Remington Park, Florida, a beautiful point nearly opposite the famous winter-resort known as Green Cove Springs, across the St. John's River which is here about seven miles wide. Mrs. Hallowes — a lady of great piety and cultivation, and the mother of an accomplished family — is the wife of Col. Hallowes, an English officer, who, after having served the Queen for several years in India, retired on half-pay and came to this country.

Drury Ledbetter and Winifred Lanier had twelve children. Of these, Nancy married a Scotch gentleman, James Gardiner; and Mary married Francis Yates, son of the Spanish Consul at St. Augustine, Florida.

The following are the names of living heads of families who represent widely distinct branches of the Laniers, but all of whom derive their lineage from our common Huguenot stock hereinbefore described. They will serve as useful clues to any member of the family who may hereafter desire to obtain some more complete account of it.

William L. Lanier, of Selma, Alabama, President of the Alabama Central Railway.

Sampson Lanier, of Greenville, Alabama.

Thomas Lanier, of Lake Griffin, Florida.

Joseph Lanier, of Quincy, Florida.

Lewis Lanier, of Fort Meade, Florida.

Robert Sampson Lanier (my father), of Macon, Georgia.

W. L. Lanier, of West Point, Georgia. (The town of Lanier, in Schley County, Georgia, owes its name to the Laniers who once lived in Screven County, and who are referred to in the Family Tree hereinbefore given.)

D. G. Lanier, of Flat Rock, South Carolina.

Lucius Lanier, of Baltimore, Maryland.

There are also distinct branches in Mississippi, Texas, Virginia, and North Carolina, the names of whose representatives I do not know. I am told that the Hon. Thomas Lanier Clingman, of the latter State, derives his lineage in part — as indicated by his name — from the Rockingham County ancestors to whom I have alluded.

The late Edmund Lanier, Commander in the United States Navy, was, I believe, the son of a Presbyterian clergyman living in Nashville, Tennessee, who is of a still different branch from any of those specified above.

There is also a group of Laniers in the island of Cuba. One family of this group attended the Centennial Exhibition last year, and I regret that I was unable to meet them. I remember to have heard you relate that you were once accosted by a young Cuban while on one of your voyages to Europe, who informed you that his mother's name was Lanier, and that she was a descendant of the Huguenot Laniers from. the South of France.

Some of the branches above indicated by a single name consist of many members, who are spread over several Southern and Northern States.

It cannot be improper for me to close this sketch by adding that I have read with great interest and profit the account of your life which you were kind enough to send me, and that I sincerely wish you a long and peaceful enjoyment of the remarkable successes therein set forth.

Very truly yours,
SIDNEY LANIER.

J. F. D. LANIER, ESQ., New York City.

James F.D. Lanier ——— Elizabeth Gardner
1899–1881     1798–1846

**Alexander—Stella Godman**
1820–1895

**Elizabeth—Wm. M. Dunn**
1822–1910   1814–1887

| | |
|---|---|
| James | 1842–1842 |
| Wm. M. | 1843–1891 |
| Charles | 1845–1849 |
| Frances | 1847–1920 |
| Lanier | 1851–1915 |
| Mary | 1853–1885 |
| George | 1856–1926 |

**Drusilla—John Cravens**
1824–1903   1819–1899

| | |
|---|---|
| John | 1844–1882 |
| Robert | 1847–1908 |
| James | 1849–1921 |
| Alexander | 1851–1895 |
| Wm. | 1853–1934 |
| Elizabeth | 1855–1927 |
| Charles | 1857–1927 |
| Joseph | 1859–1939 |
| Mary | 1861–1907 |
| Drusilla | 1864–1956 |
| Franklin | 1865–1896 |
| Margaret | 1867–1867 |

**Margaret—James Winslow**
1827–1891

| | |
|---|---|
| Lawrence | |
| Edward | |
| Marguerite | |

—Josiah Pompelly
(Margaret's second husband)

**John James**
1829–1836

**Mary—John Stone**
1832–?

| | |
|---|---|
| Elizabeth | 1859 |
| Mary | 1860 |

**Louisa**
1835–1885

**Charles—Sarah Eggleston**
1837–1926   1858–1928

| | |
|---|---|
| JF Dill | 1862–1893 |
| Sarah | 1864 |
| Fannie | 1870 |
| Elizabeth | |

Second wife of JFD Lanier—Mary McClure

| | |
|---|---|
| Jean | 1849–1849 |
| James | 1851–1856 |
| Katherine | 1858– |